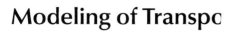

Modeling of Transpo

MW01062035

Modeling of Transport Demand

Analyzing, Calculating, and Forecasting Transport Demand

V.A. Profillidis

G.N. Botzoris

ELSEVIER

Elsevier
Radarweg 29, PO Box 211, 1000 AE Amsterdam, Netherlands
The Boulevard, Langford Lane, Kidlington, Oxford OX5 1GB, United Kingdom
50 Hampshire Street, 5th Floor, Cambridge, MA 02139, United States

Copyright © 2019 Elsevier Inc. All rights reserved.

No part of this publication may be reproduced or transmitted in any form or by any means, electronic or mechanical, including photocopying, recording, or any information storage and retrieval system, without permission in writing from the publisher. Details on how to seek permission, further information about the Publisher's permissions policies and our arrangements with organizations such as the Copyright Clearance Center and the Copyright Licensing Agency, can be found at our website: www.elsevier.com/permissions.

This book and the individual contributions contained in it are protected under copyright by the Publisher (other than as may be noted herein).

Notices
Knowledge and best practice in this field are constantly changing. As new research and experience broaden our understanding, changes in research methods, professional practices, or medical treatment may become necessary.

Practitioners and researchers must always rely on their own experience and knowledge in evaluating and using any information, methods, compounds, or experiments described herein. In using such information or methods they should be mindful of their own safety and the safety of others, including parties for whom they have a professional responsibility.

To the fullest extent of the law, neither the Publisher nor the authors, contributors, or editors, assume any liability for any injury and/or damage to persons or property as a matter of products liability, negligence or otherwise, or from any use or operation of any methods, products, instructions, or ideas contained in the material herein.

Library of Congress Cataloging-in-Publication Data
A catalog record for this book is available from the Library of Congress

British Library Cataloguing-in-Publication Data
A catalogue record for this book is available from the British Library

ISBN: 978-0-12-811513-8

For information on all Elsevier publications visit our
website at https://www.elsevier.com/books-and-journals

Working together
to grow libraries in
developing countries

www.elsevier.com • www.bookaid.org

Publisher: Joe Hayton
Acquisition Editor: Brian Romer
Editorial Project Manager: Andrae Akeh
Production Project Manager: Paul Prasad
Cover Designer: Mark Rogers

Typeset by TNQ Technologies

To my wife Areti and my son Aristeidis
V.A. Profillidis

To Nikiforos, Zoe, and Vassiliki
G.N. Botzoris

Contents

3. Methods of Modeling Transport Demand

6. Trend Projection and Time Series Methods

7. Econometric, Gravity, and the 4-Step Methods

8. Artificial Intelligence—Neural Network Methods

Preface

Forecasting the future has always been a challenge for humanity in its effort to safeguard achievements and better organize future endeavors. The future is an immense set of eventual plausible alternatives and generates hopes and fears. However, from the very early steps of rational thinking, man has realized that the future provides early signs of what will happen. It rests upon man to depict and record these early signs, and based upon them, to understand and explore plausible future evolutions, and forecast as accurately as possible what will probably happen. Thus, the core of any science is to analyze data and the events of the past in order to forecast and calculate the future values of a phenomenon under study. Sciences related to inert materials (like physics and engineering) can compile knowledge in some kind of universal laws, which are valid everywhere across the world and for every moment in the future with a high degree of certainty and objectivity. This is not the case with sciences related to economic and social phenomena, which can hardly lead to universal laws but often foresee future evolutions with a degree of uncertainty and subjectivity, and furthermore only for a small range of problems.

The aim of transport is to carry a person or a good from one place to another by using a specific transport mode (car, train, airplane, ship) which runs on appropriate infrastructure (road, railway track, airport, port). Transport permits people to work at a distance of many kilometers from home, to buy and sell goods from remote areas thousands of kilometers from the production or consumption area, and to visit other people and discover and explore other areas and civilizations even at the most distanced areas of the globe. Transport and (nowadays) the Internet give practically infinite possibilities for anyone to extend and broaden his domain of activities and interests; this new reality has in many ways transformed the whole planet into a new kind of global village.

Transport demand aims at calculating the amount of transport that people will choose and use for a specific price or other characteristics (such as travel time, frequency, punctuality, etc.) of a transport mode. It may concern both transport modes and transport infrastructure. Transport demand models are simplified constructs that attempt to describe, explain, correlate, and forecast transport demand as accurately as possible within a rational framework of assumptions. Transport demand is the outcome of technical aspects (such as travel times or the technology used for the transport mode and for the infrastructure), economic aspects (such as travel costs, revenue of the customers), lifestyle aspects of the society or preferences of a specific individual for a transport mode, psychological aspects, and so on. Thus, a transport demand model should take into account both objective aspects of demand (related to the technological and physical characteristics of the transport activity) and subjective ones (related to economic and social conditions). Transport demand models try to establish the most accurate rational correlation between transport demand and the factors (of both objective and subjective character) that affect it; this correlation can be conducted at various levels of analysis and sophistication, from purely qualitative, based on more or less subjective perceptions and assessments made by some individuals, to quantitative ones, which are based on some form of mathematical relationship between transport demand and one or more factors affecting it. Such a correlation should be explored, established, checked, and validated before it can be used for the forecast of future transport demand.

The basic computational tools for constructing a transport demand model are statistics and computational intelligence. Statistics permit a transport forecaster to analyze data of the past, to formulate an equation which describes accurately the evolution of these data, and then to use this equation for the forecast of future transport demand. The equation of a transport demand model may depend only on time or (in addition to time) on other factors which also affect transport demand. Computational intelligence is usually employed when methods based on statistical techniques fail to accurately simulate a problem; computational intelligence techniques make use of the knowledge and methods of artificial intelligence, and particularly of neural network methods and of fuzzy methods.

Transport demand modeling is a rather new branch of transport science which began to develop during the 1960s alongside the construction of new big infrastructure projects. Up until a few years ago, the basic tools for transport demand modeling were qualitative and simple statistical methods. However, evolutions in computer science and new ways of mathematical thinking have broadened the field of methods and techniques for the analysis of transport data and the forecast of their evolution. Thus, when facing any problem of transport demand, a forecaster has access to a plethora of methods, by which he should be neither impressed nor deterred. The central aim of the book is to analyze and present the available methods of forecast, the minimum theoretical background for each one of them, the appropriate formulas and computer software to be used in each case, and applications to specific problems. However, the forecaster should not have any kind of prejudice in relation to the degree of sophistication of a method: no matter how mathematically complicated or simplistic, any method of forecast can be selected if it can afford forecasted values close to reality, provided that it is previously tested for its validity and accuracy. The knowledge included in the book comes from original and applied research conducted by the authors as well as by other specialists of the sector worldwide.

The science of transport demand modeling has thus far been developed empirically on the occasion of specific problems in need of a solution and is not founded on solid theoretical considerations and background. As a result, a forecaster facing a specific problem typically comes across numerous case-studies, without a clear identification of assumptions, methods, and computational techniques used. In this book we have put great effort into founding transport demand modeling on a more axiomatic approach, by explicitly giving the assumptions for each theory and method and testing the formulas and computer software for their validity. We have tried to reduce the number of assumptions and conditions of application of a method as much as possible, in order to provide to the simulated formulation of the real problem the maximum number of degrees of freedom, so as to represent as accurately as possible the real problem under study.

Transport demand forecasts are a prerequisite for almost all activities related to transport. Any decision related to the planning, investment, and operation of both the infrastructure and the various transport modes always needs the most accurate forecast of transport demand, and even more so nowadays in the competitive national and international economic environment. Any construction of a transport infrastructure or any operation of a transport services company which is not based on the most accurate forecast of future demand runs the risk to turn into an economic adventure and often in economic disaster.

Transport demand forecasts can be conducted by specialists coming from a scientifically diversified background: engineers, economists, mathematicians-statisticians, computer and data analysts, and so on. The book addresses to all these specialists, either working in the field or studying in schools of engineering, economics, transportation, applied statistics, computer science, and business administration. A big dilemma faced at the beginning of the writing of the book related to the minimum prerequisite mathematical, and particularly statistical, background that the reader ought to have in order to read and understand in-depth the content of the book. We opted for a minimum background at the level of a first year student of engineering or economics. For this reason, we provide (in Chapter 5 and wherever it is necessary) a short analysis of the required terms and knowledge about statistics and mathematics. Thus, the book can be easily read by any student studying in the aforementioned fields, but also any professional working in the transport sector after decades from his graduation and the inevitable erosion of mathematical knowledge in his mind.

The book draws knowledge from many scientific branches, such as economics, engineering, mathematics, statistics, informatics, and even robotics and psychology. As the reader may be interested in a specific part of the book, we did not take for granted that he has already comprehended what preceded his specific area of interest. For this reason, the reader is systematically referred to which other part of the book the necessary knowledge for understanding his specific topic of interest is made available.

The first step in any effort of transport modeling, and before looking for the appropriate method to use, lies in that the forecaster understands clearly which are the factors or driving forces that affect the specific transport demand problem. All these factors and the related elasticities are analyzed in Chapter 1, together with the analysis of whether rates of growth of transport are similar (coupling) or not (decoupling) to rates of growth of gross domestic product (GDP).

As transport is a dynamic phenomenon evolving over time, the analysis of trends is a second prerequisite before modeling. Chapter 2 makes a profound analysis, over the past four decades, of passenger and freight demand for air, rail, road, and sea transport. The analysis is conducted both at world level and at the level of many countries.

Before selecting any modeling method, it is necessary for the forecaster to have a panorama of the various methods as well as of the successive steps for constructing a model. In Chapter 3, the classification of methods into qualitative (executive judgment, Delphi, scenario writing, questionnaire survey) and quantitative (trend projection, time series, econometric, gravity) is formulated, and each particular method is succinctly analyzed together with computational intelligence methods (artificial neural networks, fuzzy method). In addition to ordinary data, the application of "big data" is extensively analyzed. Utility theories, which can help to explain how an individual makes his choice for a specific transport mode, are presented.

The various qualitative methods are extensively presented and analyzed in Chapter 4 of the book along with the assumptions, characteristics, scientific background, and applications for transport demand problems. The executive judgment method is the outcome of the evaluation and assessment of a specific problem by specialists in a particular sector. The Delphi method is based on the judgment of a group of experts in successive rounds; the degree of consensus can be evaluated by means of the Kendall's coefficient of concordance. Scenario writing traces the pathways and describes the conditions of a new transport situation, by exploring the effects of past, present, and (likely or unlikely) future events, and can be projective (from the present to the future) or perspective-visionary (from the future to the present). Survey methods (of both stated and revealed preference) can monitor, detect, and quantify, based on questionnaire responses, the attitudes, trends, and prospects of customers of a transport service and hence of transport demand. For all qualitative methods, a number of applications for transport demand problems are illustrated.

Any modeling method is based on a number of statistical methods, such as simple and multiple regression analysis, which permit the correlation of transport demand with the factors affecting it, and these are explained in Chapter 5 of the book. The various statistical metrics, tests, and methods, assuring that regression analysis represents accurately a transport demand problem, are clarified: Pearson correlation coefficient, coefficient of determination, Student's t-test, F-test, multicollinearity test (detecting eventual correlation between independent variables), tests related to residuals, determination of outliers, existence or not of serial correlation in the residuals, heteroscedasticity tests, tests for the evaluation of the forecasting accuracy and forecasting ability. All the above are extensively put into practice in a specific example of multiple linear regression analysis.

Time series and trend projection, which are the two most commonly used quantitative methods for the forecast of transport demand, are analyzed in Chapter 6 of the book. The various components of a time series (trend, seasonal, cyclical, random) are identified, and a methodology for a seasonally adjusted trend projection is presented. Assumptions, methodology, successive steps, statistical tests, and the appropriate software and specific case-studies for the trend projection method of forecast of future transport demand are all analyzed in detail. It is quite useful to conduct an ex post assessment to verify or to reconsider previous forecasts. Other simple statistical methods, such as moving average and exponential smoothing, are given. The various time series processes (white noise, random walk, autoregressive, moving average, (seasonal or nonseasonal) autoregressive moving average) are analyzed and methods to check stationarity of a time series are presented. The Box—Jenkins method, the most popular iterative procedure of modeling a time series, is explained in detail, together with an extensive case-study application.

A causal correlation of transport demand to its generating forces (some of which are the independent variables) usually necessitates implementation of econometric models, which are the topic of Chapter 7 of the book. The successive steps, the assumptions, and the necessary conditions for the construction of an econometric model are described together with how the independent variables, the functional form, and the statistical tests should be selected. The statistical tests which certify the validity, accuracy, and forecasting ability of an econometric model are analyzed in detail. The appropriate econometric equations for air, rail, road transport (both for passenger and freight), public transport, and road safety are given together with the statistical tests that testify for their validity. An essential part of Chapter 7 is devoted to the four-step method for the forecast of transport demand at urban level. The various models for the four successive steps are analyzed: trip generation—first step (growth factor models, cross-classification models, regression models), trip distribution—second step (constrained growth factor models, gravity models), choice of transport mode—third step (Logit and Probit models), trip assignment—fourth step (all or nothing model, user equilibrium model, system optimum model). The appropriate modeling of freight transport demand (trend projection, four-step models, econometric models) is also presented.

The last two chapters of the book deal with applications of computational intelligence methods, which try to make machines do things that would require human intelligence, that is, to think like people, to act like people, and to think rationally and reasonably. Chapter 8 deals with artificial neural network (ANN) methods, which attempt to imitate the way biological neurons are operating (external input, activation or not, output). ANN can be used for short- and long-term forecasts of transport demand and can consider nonlinearities, a great number of input (independent) variables, and a tremendously high number of data. How an artificial neuron operates, the different forms of learning, and the various algorithms of ANN are explained. However, ANN does not provide any interpretation of the mechanism or the process of a problem. Detailed analytical examples of how ANN can be applied for transport problems are studied and applications of ANN for the forecast of air, rail, road transport demand, for the scheduling of freight transport, and for assessing maintenance needs are given.

Time series, econometric, and ANN methods are based on the measurability of a problem and employ real numbers. In contrast, a fuzzy number does not refer to one single value (as an ordinary real number) but to a set of plausible numerical values within a specified domain and around a central value. Fuzzy numbers are suitable for representing phenomena, like transport demand, with variations or oscillations around a numerical value, and can combine subjective and objective knowledge as well as take into account uncertainty, imprecision, ambiguity, series of data with missing values, linguistic variables, and even nonmeasurable data. The properties and mathematical description of fuzzy numbers are described. Detailed analytical examples of the application of fuzzy methods in regression analysis and for econometric models are studied. Applications of fuzzy regression analysis for the forecast of air, rail, road transport demand, road safety, logistics and routing of freight vehicles, and the optimization of airports are presented.

Some technical assistance was provided by Mr. Alexander Yiannopoulos, an American specialist in philosophy. We would like to express our sincere thanks to him.

The book was written parallel to our scientific, professional, and family obligations. We thank our families and collaborators for their understanding and patience.

September 2018   V.A. Profillidis and G.N. Botzoris

Chapter 1

Transport Demand and Factors Affecting It

Chapter Outline

1.1 THE BASIC DEFINITIONS RELATED TO TRANSPORT DEMAND

1.1.1 Transport and Human Life

Transport, along with food, health, energy, and home, is an essential and crucial activity of human life. Without transport the world of every human being would be limited to a few dozen kilometers around the area of his or her settlement. It is with transport that mankind has tried from the prehistoric era to broaden its horizons and the scale of its activities, to look for better conditions for survival and prosperity. Only in the case of very primitive human life, was man living, producing, and developing in a narrow geographical area. However, from the time of the first forms of human social organization, humans have realized the essential importance of meeting other people, exchanging experiences, coordinating their lives and strategies, discovering

Modeling of Transport Demand. https://doi.org/10.1016/B978-0-12-811513-8.00001-7
Copyright © 2019 Elsevier Inc. All rights reserved.
1

other civilizations and ways of living, buying and selling goods, and protecting or conquering land [1,2][1].

A good index which illustrates the importance of transport in human activity is its contribution to the gross domestic product (GDP) of a particular country. Indeed, transport represents, in 2015, 6.6% of GDP[2] for the 28 European Union (EU-28) countries (within EU-28, France 7.4%, Germany 7.8%, Italy 7.8%, Spain 7.1%, the United Kingdom 7.4%), 6.3% for the United States, 8.1% for Canada, 4.9% for China, 5.5% for India (for the year 2013), 6.1% for Russia, 5.9% for South Korea, 6.1% for Japan, and 5.3% for Australia [4,5].

1.1.2 Definition of Transport

A survey of the meaning of the word transport in the various languages and cultures of the world reveals that transport means to carry a person or a good from one place to another. It does not generate on behalf of the transporter any right on the transported person or good. Transport is a provisional situation which is completed and lost at the end of the travel. From this definition, it becomes apparent that the constituent elements of transport are the transported *person* or *good*, the *mode* with which transport is realized, and the *infrastructure* on which the mode moves [6].

1.1.3 The Various Transport Modes and Sectors

Transport modes are characterized by the type of infrastructure on which they move and can be classified as follows [7,8]:

- *road* transport, in which private cars, busses, trucks, motor bicycles, etc. are moving on a road infrastructure,
- *rail* transport, in which railway vehicles are moving on a railway track,
- *air* transport, in which aircrafts are flying in the air and landing and taking off in airports,
- *sea* transport, in which ships, ferries, etc. are sailing in the seas and approaching land in ports,
- *inland waterways*, in which river boats are moving in rivers,
- *cycling*, with the use of a bicycle, moving on a road or on a bicycle lane or on a walkway,
- *walking*, going on foot and covering a distance, usually on a walkway.

---

1. Numbers in brackets denote references, the list of which is at the end of the book.
2. Among the methods of calculation of GDP, data of this paragraph use the expenditure approach, according to which GDP is calculated as the sum of gross private consumption expenditures + gross private investment + government purchases + net exports (= exports − imports) [3].

1.1.4 Definition and Characteristics of Transport Demand

1.1.4.1 Definition of Transport Demand

Demand is a function or relationship which relates the amount Q of goods or services that will be purchased for a specific price P. The quantities Q and P are inversely related: Q increases when P decreases and vice versa (Fig. 1.1A).

Transport demand is in turn a function which relates the amount and type of transport (passenger or freight) that people will choose for a specific price and other quality conditions of the considered transport activity.

Supply is also a function relating the amount of goods or services that will be offered for purchase in a specific price P.

The price P_0 for which transport demand becomes practically zero is called the *prohibitive* price (Fig. 1.1B). On the other hand, the quantity Q_0 of a transport service corresponding to a practically zero price of this service is called the *need* of this specific transport service, and of course it is not infinite.

With the exception of strolling, for which transport is a product for final consumption, all other categories of transport demand are a pure form of derived demand, which is a consequence of the demand for something else, since transport is a means to satisfy other needs of the economy and the society. *Freight* transport and *passenger* transport for *work* satisfy specific needs of economic activity, while passenger transport for *leisure* and *tourism* satisfies specific social and cultural needs. Passenger transport for *shopping purposes* satisfies specific needs related both to the economic activity and to the personal needs of an individual or household.

Transport demand may refer to two major categories:

- Transport for *own account*: Individuals or companies own or lease transport vehicles and they perform, alone or with their staff, transport of passengers or freight on their own, without being paid for it.

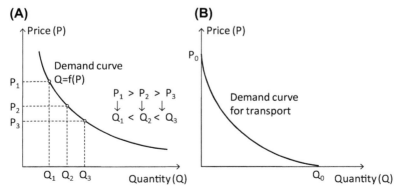

FIGURE 1.1 The demand curve relating price with quantity. (A) General demand curve. (B) Demand curve for transport.

- *Third-party* transport: A transporter (individual or company) undertakes the transport of passengers or freight under specific conditions of travel times and quality of service and is paid for this activity.

1.1.4.2 Principal Drivers of Transport Demand

The principal drivers that affect transport demand are [2,9—14]:

- *price* of the requested transport service,
- *quality* of the requested transport service (travel time, frequency, safety and security, ambience and facilities, reliability, etc.),
- price and quality of service of eventual *substitute* transport modes (e.g., high-speed trains, with $V \geq 200$ km/h, for low-cost air transport, busses and metros for private cars),
- *population* and *age* of the potential customers,
- *income* of the potential customers,
- *employment rate*,
- *lifestyle* habits and preferences (parts of the society consider busses and trains as a lower-quality product of the transport system, against private cars and airplanes),
- *land-use* patterns (distance from home to work, density of housing).

1.1.4.3 Transport Demand for an Infrastructure Facility or Operation Company

Transport demand may refer either to an infrastructure facility (e.g., an airport, a port terminal, a highway, a high-speed rail track) or to the operation of a transport company or service (e.g., passengers of an air company traveling between two airports, passengers of a bus authority of a city, passengers of a rail company between two cities, freight traffic of a shipping company between two ports).

1.1.4.4 Normal, Diverted, and Generated Demand

Demand has a dynamic character as it differs in relation to time and does not have a homogeneous character, since it incorporates diverse subsets of customers, with quite different characteristics, expectations, and requirements. To confront this latter issue, it is common practice to divide a set of demand into subsets which have more homogeneous characteristics and behavior. Thus, in relation to the transport infrastructure or mode from which demand has originated, we may distinguish the following [2,15,16]:

- *Normal* demand: This is the demand which would exist even without any change in the existing infrastructure or the transport services of an operation company. If, for instance, we transform a narrow road into a highway or replace old bus vehicles with modern ones, normal demand is that which would have existed even if the changes mentioned had not occurred.

- *Diverted* demand: This is the demand which shifts from one infrastructure element to another (e.g., from a rail track to a new highway) or from one transport mode to another (e.g., from private cars to a new metro line). This shift may be a result of the reduction of travel times, the increase of quality of transport services, reduced tariffs, improved safety, etc.
- *Generated* (or *derived*) demand: This is the demand which did not exist in the past but was created by the attractiveness of a new or improved facility or transport service (e.g., travelers of low-cost air carriers who were not traveling previously but decided to do so because of low tariffs and direct air links).

1.1.5 Definition of a Transport Model

The word model has a multitude of meanings. In science, a *model* is an effort to explain and forecast the evolution of a phenomenon of nature, society, the economy, or technology [17]. A model permits the establishment of a form of a *causal* relation between the phenomenon under study (e.g., passengers traveling by train between London and Paris) and the parameters which affect it (cost, travel times by train and other transport modes, quality of service, frequency of service, income of the traveler, etc.). Once the model is calibrated (see §3.7) and its forecasting ability is checked with the use of the appropriate statistical tests (see §5.11), it can be used to forecast future demand [14,18].

A model is a simplified representation of a reality and permits the illustration of complex phenomena and processes. To represent the real world, a model uses a set of variables which are adjusted in a logical and usually in a quantitative process. Mathematical and computational techniques are often (but not always) powerful tools for constructing models [19,20].

Models referring to physical or *technological systems* (such as an airport, a road, a railway track) have the character of *objectivity*, as they simulate physical laws which do not change in time and space. In contrast, models referring to economic and social phenomena inevitably have a *subjective* character; as most social and economic phenomena have a stochastic[3] character, they are variable in time and space and can differ from one place to another in relation to social attitudes and patterns of working conditions [2,7,21].

Transport models are constructs which employ a number of variables and parameters concerning the transport activity, economic conditions, and social attitudes, all adjusted in a logical and rational framework. This creates the possibility of understanding, explaining, and forecasting the evolution of the

---

3. A phenomenon or process is defined as deterministic when it is possible to correlate accurately ex ante what effects will be produced from specific causes (e.g., the law of gravitation in physics, see §3.9.7). By contrast, any phenomenon which can only be analyzed in a probabilistic way, with the help of statistical data and methods, is defined as stochastic.

specific transport phenomenon. Transport models have both a subjective character (related to economic and social conditions) and an objective one (related to the technological and physical characteristics of the transport activity).

1.1.6 Metrics and Units for the Description of Transport Demand

Every quantifiable phenomenon (such as transport demand) needs its *metrics*, that is, a system or standard or parameter which affords us the ability to measure, compare, evaluate, and assess a specific magnitude or property or situation. Metrics may refer to physical properties (such as weight and distance), economic properties (expressed in monetary values), socioeconomic properties (such as the number of customers of a service), and many others. Metrics must reliably and objectively represent the quantified phenomenon [22].

Transport is an activity with both technological and socioeconomic aspects. A passenger has a weight and travels a certain distance, at the same time he or she is a customer and spends money for his or her travel.

To describe the aforementioned characteristics of transport activity, a number of units are employed to define representative metrics of the phenomenon under consideration [22]:

- number of *passengers* (for passenger traffic) or *tonnes*[4] (for freight traffic): This permits to know which part of the offered capacity is used and at the same time the attractiveness of the service,
- number of *passenger-kilometers* (p-km) or *tonne-kilometers* (t-km): A passenger-kilometer is a unit to describe a passenger who travels 1 km[5], and respectively for the tonne-kilometer. These units, p-km and t-km, take into account both the number of passengers (or tonnes) and the distance traveled,
- number of *vehicles* or *vehicle-kilometers*, which permits to calculate:
  - what part of the offered capacity of a given infrastructure is used,
  - the loading and deterioration of infrastructure, which will permit to calculate its maintenance and operation conditions,
- *distance traveled* (in km or miles) and the mean distance per category of traffic,
- *revenue* (in monetary values) *generated* per unit of traffic (per p-km or t-km): This unit permits to assess the economic and financial impact of a specific transport activity.

---

4. A tonne (or metric ton) equals 1000 kg (or 9806.65 N). It should be distinguished from the short ton, a unit used in the United States (1 short ton = 2000 pounds = 0.907 metric ton) and from the long ton, a traditional British unit (1 long ton = 2240 pounds = 1.016 metric tons).
5. The unit of distance used is kilometer (km) or mile (in the United States, the United Kingdom, and elsewhere), 1 mile = 1.609344 km. The nautical mile is very seldom used, 1 nautical mile = 1.8520 km.

1.2 HISTORICAL EVOLUTION OF TRANSPORT MODES AND DEMAND

During the last 5000 years, we can identify five essential inventions—innovations in the sector of transport:

- the *wheel* (around 3500−3000 BC) in Mesopotamia,
- the technique of *navigation* (around 3000 BC in Nile, Egypt; around 2000 BC in Phoenicia),
- the technology of the *railway* (early 1800s),
- the technology of the *car* (late 1800s),
- the invention and development of the *airplane* (early 1900s).

The form of the transport sector today does not differ essentially and greatly from the situation one century ago. Private cars, trains, airplanes, and their corresponding infrastructures (roads, tracks, airports) changed, but not substantially, in one century. They are old technologies which were improved by new materials and new information-communication techniques, as well as automatization and artificial intelligence applications.

In the last two centuries, we can distinguish three great economic cycles; each one is characterized by a specific transport mode which developed rapidly during this cycle (Fig. 1.2) [7]:

- the *coal* and *steel* industrial revolution from 1800 until 1930 was accompanied by the development and expansion of the *railway*,
- the development of *electricity* and the exploitation of *oil* were accompanied from 1900 to now by the development and expansion of the *private car*. This cycle, though declining, is still in process,
- the era (from around 1960) of *computers*, the *Internet*, *automatization*, and *biotechnology*, which today is still in its developing stage, is accompanied by the development of *airplanes*, *high-speed trains*, and *high-speed ships* but also by congestion in all types of infrastructure, environmental problems, and safety issues.

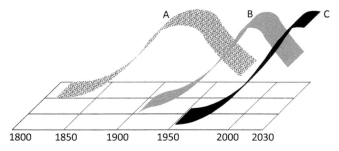

FIGURE 1.2 Economic cycles and transport technologies in the last two centuries. (A) Steel, coal, steam railway, inorganic chemistry. (B) Oil, electricity, electrified railway, private car, organic chemistry. (C) Globalization, computers, Internet, airplane, electric car, high-speed railway, biotechnology. *Source: Modified from Refs. [7,23].*

The succession of so many innovations in the transport sector for two centuries has permitted people in Europe after 1800 to increase the amount of kilometers traveled per year by 3%–3.5%, which leads to doubling every 20 years. Thus the average distance traveled per person per day increased in Europe from a few kilometers in 1800 to around 40 km in 2017. The average traveling *speed* worldwide was 5–10 km/h in 1800 (era of horse power), increased to 25 km/h in 1900 (steam power), to 40 km/h in 2000 (era of private cars, airplanes, and high-speed trains), and around 50 km/h in 2017 (due to the further expansion of air transport) [2,24–28].

Surprisingly, the average amount of time that individuals are eager to spend for transport remains almost unchanged in all historical periods and without any effect of the income level [29]. This time is estimated at 1.1 h per person per day, generally varying from 0.8 to 1.2 h [30].

Although there is always time lag between technological innovation and its applications to real problems of transport and acceptance by society, technological improvements have resulted in faster, cheaper, and more comfortable transport.

1.3 HOW TRANSPORT DEMAND AFFECTS THE TRANSPORT SYSTEM

Transport demand is an essential (and often crucial) input and a prerequisite of all aspects related to both the infrastructure and the operation of a transport activity.

1.3.1 Transport Demand and Transport Infrastructure

1.3.1.1 Planning

Good planning (see also §1.6) is necessary before any consideration of the construction of new infrastructure. No serious planning can be conducted without an accurate knowledge of future demand. All components of, e.g., a new airport (runway, apron, terminal, land access, air navigation systems, safety systems) will be planned on the basis of the estimated daily and hourly demand.

Feasibility analysis, through which the realization of a future transport project or improvement is justified (or not), also needs accurate data concerning estimated future demand. All feasibility criteria[6] (benefit/cost ratio, net present value, internal rate of return) compare future costs (construction and operation) with the benefits rendered, which may be financial (revenues) or socioeconomic (reduced travel times, increased quality of service and accessibility, increased economic output, increased safety).

---

6. An analysis of feasibility criteria can be found in Refs. [2,15,31–33].

1.3.1.2 Design and Construction

Design and construction need more technical data. Critical among them is the value of the wheel or axle load, on which is based the design of any transport infrastructure, the calculation of the thickness of the various layers, and the selection of the appropriate type of the various materials as well as their corresponding strength. Wheel or axle load is calculated on the basis of daily or hourly demand, by making choices related to the types of aircraft (airports), trains (railways), or cars and busses (road). All formulas, graphs, and nomographs of the design of the various transport infrastructures have as their necessary input the value of the wheel or axle load as well as the number of loadings, all of which depend on transport demand.

1.3.1.3 Degree of Deterioration and Maintenance

Good maintenance is essential for the efficient, safe, and economical operation of any infrastructure. The frequency, nature, and number of interventions for maintenance are a function of the loads exerted on it, which are calculated on the basis of the rates of growth of demand over time. As many transport infrastructures have high values of economic life (around 30 years for roads, around 100 years for tunnels, around 50 years for bridges, around 40 years for railway tracks, around 50 years for ports [2,34]), all demand forecasts should provide a vision for the evolution of demand over rather long periods of time.

1.3.1.4 Operation of Infrastructure

The operation of any infrastructure involves a number of activities: personnel and equipment for the survey of operation, energy to be provided (electrified railway tracks and metro tracks), lighting, equipment, and personnel for safety and security. All the above depend on demand and its evolution over time.

1.3.1.5 Level of Saturation and Measures Required

Any transport infrastructure has its own limits as to the number of passengers or tonnes that can be served under specific conditions of quality of service. This limit is called transport capacity. For instance, the capacity of a highway lane is 2000 passenger car equivalents[7]/h/direction; the maximum

---

7. The term passenger car equivalents (PCE) was introduced to define the effect of heavy (trucks and busses) or light (motorcycles) vehicles on the traffic and indicates the number of passenger cars that are displaced by a single heavy or light vehicle of a particular type under prevailing roadway, traffic, and control conditions [35]. For example, indicative values for transforming a given type of vehicle into a PCE are: private car (including taxis or pick-up), 1; motorcycle, 0.5; light commercial vehicles, 2.0; busses and trucks, 3.0.

throughput capacity[8] of a single runway with visual operation and a fleet of medium size aircraft is 60 flights/h; the capacity of a fully automated metro track is 35—45 trains/h/direction (depending on the number of vehicles per train and on the signaling system) [2,7,28].

Once demand approaches the level of capacity, saturation phenomena appear, which will require either new infrastructure or measures (such as an increase of tariffs and the introduction of tolls) to dissuade new customers from using the existing infrastructure. The path toward saturation is usually described in demand forecasts.

1.3.2 Transport Demand and Operation

1.3.2.1 Number of Cars, Aircrafts, Railway Vehicles, Ships

The fleet of a transport company (number of cars, busses, aircrafts, railway vehicles, ships, etc.) is a direct consequence of the future demand to be served. Buying or leasing one unit of the above transport modes is a costly business, which may be disastrous economically if transport demand forecasts are ignored or do not exist.

1.3.2.2 Number of Personnel

The number of personnel of a transport company (pilots, cabin, and land personnel of an air company; the number of drivers, conductors, and loco-motive engineers of a railway company; the number of drivers of busses and metros) is calculated on the basis of estimated future demand and its variations over time. Peak periods (with their additional demand) will require additional staff, whereas lower demand periods will require fewer (or part-time) staff.

1.3.2.3 Commercial and Tariff Policies, Revenues

Demand is a keystone (along with elasticities [see §1.9] and offered capacity) of future commercial and tariff policies, which aim at the maximization of revenues, while making the optimum use of the offered capacity.

1.3.3 Transport Demand and CO_2 Emissions

Transport is an important source of CO_2 emissions with a major contribution to the greenhouse effect (understood as a continuous increase in the average temperature of the planet during the prior four decades), as it contributes by

---

8. Maximum throughput capacity (MTC) defines the average number of movements (arrivals and/ or departures) that can be performed on the runway in 1 h. MTC makes the assumptions of a continuous supply of arrivals and/or departures, no simultaneous runway occupancy, safe wake vortex separation distances between two flights, and a static fleet mix (i.e., the types of aircraft do not change) [28,36].

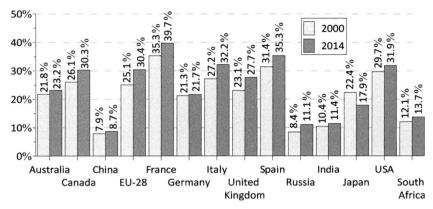

FIGURE 1.3 CO_2 emissions of the transport sector as a percentage of total CO_2 emissions for some countries worldwide. *Source: Compiled by the authors, based on data of Ref. [37].*

itself almost one-fourth of CO_2 emissions worldwide (Fig. 1.3). It is clear that any collective effort (such as the annual United Nations Climate Change conferences since 1995) to mitigate the greenhouse effect will be based on estimated future demand, which will in turn be calculated according to the measures to be undertaken, such as the internalization of external costs and taxes per tonne of emitted CO_2 (see also §1.8.4.5).

As rates of CO_2 emissions follow rates of GDP growth worldwide (Fig. 1.4), any effort to reduce CO_2 emissions, while keeping increased GDP growth rates, will require a decoupling (see §1.7) between rates of transport activity and rates of GDP growth.

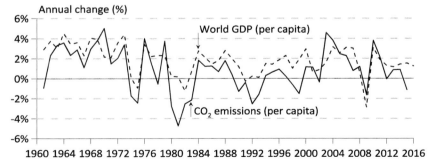

FIGURE 1.4 Annual growth rates of global gross domestic product (GDP) and per capita CO_2 emissions worldwide. *Source: Compiled by the authors, based on data of Refs. [37,38].*

1.4 THE OVERWHELMING AND REVOLUTIONARY EFFECTS OF NEW TECHNOLOGIES

New technological achievements and innovations were always a factor of changes in the economy and the everyday life of people. However, the combination of full mechanization, computers, and the Internet revolution has radically changed our way of living and dramatically affects transport.

Easy access to acquisition, transfer, and reassembling of information permits organization of a trip, seat reservation, payment of the ticket, eventual organization of car sharing (see §1.7.3.4) in an easy and no-cost way. At the same time, however, the access by unauthorized persons to personal data and the intrusion into privacy cannot be excluded.

Automation will lead to fully automated airplanes, trains, and ships, including the accurate monitoring of the position and speed of any of these. Some predict the full automation of private cars. Such an outcome is not free from problems related to liability. Furthermore, many people still prefer to drive (and not to be driven), and they are ready to pay for the joy of driving. Some will undoubtfully consider fully automated cars to be utilized as driving bombs [52].

New methods of communication among people, between man and object, and between object and object permit us to interlink processes, to select the optimum itinerary, and to take measures in real time.

In-depth understanding of the changing character of the world is necessary for a good understanding of the transport sector of tomorrow. Indeed, facts in the far future begin now. The world is becoming more open, and in any case, the course of future events is not predetermined. Innovation in transport offers so much to so many in such a short time and at a really low cost.

In contrast to what has happened in the past, when even abrupt technological changes were integrated into human-oriented patterns and structures, the combined effects of the use of machines, computers, and the Internet on the mobility of persons and goods oblige us to consider two eventual scenarios [2,52]:

1. In the *humanistic* approach, although machines and technology will govern more and more activities of the human being, they will continue to serve humanity. However, some forms of mobility will be changed or replaced (e.g., teleworking, teleconference).
2. In the *technology-oriented* approach, an alarming break in civilization habits is considered to be imminent. Technology is overcoming and governing the human being, which becomes the object and not the master of mobility. Technology will create new kinds of ethics in societies. According to this approach, it will be difficult to integrate technological achievements in the existing patterns of the economy and society, and there is the real risk for humanity to be governed by technology.

1.5 EVOLUTION OVER TIME OF THE PRINCIPAL DRIVERS OF TRANSPORT DEMAND

Transport is not a purpose in itself. It exists to satisfy other human activities, which are affected by evolutions of the economy, technology, and society. In addition, transport is an activity that cannot be stored; if it is not used, it is lost. Thus, the evolution of the principal drivers for transport demand is as follows.

1.5.1 Passenger Transport

The principal forces driving passenger transport during the last two centuries have been the following [2,7]:

- A strong increase in the *purchasing power* of individuals as the result of an almost continuous increase in *incomes*, due to the rather high rates of economic growth during the last five decades (Table 1.1). As incomes were continuously increasing, individuals were looking for transport solutions that were more expensive but at the same time more convenient to their needs and expectations. Increase in personal income is at the origin of the explosion of private cars as well as of air transport. Expenditure for transport represents a significant component of a contemporary household's expenses (Table 1.2).
- *Technological evolutions* and *improvements*, which permitted a spectacular increase in speeds and thereby the reduction of travel times, as well as increased comfort and convenience, improved accessibility, and the reduction (per unit of transport) of environmental impact. Air transport, which was an exceptional activity some decades ago, is now an ordinary, everyday practice.
- Reduction of *travel costs*, due to technological improvements, reduction of the production costs of transport vehicles as a result of the relocation of many industries to low-wage countries, economies of scale, reduction of taxes, and better methods of organization and management. Some transport activities (such as air transport and possession of a private car), which were the privilege of only a few high-income social classes some decades ago, can now be used by medium- (or even low-) income individuals. A characteristic and extreme example is the low-cost air transport companies. Fig. 1.5 illustrates reduction of average passenger traveling costs in the United States over the last decades.
- Evolution of *social attitudes* and *lifestyle*, which are characterized by the following:
  - increasing *individualism*: Transport is often seen by many as an extension of the private space of their house or office. This tendency is concealed under the explosive increase in the number of private cars,
  - *minimization* of lost time (in transport or elsewhere), something that creates the tendency toward faster and faster transport,
  - *comfort*, *ease*: The conditions of travel are expected to be similar to conditions in the house or the office,

TABLE 1.1: Growth rates of gross domestic product per capita worldwide.

	1960–1969 (%)	1970–1979 (%)	1980–1989 (%)	1990–1999 (%)	2000–2016 (%)	1960–1989 (%)	1990–2016 (%)	1960–2016 (%)
Australia	2.80	1.31	1.84	2.07	1.45	2.08	1.71	1.91
Brazil	2.92	5.81	0.07	0.77	1.32	3.14	1.18	2.08
Canada	3.55	2.77	1.70	1.54	0.88	2.58	1.24	1.88
China	0.28	4.06	8.31	9.44	8.86	4.64	9.02	6.61
EU-28		2.84	2.14	1.84	1.03	2.42	1.41	2.28
France	4.40	3.19	1.87	1.52	0.54	3.14	0.98	2.12
Germany		3.07	1.94	1.49	1.14		1.33	
Italy	5.00	3.32	2.40	1.38	−0.34	3.59	0.41	2.07
Spain	6.64	2.69	2.44	2.08	0.65	3.79	1.30	2.63
UK	2.25	2.47	3.03	1.96	1.04	2.52	1.45	1.98
India	1.73	0.26	3.22	3.76	5.74	1.86	4.90	3.29
Japan	9.09	3.44	3.92	0.90	0.76	5.06	0.88	3.10
South Korea	6.66	8.63	8.62	5.74	3.32	7.55	4.33	6.06
Russia				−5.24	3.41		0.59	
USA	3.32	2.49	2.55	2.10	0.92	2.62	1.41	2.02
World	3.52	2.16	1.36	1.13	1.52	2.27	1.44	1.87

Source: Compiled by the authors, based on data of Ref. [38].

TABLE 1.2: Expenditure for transport as a percentage (%) of the total expenditure (in US$) per capita, values of the year 2015.

Country	Consumption expenditure per capita for transport		of which:					
			Purchase of transport equipment		Operation of transport equipment		Purchase of transport services	
	US$	%	US$	%	US$	%	US$	%
Australia	3018	10.0	598	2.0	1487	4.9	933	3.1
Canada	3595	14.8	1557	6.4	1545	6.4	493	2.0
EU-28	2414	13.0	673	3.6	1209	6.5	532	2.9
France	2687	13.0	686	3.3	1511	7.3	490	2.4
Germany	3193	14.4	1021	4.6	1390	6.3	782	3.5
Italy	2337	11.8	496	2.5	1464	7.4	377	1.9
Spain	1823	10.9	476	2.8	1034	6.2	313	1.9
UK	3234	13.8	985	4.2	1280	5.5	969	4.1
India (2014)	126	14.0	18	1.9	46	5.2	62	6.9
Japan	2040	11.7			n.a.			
Russia	584	12.0	228	4.7	204	4.2	152	3.1
South Korea	1601	12.3			n.a.			
USA	3550	9.4	1257	3.3	1934	5.1	360	1.0

Source: Compiled by the authors, based on data of Refs. [5,38].

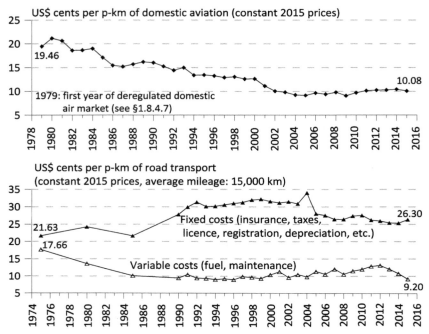

FIGURE 1.5   Evolution of average traveling costs in the United States. *Source: Compiled by the authors, based on data of Refs. [39,40].*

- An increase in the global *population* (Fig. 1.6), from 900 million in 1800, to 7.442 billion in 2016, estimated to reach 8.551 billion in 2030 and 9.771 billion in 2050.
- Changes in the pattern of urban development (Fig. 1.7), characterized by an increase in densities of population, the relocation of many urban activities (housing, services, commerce) to areas formerly considered remote, all of which require new parking and road facilities, efficient bus and metro systems, etc.

1.5.2 Freight Transport

Many of the factors driving the increase in passenger transport also apply to freight transport, the growth of which is similarly linked to economic growth. However, freight is only one component of the supply chain, which includes, in addition to transport, one or more of the following (Fig. 1.8): collection and distribution, loading of the product, assembly, warehouses, delivery to the consumer, a continuous flow of information. Transport costs constitute a small component of the total cost of a product: around 10% for agricultural products and even less for raw and manufactured materials [2]. Half of world

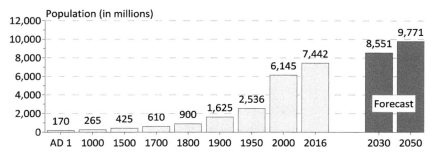

FIGURE 1.6 Evolution of world population since AD 1 and estimation for the years 2030 and 2050. *Source: Compiled by the authors, based on data of Refs. [41–43].*

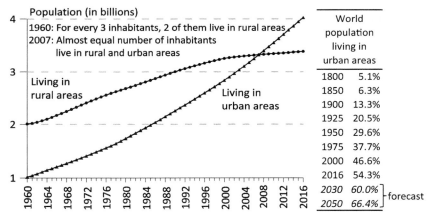

FIGURE 1.7 Evolution of world population living in rural and urban areas. *Source: Compiled by the authors, based on data of Refs. [38,43,44].*

freight travels a distance greater than 3000 km from the area of production to the area of consumption. In the supply chain, transport represents 40%–60% of the total logistics costs. The upper or lower value of the previous percentages depend on the existence of warehouses, refrigeration equipment, etc. [2,45–47].

Understanding the nature and structure of freight transport requires not only describing the route of goods from the place of production to the place of consumption but also exploring how goods are produced, where goods are sought for consumption, and what are the alternative routes, modes, and costs of transport (see also §7.11).

For many years, freight transport has been the poor child in transport science, which has principally focused on passengers. In addition, there is a lack of information and data for many categories of freight; hence our

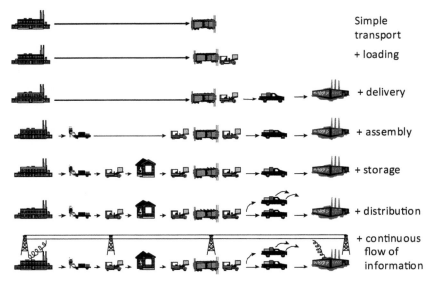

FIGURE 1.8   Freight transport as a component of the logistics chain. *Source: Compiled by the authors.*

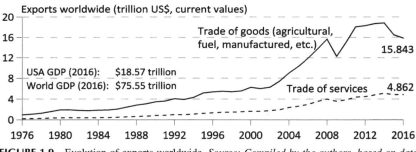

FIGURE 1.9   Evolution of exports worldwide. *Source: Compiled by the authors, based on data of Ref. [38].*

knowledge on this matter is neither accurate nor complete. The driving forces[9] for freight transport are the following:

- An increase in the *purchasing power* of consumers as a result of the increase in incomes. However, the rates of growth in physical terms are worldwide less than half of the rates of growth in monetary terms. The reason is that a large part of GDP worldwide is created by services and the knowledge-based economy, which do not need freight transport [2,7] (Figs. 1.9 and 1.10).

---

9. The terms driving forces and drivers used in this book are interchangeable.

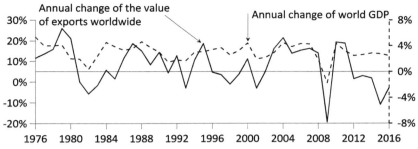

FIGURE 1.10   Rates of evolution of exports and gross domestic product (GDP) worldwide. *Source: Compiled by the authors, based on data of Ref. [38].*

- Technological innovations, new methods of organization, and digitalization have made freight transport *faster, cheaper,* and *more reliable.* Reduced freight costs are the origin of half of its growth over the last several decades [2,7,48]. It is questionable, however, whether this reduction of freight costs can continue, taking into account environmental constraints.
- Relocation of companies, in search of lower wage costs, is changing the flow of goods from emerging economies to their local markets and to markets in Europe and North America.
- Rates of growth in various industries are also changing rapidly. Growing industries include electrical products, chemicals, and plastics, whereas shrinking industries include raw materials, textiles, etc. There is a clear tendency to products with less bulk, higher value, and lighter weight.

1.6 HOW TRANSPORT DEMAND AFFECTS THE PLANNING OF THE TRANSPORT SYSTEM

1.6.1 Demand and Transportation[10] Planning

The structure, organization, and evolution of each transport mode (e.g., air transport) and its interactions with other transport modes and with the characteristics of the economy and society (population, technology, income, cost, social attitudes, etc.) are the outcome of a complex procedure known as transportation planning. *Transportation planning* is the process by which a planner tries to understand, explain, and forecast the evolution of the problem under study and suggests goals, structures, organization, and investment to meet future needs in the most efficient way by taking the maximum utility and advantages from a specific transport infrastructure or service [2].

The point of departure for any planning is the existing situation. Next, future demand is assessed, alternative solutions to meet future demand are

---

10. The terms transport and transportation used in this book are interchangeable.

surveyed, and the best among them is chosen. As it is never clear what is best, an essential characteristic of planning is collaboration between planners, transport authorities, politicians, and the public. Demand is the most critical parameter, as it affects all aspects of both the infrastructure and the operation of transport companies.

1.6.2 Demand and Business and Master Plans

Transport planning is usually incorporated into the so-called *business plan* or *master plan*, in which planners attempt to identify the strategy that should be followed in relation to the various parameters of the internal and the external environment (see §1.8.2). Planning usually results in the compilation of various scenarios, each of which requires a demand forecast. The various scenarios allow one of the several recommended solutions to be chosen in any given situation.

A business or master plan is based on the assumption that the fundamental economic and technological characteristics related to the problem under study will remain invariable or will follow a specific course. This, however, occurs only rarely; the implementation of a transportation solution, based on a business plan's projected scenario (often conducted several years earlier), can give the illusion of a scientific approach but may in fact have little to do with reality. A business or master plan constitutes nothing other than the framework within which the eventual solution of a specific problem can be explored [7,49].

The essential characteristics of a business plan are *clarity, ranking of objectives and priorities*, specific *implementation methods*, *flexibility*, and *expandability*, so as to successfully respond to future situations, which are unclear from today's perspective [7,50,51].

1.7 TRANSPORT DEMAND AND ECONOMIC ACTIVITY: COUPLING AND DECOUPLING

1.7.1 Correlation of Transport Demand With Economic Activity

For some years, to a number of economists and engineers, the prediction of future transport demand was a rather easy task: they considered that the growth rates of transport should follow a pattern similar to the growth rates of GDP. However, this is rarely the case and only occurs under specific values of per capita GDP and specific patterns of urban development. But even when growth rates of transport globally are similar to growth rates of GDP, this is not reflected in all sectors of transport. For instance, growth rates of air transport between 2000 and 2014 were almost triple the growth rates of GDP (Fig. 1.11).

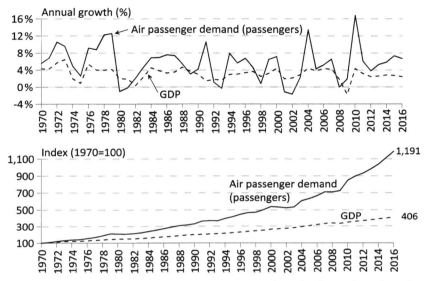

FIGURE 1.11   Rates and index of evolution of air passenger demand and gross domestic product (GDP) worldwide. *Source: Compiled by the authors, based on data of Ref. [38].*

Fig. 1.12 illustrates the evolution of GDP, passenger, and freight transport for countries representing 51.8% of world population and 73.4% of world GDP over the last 25 years. Until 2000, growth rates of passenger transport for some countries (China, France, Italy, Japan, Russia, the United States, EU-28) were almost the same as the growth rates of GDP for each country. But since 2000, the growth rates of passenger transport have diverged from the growth rates of GDP. Furthermore, the growth rates of freight transport for some countries (Australia, Germany, Italy, India, Japan, the United Kingdom until 1998, the United States) up to 2000 were almost the same as the growth rates of their GDP, but since 2000 a divergence of the evolution of both passenger and freight transport from the evolution of GDP is clear in most countries.

1.7.2 Coupling and Decoupling Between Transport Demand and Gross Domestic Product—Various Forms and Degrees of Decoupling

Coupling between transport and economic activity (expressed by the GDP per capita or the disposable personal income) is the state of affairs when the rates of change of transport activity vary with the rates of change of GDP. *Decoupling*, on the contrary, is the break in the link between transport activity and GDP and reflects a situation where the *rates of change of transport activity are not reflected to the rates of change of GDP.* Decoupling signifies the

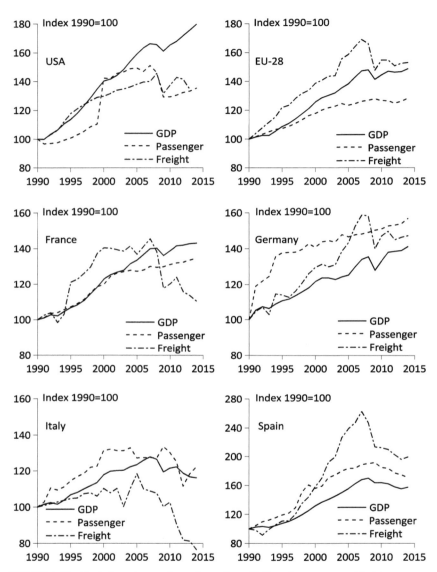

FIGURE 1.12 Evolution of gross domestic product (GDP) and passenger and freight transport for some countries of the world. *Source: Compiled by the authors, based on data of Refs. [5,38].*

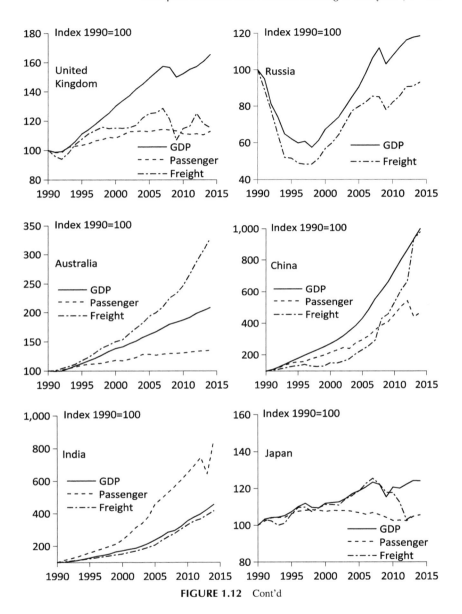

FIGURE 1.12   Cont'd

alteration of the formerly existing causal relationship (if indeed there were any) between transport and GDP [53–55].

Coupling or decoupling between transport and GDP is measured in terms of the ratio of the rate of change of transport activity to the rate of change of GDP. We will call this ratio the elasticity $\varepsilon_{transport,GDP}$ of transport in relation to GDP [53]:

$$\varepsilon_{transport,\ GDP} = \frac{\%\ \Delta\ transport}{\%\ \Delta\ GDP} \tag{1.1}$$

We define the situation as coupling when $0.8 \leq \varepsilon_{transport,GDP} \leq 1.2$ and decoupling when $\varepsilon_{transport,GDP} > 1.2$ or $\varepsilon_{transport,GDP} < 0.8$. Coupling can be defined as expansive when rates of both GDP and transport are positive and recessive when rates of both GDP and transport are negative (Fig. 1.13). Decoupling may be weak when $0 < \varepsilon_{transport,GDP} < 0.8$ or strong when $\varepsilon_{transport,GDP} < 0$. Furthermore, decoupling may be expansive when the rates of both GDP and transport activity are positive and recessive when rates of both GDP and transport activity are negative. Thus, in weak decoupling, the rates of change of both GDP and transport activity are positive, and $0 < \varepsilon_{transport,GDP} < 0.8$; in strong decoupling, the rates of change of GDP are

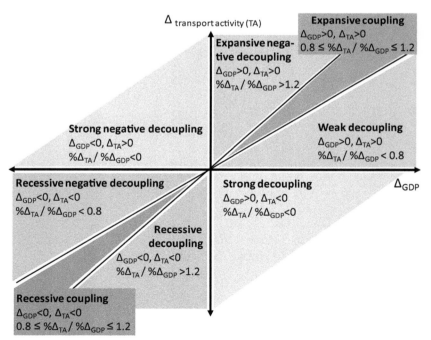

FIGURE 1.13 Degrees of coupling and decoupling between transport activity and gross domestic product (GDP). *Source: Compiled by the authors, modified from Refs. [53,57].*

positive, whereas the rates of change of transport activity are negative, and $\varepsilon_{transport,GDP} < 0$; and in recessive decoupling, the rates of change of both GDP and transport activity are negative, and $\varepsilon_{transport,GDP} > 1.2$. In the case of negative decoupling, we encounter the situation of expansive negative decoupling, when the rates of change of both GDP and transport activity are positive and $\varepsilon_{transport,GDP} > 1.2$; strong negative decoupling when rates of change of GDP are negative, rates of change of transport activity are positive, and $\varepsilon_{transport,GDP} < 0$; and weak negative decoupling when rates of change of both GDP and transport activity are negative, and $0 < \varepsilon_{transport,GDP} < 0.8$ [53,56].

The decoupling of both passenger and freight transport demand from GDP is considered an efficient way to maintain economic growth and increase GDP, while assuring efficiency of transport from an economic and environmental point of view, because:

- if transport demand has lower rates of growth compared with GDP, this will lead to fewer emissions and environmental effects, thus contributing to environmental sustainability,
- if the link between GDP and transport demand is not broken, then any increase in GDP will require the construction of new transport infrastructure and investment, thus contributing to an endless vicious circle, which is neither economically nor environmentally efficient [58−61].

1.7.3 Factors Affecting the Degree of Decoupling Between Gross Domestic Product and Transport Demand—Passenger Transport

1.7.3.1 Limits of Available Time and Money

In §1.2 it was noted that for many centuries the average time spent in transport is 1.1 h per person per day. The increase in mobility is principally due to the increase in speed, which, however, for technical and safety reasons reaches its limits [2] (Fig. 1.14).

Households spend a percentage of their revenues for transport (see Table 1.2). In periods of recession of the economy or of changes in lifestyle, individuals may decide to spend less for transport and more for other activities.

1.7.3.2 Effects of the Internet

Use of the Internet for everyday activities is spreading and causes major changes in transport:

- *Teleworking* and *teleconferencing* grant the possibility of working at home or attending a meeting at distance, and thus many trips from work to home or from one work site to another will disappear. In the United States, 4.4% of citizens were working at home in 2014, as opposed to 3.3% in 2000,

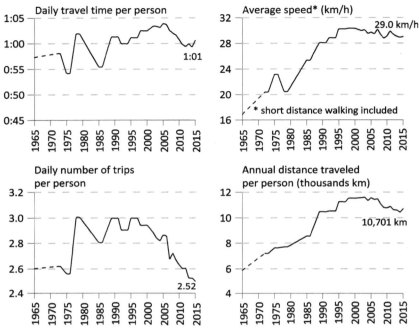

FIGURE 1.14 Trends in the time spent for traveling, the average speed, the mobility, and the distance traveled in Great Britain (after 1989 data refer to England, a change that is unlikely to affect the broad conclusions derived). *Source: Compiled by the authors, based on data of Ref. [67].*

3.0% in 1990, and 2.3% in 1980. However, up to 50% of jobs (among them accountants, advertisers, design engineers, etc.) may be suitable for teleworking. Thus, by 2050 passenger traffic may well be reduced, due to teleworking, by 10% [62–65].

- *Electronic commerce* (e-commerce) allows the sale of consumer products, delivered at home, via the Internet, (Figs. 1.15 and 1.16) [66]. Thus, some forms of passenger transport have been replaced by some forms of freight transport.
- *E-learning* and *e-management* permit the pursuit of studies and management activities from a distance and can reduce some categories of passenger transport.

1.7.3.3 Changes in Urban Development Patterns

Changes in urban development patterns are slow. If future cities are organized according to a green urban model, many daily transport activities will be performed by walking or cycling, thus reducing the number of short-distance car trips [71,72].

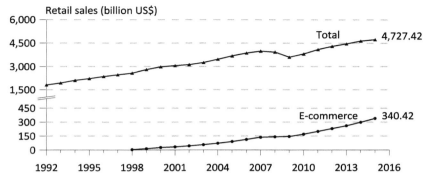

FIGURE 1.15   Evolution of annual retail sales in the United States, total and e-commerce. *Source: Compiled by the authors, based on data of Ref. [68].*

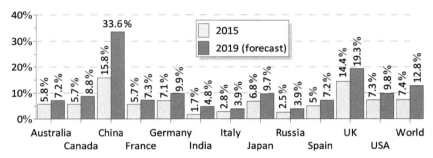

FIGURE 1.16   Retail e-commerce sales (as a percentage of total retail sales) in 2015 and forecast for the year 2019 for selected countries worldwide. *Source: Compiled by the authors, based on data of Refs. [69,70].*

1.7.3.4 Extensive Use of Global Positioning System, Car Sharing, and Carpooling

Extensive use of global positioning system (GPS) will reduce the length of passenger trips, while extensive use of *car sharing* or *carpooling* will result in fewer passenger trips.

Private cars remain immobile for 95.5% of their operational life span [2]. This fact, combined with the high costs of purchasing and operating a car (Fig. 1.5), has led to forms of ownership and use where a car can serve several households or individuals. In the simplest form of carpooling, car owners share their car with other people for specific trips (Table 1.3) [73—76]. In Europe, carpooling is used for medium distances of about 200 km [77].

Car sharing refers to forms of car rental services in which several users share a car fleet owned by a service-providing company. Members of the car sharing network pay a monthly or annual fee (usually based on both time and mileage), allowing the use of cars located at various parking points in a city

TABLE 1.3: How people travel to work in the United States.

| Year | Automobile | | Public transport (%) | Walk (%) | Bicycle/Motorcycle (%) | Other (%) | Work at home (%) |
	Drive alone (%)	Carpooled (%)					
1970	57.5	20.2	8.5	7.4	n.a.	n.a.	3.5
1980	64.4	19.7	6.2	5.6	0.9	0.9	2.3
1990	73.2	13.4	5.1	3.9	0.6	0.8	3.0
2000	75.7	12.2	4.7	2.9	0.5	0.7	3.3
2010	76.6	9.7	4.9	2.8	0.7	1.0	4.3
2016	76.3	9.0	5.1	2.7	0.7	1.2	5.0

Source: Compiled by the authors, based on data of Ref. [81].

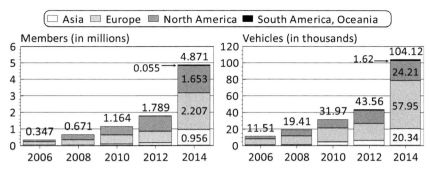

FIGURE 1.17 Evolution of car sharing in the world. *Source: Compiled by the authors, based on data of Refs. [82,83].*

for a specific time slot, and then park them at either the same or another specific parking point [78—80]. Between 2006 and 2014, the annual growth in membership of car sharing networks worldwide was 39.1%, and the annual growth of car sharing fleets was 31.7% (Fig. 1.17).

1.7.4 Factors Affecting the Degree of Decoupling Between Gross Domestic Product and Transport Demand—Freight Transport

1.7.4.1 Changes in the Composition of the Economy

Many industrialized or developing countries are transforming their economies from the agricultural and industrial sectors to the service sector (Table 1.4),

TABLE 1.4: Gross domestic product (GDP) sector composition of world economies (value added, % of GDP).

Region	Year	Agriculture sector (%)	Industry sector (%)	Service sector (%)
Low-income countries	1995	41.7	16.7	41.6
	2015	30.5	21.6	47.9
Middle-income countries	1995	15.9	37.3	46.8
	2015	8.6	33.9	57.5
High-income countries	1995	2.4	29.2	68.4
	2015	1.5	24.4	74.1
World	1995	8.1	33.6	58.3
	2015	3.8	27.2	69.0

Source: Compiled by the authors, based on data of Ref. [38].

which obviously requires less freight transport. But even outside of the service sector, there is a tendency toward lighter materials, which require less freight transport.

1.7.4.2 Relocation of Manufacturing Activities

The relocation of manufacturing activities in search of lower labor costs will continue to move furthermore many industrial activities to more distant areas, resulting in greater distances for freight transport. For instance, within the EU-28, the average distance of freight transport (129 km in 2015, 86 km in national transport, and 611 km in international transport) has been constantly increasing in recent years, with annual growth rates of 1.0%—2.5% [2].

1.7.4.3 Economies of Scale and Concentration

The continuing effects of economies of scale will lead to greater concentration. Thus, instead of many points of collection and distribution, there will be fewer, more central points (with larger warehouses), and more points of distribution near the points of sale. However, due to the saturation of many infrastructures, the tendency toward greater concentration may reach its limits in some cases.

1.7.4.4 Trade Liberalization

Trade liberalization is still in progress and will increase transactions world-wide, thus increasing freight transport (see also §1.8.4.7).

1.7.4.5 Environmental Tax

If an environmental tax is applied worldwide, this will make faster transport (such as air freight) more expensive and will lead to a shift toward other, slower modes of transport.

1.7.5 The Situation of Coupling and Decoupling for Some Countries

We have conducted the analysis described in Fig. 1.13 for some countries for the period 1990—2014 (Fig. 1.18) by considering separately the periods 1990—2000, 2000—10, and 2010—14. For many of the countries considered in Fig. 1.18, the decoupling of transport activity and GDP has been clear for some period of time. More specifically:

- United States: coupling (expansive) between GDP and both passenger and freight transport activity during the period 1990—2000; decoupling after 2000 (strong decoupling in freight transport, weak decoupling in passenger transport).
- EU-28: both passenger and freight transport activity marginally coupled with GDP for the period 1990—2000; after 2010, strong decoupling in freight transport and weak decoupling in passenger transport.

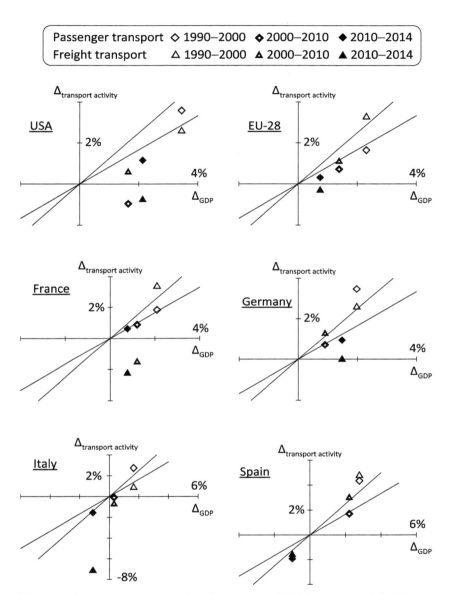

FIGURE 1.18 Coupling and decoupling of passenger and freight transport activity for some countries worldwide for the period 1990–2014. *Source: Compiled by the authors, based on data of Refs. [5,38].*

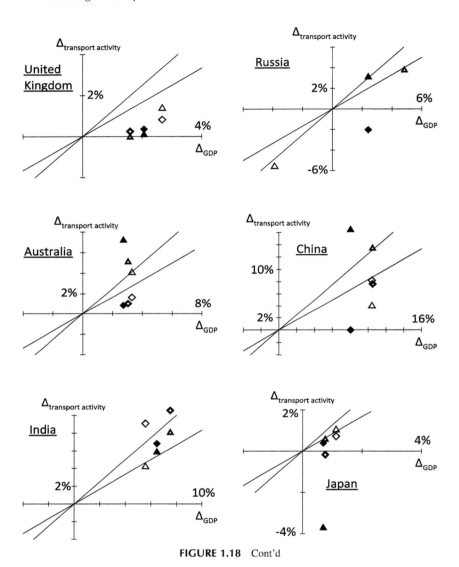

FIGURE 1.18   Cont'd

- China: marginally expansive coupling until 2010; decoupling afterward—weak decoupling in passenger transport, expansive negative decoupling in freight transport, with freight activity growing faster than GDP.
- India: more or less expansive coupling of both passenger and freight activity to GDP for the whole period of analysis, especially after 2010.

- Japan: since 2000, decoupling of both passenger and freight transport, especially after 2010; strong decoupling for freight transport.
- Australia: after 2010, weak decoupling in passenger transport, but expansive negative decoupling in freight transport.

However, a meaningful comparison of the coupling or decoupling situation is only possible among countries with comparable economic level and patterns of urban and travel development.

1.7.6 Transport Demand and Regional Development

The relationship between transport demand and regional development is complex and often unpredictable concerning the positive or negative outcome of the interaction. Transport is one component, and often not a critical one, of the many aspects of the production process. Transport infrastructure is considered an efficient way to provide better access to provincial products in large urban areas. However, at the same time, developed transport infrastructure exposes formerly safe regional monopolies to the (often higher quality and lower cost) products of other areas. New transport infrastructure that sharpens the comparative advantages of a region by making it more accessible may offer opportunities for a positive balance of new demand (principally, generated demand) and thus contribute to local economic development [84,85].

An area's *regionality* is an inverse function of the *accessibility*, which can be measured by the travel time, the distance, or the cost of transport (either direct cost or generalized cost; see Chapter 3, §3.3.3) needed to reach the area. Thus, the better the accessibility, the less peripheral a region's position is. Fig. 1.19 illustrates the two-way interaction between transport and economic activity.

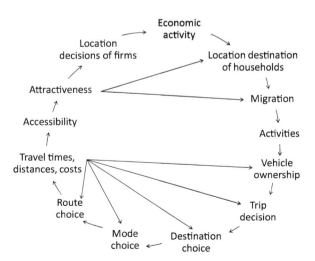

FIGURE 1.19 The interaction between transport and economic activity. *Source: Modified from Ref. [84].*

1.8 FACTORS OF THE INTERNAL AND EXTERNAL ENVIRONMENT OF TRANSPORT AND EFFECTS ON DEMAND

1.8.1 Transport as a System

In the previous sections, we analyzed the principal drivers of transport demand (§1.5), their evolution over time, and the effects of economic activity on demand (§1.7). These are some of the factors affecting a complex phenomenon such as transport. Due to its complexity, transport should always be considered as a system and be analyzed following techniques of *systems analysis* [86,87]. Thus the various components of a transport activity (technology, personnel, organization, commercial and tariff policy, financial resources, management, etc.) should be organized and adapted continuously, in relation to the changing conditions of the economy and the society in question.

1.8.2 The Internal and External Environment of Transport

The *internal* environment of an organization refers to all those components and factors occurring within the organization and which are therefore usually easier to identify, understand, and control. The *external* environment comprises factors outside the organization, the evolution of which is difficult to predict, and the control of which is practically impossible.

1.8.3 Factors of the Internal Environment That Affect Demand

The essential factors of the internal environment of a transport service affecting transport demand are the following [2]:

- *Technology.* Technology (see also §1.4, §1.5.1, and §1.5.2) and allocation of human resources are the two fundamental components so that a transport service can be rendered. Technology provides the moving vehicles and ways of efficient and safe operation of a transport activity.

   Engineers often overestimate the impact of technology by considering it the core activity of transport and by assigning it a higher priority compared with marketing and management. Such a consideration may prove disastrous. Technology is subordinate to the economy as a whole, which in turn is subordinate to society, legislation, and the environment.
- *Allocation of human resources*: As technology advances, most transport activities performed in the past by humans have been replaced by machines.
- *Planning, organization*, and *management* (see also §1.6): An efficient organization is characterized by clear objectives as well as by the utilization

of flexible and efficient methods to attain these objectives. To avoid conflicting situations, we usually distinguish between:

- Decisions at the *strategic* level, which define the critical fundamental orientations of a transport activity, such as demand, the ratio of revenues to expenses, and so on. Strategic decisions refer to the major, core choices of a company or an individual; they contribute directly to the achievement of predefined targets and their effect is long term.
- Decisions at the *tactical* level refer to the implementation of strategic decisions and have a medium-term impact. In a corporate environment, tactical decisions concern issues such as technology, allocation of human resources, commercial policy, and so on. The day-to-day implementation of tactical decisions is materialized through *operational* decisions.

Efficient management requires periodic comparison between strategic parameters and results. If, in spite of tactical decisions, the strategic objectives cannot be attained, a reorientation of strategic choices is inevitable.

1.8.4 Factors of the External Environment That Affect Demand

1.8.4.1 Economic Growth, Purchasing Power, and Available Income for Transport

See §1.5.1, §1.5.2, and §1.7.

1.8.4.2 Energy Consumption

Transport is strongly dependent on energy and cannot exist without it. Energy costs represent 15%−35% of air passenger (28.1% in 1980, 15.5% in 1990, 14.6% in 2000, 34.2% in 2008, 28.5% in 2015) and 35%−45% of air freight transport costs; 5%−10% of rail passenger and 15%−25% of rail freight transport costs; 15%−25% of road passenger and 20%−30% of road freight transport costs; and 50%−70% of ocean shipping operating costs [2,88,89], depending on the price of a barrel of crude oil, which has strong fluctuations over time (Figs. 1.20 and 1.21). It is estimated that the known reserves of liquid fuel can satisfy worldwide demand for the next four to five decades.

Transport absorbed 28.8% of energy consumption worldwide for the year 2014 (23.2% in 1973, 27.5% in 2000, 27.3% in 2008), a percentage almost equal to industry (28.9% in 2014). The rest is consumed for residential and service purposes and other uses [2].

Transport absorbs the greatest part of oil consumption in the various countries of the world (Fig. 1.22). Within the transport sector, road and air transport are the most consuming modes (Fig. 1.23).

1.8.4.3 Culture, Lifestyle, and the Expectations of Society

See §1.1.4.2, §1.5.1, and §1.7.3.1.

FIGURE 1.20 Evolution of the cost of a crude oil barrel. *Source: Compiled by the authors, based on data of Ref. [90].*

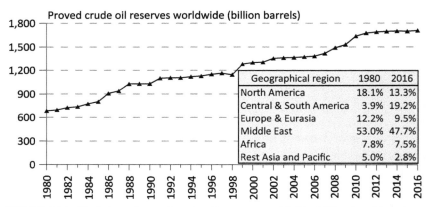

FIGURE 1.21 Evolution of proved crude oil reserves worldwide (billion barrels) and per geographical region (Eurasia: Russia and ex-USSR countries). *Source: Compiled by the authors, based on data of Ref. [90].*

1.8.4.4 Population

As transport exists for the satisfaction of human needs, any increase in population has a direct effect on transport demand. Not all age groups, however, have the same degree of mobility. The mobility of a person at the age of 70+ years is almost two-third of that person's mobility at the age of 40–49 years (Fig. 1.24).

As life expectancy is constantly increasing (worldwide, it increased from 52.5 years in 1960 to 69.4 years in 2014 for males and 73.6 years for females; Figs. 1.25 and 1.26), the aging of the population will have negative effects on transport demand. People aged more than 65 years were 5.1% of world population in 1950, 5.8% in 1980, and 8.3% in 2015 and are projected to reach 11.7% in 2030 and 16.0% in 2050 (Fig. 1.27).

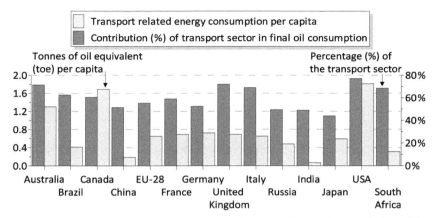

FIGURE 1.22 Transport-related energy consumption per capita and the contribution of the transport sector to oil consumption for various countries worldwide (2013). *Source: Compiled by the authors, based on data of Ref. [91].*

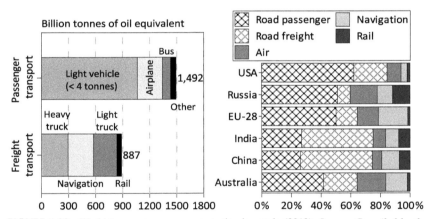

FIGURE 1.23 World transport energy consumption by mode (2012). *Source: Compiled by the authors, based on data of Refs. [4,92].*

1.8.4.5 The Environment and Transport Demand

Transport is an important air pollution emitter, accounting worldwide during the last years for about 90%–95% of carbon monoxide (CO) emissions, 60%–70% of nitrogen oxides (NO_x), 40%–50% of hydrocarbons (HCs) and volatile organic compounds (VOCs), 25% of carbon dioxide (CO_2) emissions, 5% of sulfur dioxide (SO_2), and 25% of suspended materials [93]. Fig. 1.28 presents the emissions of some air pollutants coming from the various transport modes for passenger and freight transport.

In 2012, the transport sector was responsible for 23.1% of total CO_2 emissions worldwide. Within the transport sector, the contribution of the

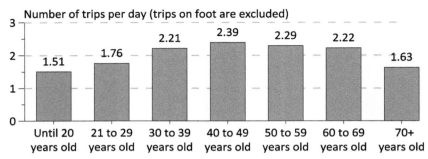

FIGURE 1.24 Average number of trips per day by age in England (2016). *Source: Compiled by the authors, based on data of Ref. [67].*

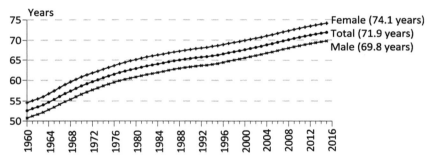

FIGURE 1.25 Evolution of the life expectancy at birth at world level. *Source: Compiled by the authors, based on data of Ref. [38].*

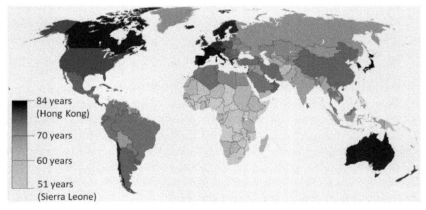

FIGURE 1.26 Life expectancy at birth at world level (data of the year 2015). *Source: Compiled by the authors, based on data of Ref. [38].*

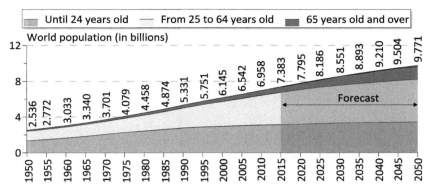

FIGURE 1.27 World population by age group between 1950 and 2015 and forecast until 2050. *Source: Compiled by the authors, based on data of Ref. [43].*

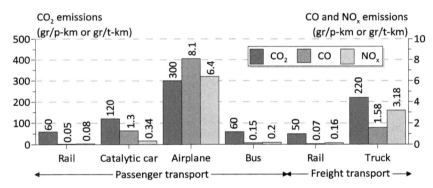

FIGURE 1.28 Emissions of pollutants provoked by various transport modes. *Source: Compiled by the authors, modified from Ref. [7].*

various transport modes that year was: roads 73.2%, navigation 10.4%, aviation 10.5%, railways 3.6%, pipelines 1.8%, other (nonspecified) 0.5% [93]. CO_2 emissions from the transport sector of various countries are given in Fig. 1.3.

Noise emissions and their effects are different depending on the transport mode. The noise level of road transport results from the overlapping of the engine noise, the rolling noise (the contact between tires and the road surface), and other recurring noises (Fig. 1.29), while the main noise emissions of railway transport result from the contact between the wheel and the rails, the motor operation, the aerodynamic effects, and the vibrations of aboveground railway structures (Fig. 1.30) [94–97]. The main noise source of airplanes is engines, the noise level of which sometimes exceeds 118 dB(A). It is estimated that noise becomes annoying for humans when the noise level exceeds the limit of 55–65 dB(A) [7,98].

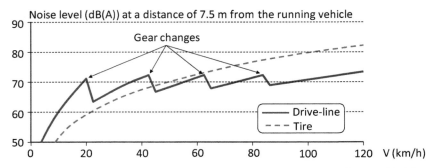

FIGURE 1.29   Noise levels from road transport. *Source: Compiled by the authors, modified from Ref. [99].*

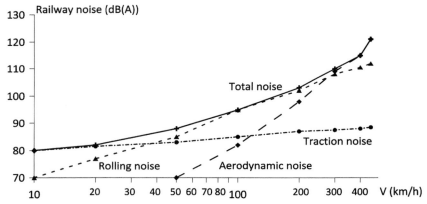

FIGURE 1.30   Noise levels from railway transport. *Source: Compiled by the authors, modified from Ref. [100].*

Other environmental effects of transport include land occupancy, alteration of the landscape, accidents, and traffic congestion [71].

Environmental effects can be translated into monetary values and are called environmental costs. An objective quantification of environmental costs in monetary values has been available for some years [71,101]. Environmental costs are a typical form of external costs, understood as the costs borne by an individual, without any prior notification or permission, and without any compensation paid to this individual by the agent causing the externality [103].

If we ask each transport mode to pay (through, e.g., fuel taxes) for the environmental (external) costs it creates, we then speak of an *internalization* of external costs [104]. Such measures are efficient policy tools to stop the environmental degradation of the planet earth and reverse the increase of median global temperatures[11]. Inevitably, any internalization of external costs will be based on the most possible accurate forecasts for the evolution of transport demand.

1.8.4.6 Institutional Framework and Transport Demand

The institutional framework includes national and international laws, as well as rules and regulations in a form of state, peripheral (like the European Union), or world (like the United Nations) policy. Legislation allocates rights to and imposes obligations on citizens and defines the ultimate form of organization for a given society; it differs from time to time and from one place to another.

Transport demand is affected by a number of general and specific arrangements of the institutional framework of each country. Thus:

- The equality of citizens results in the equality of the consumers of a transport service, no matter their sex, age, income, etc. A society of fully equal citizens (at least theoretically) results in more freedom of movement and has evidently positive effects on transport demand.
- A transport company cannot operate legally unless it respects all kinds of legislation as well as regulations related to the specific transport activity. A social environment characterized by the legal operation of economic activity assures security, which in turn extends possibilities for movement and transport.
- The organizational form of the transport market (monopoly, oligopoly, competition, etc.) is described in the legislation and defines how a new operator can enter the market, how an existing operator can leave it, the rights and obligations of customers, and so on. The more liberalized the market is, the more possibilities exist for new entrants, who will usually offer services at lower tariffs, with positive effects on transport demand.
- The form and degree of taxation on the revenues of a transport company is described in the fiscal legislation. Lower taxation paid either by the customers or by the provider of a transport service usually boosts transport demand.
- The conditions of employment and salaries of personnel working in a transport company are detailed in labor legislation. The more flexible the labor legislation is, the greater the flexibility for transport providers to select their personnel in relation to the specific requirements of the market at a given moment, which is also positive for transport demand.

---

11. Average global temperature increased by 0.7°C from 1900 to 2000. If no change occurs in the actual rates of global warming, average temperatures will rise by 1.7−4.4°C in 2100. The global sea level has risen between 1900 and 2000 by around 18 cm and between 2000 and 2015 by 4.5 cm. If no change occurs, a further rise at the global sea level between 30 and 90 cm should be expected by 2100, due principally to the melting of polar ice caps. Any increase of the earth's temperature by 1°C results in an increase of the sea level by 10−30 cm, depending on the geographical area [2,7].

- Whether public subsidies should be allocated for the financing of a deficitary transport activity (such as a rail or bus service) is a controversial issue; some economists, opting for state intervention, argue for the continuation of public subsidies, while economists in favor of a more liberal economy suggest their drastic reduction or even elimination [2,102]. While in most cases public subsidies permit the continual operation of a deficitary transport activity (primarily rail and bus services), in some cases they constitute an obstacle for new entrants into the market and are thus detrimental to demand (this is particularly the case with respect to air transport).
- The minimum technical characteristics of the fleet and the financial resources of the company are determined so that a transport service can be considered trustworthy and solvent. More stringent requirements for a transport company have positive effects on the security of customers in the specific market, while limiting the possibilities for low-quality entrants into the market.
- The accepted levels of emissions of various pollutants (CO_2, noise, etc.) are detailed in national and international environmental legislation. Stricter environmental legislation will lead to the withdrawal and replacement of old and obsolete equipment from the market.

1.8.4.7 Globalization, Liberalization, Competition, and Transport Demand

Globalization may be defined in a variety of ways. For some, globalization is the triumph of markets and free trade, for others the rise of the information economy and the Internet; for many, it constitutes the leveling of civilization and tradition; for most, it means the victory of multinationals and holding companies on national governments; for antiglobalization demonstrators, it is a spectral enemy.

What is overlooked, however, is that the globalization of production and exchanges is a very old procedure, beginning from the very moment that man sought new roads for raw materials, buyers, and labor. Nowadays, communications (Internet, transport, telematics) permit the most distant points of the planet to come into contact with each other as if they were working in the same office. Everybody looks for the competitive advantage that will grant him or her power and wealth [2].

According to Theodore Levitt, globalization describes the process of convergence of markets and technologies at a world level, through which companies tend to produce the same product in the same way worldwide and in order to conquer clients and markets they look for low-cost materials and highly skilled staff [105]. According to Kenichi Ohmae, globalization concerns the entire chain of production—that is, the creation of added value—and encompasses research and development, production, trade, transport, and financial exchanges [106]. A more political definition according to the *Financial Times* describes globalization as the process by which national and regional economies, societies, and cultures are gradually integrated through a global network of trade, communication, immigration, and transportation [107].

Some forms of globalization can be found in other eras of human history, specifically within the empire of Alexander the Great, the Roman Empire, and more recently within the British Empire. However, today's globalization constitutes a break from the past, as national economies are restructured within the globalist frame, following orientations and requirements of the world economy as opposed to the objectives of the state or (even more so) the individual citizen.

Transport is, along with the Internet, among the principal drivers of globalization today, as it permits the speedy exchange of passengers and goods. However, if a transport activity (such as rail transport) is to survive in the globalized world of today and tomorrow, it ought to adopt and realize a number of changes, such as the following:

- Liberalization from many old-fashioned and obsolete mechanisms of the transport market. This does not mean a transport market without regulations; a minimum level of regulations concerning safety, quality of service, and minimum financial requirements for a transport rending services company is essential for any deregulated market [2,7,102]. Deregulation is usually followed by the appearance of new entrants into the specific market, which usually leads to the increase in demand.
- Creation of a truly competitive environment within the specific transport market (air, rail, etc.). This means, among other things, a drastic reduction of public subsidies for specific categories of transport and allocation of transport services contracts through a public bidding process. Competition results in major changes to the specific transport market: some companies will not survive and will leave the market, while others will enter the market. The net balance is usually positive for transport demand.
- As a combined consequence of liberalization and competition, new services at lower costs are offered to customers. Low-cost air transport is one such example.
- A prerequisite for competition is the least possible involvement and interference of the state in the operation of transport companies. This leads to a minimization of public subsidies for transport activities and the limitation of such subsidies to where they are really necessary (remote and isolated areas, categories of people such as the elderly, etc.). For many countries of the world, there is no competition in the market for transport services. The more competitive the market, the more critical the effect of tariffs on transport demand. Thus many transport companies in regulated markets collapsed when the markets were liberalized and competition was introduced (TWA airlines in the United States, the freight rail company Sernam in France, etc.).

1.9 TRANSPORT DEMAND AND ELASTICITIES

1.9.1 A Definition and a Variety of Types of Elasticities

Transport serves a need in everyday life. *Elasticity* assesses whether the degree of satisfaction of a need can be reduced or not. Elasticity reflects the *sensitivity* of a good or service to changes in the essential characteristics of this (or another substitute) good or service.

The elasticity ε of a function $y = f(x)$ can be defined as follows [2,7,108]:

$$\varepsilon = \lim_{\Delta x \to 0} \frac{\dfrac{\Delta y}{y}}{\dfrac{\Delta x}{x}} = \frac{\dfrac{dy}{y}}{\dfrac{dx}{x}} \tag{1.2}$$

Elasticity is the limit on the dependent variable y of a change on the independent variable x. In transportation, y is the demand of a transport service and x may be the price of this service, the income of the users (or potential users) of the service, the travel times of the service, or the price or income of the users or travel times of substitute services. Thus, in relation to what denotes x, we may distinguish many types of elasticity. Elasticities are essential inputs in many transport demand forecasts, as they reflect the effects on demand of changes (realized in the past) in one or more of the characteristics of a transport service.

If a change in a characteristic of a transport service results in a proportionally greater change in demand, the demand is termed *elastic* in relation to the specific characteristic and the absolute value of elasticity is greater than 1.0. If, on the contrary, a change in a characteristic of a transport service results in a proportionally smaller change in demand, then demand is termed *inelastic* and the absolute value of elasticity is smaller than 1.0.

Elasticities may refer to the long run (more than 1 year) or to the short run (up to 1 year).

1.9.2 Price Elasticity

Price elasticity ε_{price} is the ratio of change of demand Q to the change of price P of a transport service. It reflects how consumers react to a change in price of a transport service [2,7,108]:

$$\varepsilon_{price} = \frac{\dfrac{dQ}{Q}}{\dfrac{dP}{P}} \tag{1.3}$$

Price elasticity of transit transport has values between -0.20 and -0.50 in the short run and between -0.60 and -0.90 in the long run [2].

Price elasticity of bus transport in urban areas has an average value -0.40 and varies between -0.20 and -0.50 in the short run and between -0.45 and -0.60 in the long run [2,109,110].

In the case of metro systems, price elasticities in the short run are -0.30 to -0.60 (on average -0.40 during peak hours and -0.50 during off-peak hours) and in the long run -0.50 to -1.00 (on average -0.60 during peak hours and -0.75 during off-peak hours) [2,110].

Rail passenger services for leisure have long-run price elasticities between -1.0 and -1.4 and for work between -0.5 and -0.7. Short-run elasticities are almost half as previous values [2,109,111,112].

In the case of freight transport, long-run price elasticities for both road and rail are between -0.25 and -0.35 [2,111,112].

In the case of air passenger transport, average price elasticities vary between -1.0 and -2.7 for leisure trips and between -0.65 and -1.15 for business trips. For air freight transport, average price elasticities vary between -0.8 and -1.6 [2].

1.9.3 Income Elasticity

Income elasticity ε_{income} is the ratio of the change in demand Q to the change in income I of the customers of a transport service. It reflects how users of a transport service react to a change in their income [2,7,108]:

$$\varepsilon_{income} = \frac{\dfrac{dQ}{Q}}{\dfrac{dI}{I}} \tag{1.4}$$

According to some authors, values of income elasticities greater than 1.0 identify so-called luxury services or goods, whereas values of income elasticities smaller than 1.0 identify so-called normal (or essential or nonluxury) services or goods [113,114].

In Europe, income elasticity for trips with private cars has values between 1.9 and 2.1; in North America, the values are between 2.0 and 2.3. Income elasticities for interurban trips with railways in Europe have values between 0.8 and 1.0, reaching as much as 2.0 for high-speed railways [114]. Income elasticities for air transport are in the range of 1.8–2.0 for leisure trips and 0.8–1.4 for nonleisure trips (all previous values refer to long-run elasticities). For busses, income elasticities are in the range of -0.3 (short run) to -0.9 (long run), and they are related to the private car ownership index [2,109,111,115,116].

The elasticity of freight transport in relation to GDP has been found to be close to 1.0: a little lower than 1.0 for developed economies and a little higher than 1.0 for developing economies [2].

1.9.4 Cross-Elasticities

Cross-elasticities relate changes in the demand for a transport service to changes in the prices of another, substitute service. Consider, for instance, transport service 1 (e.g., high-speed trains between London and Paris) and its substitute transport service 2 (e.g., air transport between London and Paris). The cross-elasticity of transport service 1 in relation to transport service 2 is the ratio of the change of demand for transport service 1 to the change in price of transport service 2 [2,7]:

$$\varepsilon_{1,2} = \frac{\dfrac{dQ_1}{Q_1}}{\dfrac{dP_2}{P_2}} \tag{1.5}$$

Cross-elasticities allow the evaluation of substitution factors and are strongly dependent on local circumstances.

1.9.5 Evolution of Elasticities Over Time

Among the few available analyses of the evolution of elasticities over time, it has been suggested that, in the case of the United Kingdom, the absolute values of both price and income elasticities have declined substantially over the last two centuries (Fig. 1.31) [117].

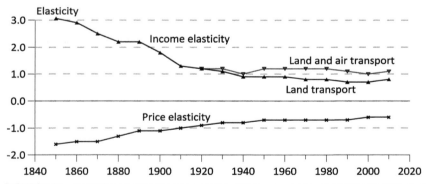

FIGURE 1.31 Evolution over the last two centuries of income and price elasticities for passenger transport in the United Kingdom. *Source: Modified from Ref. [117].*

Chapter 2

Evolution and Trends of Transport Demand

Chapter Outline

2.1 DESCRIPTION OF TRANSPORT DEMAND: DATA, SURVEYS, AND DEGREE OF ACCURACY

2.1.1 Collection of Transport Data of the Past

Analyzing trends or forecasting demand for transport is a complex undertaking, the purpose of which is to understand, explain, and foresee the evolution of transport demand. This undertaking makes use of and is based on mathematical, statistical, or other kinds of rational thinking methods. Whatever the method used, it cannot produce any kind of usable results, unless it is fed with the *appropriate data*, which permit an accurate description of the problem under study. Data may refer to any of the metrics of transport (see §1.1.6), such as the number of passengers, passenger-kilometers, vehicles, and revenues.

Forecast of demand may refer either to an existing transportation infrastructure or mode, or to a new one. In the latter case, the information and characteristics of the problem will require a survey to be carried out among eventual users of the new transportation infrastructure or service. In the former case, however, even if there exist past statistical data (such as the number

Modeling of Transport Demand. https://doi.org/10.1016/B978-0-12-811513-8.00002-9
Copyright © 2019 Elsevier Inc. All rights reserved.

of passengers), these may prove inadequate, since in many cases we need more information about transport characteristics, for example, the origin, destination, distance traveled. In such cases, a *survey* of the characteristics of transport for a given infrastructure or service will be necessary.

Data in general can be defined as the information about facts, which is critical to any rational decision-making procedure. Data should be provided within a common and systematic framework [118].

2.1.2 Characteristics of Transport Data

Transport data, which will be used for the analysis of trends of demand, must encompass the following characteristics [2]:

- *accuracy*: the correct value must be provided so as to represent the phenomenon under study in a trustworthy way,
- *consistency* and systematic development: information must be recorded and collected in the same way using the same method over time,
- *validity*: the information provided must describe the phenomenon under study in an unambiguous and consistent way. However, a valid value that has the potential to be accurate is not necessarily accurate,
- *protection of confidential data*: no invasion in the privacy of an individual should be attempted, and the information gathered should be stored securely,
- *continuity* over time: there should be no missing values for any of the years (or periods) under study,
- *easy* and inexpensive access to data for anyone interested.

2.1.3 Sources of Data

The principal sources of transport data are the following:

- *administrative statistics* of public authorities or international institutions (such as the World Bank, the European Commission, etc.),
- statistics of *private* companies,
- *processed statistics*, based on data of either public authorities or private companies,
- *surveys*, by means of which we attempt to identify, describe, and measure some characteristics of transport as they now exist or as they should exist according to the expectations of respondents. The usual tool of surveys is completion and analysis of questionnaires,
- the *Internet*, social media, etc.,
- *records* with the use of the appropriate equipment (such as traffic counters).

2.1.4 Information Related to Sources of Transport Data

The quality of transport data can be assured if the researcher who uses these data has access to the following information:

- Method of data collection: when, by whom, how often (daily, monthly, yearly, etc.).
- Possession of data: by whom, how often, who pays, how the information is made available, whether the information is filtered before being released.
- Use of data: whether only by the people who collected the information or by other individuals as well; whether they are readily available or need postprocessing; what can be made public and what should be held in private.

2.1.5 The Internet Revolution—Big Data as a New Source of Transport Data

Big data refer to data which are collected electronically with the help of the Internet, mobile telephones, global positioning system (GPS), and various other devices which can track the movement of people and goods [119–121].

Big data can improve transport statistics to a great extent, as almost all transportation systems are supported by advanced information and communication technologies. However, a particular set of big data does not necessarily represent the entire statistical population. In addition, big data are proprietary information and belong to specific private companies, which do not have any obligation to share this information with other private companies or public authorities [122].

Big data can cover the shortcomings of official statistics or provide additional information, which conventional data sources cannot offer. Users of big data include government authorities (for purposes such as planning and modeling demand, traffic control, congestion management with real-time active traffic management, and so on); private companies (for similar purposes); the travel industry; and freight and logistics companies (for establishing more complex networks of suppliers, adapting their offer of transport services to demand forecasts, and providing efficient delivery processes).

The volume of big data is so large (and will become even more so in the future) that it is difficult to process by using traditional databases or software methods. Big data require specialized software tools, which can help to determine which data are relevant and reliable and whether and how data can be analyzed to achieve a more complete knowledge of the transport problem under study.

The use of big data in the transport sector is increasing but is usually combined with traditional forms of data. Thus, it appears that some standardization is necessary to engage for clarity, consistency, and a nondiscriminatory use of big data [123]. Big data are analyzed in more detail in §3.13.

2.1.6 Sources of Transport Data Used in This Book

This book deals with all transport modes and considers both the operation and the infrastructure of each mode. The principal sources of data used in this book are the following:

- The *World Bank*. Statistical data cover population; finance; economics and growth; energy and environment; air, rail, and sea transport demand and infrastructure.
- The *Organization for Economic Co-operation and Development* (OECD). Statistical data are similar to those of the World Bank but are limited to member countries of the OECD and primarily concern road accidents, passenger and freight transport, and infrastructure investment and maintenance.
- The *Directorate-General for Mobility and Transport* of the European Commission. Statistical data cover all European Union (EU) member countries and candidate members of the EU. These data concern population, passenger and freight transport, transport infrastructure, safety, energy consumption, and the environmental effects of transport modes.
- The *Eurostat*, the statistical office of the EU. It provides data on passenger and freight, for all transport modes.
- The *United Nations Conference on Trade and Development* (UNCTAD). Statistical data concern maritime transport, seaborne trade, merchant fleet by country of ownership and flag.
- The *International Air Transport Association* (IATA), which provides data on air transport.
- The *International Union of Railways* (UIC, from its French initials Union Internationale des Chemins de Fer), which provides data concerning all aspects (passenger and freight demand, infrastructure, and rolling stock) of its member railways.
- The *International Organization of Motor Vehicle Manufacturers*, which provides data concerning passenger vehicles (private cars, taxis, and hired passenger cars) and commercial ones (light commercial vehicles, heavy trucks, coaches, and busses).
- The *European Automobile Manufacturers Association*, which provides data covering the manufacture, registration, taxation, and trade of automobiles produced by the automobile industry in EU member countries.
- The *Departments of Transportation* of the various countries, which provide updated and well-documented statistical data for transport, as well as selected market surveys on transport issues.

2.2 EVOLUTION AND TRENDS OF THE MODAL SPLIT OF EACH TRANSPORT MODE IN THE TRANSPORT MARKET

2.2.1 Passenger Transport

Parts of each transport mode in the market (also referred to as market shares or modal split) differ from one country to another, as they are affected by a number of factors [2]:

- the purchasing power of individuals and their willingness to pay for transport,
- the organization of the transport market, the degree of competition (if any), the existence or lack of state subsidies for specific transport modes (such as railways, busses, and metro),
- the level of infrastructure for each transport mode; over the years, some countries have favored railways and metro by investing huge amounts of public funds in them, whereas other countries have favored the development and expansion of highways and airports,
- the size of the country and the distances of trips: large countries such as the United States, China, and Russia are more favorable toward air transport, compared with medium- or small-size countries,
- the cost of transport services, and whether or not substitute modes exist,
- the lifestyle and social attitudes toward specific transport modes (see also §1.5.1).

Table 2.1 illustrates for the year 2015 parts of each transport mode in the transport markets of the EU, the United States, Japan, China, and Russia. As railways are not subsidized in the United States, they have a marginal share in the passenger market, which is dominated by passenger cars. However, passenger cars have a high share in the transport market in the EU, but railways also play an essential role in the market. Railways' shares are even higher in Russia, Japan, and China. Due to the size of the country, air transport has greater market shares in larger countries such as the United States, China, and Russia.

Some big countries (such as China and Russia) are still experiencing a transition from centrally planned economies to liberal economies. In other countries (such as India), regulation is still strong in their domestic transport market. Thus, the United States (Fig. 2.1) and the EU (Fig. 2.2) can be considered as representative markets for the evolution of the traffic and modal split of the various transport modes for a long period, which covers the years from 1990 to 2015 for the United States and the years from 1995 to 2015 for the EU countries. For the EU countries, the first year of analysis is 1995, as some countries (Poland, Hungary, etc.) also experienced a transition toward a liberal economy. In both cases (the United States and the EU), the market shares of the various transport modes have been more or less stable over the

TABLE 2.1: Parts in the passenger market of the various transport modes for the year 2015 and for some countries of the world.

	EU-28		United States		Japan (2014)		China		Russia	
	billion p-km	%	billion p-km	%	billion p-km	%	billion p-km	%	billion p-km	%
Passenger car	4719.39	72.9	6161.05	78.9	852.20	59.6	1074.27	35.7	127.05	19.3
Bus, trolley, coach	543.49	8.4	553.99	7.1	72.58	5.1			132.30	20.1
Rail	441.90	6.8	40.03	0.5	413.97	29.0	1196.06	38.6	120.60	18.4
Metro, tram	102.36	1.6	22.97	0.3					49.40	7.5
Waterborne	21.70	0.3	0.67	0.0	3.27	0.2	7.31	0.2	0.56	0.1
Air	649.01	10.0	1033.05	13.2	86.76	6.1	728.30	24.2	226.80	34.5
Total	6477.85		7811.76		1428.78		3005.93		656.71	

Source: Compiled by the authors, based on data of Ref. [4].

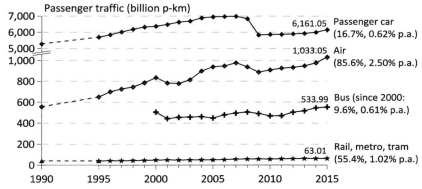

FIGURE 2.1   Evolution of passenger traffic of the various transport modes for the United States (in parentheses the total and the per annum [p.a.] growth rate of traffic between 1995 and 2015). *Source: Compiled by the authors, based on data of Ref. [4].*

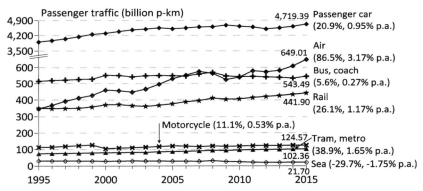

FIGURE 2.2   Evolution of passenger traffic of the various transport modes for the EU-28 countries (in parentheses the total and the per annum [p.a.] growth rate of traffic between 1995 and 2015). *Source: Compiled by the authors, based on data of Ref. [4].*

last 25 years, and the annual growth rates of traffic of each mode have been rather low, a sign of markets which have entered maturity or are well on the way toward maturity.

2.2.2 Freight Transport

The characteristics of the country (size, number, quality of seaports, etc.) and the nature of products imported or exported are more critical for the modal split of freight transport compared with passenger transport. Countries surrounded by sea (which can be used for trade and freight transport) have higher shares of sea transport in their freight markets (this includes countries such as Japan and China, as well as many EU countries). In the United States, railway tracks are used almost exclusively for freight. American railways transport products such as coal, metals, minerals, chemicals, food, equipment, automobiles, and oil; as such, they have a large share in the transport market. In Russia, distances are greater and the nature of some products (principally raw materials) is favorable for railways, which have cornered the market for freight transport together with oil pipelines. Trucks dominate the freight market in the EU and Japan (Table 2.2).

The evolution of the modal split of freight transport in the United States (Fig. 2.3) between 1995 and 2014 is characterized by a reduction in the share of pipelines and inland waterways and by a corresponding increase in the share of trucks and railways. Growth rates were low but positive for trucks, railways, and inland waterways, and negative for pipelines. The modal split of freight transport between 1995 and 2015 in the EU (Fig. 2.4) has been characterized by lowering market shares for pipelines, railways, and sea transport and a substantial increase in share for trucks, while inland waterways kept their share at the same level.

2.3 EVOLUTION AND TRENDS OF AIR TRANSPORT DEMAND

2.3.1 Rates of Growth of Air Transport, Low Margins of Profit, and Cyclic Fluctuations

Worldwide, air transport has been among the few businesses experiencing high and almost continuous growth rates, with an average annual growth rate from 1980 to 2015 of 5.6%, almost triple the average growth rate of gross domestic product (GDP) (see Fig. 1.11). When comparing the growth rates of air transport with the growth rates of GDP (Fig. 1.11), we can note a clear coupling effect: ups and downs of air passenger demand are almost parallel to ups and downs in GDP. In 2015, 3.464 billion passengers used air transport worldwide (against 2.628 in 2010, 1.674 in 2000, 1.025 in 1990, 0.642 in 1980, and 0.310 in 1970). In the period 2004−15, the revenues of the airlines worldwide almost doubled, from 379 billion US$ in 2004 to 721 billion US$ in 2015 [2,124,125].

A fundamental entrepreneurial characteristic of air transport is thin profit margins, generally not exceeding 3%−4%, combined with cyclic fluctuations and a period of return of around 10 years (Fig. 2.5). The survival of an air company depends principally on the reduction of costs and the increase in productivity.

2.3.2 Factors Affecting Air Transport Demand

A number of factors affect air transport demand: the prices of air trips, the income of customers or eventual customers, changes in the personal disposable income, the volume and growth of various industrial sectors, the attractiveness of trade and tourism, the GDP of countries on both ends of an air trip, energy

TABLE 2.2: Parts in the freight market of the various transport modes for the year 2015 and for some countries of the world.

	EU-28		USA (2014)		Japan (2014)		China		Russia	
	billion t-km	%	billion t-km	%	billion t-km	%	billion t-km	%	billion t-km	%
Road	1722.32	49.0	3810.53	44.6	210.01	50.7	5795.57	32.4	232.00	4.6
Rail	417.54	11.9	2702.74	31.6	21.03	5.1	2375.43	13.3	2306.00	45.3
Oil pipelines	115.19	3.3	1305.21	15.3			466.50	2.6	2444.00	48.1
Inland waterways	147.52	4.2	482.98	5.6			3589.12	20.0	63.00	1.2
Sea	1111.36	31.6	251.80	2.9	183.12	44.2	5688.38	31.8	40.00	0.8
Total	3513.94		8553.26		414.16		17,915.00		5085.00	

Source: Compiled by the authors, based on data of Ref. [4].

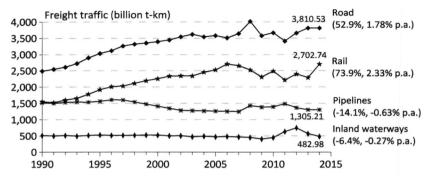

FIGURE 2.3   Evolution of freight traffic of the various transport modes for the United States (in parentheses, the total and the per annum [p.a.] growth rate of traffic between 1990 and 2014). *Source: Compiled by the authors, based on data of Ref. [4].*

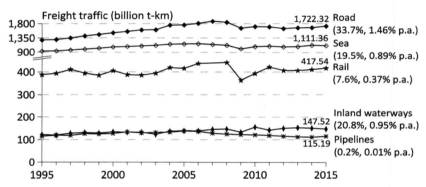

FIGURE 2.4   Evolution of freight traffic of the various transport modes for the EU-28 countries (in parentheses the total and the per annum [p.a.] growth rate of traffic between 1995 and 2015). *Source: Compiled by the authors, based on data of Ref. [4].*

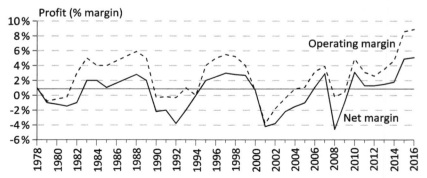

FIGURE 2.5   Profit margins and cyclic fluctuations of airlines worldwide. *Source: Compiled by the authors, based on data of Ref. [126].*

provision and costs, liberalization and competition in the air market, relaxation of various kinds of restrictions (such as visas) for transport, amount of leisure time, wars, political and economic (in)stability, diseases, lifestyle, environmental constraints, and so on.

Air transport is extremely vulnerable to any kind of national or international crisis: war, political turmoil, economic instability, energy shortage, etc. However, in spite of this vulnerability, air transport has always recovered after any event that has destabilized some region of the world. Thus, over the last 40 years the air transport sector has managed to recover after two major financial—economic crises, four periods of recession, three periods of energy shortage, several attacks (in New York on September 11, 2001 and elsewhere), epidemics, and various local and regional wars.

2.3.3 Scheduled, Charter, and Low-Cost Flights

A *scheduled* flight is a regular flight that has been planned for a certain time and date, for which any interested individual is able to purchase a ticket, the price of which is a function of airline policy, how early relative to the date of travel the ticket is bought, etc. A breakdown of operating costs of scheduled airlines is as follows: the cost of purchasing (or leasing) and maintaining airplane 22.4%, flight and cabin crew 16.2%, ground crew 10.5%, fuel 25.4%, marketing and sales 8.5%, cost of use of airport and air traffic systems 6.6%, and administration 10.4% [127].

A *charter* flight is a flight that is booked for a specific destination by a company or person. Random passengers cannot travel, unless they are authorized by the agency which has booked the flight.

A flight is characterized as *low cost* when it has not only lower fares but also fewer comforts compared with traditional scheduled airlines. Strictly speaking, low-cost flights are scheduled flights.

In this book, whenever the term air passenger demand is used, it includes passengers (both domestic and international) of scheduled, nonscheduled (charter), and low-cost flights, unless otherwise stated.

2.3.4 Evolution and Trends of Air Passenger Demand

The number of air passengers worldwide increased from 310 million in 1970 to 3.464 billion in 2015 (Fig. 2.6). It is also interesting that the number of passengers per flight increased from 32.9 in 1970 to 104.4 in 2015 (Fig. 2.6), as over time airlines preferred to use medium- or large-size airplanes (Fig. 2.7).

Air passenger demand concentrates in population, economic, or production centers. Thus, five regions of the world (USA, EU-28, China, Japan, and India) capture 61% of total air passenger demand worldwide (Fig. 2.8). Not all of the above areas, however, have similar growth rates of air transport, because of

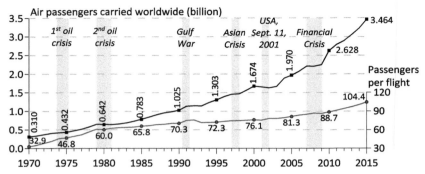

FIGURE 2.6   Evolution of air passenger demand worldwide. *Source: Compiled by the authors, based on data of Ref. [38].*

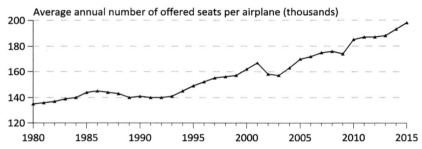

FIGURE 2.7   Average annual number of offered seats per airplane. *Source: Compiled by the authors, based on data of Ref. [124].*

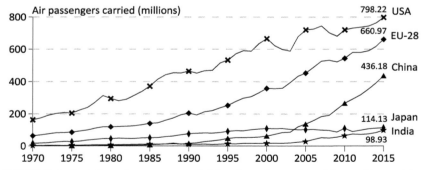

FIGURE 2.8   Evolution of passengers carried by air carriers registered in specific countries. *Source: Compiled by the authors, based on data of Ref. [38].*

different economic growth rates as well as of different levels of maturity of the specific market. Air markets in the United States and the EU-28 can be considered as mature or heading toward maturity, since they have declining growth rates. The air market in Japan is nearly saturated, as there is no (or little) growth. By contrast, the markets for air passenger transport in China and India are in the developing stage, as they have increasing growth rates. More than half (55%) of world air passenger demand originates in the airports of three regions of the world: the United States, EU-28, and China.

2.3.5 Evolution and Trends of Air Freight Demand

Although air freight has been considered for years as a very promising sector for growth, it has been almost stagnant worldwide between 2010 and 2015 (Fig. 2.9). There are many reasons for this: low growth rates in some countries, the fast relocation of productive activities, the easy transfer of information and documents through the Internet, more centralized warehouses, more competition in air freight fares, developments in substitute modes (such as fast railways, trucks, ships, and inland waterways) with just-in-time delivery practices, and so on.

Air freight markets between 2008 and 2015 have declined in the United States, EU-28, Japan, and South Korea; stagnating in India; and developing in China (Fig. 2.10).

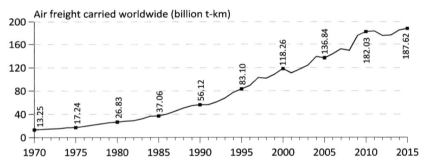

FIGURE 2.9 Evolution of air freight demand worldwide. *Source: Compiled by the authors, based on data of Ref. [38].*

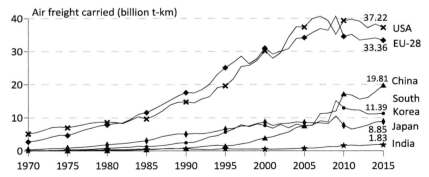

FIGURE 2.10 Evolution of air freight carried by air carriers registered in specific countries. *Source: Compiled by the authors, based on data of Ref. [38].*

2.3.6 The Rise of Demand for Low-Cost Airlines

Low-cost airlines (LCA) present a number of differences compared with full-service airlines [2,28,128−133]:

- they operate only direct air links between major population and tourism poles, and they offer lower tariffs compared with full-service airlines,
- they use regional airports (offering lower landing fees), often distant from the city served,
- reservation and sales of tickets are carried out through the Internet, and thus the costs of purchasing tickets are minimized,
- cabin luggage and checked bags that can be transported free of charge are subject to size and weight restrictions,
- they have a higher average airplane daily utilization (11.13 h for LCA, as opposed to 9.06 h for full-service airlines),
- they have a higher load factor (percentage of available seats which is sold) of passenger seats (78.2% for LCA against 74.6% for full-service airlines for the year 2014),
- as a result of the above, operating costs of LCA are 33%−45% lower compared with full-service airlines,
- they have an aggressive commercial and pricing policy.

Fig. 2.11 (left) illustrates the continuing penetration of LCA in the air transport market, with a worldwide share in 2015 of 25.4%. However, their degree of penetration is different for the various regions of the world (Fig. 2.11, right).

In their struggle to compete with LCA, full-service airlines have been forced to adopt many of the practices of LCA, such as fewer free in-flight

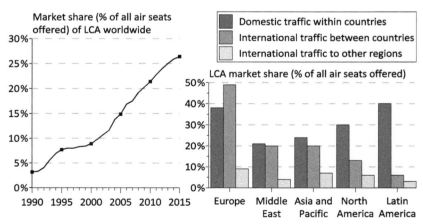

FIGURE 2.11 Evolution of market share of low-cost airlines (LCA) worldwide (left) and for the various regions of the world (right). *Source: Compiled by the authors, based on data of Ref. [134].*

services, online ticketing purchasing and check-in, and separate luggage pricing. In 2013, fares of LCA compared with those of full-service airlines were lower by 32.9% in Oceania, 36.6% in Europe, 43.7% in Asia, 43.6% in South America, and 45.0% in North America [2,129].

2.3.7 Evolution and Trends of Flight Departures

The number of flight departures worldwide of registered (scheduled + charter + low cost) airlines increased from 9.448 million in 1970 to 33.772 million in 2015, the first year in which there was one flight departure per second worldwide (Fig. 2.12). Almost two-thirds of flight departures worldwide (61.9%) take place in airports in the United States, EU-28, China, Japan, and India (Figs. 2.13 and 2.14).

2.3.8 Evolution and Trends of Demand in Airports

In the value chain of air transport, the airport and the airplane (along with the airlines) are the core activities of the business. However, both are the hard part of the product of air transport, as any changes are expensive and take time.

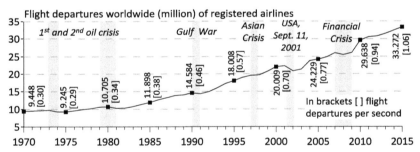

FIGURE 2.12   Evolution of flight departures worldwide of registered airlines. *Source: Compiled by the authors, based on data of Ref. [38].*

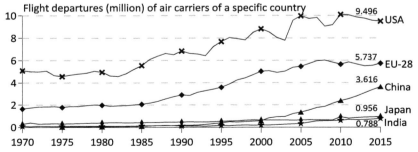

FIGURE 2.13   Evolution of flight departures of registered airlines of some countries. *Source: Compiled by the authors, based on data of Ref. [38].*

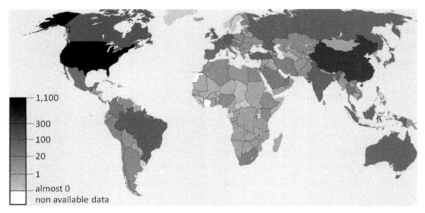

FIGURE 2.14 Flight departures per hour for the various countries for the year 2015. *Source: Compiled by the authors, based on data of Ref. [38].*

By contrast, reservation systems, pricing policies, and customer satisfaction measures are the soft part of the product, as changes can be realized in a short time and usually at low cost.

Table 2.3 illustrates the evolution of air passenger demand for the principal airports of the world between 2000 and 2015. We can remark that airports in the United States and Europe are in the maturity stage, whereas airports in China and the Middle East are in the developing stage.

Table 2.4 illustrates the evolution of air freight demand for the principal airports of the world. Airports in the United States and Europe are in the maturity stage (or even stagnating, like Los Angeles), whereas airports in China and the Middle East are in the developing stage, though with lower growth rates compared with air passenger traffic.

In order to satisfy the increasing demand for air transport, airplane manufacturers have provided a great variety of airplanes in every regard, including number of passengers, maximum distance (range) that can be traveled, safety and security, comfort and ease, lower noise and CO_2 emissions, etc. In 2015, the airplane industry was dominated by Boeing (between 2010 and 2015 deliveries of 3673 airplanes, 42.5% of the market, with a total capacity of 677,914 seats, 46.4% of the market) and Airbus (between 2010 and 2015 deliveries of 3522 airplanes, 40.7% of the market, with a total capacity of 664,486 seats, 45.5% of the market) (Fig. 2.15).

Fig. 2.16 illustrates the evolution of the number of commercial airplanes in operation worldwide between 1980 and 2015. Fig. 2.16 illustrates also prospects for the year 2035 and estimates for the share of commercial airplanes per geographical region for the years 2015 and 2035.

The air transport activity is obliged to balance between high regulation (related to airports and airplanes) and partial or full liberalization (related to the operation of airlines).

TABLE 2.3: Evolution of air passenger traffic in the principal airports of the world.

Name of the airport (Country, City)	Passengers (in millions)							2000–15 annual growth rate (%)
	2000	2005	2010	2012	2013	2014	2015	
Hartsfield–Jackson International Airport (USA, Atlanta)	80.16	85.91	89.33	94.96	94.43	96.18	101.49	1.59
Beijing Capital International Airport (China, Beijing)	21.69	41.00	73.95	81.93	83.71	86.13	89.94	9.95
Dubai International Airport (UAE, Dubai)	12.31	23.61	47.18	57.68	66.43	70.48	78.01	13.10
O'Hare International Airport (USA, Chicago)	72.14	76.51	66.77	66.83	66.88	70.00	76.94	0.43
Japan Tokyo Haneda Airport (Japan, Tokyo)	56.40	63.28	64.21	67.79	68.91	72.83	75.32	1.95
Heathrow Airport (United Kingdom, London)	64.61	67.92	65.88	70.04	72.37	73.41	74.99	1.00
Los Angeles International Airport (USA)	66.42	61.49	59.07	63.69	66.70	70.66	74.94	0.81
Hong Kong International Airport (Hong Kong)	32.75	40.27	50.35	56.06	59.61	63.12	68.28	5.02
Charles de Gaulle Airport (France, Paris)	48.25	53.80	58.17	61.61	62.05	63.81	65.77	2.09
Fort Worth International Airport (USA, Dallas)	60.69	59.18	56.91	58.59	60.44	63.55	64.07	0.36
Atatürk Airport (Turkey, Istanbul)	14.70	19.29	32.17	44.99	51.17	56.77	61.84	10.05
Frankfurt Airport (Germany, Frankfurt)	49.36	52.22	53.01	57.52	58.04	59.57	61.03	1.43
Pudong International Airport (China, Shanghai)	5.54	23.66	40.58	44.88	47.19	51.69	60.05	17.21
Schiphol Airport (The Netherlands, Amsterdam)	39.61	44.16	45.21	51.04	52.57	54.98	58.28	2.61
John F. Kennedy International Airport (USA, New York)	32.86	41.89	46.51	49.29	50.41	53.25	56.83	3.72

Source: Compiled by the authors, based on data of airport authorities.

TABLE 2.4: Evolution of air freight traffic in the principal airports of the world.

Name of the airport (Country, City)	Freight traffic tonnes (in millions)							2000–15 annual growth rate (%)
	2000	2005	2010	2012	2013	2014	2015	
Hong Kong International Airport (Hong Kong)	2.27	3.43	4.17	4.06	4.16	4.41	4.42	4.55
Memphis International Airport (USA, Memphis)	2.49	3.60	3.92	3.92	4.14	4.26	4.29	3.70
Pudong International Airport (China, Shanghai)	0.22	1.86	3.23	2.94	2.93	3.18	3.27	19.87
Ted Stevens International Airport (USA, Anchorage)	1.80	2.55	2.58	2.45	2.42	2.48	2.62	2.53
Incheon International Airport (South Korea, Seoul)	—[a]	2.15	2.68	2.46	2.46	2.56	2.60	1.90[b]
Dubai International Airport (UAE, Dubai)	0.57	1.33	2.27	2.27	2.44	2.37	2.51	10.42
Louisville International Airport (USA, Louisville)	1.52	1.82	2.17	2.19	2.22	2.29	2.35	2.95
Narita International Airport (Japan, Tokyo)	1.93	2.29	2.17	2.01	2.02	2.13	2.12	0.63
Frankfurt Airport (Germany, Frankfurt)	1.71	1.96	2.48	2.07	2.09	2.13	2.08	1.30
Taoyuan International Airport (Taiwan, Taipei)	1.21	1.71	1.77	1.58	1.57	2.09	2.03	3.50
Miami International Airport (USA, Miami)	1.64	1.75	1.84	1.93	1.95	2.00	2.01	1.34
Los Angeles International Airport (USA)	2.04	1.94	1.81	1.69	1.75	1.82	1.93	-0.36
Beijing Capital International Airport (China, Beijing)	0.77	0.78	1.55	1.79	1.84	1.83	1.89	6.13
Changi Airport (Singapore)	1.71	1.85	1.84	1.90	1.89	1.88	1.89	0.68
Charles de Gaulle Airport (France, Paris)	1.61	2.01	2.40	2.15	2.07	1.89	1.86	0.97

[a]In operation since 2001.
[b]2005–10 annual growth (%).
Source: Compiled by the authors, based on data of airport authorities.

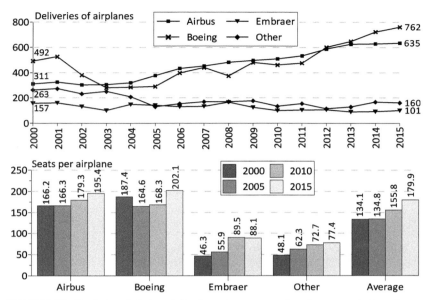

FIGURE 2.15   Evolution of airplane deliveries and average number of seats per airplane. *Source: Compiled by the authors, based on data of airplane manufacturers.*

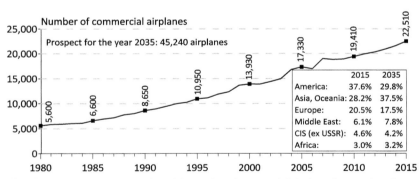

FIGURE 2.16   Evolution worldwide of the number of commercial airplanes in operation. *Source: Compiled by the authors, based on data of Ref. [38].*

2.4 EVOLUTION AND TRENDS OF RAIL TRANSPORT DEMAND

2.4.1 Rise and Decline of Railways

Steam-powered railways were developed during the first industrial revolution and since 1830 have permitted fast connections (by the standards of the time), thus leading during the 19th century to spectacular increases in transport demand.

The golden century of railways was the period 1850–1950. In spite of many technical innovations (such as diesel and electric traction in the 1890s, signaling and automatic train control in the 1950s, high-speed trains in the 1980s [with V_{max}: 300 km/h], and GPS and information technology systems in the 1990s), railways failed to efficiently confront competition from other transport modes (cars, airplanes, and more recently LCA), and as a result have lost much of their market share. Currently, railways are trying to reposition themselves in the transport market by exploiting their comparative advantages: ability to transport high volumes (of both passengers and freight), high speeds (for distances up to 700 km they achieve better door-to-door travel times compared with airplanes), less energy consumption, and lower CO_2 emissions compared with other transport modes [7,135].

2.4.2 Evolution and Trends of Rail Passenger Demand

Over the past 35 years, rail passenger demand worldwide (expressed in passenger-kilometers, p-km) (Fig. 2.17) has shown low but almost constant growth rates, principally due to high growth rates in India and China (until 2010), while stagnating in other regions such as the EU-28, Japan, and Russia (Fig. 2.18).

Railways lost some markets (particularly local and regional transport) but gained other markets, principally due to innovations in high-speed rail. Rail passenger demand does not seem to be affected (either positively or negatively) by changes in the GDP or in the income of customers. The reason is that rail services (with the exception of high speeds) have income elasticities lower than 1.0 (see §1.9), thus rail passenger transport is considered as a nonluxury product.

Average distance traveled by rail is also increasing worldwide, but this is principally due to long rail trips in China and India (Fig. 2.17). In other parts

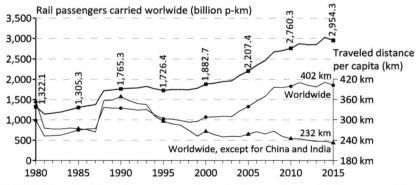

FIGURE 2.17 Evolution of rail passenger demand and per capita traveled distance worldwide. *Source: Compiled by the authors, based on data of Refs. [38,136].*

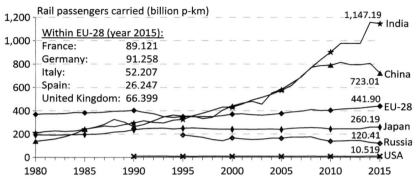

FIGURE 2.18   Evolution of rail passenger demand for some countries. *Source: Compiled by the authors, based on data of Refs. [4,38,136].*

of the world, the average traveled distance has been greatly reduced, as railways lost both long-distance trips (to air transport) and medium- and short-distance trips (to road transport).

2.4.3 Evolution and Trends of Demand for High-Speed Trains

High-speed trains were the response of railways to the transport market requirements for reduced travel times and greater comfort. For medium distances (500−700 km), the travel time of high-speed trains (with V_{max}: 320 km/h in 2017) between the departure and arrival stations is around 2−3 h. As railways enter the center of cities, door-to-door travel times of high-speed trains are more advantageous compared with road and air transport for distances up to 700 km. Demand for high-speed rail services is either diverted (from private cars, busses, airplanes), normal (from existing lower-quality rail services), or generated (new demand due to the attractiveness of the service) (see also §1.1.4.4) [137,138].

Many high-speed tracks have been constructed and are in operation in 2018, among them: London−Paris (444 km, 2 h 15 min), Madrid−Barcelona (621 km, 2 h 40 min), Madrid−Seville (472 km, 2 h 30 min), Paris−Lyon (427 km, 1 h 50 min), Berlin−Hamburg (284 km, 1 h 25 min), Rome−Milan (560 km, 2 h 55 min), Seoul−Busan (418 km, 2 h 15 min), Beijing−Shanghai (1302 km, 4 h 50 min), Beijing−Guangzhou (2298 km, 8 h 05 min), Tokyo−Osaka (515 km, 2 h 20 min), Taipei−Kaohsiung (345 km, 1 h 45 min).

Demand for high-speed rail services (Fig. 2.19) is constantly increasing, due mainly to the fact that new high-speed tracks are constructed and opened year after year for operation. Compared with ordinary rail transport, high-speed rail services have income elasticities greater than 1.0 and can therefore be considered as a luxury product (see also §1.9).

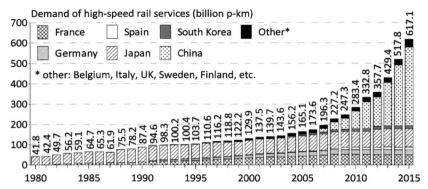

FIGURE 2.19 Evolution of demand of high-speed rail services worldwide. *Source: Compiled by the authors, based on data of Ref. [136].*

2.4.4 Evolution and Trends of Rail Freight Demand

Rail freight demand worldwide (expressed in tonne-kilometers, t-km) during the last 35 years presents fluctuations (Fig. 2.20):

- slow growth rates until 1990,
- negative growth rates between 1990 and 1995, principally due to the restructuring of the economies of formerly socialist countries in Europe, for which most freight was previously transported by rail,
- high growth rates between 2000 and 2008, due to increased freight traffic in China, the United States, and Russia, as a result of high economic growth rates; this was reflected in freight transport for products typically transported by rail (bulk commodities and raw materials),
- decline and stagnation since 2008.

Until 2008, rail freight had positive growth rates in the United States, Canada, China, Russia, and India and recessed or stagnated in the EU-28 (Fig. 2.21).

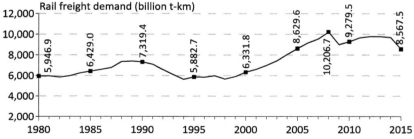

FIGURE 2.20 Evolution of rail freight demand worldwide. *Source: Compiled by the authors, based on data of Refs. [38,136].*

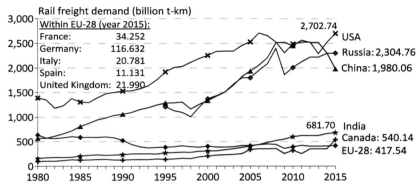

FIGURE 2.21 Evolution of rail freight demand for some countries. *Source: Compiled by the authors, based on data of Refs. [4,38,136].*

2.4.5 Trends in the Global Railway Technologies Market

The global railway technologies market may refer to the following components of the railway system [7]:

- infrastructure (subgrade, subballast, ballast, sleepers, fastenings, rails, electrification equipment),
- engineering systems (telecommunications, control/safety),
- rolling stock (locomotives [diesel or electric], passenger vehicles, freight vehicles, high-speed vehicles, metro vehicles).

The global railway technologies market (infrastructure, engineering systems, and rolling stock) is estimated at 115 billion US$ for the year 2006, 150 billion US$ for the year 2010, and 182 billion US$ for the year 2014. The share of each of the above components for the period 1990—2010 was as follows: infrastructure 50%, rolling stock 39%, and engineering systems 11%. However, the financial—economic crisis of 2008—10 resulted in the delay, postponement, or even cancellation of the construction of a number of new railway tracks (particularly in Europe). The rate of construction of new tracks in China has also declined since 2012. The combined effect of these two phenomena was a change in the share of the three railway components, which was for the year 2014 as follows: infrastructure 29%, rolling stock 60%, and engineering systems 11%. The same year, the share of the three segments of railway systems in the global railway technologies market was as follows: conventional railways 74%, urban railways 14%, and high-speed railways 12%.

Big orders in the railway technologies market come from China, the United States, and Russia, followed by Germany, France, Japan, India, the United Kingdom, Italy, and Spain (Fig. 2.22). The world rolling stock market was dominated in 2009 by the following rolling stock constructors: Bombardier

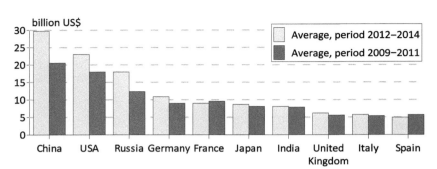

FIGURE 2.22   Turnover of the railway industry of principal countries in the railway technologies market (infrastructure, engineering systems, rolling stock). *Source: Compiled by the authors, based on data of Refs. [7,139].*

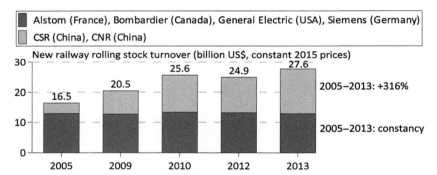

FIGURE 2.23   Principal constructors in the new rolling stock market worldwide. *Source: Compiled by the authors, based on data of Refs. [7,139].*

23%, Alstom 14%, China South Locomotive & Rolling Stock Corporation (CSR) 14%, Siemens 11.5%, China North Locomotive and Rolling Stock Industry Corporation (CNR) 11%, General Electric 7.5%, Kawasaki 5%, Construcciones y Auxiliar de Ferrocarriles (Spain) 5%, Transmashholding (Russia) 4%, other companies 5%. However, the situation has changed considerably since 2010, in favor of Chinese rolling stock constructors (Fig. 2.23).

2.5 EVOLUTION AND TRENDS OF ROAD TRANSPORT DEMAND

2.5.1 The Private Car Ownership Index

The private car ownership index (number of passenger cars per 1000 inhabitants) has been considered for years as a representative index of the development of road transport in a particular country. This is the case only to a

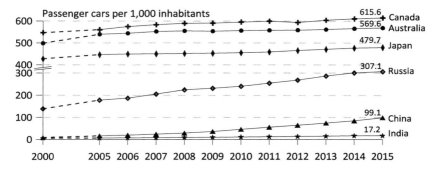

FIGURE 2.24 Evolution of the private car ownership index for some countries of the world. *Source: Compiled by the authors, based on data of Refs. [140,141].*

relatively lesser extent today and will be even less in the future due to the development of car sharing and carpooling (see §1.7.3.4). Increasing congestion and costs in many cities around the world discourage the possession of a second or third private car in one household. Individuals prefer to share a car with others, particularly for trips related to work.

Fig. 2.24 illustrates the evolution of the private car ownership index for some countries in the world over the period 2000–15. A huge increase in private cars is observed in China and Russia, which have moved toward a liberal economy and at the same time increased considerably their GDP per capita. No great changes are noticed in industrialized countries, such as Japan, Australia, or Canada.

A longer period of analysis, going back to 1950 for the United States and the world and to 1970 for the EU-28 countries, is illustrated in Fig. 2.25. In both cases, the great increase in the number of private cars took place between 1950 and 1990, as a result of economic growth, spectacular technological achievements, and a lifestyle which favored the possession of a private car.

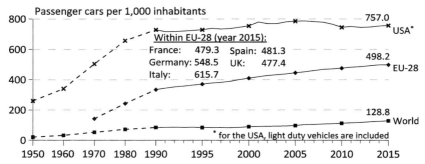

FIGURE 2.25 Evolution of the private car ownership index for the USA, the EU-28, and the world. *Source: Compiled by the authors, based on data of Refs. [140,141].*

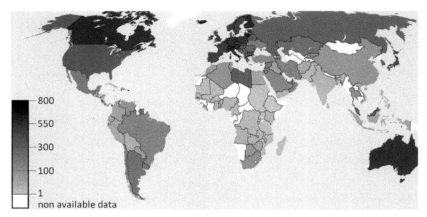

FIGURE 2.26   Private car ownership index (passenger cars per 1000 inhabitants) all over the world for the year 2015. *Source: Compiled by the authors, based on data of Ref. [140].*

Fig. 2.26 illustrates the private car ownership index all over the world.

Similar to the private car ownership index is the commercial vehicle ownership index (Fig. 2.27). Commercial vehicles refer to light commercial vehicles, heavy trucks, coaches, and busses. In the decade 2005—15, the number of commercial vehicles increased substantially in China and India but only slightly in other countries of the world, such as the United States, the EU-28, and Japan.

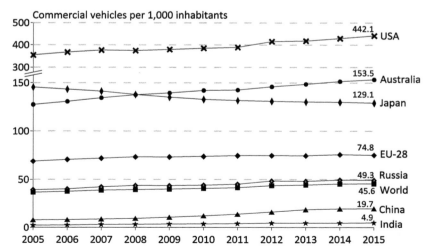

FIGURE 2.27   Evolution of the commercial vehicle ownership index for some countries. *Source: Compiled by the authors, based on data of Ref. [140].*

2.5.2 Evolution and Trends of Production of Road Vehicles

Worldwide, the production of road vehicles demonstrated constant growth over the last 35 years (Fig. 2.28). From 1970 to 2015 the production of new passenger cars worldwide has increased by 3 times and the production of commercial vehicles by 3.5 times. However, between 1970 and 2015 the production of new cars did not change substantially in Germany, the United Kingdom, Russia, or Japan and shrunk in the United States. But there has been an explosion of new car production in China, India, and South Korea, primarily due to the relocation of many car manufacturing companies to these countries (Fig. 2.29).

2.5.3 Evolution and Trends of Road Traffic

The increase in the number of private cars, combined with the increase in GDP per capita, resulted in a tremendous increase in road traffic over the years, as illustrated in Fig. 2.30 (for the United States) and Fig. 2.31 (for the United Kingdom). However, road traffic manifests fluctuations due to the effects of both domestic and international events (Fig. 2.32, case of the United Kingdom), as well as of seasonal factors (Fig. 2.33, case of the United States). Monthly fluctuations reach their peak values in August, which in the United States are 10% higher relative to average yearly values, and 15% higher relative to the yearly minimum, which usually occurs in February.

Hourly fluctuations from Monday to Friday result in peak values early in the morning and late in the afternoon (Fig. 2.34). During the weekends, road traffic usually follows the normal distribution (see Table 4.6 and Fig. 5.4) with midday peak values.

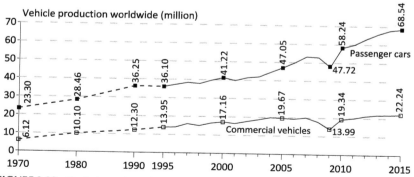

FIGURE 2.28 Evolution and trends of production of road vehicles worldwide. *Source: Compiled by the authors, based on data of Refs. [140,142].*

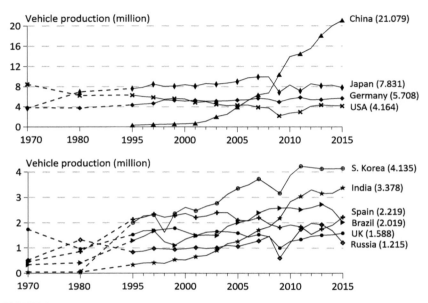

FIGURE 2.29   Evolution and trends of production of road vehicles in some countries. *Source: Compiled by the authors, based on data of Refs. [140,142].*

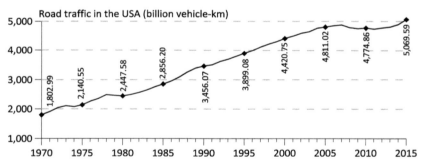

FIGURE 2.30   Evolution of road traffic in the United States. *Source: Compiled by the authors, based on data of Ref. [143].*

2.5.4 Road Safety

Transport activity ensures the mobility of people and goods but at the same time is at the origin of a number of accidents causing deaths, injuries, or material damages. The majority of such accidents take place in the road network. Fig. 2.35 illustrates the comparative risk of death by transport mode. Thus, road safety has become an issue of major concern for governments, health and transport institutions, and citizens [145–147]. In 2015, road accidents worldwide resulted in 1.34 million deaths and about 35 million injuries.

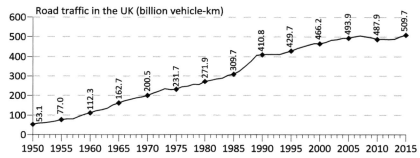

FIGURE 2.31 Evolution of road traffic in the United Kingdom. *Source: Compiled by the authors, based on data of Ref. [144].*

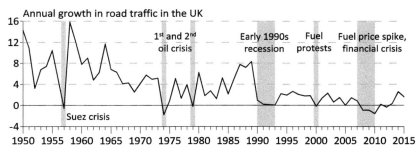

FIGURE 2.32 Effects on road traffic in the United Kingdom of some major international and domestic events. *Source: Compiled by the authors, based on data of Ref. [144].*

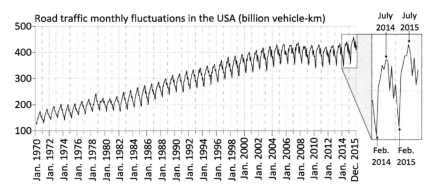

FIGURE 2.33 Monthly fluctuations of road traffic in the United States. *Source: Compiled by the authors, based on data of Ref. [143].*

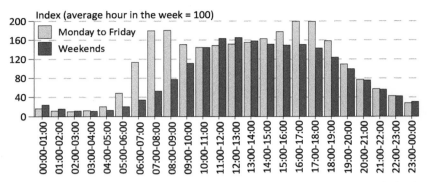

FIGURE 2.34   Hourly fluctuations of road traffic on all roads in the United Kingdom during the year 2015. *Source: Compiled by the authors, based on data of Ref. [144].*

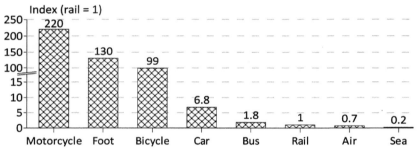

FIGURE 2.35   Risk for an accident leading to a fatality when using various transport modes. *Source: Compiled by the authors, based on data of Ref. [7,71].*

Road accidents are the leading cause of death among people aged 15−29 years [148]. Fig. 2.36 illustrates the various causes of death, among them road accidents.

However, road accidents are more frequent in low- and medium-income countries (Figs. 2.37 and 2.38, left). 90% of the total number of road accident deaths worldwide occurs in these countries, which represent 82% of world population, but only 54% of world's fleet of cars. It is noteworthy to outline that the trend concerning deaths from road accidents is declining in high-income countries but increasing in low- and medium-income countries (Fig. 2.38, right).

Although great differences in road safety may be observed among high-income countries (such as the differences between the United Kingdom and the United States; see Fig. 2.37), road fatalities are clearly higher in low- and medium-income countries compared with high-income countries, as a result of not only different levels of investment in road infrastructure, maintenance of vehicles, and awareness and sensitivity of drivers, but also of the increase in

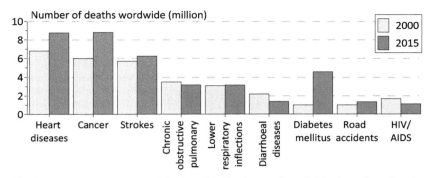

FIGURE 2.36 Principal causes of death worldwide. *Source: Compiled by the authors, based on data of Refs. [149,150].*

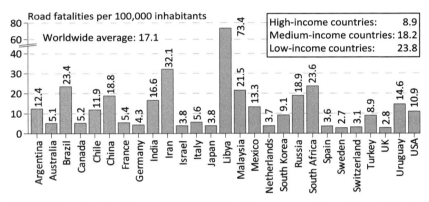

FIGURE 2.37 Road fatalities per 100,000 inhabitants for some countries of the world for the year 2015 (Brazil, China, India, Iran, Libya, and Russia for the year 2013) and various income levels. *Source: Compiled by the authors, based on data of Ref. [151].*

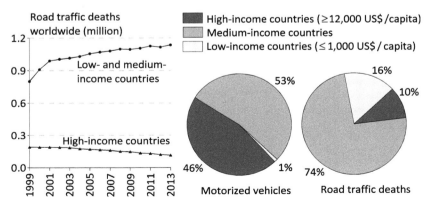

FIGURE 2.38 Road traffic deaths and registered motorized vehicles by income level. *Source: Compiled by the authors, based on data of Refs. [148,150].*

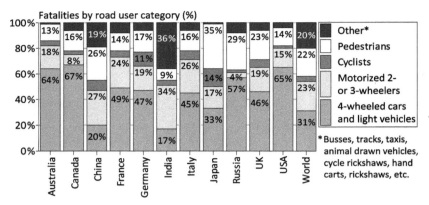

FIGURE 2.39 Fatalities by type of road user for various countries of the world. *Source: Compiled by the authors, based on data of Ref. [148].*

the private car ownership index. Pedestrians, cyclists, and motorized two- or three-wheelers are by far more vulnerable than drivers of cars (Fig. 2.39).

2.6 EVOLUTION AND TRENDS RELATED TO ELECTRIC CAR TECHNOLOGY

2.6.1 Definition and Types of Electric Cars

An electric car can be defined as an automobile which moves by means of electric motors, consuming electrical energy that is stored in rechargeable batteries or another energy storage device [152–154]. Although the first electric cars were produced in the 1880s, the higher construction and operation costs (compared with conventional cars), as well as the shorter range of traveling distance and corresponding loss of autonomy, delayed their mass production for more than one century [155]. However, since 2000 a renaissance in electric car manufacturing has occurred, due to the need to reduce greenhouse gas emissions [156,157].

There are many types of electric cars, but they can be classified into two basic categories [152–154]:

- fully electric cars, which rely entirely on their battery,
- hybrid electric cars, which have rechargeable batteries, but also possess internal combustion engines as a backup or as an integral part of their cycle.

2.6.2 Cost of Electric Cars

The purchase cost of a medium-size electric car (five-seat sedan with a range of autonomy between successive charges of about 140–160 km) was

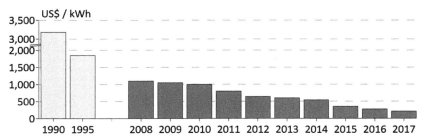

FIGURE 2.40 Evolution of the cost of a battery of an electric car. *Source: Compiled by the authors, based on data of Refs. [158,159].*

around 30,000 US$, in 2017, which is still higher compared with conventional (petrol or diesel) cars.

The cost of a lithium-ion battery in 2017 was 210 US$/kWh (80% lower compared with 2010) and is projected to drop to 70 US$/kWh (or even lower) by 2030 (Fig. 2.40). Thus, it can be estimated that during the 2020s the electric car will become, without any kind of state subsidy, a more economical option than a conventional car. The price of the oil during the 2020s is projected to be in the range of 50−70 US$ per barrel. A massive turn of consumers to electric cars in the early 2030s can only be delayed if the cost of a barrel of oil falls down to US$ 20, something very unlikely to happen, due to the high production costs of oil outside the Middle East. In addition to the reduction in cost, electric car manufactures tried to increase the range of autonomy of electric cars, which surpassed 400 km in 2017 for higher-cost electric cars.

2.6.3 Evolution and Trends of the Electric Car Market

In 2015, a total of 1.257 million electric cars were circulating in roads worldwide. Sales of electric cars worldwide were 550.57 thousand in 2015, 69% higher compared with 2014 (325.09 thousand), against only 1.67 thousand in 2005 [159]. It is important to note that 79.7% of electric cars are located in the United States (32.1%), China (24.8%), Japan (10.1%), the Netherlands (7.1%), and Norway (5.6%) (Fig. 2.41). The market share of electric cars (as a percentage of the market share of new cars) reached 23% in Norway, and nearly 10% in the Netherlands in 2015 [159]. Very long-term prospects for 2040 (which have an inherent element of prophecy) estimate sales of electric cars up to 41 million, with the worldwide share of electric cars in the new light vehicles market projected to be 35%. In 2040, electric cars are projected to represent more than 25% of the global car fleet, which entails a reduction of the consumption of oil barrels per day by 13 million.

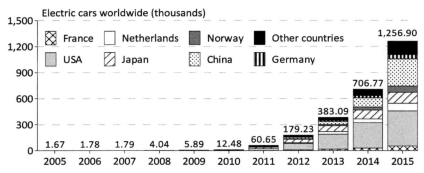

FIGURE 2.41 Evolution of the number of electric cars worldwide. *Source: Compiled by the authors, based on data of Ref. [159].*

2.6.4 Principal Driving Factors for the Electric Car Market

Wherever electric cars represent a large share of new car sales, it is the combined effect of the following:

- government subsidies for buyers of electric cars, to offset high purchase costs,
- regulation concerning CO_2 and other environmental emissions,
- efforts of manufacturers to reduce construction costs,
- integration of electric car models into the production chains; in 2017 almost every major car constructor is producing at least one electric car model,
- greater range and autonomy of electric cars,
- development of a more widespread system of charging stations and infrastructure,
- consumer perception for a new lifestyle, which favors electric cars,
- integration of electric car technology into a new conception of mobility, considered as a service which meets consumers' needs in a most efficient and least harmful way to the environment,
- fascination with new technologies,
- increased sensitivity of citizens to the protection of the environment.

Fig 2.42 illustrates possible trends for the stock of electric cars by 2030. Scenarios of future trends for electric cars are based on the practicality, sustainability, safety, and affordability of electric cars, as well as whether or not electric cars will achieve a cost parity with conventional internal combustion cars by the 2020s, and depending on the regulations that will be adopted related to CO_2 emissions.

2.7 EVOLUTION AND TRENDS OF DEMAND OF METRO AND TRAM

Metro and tram (or tramway) are also forms of guided transport (like conventional railways), since they move on rails. Both are used in urban areas and

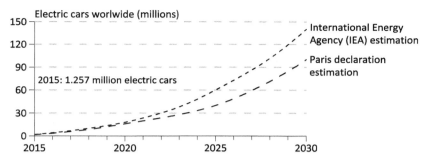

FIGURE 2.42 Possible trends for the stock of electric cars worldwide by 2030. *Source: Compiled by the authors, based on data of Ref. [159].*

permit reliable, quick, and fairly cheap transport, while alleviating congestion problems (if correctly planned) and emissions harmful to the environment. The driving forces of demand for metro and tram systems are [160−162]:

- population and particularly urban population density,
- GDP per capita,
- levels of unemployment,
- car ownership index,
- cost of oil,
- level of metro and tram fares compared with bus and taxi fares,
- distance from home to work (as this distance is constantly increasing, due to the extension of cities and productive activities, it favors the use of metro and tram systems),
- congestion,
- parking places (availability, cost).

Data concerning the evolution of demand for metro systems usually refer to a specific city or metro line and very often are not published. The share of metro and tram systems in the passenger transport market of the EU-28 was 1.58% in 2015, compared with 1.42% in 1995 and 1.54% in 2010 (Table 2.1 and Fig. 2.2).

Table 2.5 illustrates the demand for metro systems in some big cities around the world.

2.8 EVOLUTION AND TRENDS OF SEA TRANSPORT DEMAND

2.8.1 Sea Transport and Economic Activity

Sea transport has always been the most liberalized sector of transport. The critical (and principal) driving forces for the development of sea transport are the trends in worldwide GDP and trade. Other driving forces for sea transport include access, connectivity, infrastructure and warehouses, energy and labor costs, regulations related to the safety and quality of transport, responsiveness to the increased requirements of customers across supply chains, and environmental and climate change constraints [163−167].

TABLE 2.5: Passengers of metro systems for various cities worldwide.

City (Country)	First year of operation (year of last expansion)	System length (in km)	Number of stations in operation	Stations per km of line	Passengers (in billion) for a specific year	
Beijing (China)	1971 (2016)	574.0	278	0.48	3.660	2016
Tokyo (Japan)	1927 (2008)	304.1	285	0.94	3.616	2016
Shanghai (China)	1993 (2016)	588.0	337	0.57	3.401	2016
Seoul (South Korea)	1974 (2016)	331.5	307	0.93	2.857	2016
Guangzhou (China)	1997 (2016)	308.7	184	0.60	2.568	2016
Moscow (Russia)	1935 (2017)	346.1	206	0.60	2.378	2016
New York (USA)	1904 (2017)	380.2	425	1.12	1.757	2016
Hong Kong	1979 (2016)	174.7	93	0.53	1.716	2016
Mexico City (Mexico)	1969 (2012)	226.5	147	0.65	1.605	2016
Paris (France)	1900 (2013)	214.0	302	1.41	1.519	2016
London (UK)	1890 (2008)	402.0	270	0.67	1.340	2015
Cairo (Egypt)	1987 (2014)	77.9	61	0.78	1.314	2015
São Paulo (Brazil)	1974 (2017)	80.2	71	0.89	1.308	2016
Singapore	1987 (2017)	199.2	119	0.60	1.008	2014
Delhi (India)	2002 (2017)	231.0	155	0.67	1.008	2017
Osaka (Japan)	1933 (2006)	129.9	123	0.95	0.870	2016

City						
Saint Petersburg (Russia)	1955 (2012)	113.2	67	0.59	0.740	2016
Taipei (Taiwan)	1996 (2015)	131.1	117	0.89	0.740	2016
Santiago (Chile)	1975 (2017)	118.0	118	1.00	0.670	2016
Berlin (Germany)	1902 (2009)	151.7	173	1.14	0.635	2015
Madrid (Spain)	1919 (2015)	294.0	301	1.02	0.570	2015
Caracas (Venezuela)	1983 (2015)	63.6	49	0.77	0.495	2014
Kiev (Ukraine)	1960 (2013)	67.6	52	0.77	0.485	2016
Milan (Italy)	1964 (2015)	101.0	113	1.12	0.468	2014
Prague (Czech Republic)	1974 (2015)	65.2	61	0.94	0.461	2016
Vienna (Austria)	1976 (2017)	78.5	104	1.32	0.440	2016
Barcelona (Spain)	1924 (2016)	146.0	180	1.23	0.416	2014
Munich (Germany)	1971 (2010)	95.0	96	1.01	0.398	2015
Istanbul (Turkey)	1989 (2017)	105.8	82	0.78	0.385	2015
Montreal (Canada)	1966 (2007)	69.2	68	0.98	0.354	2016
Stockholm (Sweden)	1950 (1994)	105.7	100	0.95	0.330	2015
Buenos Aires (Argentina)	1913 (2016)	53.9	86	1.60	0.304	2016
Toronto (Canada)	1954 (2017)	76.9	75	0.98	0.303	2016
Minsk (Belarus)	1984 (2014)	37.3	29	0.78	0.291	2016
Athens (Greece)	1904 (2013)	84.7	61	0.72	0.264	2015
Washington D.C. (USA)	1976 (2014)	188.0	91	0.48	0.234	2016

Source: Compiled by the authors, based on data of metros' authorities.

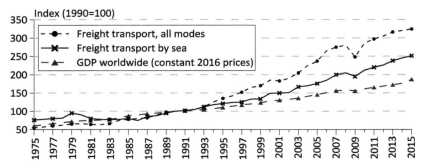

FIGURE 2.43 Evolution of sea transport and gross domestic product worldwide. *Source: Compiled by the authors, based on data of Ref. [167].*

Growth rates of sea transport are almost constantly higher than growth rates of world GDP (Fig. 2.43), due to the progressive liberalization of commercial exchanges and trade. Between 1990 and 2015 sea transport increased by 151.5%, compared with an 87.1% increase in worldwide GDP [167].

2.8.2 Products Transported by Sea

Products transported by sea and their respective share of sea freight were as follows (for the year 2014): crude oil 17%, petroleum products 9%, gas and chemicals 6%, containerized freight 15%, iron ore 13%, coal 12%, grain 4%, other dry materials 9%, minor bulks 15% [2,167].

2.8.3 Evolution and Trends of Traffic of the Various Categories of Sea Transport

Fig. 2.44 illustrates the evolution of traffic in the principal products transported by sea. The effects of the international economic crisis of 2008 were absorbed

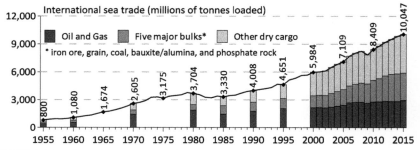

FIGURE 2.44 Evolution and trends of sea transport—Principal products transported. *Source: Compiled by the authors, based on data of Ref. [167].*

by 2010, and since then, the growth rates of sea transport of the various categories of freight have been high [167].

2.8.4 Evolution and Trends of Container Sea Traffic

Fig. 2.45 illustrates the evolution of container port traffic (in million TEU: twenty-foot equivalent unit)[1] worldwide between 2000 and 2014, which was multiplied 3.17 times during this period. This increase was mainly stimulated not only by traffic from China (Fig. 2.46), and more particularly from the ports of Shanghai, Shenzhen, Ningbo-Zhoushan, Qingdao, Guangzhou, etc., (Fig. 2.47), but also by an increase in traffic from the ports in Singapore, Busan (South Korea), and Dubai (Fig. 2.48).

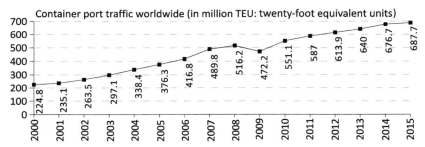

FIGURE 2.45 Evolution of container port traffic worldwide. *Source: Compiled by the authors, based on data of Ref. [38].*

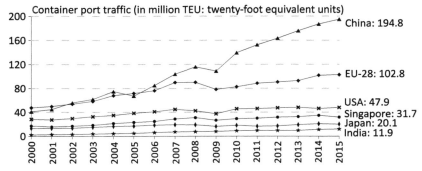

FIGURE 2.46 Evolution of container port traffic for some countries of the world. *Source: Compiled by the authors, based on data of Ref. [38].*

---

1. The twenty-foot equivalent unit is a unit of cargo capacity used to measure the capacity of container ships and terminals. It is based on the 20 ft (6.1 m) long, 8 ft (2.44 m) wide, and 8 ft 6 in. (2.59 m) heigh container. These dimensions have been set by the International Organization for Standardization.

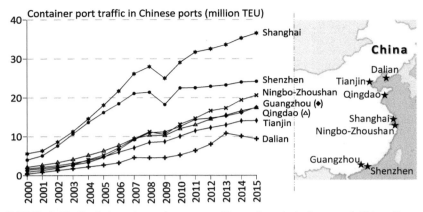

FIGURE 2.47 Evolution of container port traffic at the principal ports of China. *Source: Compiled by the authors, based on data of Refs. [167,168].*

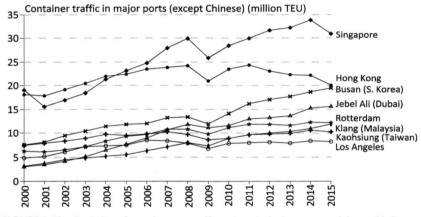

FIGURE 2.48 Evolution of container port traffic at the principal ports around the world. *Source: Compiled by the authors, based on data of Refs. [167,168].*

2.8.5 Evolution of the World Fleet

As of January 2016, the world fleet comprises 89,423 vessels with a total capacity of 1,745,921,886 deadweight tonnage (dwt). Owners of vessels may choose either the flag of their own country or so-called flags of convenience or open registration countries, such as Panama, Liberia, Malta, Antigua and Barbuda, Marshal Inlands, Cyprus, and Bahamas, which offer fiscal advantages, less regulation, and the least technical controls to ship owners [169,170].

The principal countries of ship owners of the world fleet as of January 2016, as a percentage of deadweight tonnage worldwide, were Greece 16.36%

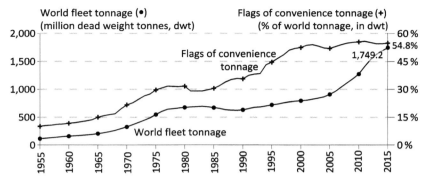

FIGURE 2.49 Evolution of world fleet tonnage and of percentage of world tonnage registered under flags of convenience. *Source: Compiled by the authors, based on data of Refs. [167,171].*

(of which 77.92% under foreign flag), Japan 12.78% (of which 87.43% under foreign flag), China 8.87% (of which 53.36% under foreign flag), Germany 6.65% (of which 90.51% under foreign flag), Singapore 5.32% (of which 35.20% under foreign flag), Hong Kong 4.88% (of which 22.72% under foreign flag), South Korea 4.40% (of which 79.57% under foreign flag), and the United States 3.36% (of which 86.47% under foreign flag). However, the trend of ship owners toward flags of convenience, in which 54.8% of world tonnage were registered in 2015 (compared with 21.6% in 1970 and 35.7% in 1990), should be noticed (Fig. 2.49).

Chapter 3

Methods of Modeling Transport Demand

Chapter Outline

3.1 STRUCTURE AND VARIABLES OF A TRANSPORT DEMAND MODEL

3.1.1 Structure of a Transport Demand Model

Transport demand is a complex phenomenon which incorporates economic aspects (such as travel costs, revenue of the customers, etc.), technical aspects (such as travel times, the technology used and the resulting convenience and comforts, etc.), lifestyle aspects of the society and of a specific individual (preferences for a specific transport mode), psychological aspects (e.g., some individuals suffer from claustrophobia and refuse to use an airplane or a lift), and the factor of time (i.e., the same individual may at different times choose different transport modes). Models of transport demand aim at providing the most accurate representation for a specific transport demand problem (e.g., passengers traveling by high-speed trains between London and Paris).

Modeling of Transport Demand. https://doi.org/10.1016/B978-0-12-811513-8.00003-0
Copyright © 2019 Elsevier Inc. All rights reserved.

89

They try to establish a more or less rational correlation between the factors that affect transport demand and the effects of these factors on transport, that is, the quantity and other characteristics of transport.

Transport demand models are simplified (though not simplistic) constructs that attempt to describe, explain, correlate, and forecast transport demand within a rational framework as accurately as possible. They are always based on a set of assumptions and subsequently have a rather limited range of application to cases for which the assumptions are valid. For this reason, transport demand models should not be extended or generalized and applied to problems and issues for which the assumptions made are not valid. Such extensions and generalizations are common mistakes that should be avoided.

A forecast may refer to a short-term, medium-term, or long-term prospect, and often refers to a very specific problem (e.g., demand of air passengers for low-cost airlines between London and Mallorca) or a more general one (e.g., demand of air passengers to tourist destinations) or an even more general one (e.g., air passenger demand worldwide). The nature and time range of the problem under study will lead the forecaster to consider a set of assumptions related to the problem and of factors affecting the problem. In order to permit the greatest possible applicability and forecasting ability of a model, the number of assumptions should be limited as far as possible and should be restricted to only the most necessary ones. The factors affecting the problem should be chosen carefully. An increased number of such factors does not necessarily mean that a successful forecast is assured. Many trustworthy models that have been valid for many years rely on just a few factors. In previous chapters, we have analyzed the driving forces of transport demand in general (§1.5) and for each transport mode specifically (e.g., §2.3.2 for air transport).

Fig. 3.1 illustrates the successive steps for a rational forecast of transport demand. The last (and often forgotten) step of a good forecast is to compare the forecasted values of transport demand with the realized ones. If there is any great difference (e.g., >15%) observed over successive forecasts between the forecasted and realized values, this is a sign that the method chosen is not appropriate and should be replaced by a more appropriate one in any similar undertaking in the future.

3.1.2 Definition of a Variable

Factors affecting transport demand may stay constant or change and vary in relation to time and other characteristics of the transport demand problem. In the latter case, we use the term *variable* to designate a characteristic or attribute of an individual or organization that can be measured or observed and that varies from individual to individual or within the organization involved in a transport demand problem [172].

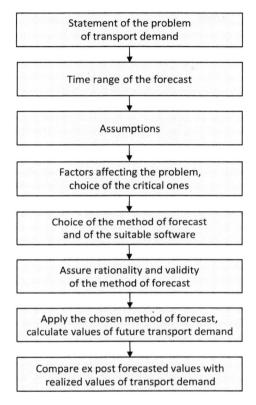

FIGURE 3.1 Successive steps for the forecast of future transport demand which is likely to occur. *Source: Compiled by the authors.*

3.1.3 Numerical and Categorical Variables

In relation to the content of a variable, we can have numerical or categorical variables:

- *Numerical* (or *quantitative*) variables: these have values that describe a measurable quantity. Since the values of numerical variables have mathematical meaning, they can be added or subtracted, multiplied, or divided. Numerical variables can be classified as follows:
  - *Continuous* (or *interval*) variables: a variable that is not restricted to specific values but can take on infinitely many uncountable values. The per capita GDP or the personal disposable income is a continuous variable.
  - *Discrete* variables: variables having only integer values. The number of possible values of a discrete variable is either finite or countably infinite. The number of private cars per family, the annual number of air passengers carried worldwide, etc., are typical discrete variables.

- *Categorical* (or *nominal or qualitative*) variables: they can take values indicating membership in one of several possible categories. These categories are often assigned numerical values used as labels. The number of possible values of a categorical variable is limited, fixed (usually), whereas its possible values are mutually exclusive. Examples of categorical variables are the day of a week (1 for Monday, 2 for Tuesday, etc.), the gender (0 for male, 1 for female), the mode of transport (on foot, by vehicles such as bicycle, motorcycle, private car, carpool, minivan, bus, tram, metro), the evaluation of quality of transport (e.g., 1: poor, 2: fair, 3: average, 4: good, 5: excellent), etc. Categorical variables can be further categorized as:
  - *Ordinal* variables: they designate the type of a categorical variable that is used to rank or order some characteristics of the variable. A well-known example of measuring of an ordinal variable is the Likert scale (see §4.4.6.4). The numbers in ordinal variables have mathematical meaning. For example, when evaluating the quality of transport, the average value of 100 responses can be calculated and encompasses a useful indicator.
  - *Nominal* variables: these designate the type of categorical variables for which the values cannot be organized in a logical sequence and do not have mathematical meaning. An example of a nominal variable is the gender or the mode of transport; in both cases the average value of the variable has no practical or logical meaning.
  - *Binary* (or *dichotomous*) variables: these are categorical variables which indicate only two states and can take only two values (i.e., yes or no, e.g., bicyclist or pedestrian, red or green light). Observations that occur in one of two possible states often take the value 0 and 1; for example, the value 1 for a binary variable could indicate the possession of a private car, whereas the value 0 the opposite. The numbers in ordinal variables may or may not have mathematical meaning.

3.1.4 Dependent and Independent Variables

We usually distinguish the variables of a transport demand model into independent and dependent ones. *Independent* variables are defined as those that probably cause, influence, or affect the outcome of the problem of transport demand under study, which usually relates to the quantity to expect of future transport demand (passengers or passenger-kilometers, tonnes or tonne-kilometers) and in some cases specific characteristics of that demand (like the origin and destination of trips). *Dependent* variables are defined as those that depend on the independent variables and are the outcome or result of the influence of the independent variables. Dependent variables in a transport demand model are usually considered to be the quantity of future transport or some of its characteristics.

Some authors use instead of the term variable the term *parameter*, instead of the term independent variable the term *explanatory* variable, and instead of the term dependent variable the term *response* variable [173,174]. However, an independent variable always has an explanatory character, but an explanatory variable may well be nonindependent, if it is correlated with another explanatory variable. An independent variable is not affected at all by any other independent variable, whereas an explanatory variable may be affected by another explanatory variable. A rational transport demand model should be based on explanatory variables that are not correlated among them, that is, on independent variables. Thus, the analysis of this book focuses on independent (and not explanatory, in general) variables. The result of the interaction of explanatory variables is the response variable, whereas the result of independent variables is the dependent variable.

3.1.5 Independent Variables of a Transport Demand Model

The independent variables of a transport demand model may refer to what has been labeled in Chapters 1 and 2 as the factors or principal drivers or driving forces of transport demand. Such variables are (see also §1.5):

- time period to which transport demand refers,
- transport costs (fares of the mode under study but of substitute or competing modes also),
- travel times (terminal to terminal, door to door),
- economic/financial indicators, like the per capita GDP, the revenue of an individual or the per capita expenditure for transport,
- institutional/legislative framework (regulation, competition, partial or full liberalization, privatization, public subsidies),
- population (present customers, eventual or potential customers),
- patterns of urban development, land uses, spatial configuration of activities (houses, production activities, services, commerce, leisure),
- environmental aspects (CO_2 emissions, noise, other disturbances),
- technology (convenience, comfort, easiness),
- energy consumption and dependence,
- lifestyle: a subjective tendency toward a transport mode as an influence of similar tendencies of other individuals; these tendencies may have little to do with the performances of the specific mode.

3.1.6 Proxy Variables

A *proxy* variable is a variable that is used in the place of a variable that cannot be measured, or is difficult to be measured, or for which we do not have access to available data or observations. The proxy variable should present a correlation, positive or negative, with the variable of interest and must be easily measurable in a reliable way. For example, the quality of service of a public transport authority is difficult to be quantified and thus we can use as a proxy variable the number of the recorded complaints of passengers. The per capita GDP of a region could be a proxy variable for the quality of life in the specific region, the car ownership index a proxy variable for the standard of living, the distance a proxy variable (however poor in many cases [175]) for international freight transport cost, the passenger or freight traffic per employee a proxy variable for the productivity of a transport company, etc.

3.1.7 Dummy Variables

Dummy variables are used, as independent variables, to indicate the presence or absence of one or more features that are expected to affect the dependent variable. Dummy variables are used to sort, according to a specific characteristic, the data or observations into mutually exclusive categories and they take the value 1 or 0; the value 1 usually denotes the presence of the specific characteristic, whereas the value 0 denotes its absence. For example, if we try to model the use of private cars in business trips, we can use as dummy variables, in addition to other independent variables, the gender (0 for male, 1 for female) and/or the marital status (0 for singles, 1 for married). The dummy variables are also used to describe specific facts of the past, such as wars, suicide attacks, general strikes, epidemics, etc., in order to quantify the effect of such a fact on the demand of a specific mode of transport.

3.1.8 Linguistic Variables

Linguistic variables are defined as variables whose values are words or sentences in a natural or artificial language (languages which emerge in computer simulations, robot interactions, etc.). For example, the transport cost could be defined as a linguistic variable if its values are linguistic rather than numerical, i.e., low, average, high, etc., rather than US$10, US$50, US$100. In addition to the primary terms, a linguistic value may involve connectives, such as *and, or, either, neither*, etc.; the negation *not*; and hedges, such as *very, more or less, completely, quite, fairly, extremely, somewhat*, etc. Linguistic variables are very common in fuzzy models (see §9.2.3 and §9.8.3) [176,177].

3.1.9 Variables Used in a Logarithmic Form

Some numerical variables are often transformed in a logarithmic (log) form and especially natural (ln) logarithms (for which the base e of the logarithm is Euler's number, approximately equal to 2.718281). This is the case of variables that refer to economic or financial terms (such as the GDP, the disposable income, revenues, etc.), which always take positive values. In addition, variables that have high positive values, such as the population of a region, can also be expressed in a logarithmic form. The logarithmic form cannot be used when the variables take zero or negative values. The advantages of the log transformation of the variables are the following:

- the range of variables is significantly reduced[1],
- the models are less sensitive to extreme data or observations of the dependent and the independent variables,
- the coefficients on the natural-log scale are directly interpretable as approximate proportional differences (i.e., percentage changes). This is because for small values x of a variable X this property of the natural logarithms implies that $\ln(1 + x) \approx x$ (e.g., for $x = 0.05$ it is $\ln(1 + 0.05) = 0.049 \approx 0.05$, for $x = 0.10$ it is $\ln(1 + 0.10) = 0.095 \approx 0.10$, etc.) [178]. Thus, when modeled, the coefficients of such variables have useful interpretations; they could represent elasticities, since an increase of the value of a variable by 1% is almost equivalent to adding 0.01 to $\ln(X)$ (see also §1.9),
- they can transform in most cases a nonstationary time series to a stationary one (see §5.1.5),
- they can confront significant problems arising when modeling, such as the heteroscedasticity (see §5.10).

3.1.10 Variables Within a Frame of Epistemological Approach

The way toward understanding and explaining a complex phenomenon like transport will need some of the previously mentioned variables to be used in the following sequence of initiatives and efforts:

1. establish a patterned set of *assumptions* (both explicit but also underlying) concerning the complex reality of transport demand to be approached,
2. make an effort to attain the appropriate *knowledge* related to the reality of transport demand (*data*, surveys, etc.),
3. look for the appropriate ways to approach knowledge of transport demand and select the most suitable *methods*.

3.1.11 Endogenous and Exogenous Variables

Variables of a transport demand model may relate to the problem under study, in which case they are called *endogenous*. In a transport demand model such variables are travel times, values of fares, etc. In contrast, variables, which are external to the problem under study, are called *exogenous*.

---

1. We remind that $\ln 1 = 0$, $\ln 5 = 1.609$, $\ln 10 = 2.303$, $\ln 100 = 4.605$, $\ln 1000 = 6.908$, $\ln 10,000 = 9.210$, $\ln 100,000 = 11.513$, $\ln 1,000,000 = 13.816$, etc.

The following can be considered as exogenous variables in a transport demand model: economic/financial indexes (like the GDP per capita, the revenue of the customers of a transport mode), land use patterns, etc. Exogenous variables should be given values according to reliable analyses of trustworthy organizations. If this is not the case, and exogenous variables are given arbitrary estimations by an analyst, this will affect inevitably the explanatory and the forecasting ability of a model.

3.2 TRANSPORT DEMAND IN A DETERMINISTIC OR PROBABILISTIC APPROACH

When selecting the appropriate method, we should decide whether the phenomenon of transport demand has a deterministic nature or a probabilistic one. If we consider it as a deterministic one, then we should make use of *deterministic* methods, which consider that under the fulfillment of certain conditions a specific result will or will not occur. On the contrary, if we consider transport demand as a probabilistic (or stochastic) phenomenon, then we turn toward *probabilistic* (or stochastic) methods, in which the fulfillment of x_1 conditions has a t_1 probability of causing the d_1 transport demand, the fulfillment of x_2 conditions has a t_2 probability of causing the d_2 transport demand, and so on. Empirical evidence suggests that this situation is not uncommon in transport mode choices; even when people tend to favor or repeat a specific transport choice or pattern consistently and continuously, this will apply to the vast majority of customers of a transport service but not to all of them, since human behavior always entails a random and unpredictable factor. Though the majority of methods of forecast of transport demand are of a deterministic nature, new methods, such as the artificial neural network (ANN) method (see Chapter 8) and the fuzzy logic method (see Chapter 9), can approach and represent the stochastic character of transport. The stochastic aspect is also essential to models of choice of transport mode at the urban level (among them the models Probit and Logit, see Chapter 7, §7.10.5).

3.3 THE CHOICE BY A TRAVELER OF A TRANSPORT MODE—UTILITY THEORIES AND GENERALIZED COST OF TRANSPORT

3.3.1 Choice Among Many Alternative Transport Modes

Any human being when trying to satisfy a particular need faces many alternatives. Consciously or subconsciously (and in many cases even instinctively) he or she chooses the alternative he or she believes will bring him or her the greatest benefit with the least effort. Thus, an individual selects a specific transport mode based on his or her knowledge and experiences on the specific issue by assessing many factors in his or her effort to maximize the benefits derived from this choice. Not all individuals, however, evaluate the various factors of transport (such as costs, travel times, comfort, etc.) in the same way, and they may have different priorities. Even the same individual at different times may have a different attitude toward the various (and mutually exclusive) transport modes (e.g., high-speed train, low-cost air transport, private car) as the result of another assessment of factors, either by neglecting some of them or by changing their prioritization. In order to assess such changes in behavior, *behavioral* theories have been developed and permit the study of the effects of social, psychological, economic, cognitive, and emotional factors on the choices of an individual among various transport modes [2,7,179]. Within such an approach, the so-called utility theories have been developed.

3.3.2 Utility Theories

An individual, before choosing a transport mode, tries to assess and trade-off the worth of one alternative mode over another and chooses the alternative that is most likely to maximize his or her benefits and welfare. *Utility* U can be defined as an indicator of the value of an individual and is derived from a subjective assessment, which is based on the attributes of eventual alternatives or sets of alternatives [180,181].

According to the *utility maximization* rule, an individual α will choose the alternative transport mode i, which provides him or her with the highest utility U_{max} among available alternatives. Thus, an alternative is chosen if its utility is greater than the utility of all other alternatives. In his choice, the individual α (with specific characteristics C_α, like revenue, lifestyle preferences, etc.) evaluates the attributes X_i related to the alternative i and ranks these attributes in a priority order by giving a weight to each attribute. Thus, among two alternatives i and j he or she will choose the alternative i if [181]:

$$U(X_i, C_\alpha) \geq U(X_j, C_\alpha) \qquad (3.1)$$

Eq. (3.1) can be generalized for many alternatives i, j, k,… and it is known as the "all-or-nothing" principle, in the sense that an individual chooses either one alternative or none.

Eq. (3.1) is of a deterministic nature and is based on the nonrealistic assumption that the decision maker has full knowledge of the attributes of each alternative and pays equal attention to all available alternatives. However, an individual may make different choices when facing the same problem at different times. Different choices are also observed among apparently similar individuals when facing the same or even identical alternatives. The reason of such a variation in choosing a transport mode is that an individual may have incomplete or incorrect information or misperceptions about the attributes of some or all of the alternatives. Different individuals, each holding different information or perceptions about the same alternatives, are likely to make different choices. In order to explain and mathematically represent this changing behavior of individuals, a probabilistic approach is more suitable than a deterministic one, as it provides probabilities (instead of certainty) that people with a given set of characteristics and facing the same set of alternatives will choose one of these alternative transport modes. In the case of the probabilistic approach, the real utility $U(X_i, C_\alpha)$ is calculated as the sum of a deterministic component V_i, as it is estimated by an analyst, and of a measurement error ε_i, which is the part of the utility, however, unknown, to the analyst. Thus [2,182]:

$$U(X_i, C_\alpha) = V(X_i, C_\alpha) + \varepsilon_{i,\alpha} \tag{3.2}$$

The deterministic component $V_{\alpha,i}$ (called also systematic component) of utility of alternative i for the individual α can be written as:

$$V_{\alpha,i} = V(C_\alpha) + V(X_i) + V(C_\alpha, X_i) \tag{3.3}$$

where

$V(C_\alpha)$ part of the utility associated with the characteristics of individual α, such as the revenue, age, gender, lifestyle preferences, etc.,

$V(X_i)$ part of the utility associated with the attributes X_i of alternative i, such as travel cost, travel time, reliability, etc.,

$V(C_\alpha, X_i)$ part of the utility which results from interactions between the attributes X_i of alternative i and the characteristics of individual α.

3.3.3 The Generalized Cost as a Specialization of the Utility Function for Transport

A specialized (and simplified) form of the utility function for transport is the generalized cost (GC) for transport, which can be written for the individual α using the transport mode i as [2,7,183]:

$$GC_{\alpha,i} = DC_{\alpha,i} + h_i \cdot T_\alpha + q_{\alpha,i} \tag{3.4}$$

where

$GC_{\alpha,i}$ generalized cost of transport for the individual α when using transport mode i,

$DC_{\alpha,i}$ direct cost in monetary values from door to door for the individual α when using the specific transport services (first or second class ticket, etc.) of a transport mode i,

$h_i \cdot T_\alpha$ monetary value of travel time when using mode i, which is the product of the total travel time h_i (door to door) multiplied by the monetary value of a man-hour of the specific individual α,

$q_{\alpha,i}$ the quality of service (in monetary values) for the individual α when using transport mode i; as the quality of service is not easily expressed in monetary values, it is often omitted in the calculation of the generalized cost for transport.

Many transport studies in countries of western Europe and the United States have concluded (for the economic conditions of these countries) a monetary value of a man-hour (for the year 2018) for professional trips of 14.5−30.0€ and for leisure trips of 7.0−8.0€ [7,184].

3.4 QUANTITATIVE AND QUALITATIVE METHODS FOR TRANSPORT DEMAND

3.4.1 Definition and Characteristics of Quantitative and Qualitative Methods

There exists a variety of methods for the forecast of transport demand, which can be classified epistemologically, ontologically, and methodologically into *quantitative* and *qualitative* ones. Their differences originate from the positivism−idealism debate in the late 19th century.

A quantitative method uses an interrelated set of variables under certain assumptions and aims to specify the relationship among the variables in terms of magnitudes. It is characterized by a *rationale* that permits us to analyze, explain, and predict a specific phenomenon that can be reduced to some variables, which represent the only truth, the objective reality that exists and is independent of human perception. The investigator and the investigated are considered as independent entities. The investigator is capable of studying a phenomenon without influencing it or being influenced by it. The goal of a quantitative method is to establish and measure a quantitative relationship between variables within a value-free framework. To do so, a quantitative method needs data which can be analyzed in terms of numbers and equations by attempting to establish a more or less general law that permits an *objective* interpretation and forecast of the phenomenon under study.

Qualitative methods demonstrate a different approach (compared with quantitative ones), as they try to explain the behavior and attitudes of individuals in a manner that is more open and responsive to its subject. They can afford a descriptive approach and an overall examination of complex issues. In the case of qualitative methods, there are multiple realities or multiple truths for transport, based on one's perception of reality, which is socially constructed and for this reason constantly changing. Their epistemological approach is that there is no access to reality independent of our minds. Qualitative methods put emphasis on the process and sense making. Thus, qualitative methods have an inherent nature of *subjectivity*.

3.4.2 Advantages and Disadvantages

Quantitative methods present a number of advantages, such as [2,7]:

- *accuracy*, as they are based on data and reliable measurements,
- *rationality* and eventually *causality*, as they try to relate rationally and eventually causally effects of the independent variables on the dependent variables,

- *numerical values*, as they are supported by statistical techniques and sophisticated software,
- *forecasting ability*, as their validity can be extended to the future,
- *control* at any time of the validity of the relationship between dependent and independent variables.

However, quantitative methods are not free of disadvantages, such as [2,7]:

- due to the *complexity* of human behavior, it is difficult to take into account all the variables of the problem and provide the correct values in a numerical application,
- not all humans take action in the same way, as is the case of inert materials in physical sciences,
- quantitative methods are based on the assumption that facts are true and the same for all people all of the time, something that is totally unrealistic,
- quantitative methods may exclude degrees of freedom and choice options,
- even though quantitative methods are considered as objective, many factors of subjectivity can interfere and depend on the analyst, interpretation techniques, etc.

Qualitative methods present also advantages and disadvantages. The following can be considered among the advantages:

- they can analyze specific cases,
- they can afford an overall examination of complex matters,
- they permit a descriptive approach.

The following can be classified among the disadvantages of qualitative methods:

- their subjective nature, which cannot assure a high level of validity and reliability,
- generalization within a wider context may be dangerous or erroneous,
- the dependence on viewpoints expressed by the analyst and the participants of a qualitative study,
- a long time is usually required.

3.5 AGGREGATE AND DISAGGREGATE MODELS

The ambition of every scientist is to construct a model which proves successful in explaining and solving various problems under study. Such models are called *aggregate* and try to analyze and interpret the society as a whole, and many of their parameters are of a general nature [2,185].

However, the transportation problem can manifest itself differently in different societies and thus the creation of models with the individual human behavior as a reference point is attempted. Such models are called *disaggregate* and usually analyze an individual transport problem. Disaggregation may refer to transport modes (road, air, rail, sea), geographical scale or country, economic level (revenue per capita), etc. [186–188].

A usual question is whether a disaggregate model can be used (and under what assumptions, conditions, or modifications) for a problem different from the one it was created for. Such modifications or generalizations of a disaggregate model should be attempted very carefully and only provided that similarities exist between the problem covered by a disaggregate model and the problem under study.

3.6 MODELS BASED ON STATISTICS AND COMPUTATIONAL INTELLIGENCE

Transportation data are most commonly modeled using two different approaches: statistics and/or computational intelligence. Statistics is the mathematics of collecting, organizing, and interpreting numerical data, particularly when these data concern the analysis of population characteristics by inference from sampling [189,190]. Statistics has solid and widely accepted mathematical foundations and can provide insights on the mechanisms creating the data. However, statistics frequently fails when dealing with complex and highly nonlinear problems. Computational intelligence combines elements of learning, adaptation, evolution, and fuzzy logic to create models that are intelligent in the sense that their structure emerges from an unstructured beginning (the data) [190−192].

3.7 MODEL SELECTION, CALIBRATION, ESTIMATION, AND VALIDATION

Model *selection* is the process of choosing the appropriate type of model of the specific qualitative or quantitative method. The selection is based on the given data or observations, the scope of the model (analysis of transport demand, forecast of transport demand, quantification of various elasticities, etc.), the time range for the forecast (from some days to many years), the available time for the forecast, the forecaster's background and capabilities, etc. (see also §3.12).

Given the type of a model, the process of allocation of the appropriate values to the various coefficients of the model is called *calibration* of the model. The calibration process is usually a trial and error effort that looks for the appropriate values for the various coefficients which can provide the best fitting of the calculated values of transport demand to the actual ones.

Model *estimation* contains both the processes of model selection and model calibration.

Model *validation* is the process of demonstrating that the calibrated model is a rational representation of an actual transport system and that it adequately simulates the specific transport problem in order to fulfill modeling objectives, which can be analysis of demand, forecast of demand, quantification of elasticities, etc. The validation process includes various statistical checks concerning the stability and the consistency of a model and examines whether the model's predictive ability is maintained when it is applied to data or observations that were not used during model calibration.

3.8 QUALITATIVE METHODS OF FORECAST OF TRANSPORT DEMAND

Qualitative methods for the forecast of transport demand are based on perceptions, evaluations, and assessments made either by transport specialists or by the users of a transport service. They have a more or less subjective and fluctuating character, as they differ from one person to another and change from one moment to another. Transport science has devised methods to transform such subjective evaluations into objectively acceptable frames of decision-making and understanding the evolution of a specific transport demand problem. However, in order to reduce the degree of subjectivity of qualitative methods, simple statistical techniques have been suggested and are in use.

There are four principal qualitative methods for the assessment, evaluation, and forecast of transport demand:

- *Executive judgment*: it is based on the experience and evaluation of transport specialists who have a deep knowledge of the transport problem under study. This method considers most of the variables of a transport problem and can be executed, particularly with the help of modern electronic communication (e-mail, video chat, forums, etc.), in rather short time periods and with a low cost.
- *Delphi method*: it is based on the global assessment made by a group of transport experts and is used for the assessment of new transport problems (with unknown for the moment effects) or for existing transport problems, for which our data are either nonexisting or inaccurate or of poor quality. Delphi is conducted in successive rounds until a level of consensus is reached among experts. It can be supported by simple statistical techniques and usually it takes a rather long time.
- *Scenario writing*: it is based on the construction of alternative scenarios, which describe one or more plausible future situations and the processes and pathways toward these situations; it should be noted that the departing point is usually the existing situation. Scenario writing can also be supported by simple statistical techniques.
- *Survey methods*: these are based on the views and aspects of transport users who are interviewed over a number of transport issues. Key constituents of a survey are the questionnaire, which includes the points and issues that will be explored; and the sample of the survey, that is, the portion of the whole population which will be surveyed. Survey methods are supported by more sophisticated statistical techniques compared with other qualitative methods.

Qualitative methods for transport demand are extensively analyzed in Chapter 4 of the book.

3.9 QUANTITATIVE METHODS OF FORECAST OF TRANSPORT DEMAND

3.9.1 Causal and Noncausal Methods

Quantitative methods of forecast of transport demand are usually classified into causal and noncausal, depending on whether they establish (or not) and express mathematically a relationship of cause and effect. As usual causal factors for transport demand are considered: time, cost of transport, population, travel times, economic product of the area, performances of competing modes, etc., and as affect the transport demand under study. Causality means that if we know the evolution of the considered as causal factors, then we can explain and forecast, as accurately as possible, the evolution of their effect, which is transport demand for the case under study.

In causal methods, the forecast for the quantity of transport which is likely to occur (dependent variable) can be derived and is a function of a number of independent variables. Thus, our knowledge of some variables (the independent ones) enables us to forecast the value of the dependent variable (demand).

The first step in any causal method is the identification of factors (the independent variables) that might influence the variable which is under forecast (the dependent one, in our case demand). The next step is to look for and establish a causal relationship between the dependent and the independent variables, which is achieved in a trial and error procedure with the help of a number of statistical checks. Once such a causal relationship is established, it can then be used for the forecast of future transport demand. It is important to emphasize that the existence of a mathematical relationship between two variables does not guarantee that there really does exist any cause and effect relationship (see §7.3). Causality is the outcome of a complex analysis which is not assured only by statistical and mathematical checks but should include rational thinking (preferably in a systems approach), the existence of trustworthy data for the independent variables, and a deep understanding of what really happens in the problem under study, what are the real reasons, what is primary and secondary, and very often what is hidden behind the appearances; in conclusion what is the real essence of the problem.

Under this last point of view, not only quantitative methods but also qualitative ones present a certain (though low) degree of causality in their analysis and forecasts. This is a central position of this book: any method, independently of its mathematically complicated or simplistic character, can be used for future forecasts, if we can assure that it provides forecasted values which are close to reality.

3.9.2 The Two Families of Quantitative Methods: Time Series and Econometric

Quantitative methods are categorized in two big families:

- *Time series methods* which rely on a series of historical data of demand and focus on the forms and patterns of evolution of demand. These try to identify what pattern of demand was followed in the past, and it is assumed that this pattern will continue in the future. Their validity is assured with a number of statistical checks. Any time series is composed of one or more of a number of components; trend, seasonal, cyclical, random (see §6.1.3). Future demand is calculated through the extension or extrapolation of patterns of past demand under the assumption that historical demand data represent an experience which is repeated over time and that the existing patterns of demand will continue in the future, which is expected to be like the past.

   The simplest forms of time series methods are trend projection (see §6.2 and §6.3), moving average (see §6.6.1), and exponential smoothing (see §6.6.2). Statistical data of the past are projected into the future under the assumption that all factors affecting demand will continue to be the same in the future and with the same degree of influence. More sophisticated time series methods include the various time series processes, which analyze various patterns of evolution of statistical data of demand and aim at identifying the specific problem of demand under study with the pattern of one time series process. Some popular time series processes for transport demand are the autoregressive (AR), the moving average (MA), the autoregressive moving average (ARMA), the autoregressive integrated moving average (ARIMA), and the seasonal autoregressive integrated moving average (SARIMA) (see §6.7).

   As trend projection and other similar methods (exponential smoothing, moving average, etc.) describe, analyze, and identify general patterns or tendencies over demand, without any regard to other (than time) factors which affect demand, they are classified in the noncausal methods. However, some authors consider time series as a method with a low degree of causality. This is particularly the case of the various time series processes (ARIMA, SARIMA, etc.).

   Any time series method aims at calculating the equation or curve that fits best to the available statistical data. This can be assured by a number of statistical checks which can provide the degree of validity and accuracy of the selected statistical method.

   Time series methods are extensively analyzed in Chapter 6 of the book.
- *Econometric* methods which try to establish the most possible complete causal relationship between evolution of demand over time and factors

affecting it: cost, travel time, income, performances of competing transport modes, etc. Econometric methods were first developed within the branch of economics, and they try to provide a quantified analysis and representation of phenomena of economics or related to economics.

3.9.3 Econometric Methods, Econometrics, and Economic Theory

For many centuries and until some decades ago, economic theories tried to understand and explain the world of economics in a more or less qualitative way. Such an approach did not permit the accurate description of economic phenomena under study and permitted arbitrary conclusions which were not consistent with the theoretical assumptions of a specific economic theory. For instance, the statement that a reduction of prices of tickets of an air company would lead to an increase of passengers does not provide for any kind of measure: how many more passengers for a specific reduction of prices, are other driving forces of demand of a secondary importance, how steady in time will be any correlation of new demand resulting from a low pricing strategy, etc.

A response to the need for quantification of economic phenomena and determination of quantified economic laws is given by econometrics, which borrows knowledge from many scientific areas, such as economic theory, mathematics, statistics, and in some cases even psychology. *Econometrics* is the branch of science that consists in the application, within a set of assumptions, of laws, methods, and techniques of mathematics and statistics so as to provide the most accurate, reliable, and consistent quantification of an economic phenomenon, which will permit to understand it, correlate it with the driving forces which affect it, and forecast its evolution in the future. Special attention should be paid to the fact that econometrics is always placed within the frame of an economic theory and thus is directly affected by the assumptions of the specific theory.

3.9.4 Econometric and Economic Models

Econometric models are the basic tool in econometrics. They are a simplified representation, with the use of mathematics and statistics, of a problem or phenomenon which is either mostly economic or combines economic and technological aspects, as is the case of transport demand. In contrast to an economic model, which is a theoretical construct based on a set of assumptions that tries to describe approximately and qualitatively an economic problem, an econometric model starts also with a set of assumptions, employs equations of mathematics and statistics in order to establish a causal relationship between the driving forces and the problem under study, assesses that some kind of errors interfere in any human effort to interpret a problem of probabilistic nature (as are economic problems but also transport problems), evaluates the impact of such errors (called often disturbances) on the validity and forecasting ability of the model, and finally forecasts specific values for the quantity under study (e.g., transport demand in the future).

Econometric models try to correlate the dependent variable to a number of independent ones with the use of a statistical technique known as regression analysis (see §5.3 and §5.4). They employ most of the statistical checks, used also by time series methods, to calibrate the equation of the econometric model and testify its validity and accuracy (see §5.7—§5.10).

Econometric models are analyzed in Chapter 7 and a specific example of how to calibrate the equation of an econometric model is given in §5.12.

3.9.5 Balance Between Simplicity and Complexity

A big dilemma for any forecaster who uses econometric models of transport demand is to balance between simplicity and complexity. A number of scientists suggest that transport demand, in contrast to its apparent and appearing complexity, is in essence a simple phenomenon which deserves a simple mathematical formulation. Others criticize this approach as oversimplistic, unrealistic, and omitting essential aspects of the complex reality of transport demand. They therefore opt for more complicated and sophisticated econometric models.

An econometric model is not an end in itself but contributes to an effort to rationally represent, in a quantitative form, transport demand. As we explain in the next chapters, we can interpret the evolution of transport demand by constructing econometric models with a few (or even just a single) independent variables affecting the dependent variable (demand). In this book we opt to begin with simple models (with a few number of variables), then build and move progressively to more sophisticated models with more variables, if and only if such a strategy increases the forecasting ability of the model and extends its area of applicability and its time range of forecasts.

3.9.6 Essential Qualities for a Good Causal Forecasting

Forecasters should not forget that the existence of any kind of mathematical relationship between demand and some variables affecting it does not guarantee that there is a real relationship among them. For this reason, previous practical experience on the field, intuition, ingenuity, and a common sense are all essential qualities of good forecasting, in addition to a deep knowledge of mathematical statistics. Traditional statistical methods can be enriched with other tools of correlating cause and effects, such as the computational intelligence (see Chapter 8), consideration that the data may incorporate a degree of inaccuracy and thus have a certain fuzziness (see Chapter 9).

3.9.7 Another Category of Quantitative Method: Gravity Models

Transportation specialists tried to use an analogy of the gravity law of mechanics (known as gravitation law) and interpret it in a transportation context. Indeed, the law of gravitation (known also after the name of the British mathematician, astronomer, and physicist Isaac Newton) calculates the force F_{ij} exerted between two bodies i and j of masses m_i and m_j situated at a distance d_{ij} to be proportional to the product of these two masses and inversely proportional to the square of their distance:

$$F_{ij} = g \cdot \frac{m_i \cdot m_j}{d_{ij}^2} \tag{3.5}$$

where g is the gravitational constant or Newton's constant.

Application of the law of gravitation to transport demand problems is conducted by replacing the body i with an area or zone of population p_i, the body j with an area or zone of population p_j, the mass m_i with the total number of trips O_i originating and generated at the origin zone i, the mass m_j with the total number of trips A_j attracted at the destination zone j, the distance d_{ij} between body i and body j by the distance d_{ij} or the transport cost or the generalized cost between centroids[2] of zone i and zone j, the power-2 term of d_{ij} in the gravity law by a coefficient β, and the gravity force F_{ij} by the number of trips T_{ij} between zone i and zone j. Thus, the gravity law for transportation demand problems can be written as [2,7,193]:

$$T_{ij} = k \cdot \frac{O_i \cdot A_j}{d_{ij}^\beta} \tag{3.6}$$

with k a constant of proportionality, which takes into account factors not included in the various other terms of Eq. (3.6).

Transportation science has (like many sectors of physics, such as thermodynamics) its own law of conservation of origins or destinations or both origins and destinations. More particularly, the case of conservation of origins means that the total number of trips from a specific origin zone i to all destinations must be equal to the total originations from origin zone i, thus:

$$\sum_j T_{ij} = O_i \tag{3.7}$$

---

2. Imaginary points within zones from which all departing trips are assumed to originate and at which all arriving trips are assumed to terminate.

By substituting Eq. (3.6) into Eq. (3.7) we take:

$$\sum_j k \cdot \frac{O_i \cdot A_j}{d_{ij}^{\beta}} = O_i \Rightarrow$$

$$\Rightarrow k \cdot O_i \cdot \sum_j \frac{A_j}{d_{ij}^{\beta}} = O_i \Rightarrow$$

$$\Rightarrow k = \frac{1}{\sum_j \dfrac{A_j}{d_{ij}^{\beta}}} \tag{3.8}$$

Now by substituting Eq. (3.8) into Eq. (3.6) we take:

$$T_{ij} = \frac{1}{\sum_m \dfrac{A_m}{d_{im}^{\beta}}} \cdot \frac{O_i \cdot A_j}{d_{ij}^{\beta}} \tag{3.9}$$

All the quantities of Eq. (3.9) can have some kind of measure on the field and thus provide values for the calculation of the quantity T_{ij}. The gravity model simulated by Eq. (3.9) is among the basic tools for calculation of transportation demand for urban areas in the (known as) four-step process, in which are successively calculated the number of trips generated by and attracted to a zone (first step), the distribution and allocation to origin–destination pairs (second step), the choice of mode of transport (third step), and finally the determination of route or path of trips (fourth step). Gravity models are used in the second step of the above process, whereas time series and econometric models are used in the first step.

The law of gravitation has also inspired (for nearly a century) forecasters in the sector of economics. They considered that the trade between two regions is a function of the population and economic output and production of each region and the distance (or generally an impedance factor) between these regions. The law of gravitation for trade has been further specialized into the calculation of freight flows and demand between two regions, and more generally for modeling the demand of freight transport (see §7.11.7).

3.10 A PANORAMA OF THE VARIOUS QUALITATIVE AND QUANTITATIVE METHODS

Fig. 3.2 illustrates the various qualitative and quantitative methods for the analysis and forecast of transport demand and where in the book each method can be traced.

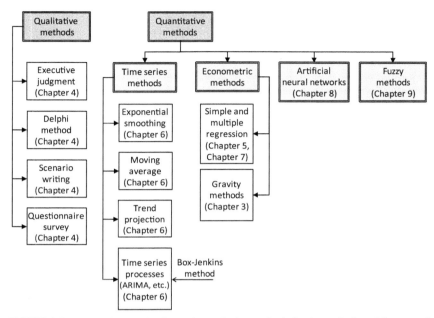

FIGURE 3.2 The various qualitative and quantitative methods for the analysis and forecast of transport demand. *Source: Compiled by the authors.*

3.11 STATISTICAL AND OTHER METHODS USED IN QUANTITATIVE METHODS

Whether causal or noncausal, the quantitative method of forecast aims to correlate the dependent variable (transport demand) to one or more independent variables. Such a correlation can be found with the use of a statistical method known as regression analysis. When a number of statistical data for the independent and dependent variables are available, regression analysis permits (through a number of statistical checks and tests) to construct the equation and find the curve which best fits to the available statistical data and then to use this equation for the forecast of future demand.

If we consider only an independent variable which is linearly related to the dependent one, then we have the case of simple linear regression. If more than one independent variables, which are linearly correlated with the dependent one, are considered, then we have the case of multiple linear regression.

Though linearity between dependent and independent variable(s) is a convenient assumption, in many cases the dependent variable is nonlinearly correlated to the independent one. Such nonlinear correlations can be transformed into linear ones by taking logarithms on both sides of the equation of demand and thus transforming the nonlinear problem to a linear one.

Regression analysis is the most basic tool when trying to construct any kind of quantitative model of transport demand. Simple regression is used in noncausal trend projection methods (with time the only independent variable) and in causal econometric models with only one independent variable (such as GDP, cost, income, etc.). Multiple regression is used in time series models and in econometric models with a number of independent variables.

Both causal and noncausal methods are characterized by the fact of rationality between cause (evolution of time, GDP, cost, etc.) and effect (transport demand). However, in many problems rationality cannot be established, and thus we can look for empirical relationships, which permit us to calculate future demand in relation to a number of data in a totally empirical way. Artificial intelligence, and in particular artificial neural networks (ANN), are suitable methods for an empirical calculation of future transport demand, when we have greatly varied data, great numbers of data, missing data, or we do not know (or we are not interested to know) the mechanism between cause and effect (demand).

Our knowledge derived from statistical data or observations is based on the certainty of the accuracy of arithmetic numbers which represent the various data. Another approach involves nontraditional numbers, but fuzzy numbers. A fuzzy number is a generalization of a regular real number, in the sense that it does not refer to one single value but rather to a connected set of possible values, where each possible value has its own weight from 0 to 1. Fuzzy methods have been used during the last 20 years for transport demand, both for rational (econometric, gravity, time series) and empirical (ANN) relationships between cause (time or/and other variables) and effect (transport demand). In fuzzy methods, traditional numbers and coefficients are replaced by fuzzy numbers. Fuzzy methods are suitable when there are missing data or data with large variations, when there is ambiguity in the measured values of data or observations, when linguistic variables are used, etc.

Fig. 3.3 summarizes the various statistical and other methods and techniques used for the construction of a transport demand model. Regression analysis (simple and multiple) is analyzed in Chapter 5, §5.2, §5.3, §5.4, nonlinear analysis in Chapter 6, §6.2.3, artificial intelligence—neural network methods in Chapter 8, and fuzzy methods in Chapter 9 of the book.

3.12 SELECTION OF THE APPROPRIATE MODEL OF FORECAST OF TRANSPORT DEMAND

As every forecasting method has specific characteristics and can be used for a limited range of applications, the question is how to ensure the selection of the most appropriate model for a particular problem of transport demand. Thus,

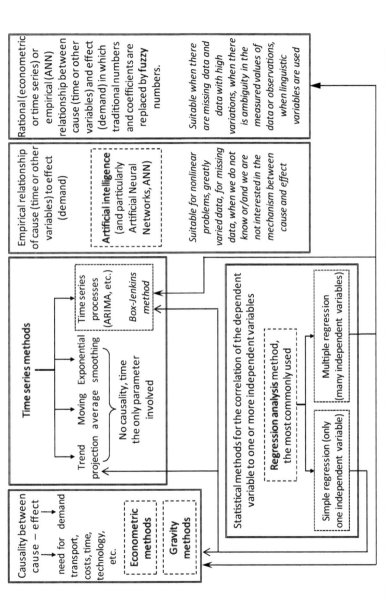

FIGURE 3.3 Application of regression analysis techniques in the various quantitative methods for transport demand. *Source: Compiled by the authors.*

the selection of the appropriate forecasting model must take into account and be based on the consideration of a number of *factors*, such as the following:

- *Time range, nature,* and *scope* of the problem under study. Thus, for a long-range problem of strategic nature, such as the construction of a new airport or a high-speed railway line or the order of a number of new aircrafts or the creation of a new transport company, an econometric model that sufficiently correlates transport demand with the driving forces which influence and generate it will be selected. On the contrary, for a short- and medium-term problem, such as the estimation and formulation of the pricing policy and strategy of any transport company (air, rail, road, sea), the demand forecast can be addressed by projecting past statistical data into the future or by searching for a similar to the problem under study time series process or even with a qualitative method.

  All qualitative methods and trend projection are suitable for short- and medium-term (up to 3—5 years) forecasts, whereas all quantitative methods are suitable for short-, medium-, and long-term forecasts.

- *Availability, relevance,* and *credibility* of statistical data. When such data are not available or are difficult to collect or are of a questionable credibility, quantitative methods cannot be used. Thus, we turn to qualitative or ANN methods, when there are no statistical data, e.g., introduction of a new transport service. Qualitative methods are based on views, opinions, and judgment of individuals, and they can employ empirical rating measures (like the Likert scale), a fact that can permit to transform qualitative information into quantitative forecasts. Among qualitative methods, executive judgment, Delphi method, and scenario writing are based on evaluations made by specialists of the sector under study (e.g., low-cost air transport specialists), whereas market surveys are based on opinions of users (or eventual users) of the sector. Trend projection and all other quantitative methods have high data requirements, something that does not apply in the case of qualitative methods.

- Appropriate identification of *turning points*. A good model should have the same (or similar, in the worst case) turning points as the problem under study.

- *Time* required to conduct a forecast. If there are time constraints in making a decision (e.g., reduced demand due to low tariffs of a new or an existing competitor), then a fast and easy-to-use method shall be selected. Such methods are the executive judgment, Delphi, scenario writing, and trend projection. Other quantitative methods and the market survey have high time requirements.

- *Cost* of the forecast. Low-cost forecasts are scenario writing and trend projection, medium-cost forecasts are executive judgment, Delphi, and ANN methods, whereas all other quantitative methods have high cost requirements.

- *Special expertise* and *skills* required. Trend projection can be conducted by a forecaster with a medium or low expertise, a market survey by a forecaster with a medium expertise, whereas all other qualitative and all quantitative methods require a high expertise.

Table 3.1 and Fig. 3.4 illustrate the suitability of the various qualitative and quantitative methods and the requirements related to expertise, time, data, and cost for each method.

3.13 BIG DATA AND TRANSPORT DEMAND

3.13.1 Definition, Sources, and Characteristics of Big Data

3.13.1.1 Definition of Big Data

All quantitative methods of forecast of future demand (whether for transport or other sectors of the economy) are based on data. In Chapter 2 we presented the various sources of data, among them *big data*, a new and revolutionary set of advanced techniques, which give the possibility to capture, manage, and analyze very large volumes of extremely varied data, generated, captured, and processed at unprecedented rates from various heterogeneous sources [121,123,194].

Never before in human history was it possible to make available so quickly such a large amount of information about people, objects, and events. In our digital era, which will be further enlarged and strengthened in the future, most of our activities are followed and recorded by a number of electronic techniques. While living in the new digital world, everybody knows more about others' activities, but at the same time a significant number of degrees of freedom of any human being is either reduced or lost. People, but also goods and freight, leave a digital trace in their everyday activity. Any electronic transaction can report on the user's location and the accurate moment in time.

Big data are the effect of a sharp decrease of costs related to the collection, storage, and processing of information; they cannot be processed with the use of existing technological tools, as they are so large, varied, and recorded at such speeds that traditional techniques of data management and analysis prove to be greatly insufficient.

3.13.1.2 Sources of Big Data

Sources of big data are very diverse; the most frequently used include the following [194,195]:

- mobile phone records,
- e-mails and sms (short message service),
- Wi-Fi access signals,
- credit card and payment transactions,
- surveillance videos,

TABLE 3.1: Performances, suitability, and requirements of the various qualitative and quantitative methods of transport demand.

		Qualitative methods				Quantitative methods		Causal methods			
		Executive judgment	Market survey	Delphi	Scenario writing	Trend projection, moving average, exponential smoothing	Time series processes (AR, MA, ARIMA, SARIMA, etc.)	Econometric	Gravity	Artificial neural networks	Fuzzy
Suitability for forecasts till	1 year	H	H	H	H	H	H	H	H	H	H
	2–3 years	M	H	M	H	H–M	H	H	H	H	H
	5 years	L	M	M	M	M–L	H	H	H	H	H
	10 years	L	L	L	M	L	M	M	M	M	M
Special expertise required		H	M	H	H	M–L	H	H	H	H	H
Time required to conduct the forecast		L	H	L	M	L	H	H	H	M	H
Data requirements		M	M	M	M	H–M	H	H	H	M	H
Cost requirements		M	H	M	L	L	H	H	H	M	H

AR, autoregressive; ARIMA, autoregressive integrated moving average; H, high; L, low; M, medium; MA, moving average.
Source: Compiled by the authors.

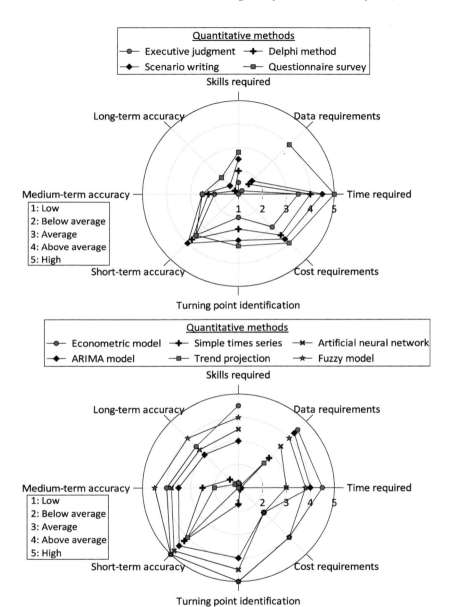

FIGURE 3.4 Comparative analysis of performances, suitability, and requirements of the various qualitative and quantitative methods of transport demand. *Source: Compiled by the authors.*

- vehicle sensor outputs,
- global positioning systems (GPS) or other techniques of georeferencing of people or of any kind of objects,
- global system for mobile (GSM), which permits to stay connected to various networks,
- data produced by devices, vehicles, and networked objects.

Big data are often classified into:

- born *digital*, when they are created by users or a computing device (GPS, GSM, Wi-Fi, e-mails, various forms of cards, etc.) in order to satisfy a specific need of record or communication,
- born *analogue*, when they result from a physical phenomenon, like emissions from magnetic, electric, or any other kind of fields, as well as light, sound, chemical, or biological stamps (video records, electromagnetic or laser reflectance of objects, etc.).

Big data are a valuable source of knowledge to better understand, anticipate, but also manipulate human behavior. They constitute both an opportunity and a challenge but also a danger and a threat. It is worthwhile mentioning that many claims of citizens have been reported for an unintended and unwanted violation of their privacy rights.

3.13.1.3 Characteristics of Big Data

The characteristics of big data are often known under the name of three V's and are the following [121,196−198]:

- *Volumes*, which are extremely large and are generated from numerous devices. The size of the digital universe is almost unthinkable: 4.4 zettabytes in 2013 (1 zettabyte $= 10^{21}$ bytes) and 16.1 zettabytes in 2016. It is estimated to reach 163 zettabytes in 2025 (Fig. 3.5).

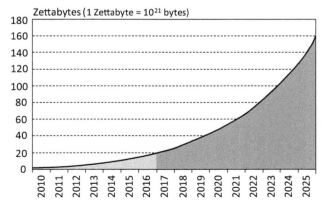

FIGURE 3.5 Evolution until 2016 and estimation for 2025 of the annual size of the digital universe. *Source: Modified from Ref. [199].*

- *Velocity*, as data are recorded and processed very rapidly.
- *Variety*, as they are generated from various sources and distributed to various recipients and can be shared or remain confidential, complete or incomplete, public or private, local or distant, structured or unstructured (e.g., video records).

Some add to the above three V's another two: *veracity* (truthfulness) and *value*.

3.13.2 Technological Aspects of Big Data

Big data combine various models, programs, software, hardware, and technologies. They constitute complicated amalgams and in order to be practical and efficient they should take into account the following: technological compatibility, deployment methods, complexity, costs, efficiency, performances, reliability, support, and security risks. Big data comprise a number of layers, in relation to their intended use: storage layer, processing layer, querying layer, access layer, and management layer. Their format can be structured (data displayed in titled columns and rows which can easily be ordered and processed), unstructured (usually binary data which have no identifiable internal structure), or semistructured.

Some important challenges before selecting or using a big data platform are:

- efficient management, which implies:
  - clean data to ensure reliability, as some data may be nonreliable, incomplete, of poor quality, or may contain errors and noises,
  - encode data for security and privacy,
- ensure a balanced and compatible system capacity,
- provide (in relation to the intended use) the appropriate techniques, which can include data mining, visualization, statistical analysis, etc.,
- as artificial intelligence (see Chapter 8) is an area of increasing applications of big data, a compatibility with the algorithms of the intended artificial intelligence use should be among the prerequisites.

When big data are provided not only by dedicated servers but by a network of connected devices, which have immense capabilities of data sharing and management, they are known under the name of *cloud computing*, which includes storage sites, computing infrastructure, various platforms, and software services. Cloud computing that covers large parts of the world with a global system of sensors, collection, and transmission of data is often referred to as the *Internet of Things* [200].

Big data will support the future knowledge economy to a great extent, by generating added value along the different stages of the data value chain, which are the following:

1. *standardization* of technology requirements, so that all connected parties can draw the maximum benefits from the calculated data,

2. design of clear *vertical applications*, so that any interested party can find the technique and data which are suitable for the problem under study. *Aggregation* of data and *interoperability* among the various generations of data are among the prerequisites to efficiently achieve this stage,
3. *integration* of heterogeneous data, development of a top-down analysis, introduction of the same (or at least similar) *metrics* to compare extremely diversified data.

The explosion of big data generated waves of an unjustified optimism. Big data can be a tool for innovative products, services, and business opportunities but they are not a panacea, as they cannot be used, for the moment at least, to address and solve all kinds of problems that traditional methods could not solve.

3.13.3 Big Data and Privacy Rights

Privacy is a cornerstone in the legislation of most countries all over the world. It means that everybody can determine for himself, when, how, and to what extent information about him or her can be communicated to others and that he or she has the right to control information about himself or herself. Privacy may have many aspects, one of them that interests transport is *geospatial privacy*, that is, the ability of an individual to move in the public space with the expectation that under normal circumstances his or her location will not be systematically and secretly monitored for later use.

Big data may constitute a serious threat for the violation of human rights, as any kind of information can be practically transferred to others, without any previous consent from the interested party. Some believe that the above definition of privacy is no longer aligned with current technological developments. Others argue that privacy rights as they are described in the legislation and were interpreted by the courts in the past cannot continue as they were.

All countries around the globe have undertaken judicial initiatives and strengthened their legislation for the purpose of safeguarding the privacy rights of their citizens and protecting them from cybersecurity threats. Let us focus on initiatives taken in some countries of the world [195].

In the United States, principles of personal data protection are as follows [195]:

- consent of a citizen is needed for the use of his or her personal data outside of the public administration space,
- any citizen has the possibility to have access to his or her personal data, check their accuracy or incompleteness,
- data controllers should keep personal data secure and accurate,
- notice should be given to citizens regarding data collection and their intended uses.

The framework of protection of personal data and privacy in the European Union can be summarized as follows [195]:

- clear and explicit consent should be granted by any citizen, so that an authority can collect and use his personal data,
- visibility and access to the transfer of data must be ensured,
- judicial remedies must be legislated for cases of violation of personal rights,
- the right to be forgotten: data pertaining to somebody must be deleted, if there are no legitimate reasons for keeping them anymore.

However, a fundamental difference between the legislation of the United States and the European Union over privacy and private rights can be traced as follows: in the United States data collection and processing is permitted, unless a specific law prohibits it, whereas the legislation of the European Union requires express legal authorization for data processing.

In Japan, explicit consent by an individual is not required if the purposes of use of the data were previously either given directly to the individual or announced publicly. Any consent of an individual is required only for cases beyond the above frame. In South Korea, explicit consent by an individual is needed for collection, use, and transfer of his or her personal data [195].

International institutions, such as the Organization for Economic Cooperation and Development (OECD), the Asia-Pacific Economic Cooperation (APEC), and others have prepared guidelines that should govern the protection of privacy and flows of personal data.

3.13.4 Applications of Big Data to Solve Some Transport Problems

Big data can be used to tackle in real time and efficiently a number of transport problems that traditional methods and techniques have failed to address:

- *Accurate monitoring* of the position of a vehicle. Knowledge in real time where a vehicle is situated can be used to confront efficiently the following transport problems:
  - Improve *road safety* dramatically. If an accident occurs, authorities can be immediately informed about the spot of the event and provide health care services in time. On the other hand, they can inform other drivers in the area of the accident, so that they can take their measures and avoid dangerous points.
  - *Optimize capacity* of all kinds of transport infrastructure and of operation vehicles. Any transport company aims at utilizing its available capacity to the maximum. Thus, if a road has capacity reserves, drivers could be informed and shifted to it, until the level of saturation is approached. If a number of seats on a bus are empty, the potential passengers may be encouraged to use a particular route.

- *Combat traffic congestion.* Drivers may be informed where traffic congestion is occurring or is likely to occur and be advised to use other itineraries,
- *Customer information and satisfaction.* Instead of conducting time and money consuming market surveys, efficient use of big data techniques enables companies to acquire information in real time about the prevailing marketing conditions of their clients. Thus, for each traveler, a transport company can construct his or her profile and priorities, establish a more personalized communication with him, and finally offer him or her the products that best suit his or her expectations and payment possibilities.
- Optimize *logistic chains* for freight transport. Big data give the possibility to freight transport companies to know accurately and in real time (which means where and how much) the location to which a transport need exists, its destination, when and to which cost they can satisfy it.
- *Predictive maintenance* of vehicles and infrastructure. Monitoring devices placed at appropriate points can inform about plausible failures to occur, thus providing the time to repair infrastructure or to inform drivers. Predictive maintenance can greatly contribute to the improvement of road safety and increase the lifecycle of a vehicle or of a spare part.
- *Optimize revenues* through a pricing strategy that is adaptable to circumstances. Transport is a product that cannot be stored; if it is not used, it is lost. In-time information about the degree of occupancy of the offered capacity gives the possibility to commercial managers to adapt their pricing strategy and to offer their clients tariffs that will lead both to clients' satisfaction as well as to the increase of revenues for the company.

3.13.5 Big Data, Social Networks, and Transport Demand

A social network can be defined as a set of persons who are linked via the internet, each member of which can reach another member or exchange information within the specific social network [121,201]. Some examples of online social networks are Facebook, Twitter, Linkedin, etc.

Information collected via social networks may be useful, particularly when traditional methods fail to provide this kind of information. However, such information lacks representativity, as it cannot be calculated to which extent the sample studied within the social network represents the population under study. Approach of transport problems with the use of social networks combines aspects of both qualitative and quantitative methods.

In the coming years, there will be an increasing number of applications of social networks big data to transport problems. Such applications may refer to:

- social networks related to air transport. Customers, actual or to be, exchange opinions and views over one or more air transport routes,

- social networks related to rail transport. Passengers, drivers, and crew can exchange information among them to make railways more secure, safe, reliable, customer-oriented, and attractive,
- social networks related to road safety. Members of the network may inform other drivers or security and police departments about locations that need more attention, about weather conditions, etc.

3.13.6 Some Applications of Big Data for the Forecast of Transport Demand

3.13.6.1 Is the Sample Representative of the Whole Population?

The major issue when using big data for transport demand problems is whether the (rather big) sample is representative of the population under study. As big data are generated from many and various sources, they may give a good image of the problem under study, but in most cases the sample studied does not represent the population under study.

3.13.6.2 Use of Big Data for the Short-Term Forecast of Passenger Demand of an Airport

Big data techniques have been used for the short-term forecast of passenger demand at the airport of Seoul, South Korea [202]. In such a study, the dependent variable D was the number of monthly passengers of the airport and the independent variable Q was the number of queries of potential passengers, related to the specific airport and provided by internet search engines on a monthly basis.

By using certain keywords, researchers recorded the number Q of queries related to the specific airport. Then, they calculated the monthly passenger demand D of the specific airport, expected within the next 8 months, by using the equation [202]:

$$D = a + b \cdot Q \tag{3.10}$$

with a high value for the adjusted coefficient of determination $\overline{R}^2 = 0.886$ (definition of the adjusted coefficient of determination is given in §5.7.4). The suggested forecasting model presented an average forecast error of 5.3%.

3.13.6.3 Use of Big Data for the Short-Term Forecast of Passenger Demand in Short-Shipping Routes

Short-shipping routes are characterized by a number of small islands in short distances among them and a varying number of passengers embarking and debarking at each island. For such a problem, conventional data (from port authorities) were complemented with a set of big data (around 44 million records) from mobile phones that were provided (in full respect of privacy regulations) from one of the three mobile communication providers. Data of mobile phones were derived from the georeferencing of the mobile phone devices of traveling passengers that were recorded by the mobile phone antennas: each time a traveler made a call, the closest antenna that routes the call was recorded, thus pinpointing the traveling passenger's approximate location. By using data fusion and table pivoting techniques, a representative matrix which contained only 3% of the initial records was constructed.

By using both conventional and big data, the researchers calibrated a gravity model (see §3.9.7) of the form [122]:

$$D_{ij} = 0.0035 \cdot \frac{P_i^{0.5} \cdot A_j^{0.8}}{T_{ij}^{0.4}} \tag{3.11}$$

where

D_{ij} number of passengers from zone i to zone j,
P_i population of zone i,
A_j number of arriving passengers in ports of zone j,
T_{ij} travel time from zone i to zone j.

However, as the researchers of the above method acknowledged, samples were not statistically representative of the whole population. Thus, the method cannot lead to accurate calculations of demand, since:

- not all mobile phone companies provided data,
- passengers who did not use mobile phones were not recorded,
- the number of foreign passengers with mobile phones registered in their country may be underestimated.

3.13.6.4 Use of Big Data for the Short-Term Forecast of Demand for Taxis of an Airport

An application of big data was conducted for the investigation of important factors that can maintain equilibrium of demand and supply of taxi services at the airport of New York [203]. The sample included all taxi trips, around 12.8 million, in April 2008. The survey focused on whether taxi drivers, when approaching the airport area, will drive toward the airport and will wait to pick up a customer or will avoid the airport and continue cruising for a customer. The model assesses the impact of the following variables: time of the day, day of the week, weather conditions, average waiting times at the airport, expected net gain of taxi drivers, etc.

3.13.7 Differences and Similarities Between Big Data and Traditional Methods for Transport Problems

Any transport specialist, before trying to use big data, must be aware of the differences of this method in comparison to traditional methods; these differences can be summarized as follows [204]:

- *Sources of data*. Traditional sources of data (see §2.1.3) are limited, whereas sources of big data are very large and spread out.
- *Statistical representativity*. In traditional methods, only a small part (the sample) of the population is surveyed, but generally (specifically for quantitative methods) it must be representative of the population under study within an accepted margin of error (see §4.4.4). Big data usually cover a much larger part of the population but lack representativity.
- *Experimental design*. A traditional method usually departs from an experimental design, which assures its statistical validity. On the contrary, big data are usually collected for other purposes than the transport question addressed.
- *Storage and structure of data*. Traditional methods usually have a single location of data, which in most cases are structured. On the contrary, big data are stored in multiple locations and may be structured or unstructured.
- *Methods of analysis*. Traditional methods are based on statistics and usually have a limited number of variables. On the contrary, big data can feed either statistical methods or pattern recognition and machine learning methods, such as the ANN method (analyzed in detail in Chapter 8). In addition, methods based on big data can have a large number of variables.

Chapter 4

Executive Judgment, Delphi, Scenario Writing, and Survey Methods

Chapter Outline

4.1 THE EXECUTIVE JUDGMENT METHOD

4.1.1 Definition

The executive judgment method is a forecasting technique for transport demand and is based on an evaluation and assessment made by specialists or managers (sometimes even top managers) of a transport company in the commercial sector, who have a broad, in-depth, and systematic understanding of the problem in question. Judgment can be defined as an individual's understanding of relationships among objects or among individuals.

4.1.2 Assumptions and Characteristics

This method considers most of the factors of the internal and external environment (see §1.8) which may have a major or minor effect on a specific problem related to transport demand. The rationale of the method is based on cause-and-effect relationships previously identified through the executives' experience in the field. The executives' understanding of the key causal relationships between transport demand and the factors affecting it is an essential prerequisite of the method. In addition to the evaluation of the existing situation, the method allows one to take into account innovations (e.g., the electric car), novelties (e.g., the use of Internet in ticket procurement), and diversification (e.g., the increasingly many alternative options for a trip) within the transport sector. The utility and efficiency of the method is related to the length and breadth of the executives' experiences, as well as the quality of the causal analysis derived from their previously accumulated experiences.

Modeling of Transport Demand. https://doi.org/10.1016/B978-0-12-811513-8.00004-2
Copyright © 2019 Elsevier Inc. All rights reserved.

125

The broader the experience of the executives, the more likely their accurate perception of the evolution of transport demand [2,7].

4.1.3 The Scientific Background of the Method

Although the method is based on empirical evidence, its scientific and epistemological foundation can be traced to contingent judgment theories, which suggest how the relationship between two variables (e.g., portion of an individual's net income which is available for use on transport activities and cost of transport) could affect a problem of transport demand by taking into account the many constraints imposed by the various factors of the internal and external environment. In general, executives conduct complicated operational research with the help of both rational and intuitive thinking. Contingent theories make possible the study of a phenomenon that is subject to change and thus dependent on factors which are conditional or uncertain [205].

The executive judgment method allows for the formulation of the assumptions of a transport demand problem in relation to changing conditions, as well as the simultaneous consideration of the vast majority of the variables related to the problem. To reduce and control the empirical and subjective nature of the method, executives are encouraged to support their assessment with some form of quantification. The method is highly adaptable to changing conditions.

4.1.4 Applications

The method requires a rather short time (some days or weeks) and can have a low cost, as it can be conducted through a teleconferencing. It is advisable to select executives with a high level of expertise and knowledge of the problem and to provide them with a sufficient amount of trustworthy data. Among the organizations that make use of the executive judgment method for the forecast of transport demand is the International Air Transport Association.

4.2 THE DELPHI METHOD

4.2.1 Definition and Fundamentals

The Delphi method is the evolution of the executive judgment method. It takes its name from the famous oracle from antiquity, situated in Delphi (central Greece, 120 km northwest of Athens), where the priestess Pythia of Apollo provided answers to individuals' queries and forecasts of their future endeavors. However, these answers were usually given in an ambiguous form and often only provided after a rather long time, during which information was collected from a network of intelligence and espionage operatives that the oracle had organized along the most influential cities of the time around the Mediterranean.

Delphi can be defined as a method of structuring a group communication process to allow a group of experts to deal *as a whole* with a complex problem and suggest eventual future evolutions [206,207]. The method is organized in successive rounds, during which the experts are surveyed with the use of a questionnaire. The goal is to reach consensus among the experts and thus assure the reliability and validity of the Delphi method [208].

Delphi is a flexible research technique which can explore new concepts based on the judgments of experts and thus expand the existing horizons of knowledge. Delphi grants the possibility to transform the subjective judgment of experts into objective conclusions on a collective basis by exploiting human intelligence. It follows the Hegelian dialectic of the thesis, antithesis, and synthesis, with the synthesis being the consensus aimed at among the experts. Although the departing point of the method is the experts' subjective opinions rather than objective facts, it seeks to combine and refine these opinions so as to express a more or less objective judgment.

Delphi is in principle a qualitative method of forecasting. However, quantitative criteria have been suggested to test and ensure the validity and reliability of the method (see §4.2.8).

4.2.2 Cases of Use

The Delphi method is used when there is *incomplete* or *nonexistent* knowledge about a problem or a phenomenon. It is an *iterative process*, which is used to collect, analyze, and synthesize the anonymous judgments of a group of experts. This is accomplished by synthesizing the views expressed by the experts in successive steps, based on the feedback received.

Some indicative cases for which Delphi can be used are the following [207,208]:

- the data necessary for identifying the problem are unavailable or of poor quality,
- analytical techniques cannot be used; instead, Delphi exploits benefits from the subjective judgment of experts on a collective basis,
- the problem is so complex that it is difficult to divide it into specific components,
- diverse backgrounds, specialties, and experiences are needed to analyze a problem,
- strong disagreements exist among experts with knowledge of the problem,
- it is possible via structural communication among experts to create a form of collective human intelligence.

4.2.3 Objectives

The principal objective of the method is to forecast the plausible evolution of a complex phenomenon by exploiting the specialized knowledge and intuition of a group of experts, through developing a technique which facilitates the attainment of the most reliable consensus among experts [209].

4.2.4 Procedure and Successive Stages

The group of experts is not necessarily a statistical sample that attempts to be representative of any population. What is required is simply that the experts possess a deep knowledge and experience of the issues examined.

When employing the Delphi method, the procedure usually includes the following stages:

1. Definition of the problem, description of the topic under investigation, and unavailability or unsuitability of other methods.
2. Design of analysis, organization of the process, estimation of costs.
3. Choice of experts. Essential *qualities* of an expert should be the following:
   a. knowledge of and experience related to the problem,
   b. capacity and willingness to participate,
   c. sufficient time and availability to participate,
   d. effective communication skills.
   Experts should be considered as consultants for tackling a particular problem, and it is desirable that some form of compensation should be offered to them for their time and effort. Experts are divided into panels, which represent different stakeholder groups such as practitioners, academics, and government officials [210]. A typical panel usually includes 10–20 experts [211].
4. Design of the *questionnaire* of the survey. In its initial form, the questionnaire is rather simple. It states the problem in broad terms and invites answers and comments from the experts. According to replies of experts, the constructed questionnaire is designed.
5. First round of the questionnaire is completed by the experts.
6. Evaluation of the first round, and the return of a new questionnaire to experts, with more specific questions. Each expert is informed about the responses of the other experts.
7. The procedure continues with successive rounds until a *consensus* is reached. Usually two to three *rounds* are necessary, but the process may take up to five to six rounds before consensus is achieved. The level of consensus can be measured either by the percentage of experts agreeing on a point of view or by Kendall's coefficient of concordance (see §4.2.8.2).
8. Based on the consensus reached by the experts, evaluate, conclude, and answer the problem posed.

4.2.5 Characteristics and Features

The Delphi method presents the following characteristics and features [212–214]:

- *anonymity* of experts, which assures free expression of opinions provided by the experts. This method helps to avoid social pressure from dominant or dogmatic individuals or even from the majority or minorities,
- *iteration*—At any point, experts can change their opinions or judgments without fear of being exposed to public criticism,
- *controlled feedback*—Experts are informed about views of other experts who participate in the study,
- some form of *statistical aggregation* permits a quantitative analysis. Thus, though qualitative, the Delphi method can provide quantitative results.

4.2.6 Areas and Sectors of Application

The Delphi method was used for the first time during the 1950s in the United States for the estimation of how many atomic bombs the Soviet Union would deploy in the event of an atomic war. Although estimates in the first round were spread in the wide range of 150–5000, a final consensus was reached in the range of 167–360.

Since then, Delphi has been used and applied in almost every area of human activity: business, education, health care, real estate, engineering, transport, environment, social sciences, and so on.

4.2.7 Criticism and Reasons of Failure

The principal criticism of Delphi is that it constitutes a judgmental technique based on subjective views of individuals and thus it lacks internal validity. However, quantitative criteria have been suggested (see §4.2.8) as a way to check the validity of the method.

The method merits many successful forecasts but has also experienced a number of failures, due to the following principal reasons [207]:

- overspecifying the topic and structure, thus not allowing exploration of other alternatives,
- poor techniques of summarizing and presenting the views of the experts, thus failing to reach a common interpretation and evaluation,
- ignoring and not exploring disagreements; thus dissenting experts may be discouraged from continuing and are led to dropout; inevitably, the consensus generated is artificial,
- misunderstandings may arise from differences in language, logic, or cultural background,
- not all participants express the same degree of honesty.

4.2.8 Quantification and Criteria to Check the Validity of the Delphi Method

4.2.8.1 Degree of Consensus

Although Delphi is a qualitative method, efforts have been made to process its results within a quantifiable and rational frame. In most cases, the responses of the experts can be recorded on a 5-point Likert scale (see §4.4.6.4), in which 1 designates high negative evolution, 5 designates high positive evolution, and 2, 3, and 4 designate intermediate situations. Respondents with answers deviating by more than 2 points on the 5-point Likert scale from the consensus answers are asked to justify, explain, and eventually modify their statements [215]. It has been suggested to consider that a strong consensus is reached when more than 65% of experts agree on a specific issue, whereas no consensus is reached when less than 40% of experts agree. For percentages of agreement between 40% and 65%, the level of consensus is considered moderate (Table 4.1). In some cases, instead of the 5-point Likert scale, a 7-point Likert scale has been used. The quantitative analysis can be strongly facilitated with the use of appropriate software, such as IBM SPSS Statistics (SPSS: Statistical Package for the Social Sciences), R, PSPP (it does not have any official acronymic expansion), Stata (a syllabic abbreviation of the words statistics and data), and others.

4.2.8.2 Kendall's Coefficient of Concordance

A more detailed and analytical criterion to check the validity of a Delphi survey is Kendall's coefficient of concordance, which testifies whether experts are applying essentially the same standards in ranking the objectives under study.

Kendall has suggested a coefficient of concordance W, which measures the level of agreement among several (m) experts who are assessing a given set of k objects (or parameters) in a Delphi survey [214,216−219]:

$$W = \frac{12S^2 - 3m^2k(k+1)^2}{m^2(k^3 - k) - mT} \tag{4.1}$$

The quantities S and T are explained below.

TABLE 4.1: Degree of consensus among experts of a Delphi survey in relation to the percentage of agreement on a specific issue.

Percentage (%)	Level of consensus
>65	strong consensus
50−65	consensus
40−50	weak consensus
<40	no consensus

Source: Compiled by the authors, based on Ref. [215].

For a set of r_{ij} ranks assigned to objects (or parameters) i (i = 1, 2,..., k) by the expert j (j = 1, 2,..., m), first the sum S^2 is calculated:

$$S^2 = \sum_{i=1}^{k} R_i^2, \quad R_i = \sum_{j=1}^{m} r_{ij} \tag{4.2}$$

T is a correction factor for tied ranks (see §4.2.8.3). For each expert j, we define:

$$T = \sum_{j=1}^{m} T_j, \quad T_j = \sum_{i=1}^{g_j} (t_i^3 - t_i) \tag{4.3}$$

where

t_i the number of tied ranks in the i-th group. A group can be defined as a set of values with a constant (tied) rank,

g_j the number of groups of ties in the set of ranks (from 1 to k) for the expert j.

Thus, the coefficient T_j is the correction factor for the set of ranks R_i of the expert j.

The value W = 1 reflects unanimity of experts, whereas the value W = 0 testifies total disagreement. Values of W > 0.7 are considered indicative of a strong consensus, and values of W < 0.3 are indicative of weak consensus. The level of agreement is considered good for values 0.5 < W < 0.7 and moderate for values 0.3 < W < 0.5 (Table 4.2).

TABLE 4.2: Degree of consensus among experts of a Delphi survey in relation to the values of Kendall's coefficient of concordance W.

Values of Kendall's coefficient of concordance W	Level of consensus
W = 1	unanimity
W > 0.7	strong consensus
0.5 < W < 0.7	consensus
0.3 < W < 0.5	moderate consensus
W < 0.3	weak consensus
W = 0	disagreement

Source: Compiled by the authors, based on Ref. [214].

TABLE 4.3: Example of ranking of eight parameters by seven experts in a Delphi survey.

		Parameters i (i = 1 to k, k = 8)							
		i_1	i_2	i_3	i_4	i_5	i_6	i_7	i_8
	j_1	1	2	3	4	5	6	7	8
	j_2	3	4	1	2	5.5	5.5	7	8
	j_3	2	1	3.5	5	3.5	7.5	7.5	6
Experts j (j = 1 to m, m = 7)	j_4	1	2.5	2.5	5	4	8	7	6
	j_5	4	3	2	1	8	5	6	7
	j_6	1.5	2.5	1.5	2.5	6	5	8	7
	j_7	3	2	1	5	5	8	7	5
Summation		15.5	17	14.5	24.5	37	45	49.5	47

Source: Compiled by the authors.

4.2.8.3 Example of Application of Kendall's Coefficient of Concordance

We will illustrate the calculation of tied ranks and Kendall's coefficient with the following example. Take the case of a Delphi survey among seven experts (m = 7) who rank eight parameters (k = 8) from 1 to 8. If, for instance, one expert ranks two parameters in the third position (that is in the third and the fourth position with the same note), then he or she will allocate for both the note 3.5 (=(3 + 4)/2). However, if he or she had ranked them in the third and the fourth position, then he or she would have given them the notes 3 and 4. Table 4.3 gives the ranking of experts.

From Table 4.3, we can deduce that for the experts 1 and 5 there are no tied ranks, therefore $T_1 = 0$ and $T_5 = 0$. For expert 2, there is one group of tied ranks, specifically for parameters 5 and 6, therefore $T_2 = 2^3 - 2 = 6$. Similarly, we calculate that $T_4 = 6$. For expert 3, there are two groups of tied ranks, specifically for parameters 3 and 5 and for parameters 6 and 7, therefore $T_3 = 6 + 6 = 12$. Similarly, we calculate that $T_7 = 12$. For expert 6, there is one group with three ties (parameters 4, 5, and 8), therefore $T_6 = 3^3 - 3 = 24$. Hence, we can calculate:

$$S^2 = \sum_{i=1}^{k} R_i^2 = 15.5^2 + 17^2 + 14.5^2 + 24.5^2 + 37^2 +$$
$$+ 45^2 + 49.5^2 + 47^2 = 9,393$$

$$T = \sum_{j=1}^{7} T_j = T_1 + T_2 + T_3 + T_4 + T_5 + T_6 + T_7 =$$

$$= 0 + 6 + 12 + 6 + 0 + 24 + 12 = 60$$

and

$$W = \frac{12S^2 - 3m^2k(k+1)^2}{m^2(k^3-k) - mT} = \frac{12 \cdot 9,393 - 3 \cdot 7^2 \cdot 8(8+1)^2}{7^2(8^3 - 8) - 7 \cdot 60} = 0.72$$

The value $W = 0.72$ indicates a strong consensus among the experts in this specific example of a Delphi survey.

4.2.9 Use of the Delphi Method to Predict Trends in Transport Sectors

Table 4.4 summarizes a number of sectors of transport for which the Delphi method has been used to assess the plausible trends of a specific problem and the principal characteristics of these studies, such as [211]:

- sectors of transport: All sectors of transport have used the Delphi method for their forecasting needs,
- topic of the study: Topics vary from rather general to very specific,
- number of experts who participated in the study: Most of the studies used the views of a great number of experts (>50), while only a few number of studies were based on a very limited (<10) number of experts,
- number of rounds to reach consensus: Most of the studies used two rounds, before reaching consensus among the experts,
- whether a consensus analysis is conducted or not: Most of the Delphi applications for transport problems included a consensus analysis.

4.2.10 Use of the Delphi Method to Assess the Degree of Competition in Transport

Many countries around the world have introduced measures and policies of deregulation and liberalization to promote competition and have encouraged new operators to enter the market. However, it is never easy to assess ex ante the degree of competition that will be achieved and the number of new entrants in the market. To evaluate and forecast such evolutions in the rail freight market in Finland, a survey that made use of the Delphi method was conducted among 50 experts who represented all parties interested in the matter. More specifically, the survey included the ministry of transportation, the state operator of rail freight transport, the rail infrastructure authority, the safety authority, labor organizations, national antitrust regulators, logistics specialists, and representatives from manufacturing industries [220].

TABLE 4.4: Some transport sectors for which Delphi method has been applied.

Section of transport	Topic of study	Number of experts	Number of rounds	Consensus analysis is conducted
Low-cost carriers' destination selection	Ascertaining on which attributes passengers finalize their preferences [221]	nonavailable	2	yes
Airlines (owned by the state or the private sector)	Determining goals and criteria to evaluate performances related to the goals [222]	21	2	no
Transportation planning	Predicting future developments [223]	46	1	no
Evaluation of hazardous waste transportation firms	Criteria definition and evaluation [224]	15	3	yes
Vehicle emissions control, policy-making criteria	Criteria evaluation [225]	300	3	no
Aviation industry	Anticipating probable and extreme future scenarios [226]	57	3	yes
Transshipment port selection	Criteria verification and categorization [227]	10	2	no
Driver support systems	Predicting future developments [228]	117	3	yes
Transport telematics implementation	Criteria evaluation [229]	66	nonavailable	no
External sources of vehicle propulsion	Predicting future developments [230]	45	3	yes
Road freight transport	Indicators determination and evaluation [231]	100	2	yes
Traffic safety	Criteria definition and their weight evaluation [232]	40	2	yes

TABLE 4.4: Some transport sectors for which Delphi method has been applied.—cont'd

Section of transport	Topic of study	Number of experts	Number of rounds	Consensus analysis is conducted
Efficiency of goods transportation	Criteria evaluation [233]	15	2	yes
Sustainable transport system	Scenarios construction and their evaluation [234]	63	2	yes
Public transport	Determining inputs for multicriteria decision-making [235]	nonavailable	2	yes
International distribution center location	Determining inputs for multicriteria decision-making [236]	3	2	yes
Bus scheduling	Determination and evaluation of indicators [237]	20	2	no

Source: Compiled by the authors, modified from Ref. [211].

Topics for this Delphi survey included the willingness of new operators to enter the market, the length of the initial entry period, and the projected market share of new entrants. To quantitatively assess the answers given by the experts, a 7-point Likert scale was used. An ex post assessment of the results of this Delphi survey revealed that experts were overpositive regarding the number of new entrants with strongly different points of view among them, and they did not reach consensus on the level of competition to be expected. Concerning the market share of new entrants, the accuracy of the method was rather poor [220].

4.2.11 Use of the Delphi Method to Assess Transportation Safety

Transportation safety is a complex issue, with many factors involved [146,147,238,239]. A Delphi survey was conducted to assess bus safety [240]. Experts were asked to answer eleven questions divided into three areas: drivers, traffic conflicts, and vehicles. Several solutions were proposed to the respondents, who were asked to assess the effectiveness of these solutions by using a 5-point Likert scale. For each question surveyed, the ranking of priorities was calculated according to the notations of answers provided by the respondents on the 5-point Likert scale. In addition, for each question, the Kendall's coefficient of concordance W was calculated. For three questions (out of eleven), values of W were greater than 0.5, thus a consensus was reached. For three more questions, values of W were 0.486, 0.463, and 0.366, indicating a moderate consensus. For five questions, values of W were lower than 0.3, and for these questions the answers reached were considered either weak or nonexistent (since W was very close to 0.0) [240].

4.2.12 Use of the Delphi Method to Assess the Interaction Between Transport and Tourism

The interaction between two sectors of economic activity, such as transport and tourism, can be studied with the use of either the Delphi method or a causal econometric method. In the case of such a complex problem, the Delphi approach may be more suitable, as it examines the interaction between many components which otherwise are difficult to quantify in an econometric approach. With such a study, the Delphi method can reveal key factors and plausible evolutions, as well as highlight any areas of uncertainty and contention.

To assess the interaction between transport and tourism, the Delphi method was employed among 45 experts of both sectors in the United Kingdom [215]. Results were quantified according to a 5-point and a 3-point Likert scale. The 3-point Likert scale was more efficient for achieving consensus in some issues among the experts who considered the following criteria:

- type of work (research, practice, policy development and implementation, marketing, planning),
- type of organization (local and regional authorities, private sector suppliers, university and research organizations, passenger transport companies, professional bodies, consultancy),
- geographical coverage (international, national, regional, local).

The Delphi survey was conducted in two rounds and proved successful for most questions, since a satisfactory level of consensus among the experts was reached. The questionnaire of the survey included statements related to the following issues:

- predicted number of tourist trips: international, domestic, and day trips,
- preference of mode of transport to be used by tourists: airplane, private car, train, coach, ferry, waterborne, local bus, motorcycle, cycling, walking, integrated transport (train and bus),
- projected changes to the size, quality, and quantity of transport infrastructure and effects on tourism,
- the effect on the demand for tourism of transport issues such as high fares, fuel prices, congestion, parking facilities, and others,

- the effect on the demand for tourism of environmental issues such as climate change, levels of air and noise pollution, abnormal weather conditions, and high temperatures,
- prediction of changes in policy over environmental constraints (reduction of CO_2 emissions, etc.) and their eventual effects on tourism.

4.3 THE SCENARIO WRITING METHOD

4.3.1 Definition

A scenario is a set of rational facts and plausible events that could lead to a future situation. By departing from the existing situation, a scenario describes one or more plausible or eventually desired situations in the future and describes facts and events that could lead to the desired future situation [234,241].

Strictly speaking, scenarios do not constitute a forecast. Their aim is to span the range of possible future situations which might reasonably be expected to occur [234,241−243]. Scenarios complement the deficiencies and limitations in forecasting ability of other methods, which are based on a set of assumptions that try (not always successfully) to establish relations between causes and effects. Instead, scenarios describe *processes* in time and through a range of intermediate variables. They help us to understand and clarify what effects those changes in the various factors of the internal and external environment of transport will have. They trace pathways and describe conditions to a new situation, by exploring the effects of past, present, and (likely or unlikely) future events.

4.3.2 Constituent Elements of a Scenario

In their usual form, scenarios have three constituent elements [2,7,242]:

1. the starting point is the existing situation, which is called the original situation or baseline analysis,
2. one or more plausible future situations, which are not necessarily probable to occur,
3. one or more future processes, which from the existing situation can lead to the (plausible or desired) future one.

Fig. 4.1 illustrates the constituent elements of a scenario. If one of these elements is missing, we do not have a complete scenario.

4.3.3 Typologies of Scenarios

There are many types of scenarios in relation to their point of departure, their complexity, the level of knowledge on which they are based, etc. [242].

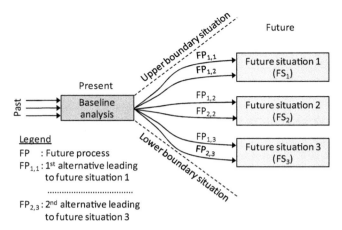

FIGURE 4.1 Constituent elements of the scenario writing method. *Source: Compiled by the authors, modified from Ref. [242].*

In relation to the point of departure and the pathway followed, a scenario may be:

- *projective*: Departing from the past or the present, the future is explored,
- *prospective* (called also *visionary*): Departing from a plausible or desired future situation, rational paths back to the present are explored.

In relation to the knowledge, on which the scenario is based, a scenario may be:

- *normative*: Based on norms (wishes, choices, interests) of users or decision makers. Most analyses show that a lack of involvement on the part of end users from the early stages may be counterproductive. The views of users may be taken into account with the help of a series of structural interviews,
- *descriptive*: Based on available facts. Descriptive scenarios limit degrees of subjectivity as much as possible.

In relation to the predictability of events and the complexity of situations, a scenario may be:

- *dominant*: It follows developments considered highly probable, without essentially deviating from them,
- *limit* or *boundary*: It describes extreme limits of eventual future evolutions, which today may look improbable or unrealistic, and presents ways to counteract such an undesired evolution.

In relation to the scale of the society taken into account, a scenario may be:

- *preferential*: It represents the preferences of large groups within society,
- *aprioristic*: It represents the opinions of elites or other small groups.

4.3.4 Scope of Constructing Scenarios for Transport Demand Problems

There are many reasons and targets that lead to the construction of scenarios for a transport demand problem:

- *scientific justification* of expected demand: Understand the complexity of the problem and the factors that affect it,
- *crisis management*: Prepare strategies to tackle eventual undesired evolutions of transport demand,
- *commercial policy* and *marketing*: Provide key factors and parameters and suggest domains to intervene to achieve desired demand levels,
- *personnel*: Convince employees of the correctness of the path to be followed and identify for each path conditions that may lead to desired future demand levels,
- *clients*: Improve the image of transport services to achieve targeted demand levels.

4.3.5 Scenarios, Quantifying, and Probabilistic Techniques

Scenarios can be supported by a great variety of techniques, ranging from the mathematically sophisticated to the purely intuitive. Statistical and mathematical tools may be used to provide a rational methodological structure as well as to suggest a probability for the realization of a specific scenario. A probabilistic analysis may refer to [241]:

- the probability of each event to occur,
- the probability of each event occurring if each other event does or does not occur,
- removing inconsistencies among previous probabilistic estimates,
- computing compound probability estimates for all possible scenarios,
- computing probability elasticities.

4.3.6 Scenario Writing and Other Qualitative and Quantitative Methods

Scenario writing may be used on its own or support other methods or being supported by other methods, such as:

- executive judgment or expert consultations (see §4.1),
- brainstorming to generate ideas and support creativity,
- Delphi survey (see §4.2),
- trend projection (see §6.2 and §6.3),
- process management: the successive steps to be followed.

4.3.7 Timescale of Scenarios

The time horizon of scenarios may be:

- short-term: up to 3 years ahead,
- medium-term: the following 7 years after the short-term period,
- long-term: the following 10 years after the medium-term period.

4.3.8 Application of Scenario Writing to a Transport Demand Problem

4.3.8.1 Scope of the Study

Among the many applications of the scenario writing method, we will refer to a study conducted on behalf of the European Commission, aiming to assess the influence of nontransport-related factors on mobility and transport [244]. The scenarios in this study had a very long time horizon (going up to 20 years) and combined a variety of methods: executive judgment, brainstorming, a Delphi survey (among 455 experts in two rounds for 9 months), and trend projection of key factors.

4.3.8.2 Identification of the Key Factors of the Problem

The following were identified as the key factors and principal drivers affecting mobility and transport: population and demographic characteristics, the economy, trade, technology, the environment, lifestyle and social attitudes, the form and organization of society, legislation, and state and international policies.

4.3.8.3 Scenarios Suggested

Three types of scenarios were suggested:

- projective: Based on a systematic analysis of current trends, a number of future evolutions (two to four alternatives) are described,
- prospective: By contemplating a desired future, strategies and actions to reach this future are described to explore the path from the future to today,
- limit or boundary scenario: Make explicit eventual negative consequences of present actions and elaborate ways to counteract them.

4.3.8.4 Comparative Analysis of Scenarios Suggested

Table 4.5 illustrates a comparative analysis of characteristics of the suggested scenarios for the long-term prospects of mobility and transport in the EU-15 countries (Austria, Belgium, Denmark, Finland, France, Germany, Greece, Ireland, Italy, Luxembourg, the Netherlands, Portugal, Spain, Sweden, and the United Kingdom).

TABLE 4.5: Comparative characteristics of scenarios for the long-term prospects of mobility and transport in Europe.

	Projective (most likely scenario)	Perspective (most desirable scenario)	Limit—boundary (most feared scenario)
Population—demographic	aging of population will continue	age balance will be achieved	aging will continue and aggravate
Economy	stabilization at low rates of growth	increased and sustainable rates of growth	recession
Environment	weak sustainability	strong sustainability	environmental degradation
Technology	low levels of innovation	high levels of innovation	technological breakdown
Lifestyle, social attitudes	individualism prevails	pluralism and tolerance	individualism and friction increase
Society	inequalities continue	inequalities decrease, a real welfare state	inequalities increase, risk of social unrest
Legislation	moderate liberalization	balance of liberalization and regulation	increased liberalization and least regulation
State and international policies	balance of freedom and social policies, international cooperation continues	freedom and welfare increase substantially at national and international level	a polarized world, tensions increase, inequalities are strengthened
Transport	increased demand, weak (or none) internalization of external costs, congestion and environmental problems persist	an ecological and sustainable transport	further aggravating of today's transport problems

Source: Modified from Ref. [244].

4.3.8.5 Evolution of Demand According to the Suggested Scenarios

The evolution of demand in the various sectors of transport was speculated on after the compilation of the answers of the experts (in total 455) who

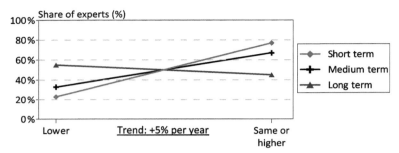

FIGURE 4.2 Anticipated development of the market share of air transport in the passenger market according to the most likely (projective) scenario to occur in the EU-15. *Source: Modified from Ref. [244].*

participated in the study. Fig. 4.2 illustrates the plausible evolutions in the share of air transport in the passenger transport market in the EU-15, according to the answers of the experts who participated in the study. Most experts agreed that for the short and medium term (in relation to the time of the study) the share of air transport would increase in the passenger transport market. However, respondents disagreed over the prospects of air transport in the long term. Nevertheless, the estimated annual growth rate for air transport between 2004 and 2014 was 5%, far higher from what was finally realized (1.9%) for that period of time in the EU-15.

Fig. 4.3 illustrates the plausible evolutions for freight transport in the EU-15. Experts agreed on a growth rate of 4.7% for the modal share of road freight transport during the years 2004—09, stabilization for the next 10 years, and decrease over the following 15 years.

Fig. 4.4 illustrates plausible evolutions for congestion in cities in the EU-15. The majority of experts considered that congestion will persist and will even be aggravated, a projected evolution which was verified by reality during the period 2004—14.

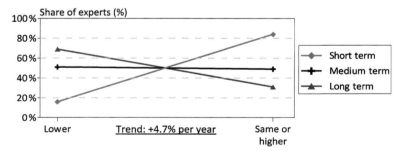

FIGURE 4.3 Anticipated development of the market share of road transport in the freight market according to the most likely (projective) scenario to occur in the EU-15. *Source: Modified from Ref. [244].*

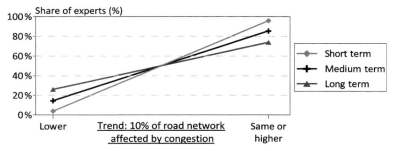

FIGURE 4.4   Anticipated development of congestion in European cities according to the most likely (projective) scenario to occur in the EU-15. *Source: Modified from Ref. [244].*

4.4 SURVEY METHODS

4.4.1 Definition

The target of any science consists in understanding, explaining, and fore-casting the real essence of things and processes as objectively as possible, while avoiding being misled by appearances that often have little to do with the phenomenon under study. Experimentation is the common tool which permits us to repeatedly study a phenomenon and clarify its characteristics. In many cases, however, before experimenting we must provide the most accu-rate description of the phenomenon under study. Whenever and wherever humans are involved, the only efficient way to understand their behavior and experiment on their attitudes is to conduct some kind of a survey. This applies to transport as well. Indeed, transport is nothing but the expression of a specific behavior of a human, who decides to move or ship a good from one point to another.

A *survey* is a description or experimentation of the trends, attitudes, or opinions of a population and this is achieved by studying a very small portion (called a *sample*) of that population. By means of surveys we can collect information on attitudes and behavior and thus describe as accurately as possible what happens or what could happen. Surveys are based on a number of answers provided by the respondents of the sample to the questions that were submitted to them, which are usually ordered in a questionnaire. For this reason, surveys are sometimes called questionnaire surveys.

Surveys based on a questionnaire are classified as qualitative methods, since they are based on subjective and changing views and aspects of respondents. Data are collected in the field, at the site where participants experience the issue or problem under study. Thus, we can uncover the participants' points of view about a problem or issue. Although qualitative in principle, however, many surveys have quantitative and numeric characteris-tics, which facilitate the accurate description and classification of what is observed.

4.4.2 Types of Surveys—Advantages and Disadvantages

There are many technical means which can be employed to conduct a survey, such as *mail, telephone, Internet, personal interview*. Each of the above has strengths and weaknesses, and the selection must be made in relation to the nature of data which will be collected, as well as cost, convenience, and availability of researchers.

In relation to the time horizon, surveys are classified into:

- *cross-sectional*: They record what is happening at one point of time,
- *longitudinal*: They provide a picture of events or attitudes over time.

In relation to the descriptive or explanatory character, a survey can be:

- *descriptive*: It aims at a description of some or most aspects of the problem,
- *explanatory* or *correlative*: It aims to explore relationships between two or more variables of the problem.

A core element of any survey is its validity, that is, *whether meaningful and useful conclusions can be drawn from the survey*. Validity may concern one of the following forms:

- content validity: Do metrics used in the survey measure the content and issues they intended to measure?
- predictive validity: Do scores predict a criterion measure? Do results correlate with other results?
- construct validity: Do results measure hypothetical constructs or concepts?

A survey based on a questionnaire presents both advantages and disadvantages. Among the advantages are validity (under certain conditions), efficiency, and flexibility. What can be considered as a principal disadvantage is that a survey explains how, but not why, people behave in a certain way; in addition, it must fulfill some prerequisites, such as a representative sample (see §4.4.3), a well-structured questionnaire (see §4.4.6), and an efficient interviewer.

4.4.3 The Sample of the Survey

Any survey is founded on the assumption that we can deduce conclusions about a population (which may be hundreds of thousands or millions of people) by studying the behavior of a small portion (called a *sample*) of the population; a sample can range from some hundreds to some thousands of people. The use of a sample permits a reduction in the number of participants, without biasing the conclusions. But this only happens when the sample is representative of the population [2,7,298].

Sampling methods are divided into probability and nonprobability types. In *probability* samples, each member of the population has a known nonzero probability of being selected, whereas in *nonprobability* samples, the members are selected from the population in a nonrandom way.

Probability samples permit higher statistical validity, as they avoid selection bias and permit a trustworthy generalization of the findings of the sample to the totality of the population under investigation. However, as a probability sample is based on chance, there is always the risk of missing some respondents whose opinions may be different or more important in comparison with others.

Nonprobability samples permit the adaptation of the selection process to the targets of the study and allow the researcher to monitor the views of those respondents considered to be more important. However, the nature of this method does not deter the presence of bias and thus inherently limits any effort to generalize findings of the sample to the population under study.

A sample may be restricted to a few number of decision makers (called an elite survey), who may reflect general views of the population, correlate many facts, or uncover reasons that the public often ignores, provided that the decision makers are not isolated from the real world [245].

There are three basic techniques of probability methods for sampling a survey [246–248]:

- *Random* sampling: Every individual in the population has an equal and known chance of being tested in the sample. Random sampling techniques can be further subdivided into *simple random* sampling, in which selection of participants is made purely by chance, and *systematic random* sampling. In the latter technique, the first individual is taken using a random number (say from a telephone directory) and then subsequent participants are selected by using a fixed sampling interval (say after n persons).
- *Stratified* sampling: Specific characteristics of individuals (age, gender, nationality, etc.) are represented at the same percentages in both the sample and the population. Take for instance an airport with an annual demand of 6 million passengers, 23% of whom travel from or to China. A stratification concerning the parameter origin and destination of passengers is assured if in the sample of the survey 23% of respondents are passengers who travel from or to China. *Stratification means that the sample reflects the true proportions of individuals with certain characteristics.* Above all, stratification ensures proportional representation. Within each stratum, the sample should include individuals with a specific characteristic in the same proportion as this characteristic appears in the entire population.
- *Cluster* sampling: The population of the study is divided by the researcher into separate groups, which are called clusters. Each cluster must be representative of the whole population, and each member of the population must be included in only one cluster (the clusters do not overlap). Then, the researcher selects a random sample of clusters to be surveyed. Whereas in stratified sampling each stratum has as a basic characteristic the similarity

of respondents' certain futures within the specific stratum, in cluster sampling all clusters are essentially the same, and any omission of some clusters from the survey does not affect conclusions of the survey. Cluster sampling is suitable for surveys spread over a large geographical area.

In nonprobability sampling methods, respondents are selected by the researcher because they are easily accessible (*convenience* or *opportunistic* sampling) or stratified by the researcher in the sample by deciding certain key characteristics in advance (*quota* sampling). The difference between a stratified and a quota sample entails that the respondents in a quota sample are not randomly selected within the strata [247].

4.4.4 The Relationship Between Sample Explored and the Population Investigated

The key and fundamental issue in any kind of survey is the extent to which the sample we explore represents the population as a whole. As the image of the sample and the truth of the population can hardly coincide, we must know as accurately as possible how close the snapshot of the sample is to the reality and truth of the population.

The sample size n will be calculated with the use of the following formula [249–251]:

$$n \geq N \cdot \left(1 + \frac{N-1}{p \cdot (1-p)} \cdot \left(\frac{d}{z_{\alpha/2}}\right)^2\right)^{-1} \tag{4.4}$$

where

N   size of the *population*, e.g., the annual number of passengers of an airport,

n   *sample* size, that is, the number of individuals required to respond to achieve the desired level of accuracy,

p   a probability parameter estimating the chance that the sample contains a specific characteristic. The parameter p is an estimation of the proportion of people (with a specific characteristic) falling into the group for which we are interested within the population. If no previous experience exists, then a percentage p = 50% is considered as the worst case [249],

d   *margin of error* that we could accept or tolerate, such as say ±5%. The margin of error describes how close the answer of the sample is to the true value of the population. It is evident that the smaller the margin of error is, the closer the findings of the survey are to the reality,

$z_{\alpha/2}$ parameter related on the confidence level (c), calculated from Table 4.6. Confidence level (c) measures how certain we can be that the sample accurately reflects the population, within its margin of error.

TABLE 4.6: Values z of (one-tailed and two-tailed) standard normal distribution.

Confidence level c (the shaded area represents the probability that a standard normal random variable is between −z and +z)	$\alpha = 1 - c$	z_α	$z_{\alpha/2}$
0.50 (50%)	0.50	0	0.674
0.80 (80%)	0.20	0.842	1.282
0.90 (90%)	0.10	1.282	1.645
0.95 (95%)	0.05	1.645	1.960
0.98 (98%)	0.02	2.054	2.326
0.99 (99%)	0.01	2.326	2.576
0.995 (99.5%)	0.005	2.576	2.807
0.998 (99.8%)	0.002	2.878	3.090
0.999 (99.9%)	0.001	3.090	3.291

Source: Compiled by the authors.

Suppose that a survey based on a questionnaire is conducted for passengers of the Eurostar trains, with 10.399 million passengers in 2015. We consider for the required number of questionnaires the worst value for the probability p, p = 0.50. The number of questionnaires to be completed correctly is a relation of the margin of error (d) and the confidence level (c) (see Table 4.6) and will be calculated as follows:

d = 10%	c = 0.80 (80%)	$z_{0.20/2} = 1.282$	→	41 questionnaires
d = 10%	c = 0.90 (90%)	$z_{0.10/2} = 1.645$	→	68 questionnaires
d = 10%	c = 0.95 (95%)	$z_{0.05/2} = 1.960$	→	96 questionnaires
d = 10%	c = 0.99 (99%)	$z_{0.01/2} = 2.576$	→	166 questionnaires
d = 5%	c = 0.80 (80%)	$z_{0.20/2} = 1.282$	→	164 questionnaires
d = 5%	c = 0.90 (90%)	$z_{0.10/2} = 1.645$	→	271 questionnaires
d = 5%	c = 0.95 (95%)	$z_{0.05/2} = 1.960$	→	384 questionnaires
d = 5%	c = 0.99 (99%)	$z_{0.01/2} = 2.576$	→	663 questionnaires
d = 3%	c = 0.80 (80%)	$z_{0.20/2} = 1.282$	→	456 questionnaires
d = 3%	c = 0.90 (90%)	$z_{0.10/2} = 1.645$	→	751 questionnaires
d = 3%	c = 0.95 (95%)	$z_{0.05/2} = 1.960$	→	1067 questionnaires
d = 3%	c = 0.99 (99%)	$z_{0.01/2} = 2.576$	→	1843 questionnaires
d = 1%	c = 0.80 (80%)	$z_{0.20/2} = 1.282$	→	4104 questionnaires
d = 1%	c = 0.90 (90%)	$z_{0.10/2} = 1.645$	→	6759 questionnaires
d = 1%	c = 0.95 (95%)	$z_{0.05/2} = 1.960$	→	9595 questionnaires
d = 1%	c = 0.99 (99%)	$z_{0.01/2} = 2.576$	→	16,561 questionnaires

This example illustrates the strongly nonlinear character of the problem. Even a small improvement in the value of the margin of error (d) or the confidence level (c) of the survey results in a considerably greater number of questionnaires to be completed. In most transport surveys, a confidence level of 95% for a margin of error of 5% is considered satisfactory.

4.4.5 Principles of a Survey

Any survey is based on the voluntary *consent* of respondents to participate in the survey and express freely and responsibly their point of view. To create an environment of confidence within a free conversation, participants must be provided with significant information on:

- the name of the organization and the individual conducting the survey,
- the purpose of the survey,
- the general subject of the survey,
- the length of the survey (in minutes),
- who is likely to have access to the information.

The researcher conducting the survey does not have any right to intrude on the participants' *privacy* and should express *respect* for the values held by the participants. Special *sensitivity* should be attributed to religious, cultural, political, or personal aspects related to the respondents and to their past history, behavior, or attitudes.

The participants of a survey must be given full freedom to express *freely* their views and what they believe or want really to express.

The process for conducting the survey must be appropriate for the participants who will be surveyed. It must take into account whether questionnaires will be self-completed or not, the literacy level of the respondents, the availability of researchers, the expected response rate, the topic, and the population of interest.

The questionnaire of a survey should decode respondents' points of view.

Some negative characteristics to avoid in a survey include lack of honesty, lack of transparency, excessively lengthy questionnaires, very restrictive space for respondents, and insufficient opportunity to express their views [252].

4.4.6 Design of a Questionnaire

4.4.6.1 Rules for the Structuring of a Good Questionnaire

The psychology of human behavior and experiences from surveys conducted in the past have led to the formulation of the following rules when structuring a questionnaire [2,7,21,252−254]:

- the questionnaire must be *appropriate* for the participants being researched,
- the collection process should fit the purpose of the questionnaire,

- questions should be phrased in such a way that the responses are given and interpreted in an *unambiguous* way,
- participants can *express freely* what they think or believe,
- participants *are not led* (through a misleading questionnaire) to a particular point of view,
- personal data collected should be *relevant*,
- *excessive complexity* should be avoided.

4.4.6.2 Order of Questions

It is preferable to order the topics raised in the questionnaire in such a way that general topics appear before particular ones. It is preferable that questions of a personal or sensitive nature (e.g., related to age, social class, economic level) should be placed in the end of the questionnaire, when confidence has been established or in any case once the critical questions have already been answered.

4.4.6.3 Types of Questions

In relation to the degree of freedom given to the respondent, questionnaires can be classified into three types:

- *closed*: The respondent is limited to one of the precoded responses given,
- *open-ended*: The respondent is given the opportunity to provide his or her own response to the question posed,
- *mixed*: Questions are open-ended with partial precoding.

4.4.6.4 Use of Scales

If the aim of the survey is to quantify the attitudes, views, or desires of respondents, then some form of scale should be used for those questions for which the responses will be quantified. It should be kept in mind, however, that a scale is not a precise measure of an attitude but merely a way to assess quantitatively the various attitudes and to classify answers in an approximate order. The usual form of scale is the 5-point (and less frequently the 7-point or 9-point) Likert scale [255].

Thus, if we want to assess whether performances of the check-in staff of an airport are helpful and courteous, we can ask respondents to note their views on a scale from 1 to 5:

Totally dissatisfied	Partially dissatisfied	Neither satisfied nor dissatisfied	Partially satisfied	Totally satisfied
[1]	[2]	[3]	[4]	[5]

Some surveys have used a 10-point scale [256]. If for instance we investigate to what extent the expectations of respondents in relation to a specific transport product or service have been fulfilled, we may give them the possibility to choose among the following:

Much worse ① ② ③ ④ ⑤ ⑥ ⑦ ⑧ ⑨ ⑩ Much better
than expected   than expected

However, a 10-point scale is likely to produce slightly lower mean scores relative to the highest possible attainable score, compared with the score produced from a 5-point or a 7-point scale [257].

The use of scales may take a semantic differential form when the purpose is to rate individual statements.

Thus, if we want to assess the degree of agreement of respondents to a specific statement of the type: "The bicycle lanes improve the cyclist safety," we may use a 5-point or a 7-point scale of answer:

| Strongly disagree [1] | Disagree [2] | Neither agree nor disagree [3] | Agree [4] | Strongly agree [5] |

| Strongly disagree [1] | Disagree [2] | Somewhat disagree [3] | Neither agree nor disagree [4] | Somewhat agree [5] | Agree [6] | Strongly agree [7] |

Semantic differential scales work well when the concepts at either end of the scale are mutually exclusive, as it was the case of the previous example.

An alternative to a strict scale of measurement is the visual analogue scale, in which respondents indicate their choice visually or spatially. For instance, in the question "*I consider traffic congestion as an important factor that would result in taking a bus or metro system*," respondents may be asked to place their answer in the line below:

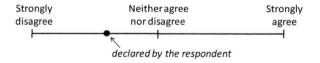

declared by the respondent

As a visual analogue scale is very difficult to interpret, it is not recommended.

4.4.6.5 Pilot Survey

Before embarking in a survey, a pilot survey should be carried out to test the feasibility and appropriateness of the questionnaire. The pilot stage of the survey permits the assessment of whether:

- the time given to the respondents is enough,
- the issues under study are identified,

- the order of questions is correct,
- the precodes used allow the respondents to express their real views,
- the scales used allow for the quantification of the real attitudes of respondents,
- all issues are included in the questionnaire, or some of them are forgotten or omitted,
- personal or sensitive questions make respondents uncomfortable and should eventually be modified.

4.4.6.6 Data Analysis and Choice of Software

Before finalizing the questionnaire, it should be decided how data and findings will be analyzed, and which software packages will be used (such as Excel, SPSS, PSPP, etc.). The findings of the survey should be adequately supported by the data, that is, the answers given by the respondents. When arriving at the stage of results and calculations, we must distinguish between facts, opinions, and interpretations.

4.4.7 Stated Preference and Revealed Preference Surveys

4.4.7.1 Definition

The massive construction of transport infrastructure during the 1960s and 1970s in Western countries, combined with increases in revenues, resulted in an increase in trips and mobility. All these have led to the necessity for a better and more accurate understanding of the various factors and characteristics of transport (affecting the choice of a specific mode), as well as whether users of a transport mode are satisfied by the services offered to them, and what changes to some characteristics of transport services (or even new services) they are willing to welcome or accept. All of the above are crucial for the study and forecasting of the evolution of demand.

Thus, transport specialists started making extensive use of surveys to assess the views, evaluations, and choices of travelers.

Such surveys may include statements of respondents that can be classified into two broad categories [2,7,254]:

- *revealed preference* statements: They refer to changes in transport characteristics and services (existing or new), for which respondents do not have previous experience,
- *stated preference* statements: They refer to characteristics of transport services and choices of travelers that have already been realized.

A questionnaire survey for transport may include questions of revealed or stated preference, or both. As will be explained later, most transport surveys include questions with the character of stated preference, which can be directly translated into predictions of demand and shares of transport [258].

4.4.7.2 Characteristics and Areas of Application of Revealed Preference Surveys

Revealed preference surveys analyze the choices and aspects of individuals in order to compare and assess ex ante effects of changes of transport quality characteristics and policies or evaluate the reactions of individuals in the event of new transport services. Conclusions based on revealed preference surveys assume that an individual's preferences are stable over time. This assumption introduces a factor of inconsistency into the revealed preference method, as individuals can hardly maintain the same value scale over time. Revealed preference surveys are usually restricted to primary service variables (such as travel time and fare) and are rarely used to evaluate the impact of changes in secondary variables (such as seat selection, station facilities, etc.) [2,7].

Revealed preference methods require that the independent (or explanatory) variables can be expressed in objective and measurable units. Revealed preference methods cannot be used in a direct way to evaluate demand under conditions which do not yet exist. In addition, they always have the inherent uncertainty whether people will do what they say, as many individuals are reacting verbally in a positive way to changes or new situations. However, when the time to realize their initial statement arrives, many of these individuals change their initially expressed point of view. And since in revealed preference surveys previous experiences do not exist, it is practically difficult to assess what percentage of expressed statements will be finally realized.

4.4.7.3 Types of Stated Preference Surveys

Stated preference surveys may focus either on choice of a specific transport mode or on evaluation (more or less of quantitative nature) of preferences of individuals. Thus, we can distinguish two types of stated preference surveys:

- *Stated choice* surveys. An individual is asked to choose one of the combinations of attributes of the various alternatives that are presented to him or her. If, for instance, we explore what will be the choice of a traveler between an airplane and a ferry service, we may present to him or her the three alternatives illustrated in Table 4.7 and ask him or her to select one of them. The respondent will select one specific combination of fare, travel time, and frequency.
- *Stated preference ranking* or *ordering* or *scaling* of the various attributes of one or more transport alternatives. An individual is asked to quantify his or her evaluation for a transport mode or for a specific attribute of a transport service, such as travel time, fare, comfort, frequency, etc.

TABLE 4.7: A stated choice survey for the selection among three alternatives of prespecified combination of attributes of air and ferry services.

	Airplane			Ferry		
	Fare	Travel time (min)	Service frequency	Fare	Travel time (min)	Service frequency
Alternative 1	£60	60	hourly	£30	180	bi-hourly
Alternative 2	£70	45	half-hourly	£30	180	hourly
Alternative 3	£70	45	half-hourly	£45	150	bi-hourly

Source: Modified from Ref. [259].

4.4.7.4 Measurement Scales in Surveys

A quantified assessment and evaluation of individuals for a specific transport attribute or alternative transport mode can be attained with the use of the following methods:

- *Ranking* or *ordering* of alternatives. A nonmetric analysis is employed in which the individual is asked to rank or order the various alternatives that are presented in front of him or her. With the use of the random utility theories (see §3.3 and §4.4.7.6), it is possible to transform ranking responses into expected choice frequencies [258]. The usefulness of this method has been questioned, since it was found that the response data from different ranking ranges are unequally reliable [193].
- *Scaling* of preferences. A response metric which uses a 10-point or 100-point scale can permit respondents a rough quantification of attributes of alternative transport choices. The use of scales is an efficient tool for a more objective evaluation of views expressed by respondents of the survey.

4.4.7.5 Successive Steps in a Stated Preference Survey

A successful stated preference survey should include the following successive steps [258]:

- identification of the attributes which must be considered and of the attributes which can be omitted, without affecting the reliability of results,
- selection of the measurement scale and unit for each attribute,
- checking whether the attributes selected are truly independent or are interrelated,
- construction of the questionnaire in relation to decisions of previous steps.

4.4.7.6 The Theoretical Background of Stated and Revealed Preference Surveys

When an individual expresses his or her preferences or choices in a survey, he or she tries to maximize his or her benefits. Thus, utility theories can help us to understand and interpret preferences and choices of individuals [2,182,260]. If i attributes (factors) are evaluated by an individual, with x_i value for each attribute and α_i the utility weight that the individual allocates for this value, the individual's choices will tend to a maximization of the total utility U, which is usually calculated as sum of partial utilities:

$$U = \sum_{i=1}^{n} \alpha_i \cdot x_i \qquad (4.5)$$

Clearly, Eq. (4.5) considers total utility U as a linear additive quality of partial qualities. However, nonlinearities (of quadratic or higher order form) have been tested in some surveys, when interrelationships were observed between the partial utility of two or more variables.

In surveys, which combine both stated and revealed preferences, the calculation of the total utility function will take into account variables that:

- are common to both stated preference and revealed preference questions,
- are specific to either stated preference and revealed preference questions,
- reflect unobserved effects associated either with stated preference or with revealed preference questions,
- take into account parameters which can be introduced as a dummy variable (see §3.1.7).

4.4.8 Questionnaire Design for Surveys for Various Transport Modes

4.4.8.1 The Uniqueness of Any Survey

Any survey based on a questionnaire has specific targets which are related to the problem under study, the prevailing conditions, the conclusions to be reached, and the practical decisions to be taken in the light of the findings of the survey. Questionnaires of similar studies carried out in the past should not be literally replicated but should be studied and modified carefully by comparing the conditions of the situation under study with the situation used as a reference.

Every survey has unique characteristics and is different from all others. In the following we will provide some guidelines for the design of a questionnaire. It is noteworthy that a questionnaire may have primary targets as varied as the assessment of impact on demand from changes made in relation to some attributes of the transport service, the measurement of customer satisfaction, or simply recording passengers' perceptions of the relative importance of the various attributes of the transport service. Thus, the questions may be either of stated or revealed preference, or of both. Respondents may be asked whether they agree or disagree with specific statements, to choose among several different alternatives, or to quantify their views on some form of scale (such as the 5-point or 7-point Likert scale, a 100-point scale, and so on).

4.4.8.2 Questionnaire Design for Surveys in Airports

In the design of a questionnaire for an airport, we may distinguish processing and nonprocessing activities, both for the departure and the arrival domains.

The departure domain includes, successively, the following: access to the airport, facilities before check-in (food and drink, currency exchange and cash machines, postal services, shopping stores, information desks, internet access points, etc.), check-in (when needed, passengers can check in before arriving at the airport), baggage drop, waiting areas, security screening, immigration and customs, retail (food, shops, and entertainment), and boarding.

Similarly, the arrival domain includes successively the following: disembarkation, immigration, baggage claim, customs and (occasionally) quarantine, retail (food, shops, and entertainment), waiting areas, and access from the airport to the final destination.

The various domains of an airport and attributes for each domain are as follows [28,261–264]:

- Processing airport domain
  - Check-in
    - perception by passengers of waiting time and queue length,
    - staff behavior and availability,
    - check-in efficiency,
    - easiness of use of equipment.
  - Immigration and customs
    - staff behavior and availability,
    - perception of waiting time or queue length.
  - Boarding
    - efficiency of boarding procedures,
    - staff behavior and availability,
    - efficiency of technical equipment (moving escalators, lifts, aerobridges, use of bus, etc.).
  - Transit screening
    - staff behavior and availability,
    - perception of level of security,
    - perception of waiting time or queue length.

- Baggage transfer
  - availability and efficiency of equipment,
  - perception of level of security.
- Disembarkation
  - efficiency of equipment (aerobridges, use of bus, etc.),
  - easiness, signaling, and orientation.
- Arrival—immigration
  - staff behavior and availability,
  - perception of waiting time or queue length.
- Baggage claim
  - perception of baggage delivery time,
  - security of baggage delivery procedure.
- Customs and quarantine
  - staff behavior and availability,
  - perception of waiting time or queue length,
  - clarity of information concerning objects to declare.
- Nonprocessing airport domain
  - Accessibility of airport
    - availability of many land transport alternatives (bus, metro, taxi, private car),
    - cost of transport to access the airport,
    - availability and cost of parking facilities,
    - travel time to access the airport.
  - Airport's facilities (departure, arrival, transfer)
    - comfort of waiting areas,
    - sanitary conditions,
    - easiness of connection among terminals,
    - separation of smoking and nonsmoking areas,
    - feeling of security.
  - Shops—entertainment—retail area
    - perception of the variety and quality of shops,
    - cost of products offered,
    - staff behavior and availability,
    - cost of services in bars and restaurants.

Each attribute can be measured by passengers with the use of a 5-point or 7-point Likert scale and thus the questionnaire can help for the planning of changes and of new services as well as of priorities among the various changes.

Airport performance Y can be modeled and expressed in relation to the various attributes previously described by a multiple regression analysis (see §5.4), which, under the assumption of linearity, can take the form:

$$Y = \alpha_0 + \alpha_i \cdot X_i \qquad (4.6)$$

where

α_0 intercept (often labeled as the constant), that is, the expected mean value of Y when all $X_i = 0$,

X_i value for each attribute X_i (previously described),

α_i weight factor of the importance of each attribute in the overall performance of an airport.

In addition to the questions posed to passengers regarding facilities and services of the airport, a questionnaire usually includes questions about the following issues [28]:

- origin and final destination of passengers,
- reason of trip: professional (related to public sector, private sector, liberal profession, studies, congress, military activity), nonprofessional (related to tourism—vacations, family—personal, medical, etc.),
- frequency of using the specific airport,
- whether the trip is organized by the passenger or a travel agency,
- reasons for choosing air transport (travel time, cost, easiness) instead of an alternative transport mode (rail, road, sea),
- how long before traveling the ticket was bought,
- number of people who accompanied the passenger to the airport,
- overall assessment of the image of the specific airport (whether the airport meets expectations of passengers, etc.).

4.4.8.3 Questionnaire Design for Surveys in Airlines

All airlines struggle to attract new passengers. They regularly conduct surveys to understand their customers' expectations, uncover what annoys them, discover what can be offered to them to increase their level of satisfaction, and thereby achieve higher levels of demand. Questionnaires may differ greatly in relation to the type of airline (full service, low cost), the range of flying (long-haul, short-haul), whether the airline participates or not in an alliance, etc. Some issues raised in a questionnaire regarding airline services are the following [28,265,266]:

- purpose of the trip (work—business, tourism—leisure, visiting friends or relatives, education, medical),
- reasons for selecting the specific airline (low price, suitable flight schedule, services in flight, Frequent Flyer Program, positive previous experience, recommended by friends, absence of alternatives, efficient ground services),
- frequency of traveling with the specific airline,
- how long from the flight date the ticket was purchased,
- day of preference for traveling,
- slot (e.g., from 08.00 a.m. to 09.00 a.m.) of preference for traveling,

- cabin class (first, business, economy) and reasons for selecting it,
- willingness to pay more in order to upgrade cabin class,
- flexibility of ticket regarding departure and arrival time,
- one way or round trip,
- assessment of the cost of the ticket (low, moderate, high),
- who paid the ticket (the traveler, his company),
- assessment of airport services related to the airline (waiting times for check-in and baggage, cleanliness, easiness to find counters and gates, clarity of boarding announcements, etc.),
- assessment of access to the airport,
- assessment of ground staff of the airline,
- assessment of in-flight services and staff (friendliness, appearance, professionalism, courtesy, availability of flight attendants, pilot's communication during flight, quality of food and beverages [if any], overall quality of service),
- assessment of aircraft (available space for baggage, comfort of seats, cleanliness, noise level, seating arrangement, watching music or TV),
- offer of products for shopping during the flight,
- assessment of benefits from Frequent Flyer Programs (free tickets, lower prices, other benefits).

4.4.8.4 Questionnaire Design for Surveys of Rail Services

Most surveys for rail services focus on passenger transport. Questionnaire design should be based on the issues under survey for a specific problem, which can be [2,7,268−272]:

- purpose of traveling by train (similar to airlines, see §4.4.8.3),
- type of train (suburban, intercity, high speed),
- degree of satisfaction from the specific railway services (travel time, punctuality and reliability, frequency, cleanliness, behavior of staff in trains),
- ease of preparing the specific railway trip (information about timetables and prices of tickets, provision of tickets),
- time to access the railway station (<15 min, 15−30 min, 30−60 min, >60 min),
- transport mode to access the railway station (private car, bus, taxi, metro, on foot),
- assessment of services in the railway station (booking systems, ticket offices, accessibility to platforms, waiting areas, Internet and TV facilities, quality and costs of food and beverages in restaurants and bars),
- easiness of preparing this railway trip (information about timetables and prices of tickets, purchase of tickets),
- assessment of in-train services,

- assessment of train facilities,
- frequency of traveling by train (daily, several times a week, once a week, several times per month, several times per year, once a year, never),
- reasons that deter passengers from using railway services (long travel times, too many stops, delays, cleanliness, train personnel behavior, station personnel behavior),
- whether the passenger possesses a private car or not.

4.4.8.5 Questionnaire Design for a Sustainable Mobility in Urban Areas

Urban areas are densely populated and usually the existing infrastructure (particularly the road network and parking facilities) are saturated, especially during peak hours. Surveys based on questionnaires are essential tools for planning measures which will establish an equilibrium between transport supply and demand, thus avoiding congestion, reducing transport costs, and minimizing environmental impact.

A questionnaire designed to survey conditions of sustainable urban mobility may include the following questions [2,267,273—279]:

- possession of a private car, number of private cars in the household,
- car sharing or carpooling,
- choice of transport mode (private car, bus, metro, taxi, bicycle, on foot) in relation to the purpose of trip: work-based (trips toward the workplace, trips from the workplace to a business destination) and nonwork-based (trips related to shopping, education, recreational, medical, social, etc.) reasons,
- frequency of using a specific transport mode in relation to the purpose of the trip,
- reason of traveling (work-based, nonwork-based),
- reason for nontraveling (working at home, age, health issues, mobility impairments),
- origin and destination of trip,
- share of each transport mode in the total number of trips and by age group, working status, gender, household income,
- time spent (for traveling, from origin to destination),
- distance traveled,
- number of trips per person and per day (total, per area of residence, by purpose),
- assessment of sufficiency of transport infrastructure (roads, pedestrian zones, bus lanes, bicycle lanes),
- assessment of parking facilities and of cost of their use,
- need for more pedestrian zones,

- perception by the respondent of the level of safety and security of each transport mode,
- noise level and annoyance provoked,
- reaction of the respondent in the case of imposing tolls for the use of road infrastructure (shift to other transport mode, etc.),
- eventual change (and under what conditions) from one transport mode to another.

4.4.8.6 Questionnaire Design for Surveys for Sea Transport

Surveys for sea transport may focus on the products transported, the shipping routes, port services, logistics, and other services. Questions regarding the following could be included in a questionnaire [280–282]:

- origin and destination of products,
- annual cargo volume (total, by product, by area, etc.),
- ship size, service frequency, and transit time,
- volume of import and export,
- rating of port services (e.g., on a 5-point Likert scale) compared with other ports,
- assessment of the port facilities' competitiveness of prices,
- type of container used (dry storage, flat rack, open top, refrigerated, tank, insulated or thermal, etc.) and size (20-ft, 40-ft),
- estimation of container ship costs,
- quality and availability of intermodal equipment,
- assessment and rating of logistics and value-added services,
- shipper's expectations and opinion on what should be done to improve shipping services,
- assessment of costs of land transport (road, rail).

4.4.8.7 A Usual Dilemma: Place Personal Questions at the End or the Beginning of a Questionnaire

All questionnaires include some questions of a more personal character regarding the specific respondent. When designing the questionnaire, one faces the following dilemma [2]:

- to address such questions at the end, once confidence of the respondent has been gained; in any case, the other essential questions have already been answered by him or her,
- to put such questions in the beginning, with the hope to create a climate of familiarity: however, there is always the risk of losing the confidence of the respondent.

Personal questions may include the following:

- gender,
- age group. Usual classifications are:
  - <25 years, 25–45 years, 45–65 years, more than 65 years,
  - <25 years, 25–35 years, 35–50 years, 50–65 years, more than 65 years.
- profession (public servant, private sector employee, freelance professional, university or college student, pupil, military, pensioner, housewife, unemployed),
- nationality,
- approximate annual revenue of the respondent. This is the most personal question, which may annoy the respondent, who could be afraid that this piece of information finds its way to the fiscal authorities or the public. It should be avoided, unless it is considered absolutely necessary for the correct evaluation and assessment of the problem under study. It should also be kept absolutely confidential.

Chapter 5

Statistical Methods for Transport Demand Modeling

Chapter Outline

5.1 AN OVERVIEW OF THE MINIMUM STATISTICAL BACKGROUND FOR TRANSPORT DEMAND MODELING

5.1.1 Definition of the Fundamental Statistical Terms

Statistical methods are the essential tool in all methods (i.e., qualitative and quantitative) of transport demand modeling. At this point, we make an overview of some statistical terms, measures, and probability distributions, so as to help the reader in accessing statistical methods. As the purpose of statistics is to derive conclusions about a phenomenon by studying only a part of data of this phenomenon, to check of the representativity of the available data for the whole phenomenon and to study the characteristics and the forms of evolution of the specific phenomenon, we usually distinguish between the following:

- the population, which is the set of all entities, elements, or individuals under study,

Modeling of Transport Demand. https://doi.org/10.1016/B978-0-12-811513-8.00005-4
Copyright © 2019 Elsevier Inc. All rights reserved.

- the *sample*, which is the subset (portion) of the population that is considered as representative of the population, from which it is selected,
- the *expected value* of a random variable X, denoted as E(X), which is the mean value in the long run for many repeated samples,
- the *estimation*, which is the generalization for the population of numerical values of a variable that are derived from a sample,
- the *estimate*, which is the result of the estimation,
- the *estimand*, which refers to the population from which a sample is drawn and is the quantity being estimated,
- the *estimator*, which refers to a sample and is the rule for calculating an estimate of a given quantity (the estimand) based on observed data,
- the *statistic*, which is the calculated numerical value that characterizes some aspects or attributes of a sample. The statistic is used as an estimate of a corresponding *parameter* of the problem and is the numerical characteristic of the population from which the sample has come about. A statistic may be *biased*, when it is calculated in such a way that it is systematically different from the population parameter being estimated. The bias of an estimator is the difference between the estimator's expected value and the true value of the parameter being estimated.

5.1.2 Definition of the Most Frequently Used Statistical Measures

Let us consider a phenomenon that can be described by one independent variable X and one dependent variable Y. The phenomenon can be described by a number n of observations (set of data) x_1, x_2, ..., x_n for the independent variable X and the corresponding observations y_1, y_2, ..., y_n for the dependent one Y. We present some definitions of the most frequently used statistical measures:

- *Mean* value (or arithmetic mean or mathematical expectation or average), which refers to the central value of a discrete data set and is the sum of the values of the data set divided by the number of items in the data set:

$$\bar{x} = \frac{1}{n} \cdot \sum_{i=1}^{n} x_i, \quad \bar{y} = \frac{1}{n} \cdot \sum_{i=1}^{n} y_i \tag{5.1}$$

- *Variance* of X (or Y), which is a measure of the spread of the values of a data set, in other words it measures how far each number in the set is from the mean value. Variance is denoted as σ^2 (when it refers to the population) or s^2 (when it refers to the sample) or in general as var and is calculated as follows:
  - for the population:

$$\sigma_X^2 = \frac{1}{n} \cdot \sum_{i=1}^{n} (x_i - \bar{x})^2, \quad \sigma_Y^2 = \frac{1}{n} \cdot \sum_{i=1}^{n} (y_i - \bar{y})^2 \tag{5.2}$$

- for the sample:

$$s_X^2 = \frac{1}{n-1} \cdot \sum_{i=1}^{n} (x_i - \bar{x})^2, \quad s_Y^2 = \frac{1}{n-1} \cdot \sum_{i=1}^{n} (y_i - \bar{y})^2 \qquad (5.3)$$

- *Standard deviation* of X (or Y), which is a measure that is used to quantify the amount of variation of the values of a data set. A low standard deviation indicates that the data points tend to be close to the mean of the data set, while a high standard deviation indicates that the data points are spread out over a wider range of values. The standard deviation of a variable is equal to the squared root of its variance and is denoted as σ (when it refers to the population) or s (when it refers to the sample).
- *Covariance* between X and Y, which is a measure of the joint variability of these two random variables (X and Y). If the greater values of one variable mainly correspond to the greater values of the other variable, and the same holds for the lesser values, the covariance is positive. In the opposite case, when the greater values of the one variable mainly correspond to the lesser values of the other variable, then the variables tend to show opposite behavior and the covariance is negative. The covariance between X and Y is calculated as follows:
  - for the population:

$$\text{cov}(X, Y) = \frac{1}{n} \cdot \sum_{i=1}^{n} (x_i - \bar{x}) \cdot (y_i - \bar{y}) \qquad (5.4)$$

  - for the sample:

$$\text{cov}(X, Y) = \frac{1}{n-1} \cdot \sum_{i=1}^{n} (x_i - \bar{x}) \cdot (y_i - \bar{y}) \qquad (5.5)$$

5.1.3 Hypothesis of a Statistical Statement and Tests That Confirm or Reject It

Any statistical application may lead to one or more possible outcomes, called *experiments*, which constitute the event space. While trying to generalize findings of a sample to the whole population, we formulate a number of assumptions, which constitute the *hypothesis test*. Hypothesis testing aims at determining whether an assumed statement based on a set of assumptions is true or false and usually is conducted in six successive steps:

1. *null hypothesis* (denoted as H_0): A statement is assumed to be true as long as a number of tests assure for its validity; otherwise, the null hypothesis is rejected,
2. the *alternative hypothesis* (denoted as H_1): A statement that is accepted as true if the null hypothesis is rejected,
3. the *level of significance* (denoted as α): The probability of rejecting the null hypothesis, when this hypothesis is true. In most applications for transport

demand problems, the level of significance is given the value of 0.05 (5%), whereas the less used value for the level of significance is 0.01 (1%),
4. the *test statistic*: A numerical measure, derived from statistical calculations based on sample data, which leads to the decision to accept or reject the null hypothesis,
5. the *critical value*: A specific value of a statistical index, to which the value of test statistic is compared,
6. *decision about the acceptance or rejection of the null hypothesis*: It is based on two criteria:
   a. comparison of the test statistic with the critical value,
   b. comparison of the probability value (called p-value) to the level of significance (α). A very small (smaller than α) p-value indicates that the null hypothesis in unlikely to be true.

5.1.4 The Various Probability Distributions

Many statistical applications do not lead to specific outcomes but rather to a range of values. In such cases, the study of a phenomenon leads to a probability distribution. There are different types of probability distributions, and the most commonly used in transport demand problems are the following:

- *Binomial distribution*: It is used to analyze variables that can assume two values (success or failure, yes or no, 0 or 1, true or false, pass or stop, etc.).
- *Poisson's distribution*: It is used to describe the likelihood of a given number of events occurring over an interval of time.
- *Normal distribution* (see Table 4.6 and Fig. 5.4): It is used for variables for which the probability of being at a specific distance below the mean equals the probability of being at the same distance above the mean.
- *Student's t-distribution* (see Table 5.2): It is similar to the normal distribution but differs in that in the case of Student's t-distribution small or large values are more likely to occur. It is often used in situations where a variable presents high variations or for the analysis of small samples. It is named after the pseudonym Student of the English statistician William Gossett and presents the following common characteristics with the standard normal distribution (a normal distribution with zero mean and unit variance):
  - mean value = 0,
  - it is symmetrical about the mean,
  - its graphical representation has the form of a bell-shaped curve.

However, the variance and standard deviation of the Student's t-distribution are larger than those of the standard normal distribution; for this reason t-distribution has more area in the tails and less area in the mean compared with the standard normal distribution.

Student's t-distribution is composed of an infinite set of distributions, each one being characterized by the number of degrees of freedom (df), defined as the number of values in the final calculation of a statistic that are free to vary.

For a number of degrees of freedom exceeding 30 (df > 30), the Student's t-distribution is similar to the standard normal distribution.

- *Chi-square* (χ^2) *distribution* (see Table 5.5): Named after the Greek letter chi (χ), it resembles to Student's t-distribution, but it is not symmetrical with regard to its mean. It is used to testify whether a population follows a specific probability distribution, whether the variance of a population equals to a specific value and whether two data sets are independent or not.
- *F-distribution* (see Table 5.3): It is used to compare variances of two populations and in this way to testify the hypotheses concerning the specific two populations. In addition, when correlating two variables and trying to calculate the coefficients of such a correlation, F-distribution provides particular criteria to testify whether the calculated values of co-efficients are compatible with a set of hypotheses. Though similar to the chi-square distribution, F-distribution has two different types of degrees of freedom, which are known as numerator and denominator.

5.1.5 Stationarity and Nonstationarity of a Series of Statistical Data

If the observed values of a variable are arranged as a series of data in a time order, then they constitute a time series. An example of time series is the number of passengers arriving or departing from an airport during a certain time period (e.g., a 10-year period), recorded at specific time intervals (per year, per month, per day). A characteristic of time series is stationarity or nonstationarity, which reflects whether the beginning time point of the time series affects its pattern and evolution over time. A time series is defined as *stationary* when its statistical characteristics (such as the mean, variance, and covariance) are time invariant and do not change if time series is shifted in time (Fig. 5.1). On the contrary, in *nonstationary* time series any shift in time results in differentiated statistical characteristics and thus in a different pattern of evolution of the problem under study [283].

Most statistical methods are based on the assumption that the time series is stationary or can become stationary through the use of mathematical transformations, such as:

- The differencing (computation of the first or of the second differences between consecutive data or observations) which helps us to stabilize the mean of a time series by removing changes, and thus to eliminate trend and seasonality (see §6.1.3). The first difference of a time series is the series of changes from one period to the next one. If Y_t denotes the value of the time

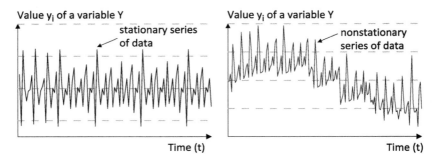

FIGURE 5.1 Typical pattern of a stationary and a nonstationary series of data. *Source: Compiled by the authors.*

series Y at the period t, then the first difference of Y at the same period t is equal to $Y_t - Y_{t-1}$. If the differenced data are nonstationary, then it is necessary to differentiate the already once-differenced data a second time in order to obtain a stationary time series. Time series that can become stationary by differencing are called *integrated processes*. When d differences are required to make a series stationary, that series is said to be integrated of order d and is denoted as I(d). Processes with $d \geq 1$ are often said to have a unit root (see 6.9.3). Thus, a time series which is stationary after being differentiated d times is said to be *integrated of order* d.

- The use of natural logarithms for the data or observations in order to stabilize the variance of a time series.

5.2 CORRELATION BETWEEN TWO VARIABLES AND REGRESSION ANALYSIS

5.2.1 Data Analysis, Correlation, and Regression Analysis

As analyzed in Chapter 3, transport demand can be modeled and quantified as the dependent variable resulting from the effects of one or more independent variables, such as transport costs, travel times, etc. Two variables may be correlated when there is some form of evidence that the one variable has direct effects on the value of the other. The statistical method used most frequently to testify whether two variables are correlated or not is known as *regression* analysis. The term was first used by the British statistician, sociologist, and anthropologist Francis Galton (1822−1911), who tried to correlate the height of children with the height of their parents one century and a half ago [284]. Galton analyzed a series of numbers, a convergence toward an average, and used the term regression to denote that any reliable extension into the future of data relating two variables should have as departing point a former or earlier situation. For this reason, prediction analysis should be able to *regress*, i.e., to return to the former situation.

5.2.2 Simple and Multiple Linear Regression Analysis

Simple linear regression is the simplest form of regression analysis between two continuous numerical variables: There is only one independent variable X and the relationship between the dependent variable Y and the (only one) independent variable X is linear (which means that graphically it is represented by a straight line). If the dependent variable Y is linearly related to more than one independent variables $X_1, X_2, X_3, \ldots$, then we have the case of *multiple linear regression* (see §5.4).

5.3 SIMPLE LINEAR REGRESSION ANALYSIS

5.3.1 Definition and Mathematical Description of Simple Linear Regression Analysis—Regression Coefficients and Error Term

The first step in any kind of regression analysis is to plot in a scatter diagram data or observations that refer to the independent variable and the dependent one. Take for instance data illustrated in Fig. 5.2. We will try to find which line best fits to the specific data set. We will use the following symbols:

X	independent variable,
Y	dependent variable,
y_i	actual (observed or recorded) value for the dependent variable Y for its i-th measurement,
$\widehat{y}_i$	the fitted (or calculated) value by the equation of linear regression of the variable Y for the value x_i of the variable X,
$\widehat{Y}$	variable that denotes the fitted (or calculated) form of the variable Y that results from linear regression,
ε_i	error term[1] (also called disturbance or noise) of the dependent variable Y. For a given sample, it is estimated (and is denoted as $\widehat{\varepsilon}_i$) by the residuals, the differences between the actual and the fitted (by the simple linear regression) values of the dependent variable Y, that is $y_i - \widehat{y}_i$.

Linear regression tries to tackle the fundamental problem of human knowledge. We explore the evolution of the real variable Y (which refers to the population) via a number of data or observations y_i (which represent a sample of the population) and we construct an artificial variable $\widehat{Y}$, through the values $\widehat{y}_i$, that we substitute with Y. The smaller the difference $Y - \widehat{Y}$, the better the adjustment. Again, human knowledge faces the critical dilemma of

---

1. Strictly speaking, the error term is the deviation of an observed value from the (unobservable) true value of the entire population, whereas the residual is an observable estimate of the unobservable statistical error (see §5.9).

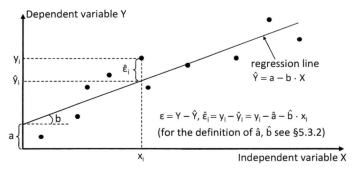

FIGURE 5.2 Symbols of simple linear regression. *Source: Compiled by the authors.*

all epistemology: to which extent do our observations record the real essence of things and phenomenon under survey?

The linear regression line of Fig. 5.2 can be represented by a regression equation of the form:

$$y_i = a + b \cdot x_i \tag{5.6}$$

where (Fig. 5.2)

b   the slope of the regression line,
a   the intercept, which is the value of y when x = 0.

Regression equation $y_i = a + b \cdot x_i$ is of a deterministic nature and implies that knowledge of the values x_i of the independent variable X is sufficient to determine accurately the value y_i of the dependent variable Y. This would be an ideal situation which, however, occurs very rarely, as many sources or errors can interfere to the regression equation, resulting from:

- measurement errors of y_i,
- the effect of a number of independent variables (other than variable X) which are omitted,
- randomness of the phenomenon under study, particularly if it is related to human behavior (as is the case of transport demand).

When such errors interfere, the regression equation takes the following probabilistic form:

$$y_i = a + b \cdot x_i + \varepsilon_i \tag{5.7}$$

where ε_i designates the random component of the regression, the probabilistic error term that accounts for the variability in Y that cannot be explained by the linear relationship with X.

5.3.2 Assessment of Fitness of the Linear Regression Line to the Data of the Problem

The ideal regression line is the one for which the residuals (all values of ε_i) are null. However, this is very rarely the case and the problem of the best fit of the regression line to the data of the problem is reduced to a minimization of the sum $\Sigma \varepsilon_i$ of the differences between actual and fitted values of the dependent variable for the various values of the independent variable. Thus, the best regression line is the one for which coefficients a and b take such values (which are referred to as estimators $\hat{a}$ and $\hat{b}$) which minimize the error term $\Sigma \varepsilon_i$. The estimator $\hat{b}$ of the slope of a simple regression is also known as *regression coefficient*.

There are a number of statistical methods which permit us to measure how close the regression line is to the data of the problem. These methods can use as a criterion for the degree of goodness of fit of the regression line measures such as the mean error, the mean absolute error, the sum of squared errors, the standard deviation of errors, etc. [285]. The most suitable and more often used among them is the method known as ordinary least squares (OLS) which is based on the *minimization of the sum of squared errors* between the actual and the fitted (by the regression) values of the dependent variable, since in this method there are no cancellations between positive and negative values of errors. Other advantages of OLS estimators are that they are unbiased and have minimum variance among the various linear unbiased estimators. This minimization of squared errors leads to statistical measures known under the name Pearson correlation coefficient (r) and coefficient of determination (R^2) (see §5.6 and §5.7), which permit us to assess how well the regression equation and line fit to the data of the problem.

5.3.3 Calculation of Parameters of the Simple Linear Regression Equation With the Ordinary Least Squares Method

Based on a data set of x_i and y_i (i = 1, 2, ..., n), the regression between the dependent variable Y and the independent variable X is described by the equation $y_i = a + b \cdot x_i + \varepsilon_i$, in which the part $a + b \cdot x_i$ represents the nonrandom component of the regression and the part ε_i the random component that must be minimized by using the OLS method. We assume that the error term has an expected value $E(\varepsilon) = 0$ and a variance $var(\varepsilon) = \sigma^2$ and that the errors are uncorrelated (among them). By using the OLS method, the minimization of the sum of squared errors $\sum(\hat{\varepsilon}_i)$ between the actual y_i and the fitted (by the regression equation) values $\hat{y}_i$ of the dependent variable Y is achieved with the calculation of the appropriate estimators $\widehat{a}$ and $\widehat{b}$ for the parameters a and b of the linear regression (Fig. 5.2):

$$\min_{a,b} \sum_{i=1}^{n} (\widehat{\varepsilon}_i) = \min_{a,b} \sum_{i=1}^{n} (y_i - \widehat{y}_i) = \min_{a,b} \sum_{i=1}^{n} \left(y_i - \widehat{a} - \widehat{b} \cdot x_i\right) \qquad (5.8)$$

Minimization of Eq. (5.8) requires the calculation of the first-order conditions with respect both to $\widehat{a}$ and $\widehat{b}$, that is the partial derivatives of Eq. (5.8) both to $\widehat{a}$ and $\widehat{b}$ will be set equal to zero:

$$\text{I}: \frac{\partial \sum_{i=1}^{n} \left(y_i - \widehat{a} - \widehat{b} \cdot x_i\right)}{\partial \widehat{a}} = 0 \Rightarrow -2 \cdot \sum_{i=1}^{n} \left(y_i - \widehat{a} - \widehat{b} \cdot x_i\right) = 0$$

$$\text{II}: \frac{\partial \sum_{i=1}^{n} \left(y_i - \widehat{a} - \widehat{b} \cdot x_i\right)}{\partial \widehat{b}} = 0 \Rightarrow -2 \cdot \sum_{i=1}^{n} \left(y_i - \widehat{a} - \widehat{b} \cdot x_i\right) \cdot x_i = 0$$

This is a linear system of two equations (I and II) with two unknown parameters ($\widehat{a}$ and $\widehat{b}$). Solving equation (I) for $\widehat{a}$ we have:

$$\text{I}: \sum_{i=1}^{n} \left(y_i - \widehat{a} - \widehat{b} \cdot x_i\right) = 0 \Rightarrow \widehat{a} = \overline{y} - \widehat{b} \cdot \overline{x} \qquad (5.9)$$

where $\overline{x}$ is the mean value of x_i and $\overline{y}$ is the mean value of y_i.
Solving equation (II) for $\widehat{b}$ we have:

$$\text{II}: \sum_{i=1}^{n} \left(y_i - \widehat{a} - \widehat{b} \cdot x_i\right) \cdot x_i = 0 \Rightarrow \sum_{i=1}^{n} y_i \cdot x_i - \widehat{a} \cdot x_i - \widehat{b} \cdot x_i^2 = 0$$

$$\Rightarrow \sum_{i=1}^{n} y_i \cdot x_i - \left(\overline{y} - \widehat{b} \cdot \overline{x}\right) \cdot x_i - \widehat{b} \cdot x_i^2 = 0 \Rightarrow$$

$$\Rightarrow \sum_{i=1}^{n} y_i \cdot x_i - \overline{y} \cdot x_i + \widehat{b} \cdot \overline{x} \cdot x_i - \widehat{b} \cdot x_i^2 = 0 \Rightarrow$$

$$\Rightarrow \sum_{i=1}^{n} \left(y_i - \overline{y} + \widehat{b} \cdot \overline{x} - \widehat{b} \cdot x_i\right) \cdot x_i = 0 \Rightarrow$$

$$\Rightarrow \sum_{i=1}^{n} y_i - \overline{y} + \widehat{b} \cdot (\overline{x} - x_i) = 0 \Rightarrow \sum_{i=1}^{n} (y_i - \overline{y}) = -\widehat{b} \cdot \sum_{i=1}^{n} (\overline{x} - x_i) \Rightarrow$$

$$\Rightarrow \widehat{b} = \frac{\sum_{i=1}^{n} (y_i - \overline{y})}{\sum_{i=1}^{n} (x_i - \overline{x})} \Rightarrow \widehat{b} = \frac{\sum_{i=1}^{n} (y_i - \overline{y}) \cdot (x_i - \overline{x})}{\sum_{i=1}^{n} (x_i - \overline{x})^2}$$

$$(5.10)$$

5.3.4 The Standard Error of the Regression Equation and the Standard Error of the Estimated Parameters

The *standard error of the regression* equation of the form $\widehat{y}_i = \widehat{a} + \widehat{b} \cdot x_i + \widehat{\varepsilon}_i$, which is based on a data set of x_i and y_i ($i = 1, 2, \ldots, n$), represents the average distance that the actual values fall from the regression line. Smaller values for the standard error are an indication that the actual data or observations are closer to the fitted line. This standard error is also known as *standard error of the estimate* or *standard error of the predicted value y*. The standard error $SE_{\widehat{Y}}$ of the regression can be calculated by the equation:

$$SE_{\widehat{Y}} = \sqrt{\frac{1}{n-2} \cdot \left[\sum_{i=1}^{n} (y_i - \bar{y})^2 - \frac{\left(\sum_{i=1}^{n} (y_i - \bar{y}) \cdot (x_i - \bar{x}) \right)^2}{\sum_{i=1}^{n} (x_i - \bar{x})^2} \right]} \qquad (5.11)$$

As far as the estimated parameters slope and intercept of the regression equation $\widehat{y}_i = \widehat{a} + \widehat{b} \cdot x_i + \widehat{\varepsilon}_i$ are concerned, the standard error of the slope $\widehat{b}$ is calculated by the equation:

$$SE_{\widehat{b}} = \sqrt{\frac{\sum_{i=1}^{n} \widehat{\varepsilon}_i^2}{(n-2) \cdot \sum_{i=1}^{n} (x_i - \bar{x})^2}} \qquad (5.12)$$

whereas the standard error of the intercept $\widehat{a}$ is calculated by the equation:

$$SE_{\widehat{a}} = SE_{\widehat{Y}} \cdot \sqrt{\frac{1}{n} + \frac{\bar{x}^2}{\sum_{i=1}^{n} (x_i - \bar{x})^2}} \qquad (5.13)$$

5.4 MULTIPLE LINEAR REGRESSION ANALYSIS

5.4.1 Definition and Forms of Multiple Linear Regression Analysis

Simple regression analysis applies to phenomena for which the dependent variable Y is related with only one independent variable X. In most problems, however, the dependent variable Y is related with a number of k independent variables X_j ($j = 1, 2, \ldots, k$).

If Y is linearly related to each one of X_j and we look for the appropriate equation which best fits Y to X_j, then we have a form of *multiple* linear regression analysis, in which the dependent variable Y is expressed in relation to the independent variables X_j by the following equation:

$$Y = a + b_1 \cdot X_1 + b_2 \cdot X_2 + \cdots + b_k \cdot X_k + \varepsilon \qquad (5.14)$$

The term linear can still be used for regression analysis with multiple independent variables because Eq. (5.14) is a linear function of the unknown parameters $a, b_1, b_2, \ldots, b_k$. Each parameter b_j represents the expected change of the dependent variable Y per unit change in the independent variable X_j, when the other independent variables X_i ($i \neq j$) remain unchanged. For this reason, the parameters $b_1, b_2, \ldots, b_k$ are also known as *partial regression coefficients*.

Models with a more complex structure than Eq. (5.14) could be calibrated by multiple linear regression analysis, if previously are appropriately transformed. For example, in the k-th degree polynomial equation of the form:

$$Y = a + b_1 \cdot X + b_2 \cdot X^2 + \cdots + b_k \cdot X^k + \varepsilon \qquad (5.15)$$

by substituting X with X_1, X^2 with X_2, and finally X^k with X_k, Eq. (5.15) can be written as:

$$Y = a + b_1 \cdot X_1 + b_2 \cdot X_2 + \cdots + b_k \cdot X_k + \varepsilon \qquad (5.16)$$

Models that include interaction effects[2] could also be calibrated as multiple linear regression models; for instance the equation:

$$Y = a + b_1 \cdot X_1 + b_2 \cdot X_2 + b_3 \cdot X_1 \cdot X_2 + \varepsilon \qquad (5.17)$$

can be written, by substituting $X_1 \cdot X_2$ with X_3, as:

$$Y = a + b_1 \cdot X_1 + b_2 \cdot X_2 + b_3 \cdot X_3 + \varepsilon \qquad (5.18)$$

Finally, a combined form of polynomial equation that includes interaction effects could also be calibrated as a multiple linear regression model. Take an equation of the form:

$$Y = a + b_1 \cdot X_1 + b_2 \cdot X_2 + b_3 \cdot X_1^2 + b_4 \cdot X_2^2 + b_5 \cdot X_1 \cdot X_2 + \varepsilon \qquad (5.19)$$

By substituting X_1^2, X_2^2 with X_3, X_4 and $X_1 \cdot X_2$ with X_5, the above equation can be written as:

$$Y = a + b_1 \cdot X_1 + b_2 \cdot X_2 + b_3 \cdot X_3 + b_4 \cdot X_4 + b_5 \cdot X_5 + \varepsilon \qquad (5.20)$$

For the majority of transportation problems, the values of the intercept a, of the partial regression coefficient $b_1, b_2, \ldots, b_k$, and of the error variance σ^2

---

2. An *interaction effect* occurs when an independent variable interacts with another independent variable before both of them simultaneously influence the dependent variable [286]. It must be distinguished from the *main effect*, where the independent variables interact directly with the dependent variable.

are unknown. These values must be estimated from sample data. The OLS method, as in the case of simple linear regression, will be used for the necessary calculations.

5.4.2 Calculation of Parameters of the Multiple Linear Regression Equation With the Ordinary Least Squares Method

Let us consider a passenger transport demand problem for which the dependent variable Y has a kind of correlation with k independent variables X_j (j = 1, 2, ..., k). For instance, X_1 can be the cost of travel, X_2 the travel time, X_3 the personal disposable income of the passenger, etc. Suppose that n (with $n > k$) sample data or observations are available for each one of the dependent and the independent variables. The data or observations are presented in Table 5.1. Assuming that the error term ε has an expected value $E(\varepsilon) = 0$ and $var(\varepsilon) = \sigma^2$ and that the errors are uncorrelated, Eq. (5.14) can be written in the form of a multiple regression equation as:

$$y_i = a + b_1 \cdot x_{i1} + b_2 \cdot x_{i2} + \cdots + b_k \cdot x_{ik} + \varepsilon_i \Rightarrow$$

$$\Rightarrow y_i = a + \sum_{j=1}^{k} b_j \cdot x_{ij} + \varepsilon_i \quad (i = 1, 2, ..., n) \tag{5.21}$$

As in simple linear regression, we will look for the least squares function, which consists in minimizing the sum of the error term:

$$\sum_{i=1}^{n} (\varepsilon_i)^2 = \sum_{i=1}^{n} \left(y_i - a - \sum_{j=1}^{k} b_j \cdot x_{ij} \right)^2 \tag{5.22}$$

TABLE 5.1: Sample data or observations for a multiple linear regression.

Data or observation i	Dependent variable Y	Independent variables			
		X_1	X_2	...	X_k
1	y_1	x_{11}	x_{12}	...	x_{1k}
2	y_2	x_{21}	x_{22}	...	x_{2k}
⋮	⋮	⋮	⋮	⋮	⋮
n	y_n	x_{n1}	x_{n2}	...	x_{nk}

Source: Compiled by the authors.

Minimization of Eq. (5.22) requires the calculation of the first-order conditions with respect to the estimators of the parameters a, b_1, b_2, ..., b_k. By setting partial derivatives equal to zero we will have:

$$\text{I}: \left. \frac{\partial \sum_{i=1}^{n}(\varepsilon_i)^2}{\partial \hat{a}} \right|_{\hat{a},\,\hat{b}_1,\,\hat{b}_2,\dots,\,\hat{b}_k} = 0 \Rightarrow -2 \cdot \sum_{i=1}^{n}\left(y_i - \hat{a} - \sum_{j=1}^{k}\hat{b}_j \cdot x_{ij} \right) = 0$$

$$\text{II}: \left. \frac{\partial \sum_{i=1}^{n}(\varepsilon_i)^2}{\partial \hat{b}_j} \right|_{\hat{a},\,\hat{b}_1,\,\hat{b}_2,\dots,\,\hat{b}_k} = 0 \Rightarrow -2 \cdot \sum_{i=1}^{n}\left(y_i - \hat{a} - \sum_{j=1}^{k}\hat{b}_j \cdot x_{ij} \right) \cdot x_{ij} = 0$$

$$(5.23)$$

Eq. (5.23) provides the set of k+1 least squares equations which are necessary for the calculation of the estimators $\hat{a}, \hat{b}_1, \hat{b}_2, \dots, \hat{b}_k$:

$$
\begin{aligned}
n \cdot \hat{a} \quad &+ \quad \hat{b}_1 \cdot \sum_{i=1}^{n} x_{i1} \quad + \quad \hat{b}_2 \cdot \sum_{i=1}^{n} x_{i2} \quad + \quad \cdots \quad + \quad \hat{b}_k \cdot \sum_{i=1}^{n} x_{ik} \quad = \quad \sum_{i=1}^{n} y_i \\
\hat{a} \cdot \sum_{i=1}^{n} x_{i1} \quad &+ \quad \hat{b}_1 \cdot \sum_{i=1}^{n} x_{i1}^2 \quad + \quad \hat{b}_2 \cdot \sum_{i=1}^{n} x_{i1} \cdot x_{i2} \quad + \quad \cdots \quad + \quad \hat{b}_k \cdot \sum_{i=1}^{n} x_{i1} \cdot x_{ik} \quad = \quad \sum_{i=1}^{n} x_{i1} \cdot y_i \\
&\vdots \\
\hat{a} \cdot \sum_{i=1}^{n} x_{ik} \quad &+ \quad \hat{b}_1 \cdot \sum_{i=1}^{n} x_{ik} \cdot x_{i1} \quad + \quad \hat{b}_2 \cdot \sum_{i=1}^{n} x_{ik} \cdot x_{i2} \quad + \quad \cdots \quad + \quad \hat{b}_k \cdot \sum_{i=1}^{n} x_{ik}^2 \quad = \quad \sum_{i=1}^{n} x_{ik} \cdot y_i
\end{aligned}
$$

$$(5.24)$$

There are many computer software packages[3] that can solve the system of Eq. (5.24) and calculate the values for the intercept $\hat{a}$ and the regression coefficients $\hat{b}_1, \hat{b}_2, \dots, \hat{b}_k$.

5.5 EVALUATION OF THE SIGNIFICANCE OF THE PARAMETERS OF A REGRESSION ANALYSIS

5.5.1 Student's t-test

Any regression constitutes a human effort to devise a mathematical description (through the estimated parameters) for a phenomenon described by a series of empirical data. It is crucial, however, to evaluate the degree of accuracy (or error) of assessment of the real phenomenon under study.

The *t-statistic* indicates how strongly each one of the estimated parameters (the slope b and the intercept a) of the simple linear regression (described by Eq. 5.7) *is associated* with the dependent variable. Similarly, for multiple linear regression (described by Eq. 5.14), t-statistic indicates how strongly

---

3. Such as EViews, MATLAB, Microfit, Minitab, NumXL, PcGive, R, SPSS, Stata, XLSTAT, etc.

each one for the regression coefficients b_1, b_2, ..., b_k and the intercept a is associated with the dependent variable. The t-statistic is calculated as the ratio of the estimator $\hat{a}$ or $\hat{b}_1$ or $\hat{b}_2$ or ... or $\hat{b}_k$ of the parameters a or b_1 or b_2 or ... or b_k of a multiple linear regression to its standard error:

$$\text{t-statistic} = \frac{\text{Estimator } \hat{a} \text{ or } \hat{b}_1 \text{ or } \hat{b}_2 \text{ or ... or } \hat{b}_k \text{ for the parameter a or } b_1 \text{ or } b_2 \text{ or ... or } b_k}{\text{Standard error of each estimator}}$$

(5.25)

The t-statistic applies for simple and multiple regression analysis the *Student's t-test* for the significance of each of the parameters (all independent variables and the intercept) of a regression model. Student's t-test is based on the Student's t-distribution (Table 5.2), with $n-k-1$ degrees of freedom, where n is the number of available data or observations and k is the number of independent variables (or generally of the regressors). In the case of simple linear regression, the number k is equal to the number of independent variables, thus $k = 1$. The *null hypothesis* of the Student's t-test is that the estimated regression coefficient $\hat{b}$ and the intercept $\hat{a}$ are equal to zero (H_0: regression coefficient = 0, intercept = 0), against a two-tailed (see Table 5.2) alternative that they differ from zero (H_1: regression coefficient $\neq$ 0, intercept $\neq$ 0).

5.5.2 Evaluation of the Overall Significance of the Regression Analysis—The F-test

The *F-test* applies for multiple linear regression and provides an overall significance of the regression analysis employed[4]. Thus, the F-test for the assessment of the overall significance of the regression compares a theoretical model (known also as *intercept-only model*) with no independent variables (or generally without regressors) to the regression model that we have calibrated. In contrast to the Student's t-test that can evaluate only one regression parameter at a time, the F-test can evaluate simultaneously all the regression parameters of all independent variables (or generally of all regressors).

In regression analysis the F-test follows the F-distribution (Table 5.3A–C), with k degrees of freedom for the numerator and $n-k-1$ degrees of freedom for the denominator, with n and k as in the Student's t-test. The null hypothesis for the F-test is that the regression coefficients (except for the intercept) are jointly all equal to zero, thus the fitness of the intercept-only model is equal to the fitness of the calibrated model under evaluation; the alternative hypothesis is that the fitness of the intercept-only model is significantly reduced compared with the fitness of the calibrated model under evaluation. The F-test is applied with the use of the F-statistic, which is calculated as the ratio of the explained

---

4. For the simple linear regression where only one independent variable is associated with the dependent one, the F-test can be omitted since the Student's t-test covers the significance test.

TABLE 5.2: Critical values of the Student's t-distribution.

This table gives, for specific degrees of freedom (df),
the critical value t_c of t-statistic with probability α lying to
its right (one-tailed hypothesis testing) and confidence interval
c lying between $-t_c$ and $+t_c$ (two-tailed hypothesis testing).

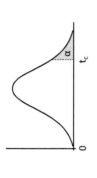

df	Values of α									
	0.25	0.20	0.10	0.05	0.025	0.01	0.005	0.0025	0.0005	
1	1.000	1.376	3.078	6.314	12.706	31.821	63.657	127.32	636.61	
2	0.816	1.061	1.886	2.920	4.303	6.965	9.925	14.089	31.599	
3	0.765	0.978	1.638	2.353	3.182	4.541	5.841	7.453	12.924	
4	0.741	0.941	1.533	2.132	2.776	3.747	4.604	5.598	8.610	
5	0.727	0.920	1.476	2.015	2.571	3.365	4.032	4.773	6.869	
6	0.718	0.906	1.440	1.943	2.447	3.143	3.707	4.317	5.959	
7	0.711	0.896	1.415	1.895	2.365	2.998	3.499	4.029	5.408	
8	0.706	0.889	1.397	1.860	2.306	2.896	3.355	3.833	5.041	
9	0.703	0.883	1.383	1.833	2.262	2.821	3.250	3.690	4.781	
10	0.700	0.879	1.372	1.812	2.228	2.764	3.169	3.581	4.587	
11	0.697	0.876	1.363	1.796	2.201	2.718	3.106	3.497	4.437	
12	0.695	0.873	1.356	1.782	2.179	2.681	3.055	3.428	4.318	
13	0.694	0.870	1.350	1.771	2.160	2.650	3.012	3.372	4.221	
14	0.692	0.868	1.345	1.761	2.145	2.624	2.977	3.326	4.140	

	50%	60%	80%	90%	95%	98%	99%	99.5%	99.9%
15	0.691	0.866	1.341	1.753	2.131	2.602	2.947	3.286	4.073
20	0.687	0.860	1.325	1.725	2.086	2.528	2.845	3.153	3.850
25	0.684	0.856	1.316	1.708	2.060	2.485	2.787	3.078	3.725
30	0.683	0.854	1.310	1.697	2.042	2.457	2.750	3.030	3.646
35	0.682	0.852	1.306	1.690	2.030	2.438	2.724	2.996	3.591
40	0.681	0.851	1.303	1.684	2.021	2.423	2.704	2.971	3.551
45	0.680	0.850	1.301	1.679	2.014	2.412	2.690	2.952	3.520
50	0.679	0.849	1.299	1.676	2.009	2.403	2.678	2.937	3.496
55	0.679	0.848	1.297	1.673	2.004	2.396	2.668	2.925	3.476
60	0.679	0.848	1.296	1.671	2.000	2.390	2.660	2.915	3.460
70	0.678	0.847	1.294	1.667	1.994	2.381	2.648	2.899	3.435
80	0.678	0.846	1.292	1.664	1.990	2.374	2.639	2.887	3.416
90	0.677	0.846	1.291	1.662	1.987	2.368	2.632	2.878	3.402
100	0.677	0.845	1.290	1.660	1.984	2.364	2.626	2.871	3.390
200	0.676	0.843	1.286	1.653	1.972	2.345	2.601	2.839	3.340
∞	0.674	0.842	1.282	1.645	1.960	2.326	2.576	2.807	3.291

Confidence interval c

Source: Compiled by the authors, based on the TINV function of Excel.

TABLE 5.3A: Critical values of the F-distribution ($\alpha = 0.01$).

This table gives the F-statistic for df_n degrees of freedom for the numerator and df_d degrees of freedom for the denominator and probability $\alpha = 0.01$.

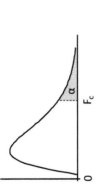

$df_d = 1$	$df_n = 1$	2	3	4	5	6	8	10	20	60	∞
1	4052	5000	5403	5625	5764	5859	5981	6056	6209	6313	6366
2	98.50	99.00	99.17	99.25	99.30	99.33	99.37	99.40	99.45	99.48	99.50
3	34.12	30.82	29.46	28.71	28.24	27.91	27.49	27.23	26.69	26.32	26.13
4	21.20	18.00	16.69	15.98	15.52	15.21	14.80	14.55	14.02	13.65	13.46
5	16.26	13.27	12.06	11.39	10.97	10.67	10.29	10.05	9.55	9.20	9.02
6	13.75	10.93	9.78	9.15	8.75	8.47	8.10	7.87	7.40	7.06	6.88
7	12.25	9.55	8.45	7.85	7.46	7.19	6.84	6.62	6.16	5.82	5.65
8	11.26	8.65	7.59	7.01	6.63	6.37	6.03	5.81	5.36	5.03	4.86
9	10.56	8.02	6.99	6.42	6.06	5.80	5.47	5.26	4.81	4.48	4.31
10	10.04	7.56	6.55	5.99	5.64	5.39	5.06	4.85	4.41	4.08	3.91
11	9.65	7.21	6.22	5.67	5.32	5.07	4.74	4.54	4.10	3.78	3.60
12	9.33	6.93	5.95	5.41	5.06	4.82	4.50	4.30	3.86	3.54	3.36
13	9.07	6.70	5.74	5.21	4.86	4.62	4.30	4.10	3.67	3.34	3.17
14	8.86	6.52	5.56	5.04	4.70	4.46	4.14	3.94	3.51	3.18	3.00

15	8.68	6.36	5.42	4.89	4.56	4.32	4.00	3.81	3.37	3.05	2.87
16	8.53	6.23	5.29	4.77	4.44	4.20	3.89	3.69	3.26	2.93	2.75
17	8.40	6.11	5.19	4.67	4.34	4.10	3.79	3.59	3.16	2.84	2.65
18	8.29	6.01	5.09	4.58	4.25	4.02	3.71	3.51	3.08	2.75	2.57
19	8.19	5.93	5.01	4.50	4.17	3.94	3.63	3.43	3.00	2.67	2.49
20	8.10	5.85	4.94	4.43	4.10	3.87	3.56	3.37	2.94	2.61	2.42
21	8.02	5.78	4.87	4.37	4.04	3.81	3.51	3.31	2.88	2.55	2.36
22	7.95	5.72	4.82	4.31	3.99	3.76	3.45	3.26	2.83	2.50	2.31
23	7.88	5.66	4.77	4.26	3.94	3.71	3.41	3.21	2.78	2.45	2.26
24	7.82	5.61	4.72	4.22	3.90	3.67	3.36	3.17	2.74	2.40	2.21
25	7.77	5.57	4.68	4.18	3.86	3.63	3.32	3.13	2.70	2.36	2.17
30	7.56	5.39	4.51	4.02	3.70	3.47	3.17	2.98	2.55	2.21	2.01
40	7.31	5.18	4.31	3.83	3.51	3.29	2.99	2.80	2.37	2.02	1.81
60	7.08	4.98	4.13	3.65	3.34	3.12	2.82	2.63	2.20	1.84	1.60
120	6.85	4.79	3.95	3.48	3.17	2.96	2.66	2.47	2.04	1.66	1.38
∞	6.64	4.61	3.78	3.32	3.02	2.80	2.51	2.32	1.88	1.47	1.00

Source: Compiled by the authors, based on the FINV function of Excel.

TABLE 5.3B: Critical values of the F-distribution ($\alpha = 0.05$).

This table gives the F-statistic for df_n degrees of freedom for the numerator and df_d degrees of freedom for the denominator and probability $\alpha = 0.05$.

$df_d = 1$	$df_n = 1$	2	3	4	5	6	8	10	20	60	∞
1	161.4	199.5	215.7	224.6	230.2	234.0	238.9	241.9	248.0	252.2	254.3
2	18.51	19.00	19.16	19.25	19.30	19.33	19.37	19.40	19.45	19.48	19.50
3	10.13	9.55	9.28	9.12	9.01	8.94	8.85	8.79	8.66	8.57	8.53
4	7.71	6.94	6.59	6.39	6.26	6.16	6.04	5.96	5.80	5.69	5.63
5	6.61	5.79	5.41	5.19	5.05	4.95	4.82	4.74	4.56	4.43	4.37
6	5.99	5.14	4.76	4.53	4.39	4.28	4.15	4.06	3.87	3.74	3.67
7	5.59	4.74	4.35	4.12	3.97	3.87	3.73	3.64	3.44	3.30	3.23
8	5.32	4.46	4.07	3.84	3.69	3.58	3.44	3.35	3.15	3.01	2.93
9	5.12	4.26	3.86	3.63	3.48	3.37	3.23	3.14	2.94	2.79	2.71
10	4.96	4.10	3.71	3.48	3.33	3.22	3.07	2.98	2.77	2.62	2.54
11	4.84	3.98	3.59	3.36	3.20	3.09	2.95	2.85	2.65	2.49	2.40
12	4.75	3.89	3.49	3.26	3.11	3.00	2.85	2.75	2.54	2.38	2.30
13	4.67	3.81	3.41	3.18	3.03	2.92	2.77	2.67	2.46	2.30	2.21

14	4.60	3.74	3.34	3.11	2.96	2.85	2.70	2.60	2.39	2.22	2.13
15	4.54	3.68	3.29	3.06	2.90	2.79	2.64	2.54	2.33	2.16	2.07
16	4.49	3.63	3.24	3.01	2.85	2.74	2.59	2.49	2.28	2.11	2.01
17	4.45	3.59	3.20	2.96	2.81	2.70	2.55	2.45	2.23	2.06	1.96
18	4.41	3.55	3.16	2.93	2.77	2.66	2.51	2.41	2.19	2.02	1.92
19	4.38	3.52	3.13	2.90	2.74	2.63	2.48	2.38	2.16	1.98	1.88
20	4.35	3.49	3.10	2.87	2.71	2.60	2.45	2.35	2.12	1.95	1.84
21	4.32	3.47	3.07	2.84	2.68	2.57	2.42	2.32	2.10	1.92	1.81
22	4.30	3.44	3.05	2.82	2.66	2.55	2.40	2.30	2.07	1.89	1.78
23	4.28	3.42	3.03	2.80	2.64	2.53	2.37	2.27	2.05	1.86	1.76
24	4.26	3.40	3.01	2.78	2.62	2.51	2.36	2.25	2.03	1.84	1.73
25	4.24	3.39	2.99	2.76	2.60	2.49	2.34	2.24	2.01	1.82	1.71
30	4.17	3.32	2.92	2.69	2.53	2.42	2.27	2.16	1.93	1.74	1.62
40	4.08	3.23	2.84	2.61	2.45	2.34	2.18	2.08	1.84	1.64	1.51
60	4.00	3.15	2.76	2.53	2.37	2.25	2.10	1.99	1.75	1.53	1.39
120	3.92	3.07	2.68	2.45	2.29	2.18	2.02	1.91	1.66	1.43	1.25
∞	3.84	3.00	2.60	2.37	2.21	2.10	1.94	1.83	1.57	1.32	1.00

Source: Compiled by the authors, based on the FINV function of Excel.

TABLE 5.3C: Critical values of the F-distribution ($\alpha = 0.10$).

This table gives the F-statistic for df_n degrees of freedom for the numerator and df_d degrees of freedom for the denominator and probability $\underline{\alpha = 0.10}$.

	$df_n = 1$	2	3	4	5	6	8	10	20	60	∞
$df_d = 1$	39.86	49.50	53.59	55.83	57.24	58.20	59.44	60.19	61.74	62.79	63.33
2	8.53	9.00	9.16	9.24	9.29	9.33	9.37	9.39	9.44	9.47	9.49
3	5.54	5.46	5.39	5.34	5.31	5.28	5.25	5.23	5.18	5.15	5.13
4	4.54	4.32	4.19	4.11	4.05	4.01	3.95	3.92	3.84	3.79	3.76
5	4.06	3.78	3.62	3.52	3.45	3.40	3.34	3.30	3.21	3.14	3.11
6	3.78	3.46	3.29	3.18	3.11	3.05	2.98	2.94	2.84	2.76	2.72
7	3.59	3.26	3.07	2.96	2.88	2.83	2.75	2.70	2.59	2.51	2.47
8	3.46	3.11	2.92	2.81	2.73	2.67	2.59	2.54	2.42	2.34	2.29
9	3.36	3.01	2.81	2.69	2.61	2.55	2.47	2.42	2.30	2.21	2.16
10	3.29	2.92	2.73	2.61	2.52	2.46	2.38	2.32	2.20	2.11	2.06
11	3.23	2.86	2.66	2.54	2.45	2.39	2.30	2.25	2.12	2.03	1.97
12	3.18	2.81	2.61	2.48	2.39	2.33	2.24	2.19	2.06	1.96	1.90

13	3.14	2.76	2.56	2.43	2.35	2.28	2.20	2.14	2.01	1.90	1.85
14	3.10	2.73	2.52	2.39	2.31	2.24	2.15	2.10	1.96	1.86	1.80
15	3.07	2.70	2.49	2.36	2.27	2.21	2.12	2.06	1.92	1.82	1.76
16	3.05	2.67	2.46	2.33	2.24	2.18	2.09	2.03	1.89	1.78	1.72
17	3.03	2.64	2.44	2.31	2.22	2.15	2.06	2.00	1.86	1.75	1.69
18	3.01	2.62	2.42	2.29	2.20	2.13	2.04	1.98	1.84	1.72	1.66
19	2.99	2.61	2.40	2.27	2.18	2.11	2.02	1.96	1.81	1.70	1.63
20	2.97	2.59	2.38	2.25	2.16	2.09	2.00	1.94	1.79	1.68	1.61
21	2.96	2.57	2.36	2.23	2.14	2.08	1.98	1.92	1.78	1.66	1.59
22	2.95	2.56	2.35	2.22	2.13	2.06	1.97	1.90	1.76	1.64	1.57
23	2.94	2.55	2.34	2.21	2.11	2.05	1.95	1.89	1.74	1.62	1.55
24	2.93	2.54	2.33	2.19	2.10	2.04	1.94	1.88	1.73	1.61	1.53
25	2.92	2.53	2.32	2.18	2.09	2.02	1.93	1.87	1.72	1.59	1.52
30	2.88	2.49	2.28	2.14	2.05	1.98	1.88	1.82	1.67	1.54	1.46
40	2.84	2.44	2.23	2.09	2.00	1.93	1.83	1.76	1.61	1.47	1.38
60	2.79	2.39	2.18	2.04	1.95	1.87	1.77	1.71	1.54	1.40	1.29
120	2.75	2.35	2.13	1.99	1.90	1.82	1.72	1.65	1.48	1.32	1.19
∞	2.71	2.30	2.08	1.94	1.85	1.77	1.67	1.60	1.42	1.24	1.00

Source: Compiled by the authors, based on the FINV function of Excel.

variance of the dependent variable to its unexplained variance and more specifically by the equation:

$$\text{F-statistic} = \cfrac{\cfrac{\sum\limits_{i=1}^{n}\left(y_i - \bar{y}_i\right)^2 - \sum\limits_{i=1}^{n}\left(y_i - \hat{y}_i\right)^2}{k}}{\cfrac{\sum\limits_{i=1}^{n}\left(y_i - \hat{y}_i\right)^2}{n - k - 1}} \tag{5.26}$$

5.6 PEARSON CORRELATION COEFFICIENT

5.6.1 Definition of Pearson Correlation Coefficient

For two variables X and Y, the Pearson correlation coefficient (r_{XY}), named after the English mathematician and biostatistician Karl Pearson, is a statistical measure of the degree of linear correlation between these two variables and is defined as follows [287]:

$$r_{XY} = \frac{\text{cov}(X, Y)}{\sigma_X \cdot \sigma_Y} \tag{5.27}$$

where

cov(X, Y) covariance between X and Y (see Eq. 5.5),
σ_X, σ_Y standard deviation of X and standard deviation of Y (see Eq. 5.4).

By substituting Eqs. (5.4) and (5.5) in Eq. (5.27), we can take for the Pearson correlation coefficient the analytical value:

$$r_{XY} = \frac{n \cdot \sum\limits_{i=1}^{n} x_i \cdot y_i - \left(\sum\limits_{i=1}^{n} x_i\right) \cdot \left(\sum\limits_{i=1}^{n} y_i\right)}{\sqrt{n \cdot \sum\limits_{i=1}^{n} x_i^2 - \left(\sum\limits_{i=1}^{n} x_i\right)^2} \cdot \sqrt{n \cdot \sum\limits_{i=1}^{n} y_i^2 - \left(\sum\limits_{i=1}^{n} y_i\right)^2}} \tag{5.28}$$

Instead of r_{XY}, some authors denote the Pearson correlation coefficient as Pearson's r. When applied to the total population (instead of a sample), Pearson correlation coefficient is denoted by the Greek letter ρ as ρ_{XY}.

5.6.2 Degrees of Correlation and the Resulting Values of the Pearson Correlation Coefficient

The Pearson correlation coefficient r_{XY} is a measure of the strength of the *linear* relationship between two variables X and Y and it takes values in the closed interval [−1, +1]. The value $r_{XY} = +1$ reflects a perfect positive correlation between X and Y, whereas the value $r_{XY} = 0$ indicates that no correlation can be found (based on the available data and observations) between X and Y. The value $r_{XY} = -1$ reflects a perfect negative correlation between X and Y.

In relation to the range of values of the Pearson correlation coefficient between X and Y, we can distinguish the following cases:

- $r_{XY} = 1$, the dependent variable Y is perfectly correlated positively with the independent variable X.

- $0.8 < r_{XY} < 1$, it testifies a strong positive correlation of the dependent variable Y with the independent variable X.

- $0.3 < r_{XY} < 0.6$, it testifies a moderate positive correlation of the dependent variable Y with the independent variable X.

- $0 < r_{XY} < 0.3$, it testifies a weak positive correlation of the dependent variable Y with the independent variable X.

- $r_{XY} \approx 0$, what was considered as dependent variable Y does not have any kind of linear correlation with what was considered as independent variable X.

- $0 < r_{XY} < -0.3$, it testifies a weak negative correlation of the dependent variable Y with the independent variable X.

- $-0.3 < r_{XY} < -0.6$, it testifies a moderate negative correlation of the dependent variable Y with the independent variable X.

- $-0.8 < r_{XY} < -1$, it testifies a strong negative correlation of the dependent variable Y with the independent variable X.

- $r_{XY} = -1$, the dependent variable Y is perfectly correlated negatively with the independent variable X.

5.6.3 Values of the Pearson Correlation Coefficient Than Can Be Considered as Satisfactory

A crucial question that arises is which is the value of r_{XY} for which a correlation between the variables X and Y can be considered strong or in any case satisfactory. The answer to this question depends on the nature of the problem under study. Thus, for physical sciences (for example) there should be no doubt about the high degree of accuracy between the dependent and the independent variable, so a value $r_{XY} = 0.80$ may be considered low.

As a very rough threshold for the limit value of r_{XY}, illustrating a linear relationship between two variables, we may use the quotient $2/\sqrt{n}$, where n is the number of available data [288].

Transport demand problems present many fluctuations, due to the attitudes and choices related to human behavior. For such problems, the Pearson correlation coefficient between X and Y is considered as satisfactory when $r_{XY} > 0.70$ and very satisfactory when $r_{XY} > 0.85$.

5.7 COEFFICIENT OF DETERMINATION

5.7.1 Definition of the Coefficient of Determination

The calibration of a multiple linear regression equation of the general form $Y = a + b_1 \cdot X_1 + b_2 \cdot X_2 + \cdots + b_k \cdot X_k$ between the dependent variable Y and the independent one(s) X_k on a given data set of x_{ij} and y_i (i = 1, 2, ..., n and j = 1, 2, ..., k) does not give any measure of how accurately this regression line represents and simulates the phenomenon under study. Indeed, it is possible that the actual values of the dependent variable are scattered, dispersed, and very distant from the regression line. Under such conditions, the question that arises is how accurate the correlation is between Y and X_k, and therefore whether the regression equation can be used to forecast future values of Y.

The above question can be tackled rather easily with the use of the coefficient of determination R^2 between the independent variable(s) X_k and the dependent one Y which is defined as follows:

$$R^2 = 1 - \frac{SS_{res}}{SS_{tot}} = 1 - \frac{\sum\limits_{i=1}^{n}\left(y_i - \widehat{y}_i\right)^2}{\sum\limits_{i=1}^{n}\left(y_i - \overline{y}_i\right)^2} \qquad (5.29)$$

where

SS_{res} the sum of the squared residuals of the regression,
SS_{tot} the sum of the squared differences of the actual data or observations of the dependent variable and its mean value.

5.7.2 Meaning of the Coefficient of Determination

The coefficient of determination R^2 is a positive number which takes values in the closed interval [0, 1] and represents the proportion of variance of the dependent variable which may be attributed to some linear combination of the independent variables.

The value $R^2 = 1$ indicates that the regression line derived fits perfectly to data and explains any variability in the dependent variable Y resulting from variabilities of the independent variable(s). The value $R^2 = 0$ indicates that no linear relationship between the dependent and the independent variable(s) can be found. A value, e.g., of $R^2 = 0.88$ indicates that a 88% variance in the dependent variable can be explained by changes of the independent variable(s), whereas the remaining 12% cannot be explained and can be attributed to variables omitted in the regression equation and to eventual measurement errors.

It must be emphasized that R^2 is a measure of the correlation between the dependent and the independent variable(s) but it does not testify *any kind of cause and effect* situation between the independent variable(s) and the dependent one (see §7.3).

5.7.3 Coefficient of Determination and Pearson Correlation Coefficient

The coefficient of determination R^2 is mostly used to multiple regression analysis between one dependent variable and a number of independent variables. When a dependent variable Y is related to only one independent variable X (case of simple linear regression), then the coefficient of determination R^2 equals the square of the coefficient of correlation r_{XY}, $R^2 = r_{XY}^2$.

5.7.4 Adjusted Coefficient of Determination

We may establish a trustworthy correlation (that is, one with a high value of R^2) between the dependent variable with one or a small number of independent ones. However, when R^2 does not have a satisfactory value, the forecaster may attempt to consider additional independent variables. The new coefficient of determination, when increasing the number of independent variables, is called the *adjusted* coefficient of determination and is denoted by $\overline{R}^2$. However, any addition of a new independent variable introduces additional limitations in the representation of the problem under study, and in this way it reduces the degrees of freedom of the problem.

The adjusted coefficient of determination $\overline{R}^2$ is defined as:

$$\overline{R}^2 = 1 - \frac{SS_{res}/(n-1)}{SS_{tot}/(n-k-1)} = 1 - \left(1 - R^2\right) \cdot \frac{n-1}{n-k-1} \qquad (5.30)$$

where

n   the number of available data or observations,
k   the number of independent variables (or generally the regressors).

5.7.5 Values of the Coefficient of Determination That Can Be Considered Satisfactory

The value of the coefficient of determination R^2 or of the adjusted coefficient of determination $\overline{R}^2$ (adjusted to the degrees of freedom) that can be considered as satisfactory depends on the acceptable value of the variability of the dependent variable resulting from the variabilities of the independent variables. As a rule of thumb, it is customary in transportation demand problems to consider values of R^2 (or $\overline{R}^2$) > 0.50 for simple or multiple linear regression as acceptable [289], values of R^2 (or $\overline{R}^2$) > 0.75 as satisfactory, and values of R^2 (or $\overline{R}^2$) > 0.85 as very satisfactory.

5.8 TEST OF CORRELATION BETWEEN INDEPENDENT VARIABLES—MULTICOLLINEARITY, DETECTION, AND REMOVAL

We underlined that the basic assumption for multiple linear regression is that the independent variables X_j are uncorrelated to each other. *Multicollinearity* is the presence of high correlation between two or more variables of a multiple linear regression equation, considered as independent [290]. In fact, it is inevitable to have some kind of (even small) multicollinearity between the various driving forces that affect human behavior and decisions concerning transport, as they cannot be totally independent among them. Thus, the question is to identify when multicollinearity is significant and becomes a serious problem for the validity and forecasting ability of the calibrated model.

When multicollinearity exists, the collinear independent variables contain the same information that affects the dependent variable (the case of independent variables X_3 and X_4 of Fig. 5.3) and thus the estimate (by means of the partial regression coefficients) of one independent variable's impact on the dependent variable tends to be less precise compared to the situation where independent variables are uncorrelated to each other.

The presence of multicollinearity violates the principle that each parameter b_j of the multiple linear regression should indicate the expected change in the dependent variable Y for a unit change in the independent variable X_j, while all the remaining independent variables X_i ($i \neq j$) are held unchanged.

Some indications for the presence of multicollinearity between the independent variables are the following:

- variances and standard errors of partial regression coefficient estimators are high, and therefore the significance of estimators and their t-statistic is low,
- values or the signs of the partial regression coefficient estimators are different from what is expected (according to the experience or findings of other researchers), they vary significantly and/or they change their sign when an independent variable is added or removed from the calibrated equation,
- high values of the coefficient of determination (and of the adjusted coefficient of determination) and high values for the F-test statistic are recorded.

The remedy for multicollinearity is the elimination from the multiple regression analysis of the independent variable(s) which appear to be highly correlated with each other. The use of a different and more extended data set for the dependent and the independent variables could also be beneficial for

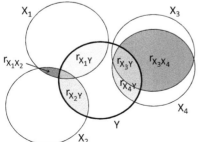

Correlation of the independent variables with the dependent one: r_{X_1Y}, r_{X_2Y}, r_{X_3Y}, r_{X_4Y}

Correlation between the independent variables: $r_{X_1X_2}$, $r_{X_3X_4}$

FIGURE 5.3 The multiple linear regression and the role of independent variables for the explanation of the dependent one. *Source: Compiled by the authors.*

the remedy of multicollinearity. The expression of one or more independent variables in a different way could affect multicollinearity, for example, the use of the personal disposable income instead of the per capita GDP as the variable that measures the individual's income.

Although collinearity is a multivariate (that is depending on many variables) phenomenon, the calculation of the Pearson correlation coefficient between the variables of the multiple linear regression and the construction of the *correlation matrix* (Table 5.4) could yield indications for the presence of multicollinearity between the independent variables. As a rule of thumb, values for Pearson correlation coefficient between the pairs of independent variables of at least 0.40 (the higher, the more likely that collinearity exists) indicate the existence of multicollinearity. The correlation matrix is symmetric and the values of diagonal are equal to 1, since these values represent correlations between each variable and itself (self-correlations).

Once again, the correlation matrix must be used with care, since although the Pearson correlation coefficient for any pair between X_1, X_2, X_3 variables might be small, the same variables as a group may nevertheless be highly correlated among them. For this reason, a more detailed statistical index is necessary. This is called the *variance inflation factor (VIF)*, and it quantifies the severity of multicollinearity between the independent variables of a multiple linear regression.

Consider the general form of a multiple linear regression, Eq. (5.20), appropriately modified for the regression between one dependent variable Y and, for example, four independent variables X_j (j = 1, 2, 3, 4):

$$Y = a_0 + b_1 \cdot X_1 + b_2 \cdot X_2 + b_3 \cdot X_3 + b_4 \cdot X_4 + \varepsilon$$

TABLE 5.4: Correlation matrix of a multiple linear regression.

	X_1	X_2	X_3	...	X_{k-1}	X_k
X_1	1	$r_{X_1 X_2}$	$r_{X_1 X_3}$	...	$r_{X_1 X_{k-1}}$	$r_{X_1 X_k}$
X_2		1	$r_{X_2 X_3}$	...	$r_{X_2 X_{k-1}}$	$r_{X_2 X_k}$
X_3			1	...	$r_{X_3 X_{k-1}}$	$r_{X_3 X_k}$
⋮	⋮	⋮	⋮	⋮	⋮	⋮
X_{k-1}				...	1	$r_{X_{k-1} X_k}$
X_k				...		1

Source: Compiled by the authors.

We will calibrate j (the number represents the number of independent variables) multiple linear regression models between each one of the independent variables on the left and the remaining independent variables on the right of the above equation and we will calculate the corresponding, for each model, coefficient of determination R_j^2:

$$X_1 = a_1 + b_5 \cdot X_2 + b_6 \cdot X_3 + b_7 \cdot X_4 + \varepsilon_1 \qquad \text{with coef. of determination } R_1^2$$
$$X_2 = a_2 + b_8 \cdot X_1 + b_9 \cdot X_3 + b_{10} \cdot X_4 + \varepsilon_2 \qquad \text{with coef. of determination } R_2^2$$
$$X_3 = a_3 + b_{11} \cdot X_1 + b_{12} \cdot X_2 + b_{13} \cdot X_4 + \varepsilon_3 \qquad \text{with coef. of determination } R_3^2$$
$$X_4 = a_4 + b_{14} \cdot X_1 + b_{15} \cdot X_2 + b_{16} \cdot X_3 + \varepsilon_4 \qquad \text{with coef. of determination } R_4^2$$

The variance inflation factor (VIF) for each one of the above models is equal to the ratio:

$$VIF_j = \frac{1}{1 - R_j^2} \qquad (5.31)$$

The ideal value for VIF is 1, which means that the corresponding model has a coefficient of determination $R^2 = 0$ (variables totally uncorrelated with each other). If the VIF of an independent variable is calculated to be equal to z, this means that the standard error of the regression coefficient of that variable is $\sqrt{z}$ times greater than it would be if the specific independent variable was uncorrelated with the other independent variables.

A rule of thumb is that if $VIF_j > 10$, then the multicollinearity between the variables of the corresponding model is harmful. For values $5 < VIF_j < 10$ multicollinearity is possible, whereas for values $VIF_j < 5$ there is no evidence for multicollinearity [291].

5.9 RESIDUALS OF LINEAR REGRESSION

5.9.1 Definition

Even the best fitted to data regression line will not coincide perfectly with all the data or observations on which it has been calculated. As we analyzed in §5.3.1, a residual is the difference between the actual value y_i and the fitted by the linear regression value $\hat{y}_i$ of the dependent variable for the value x_i of the independent variable. Recall the distinction between error and residual: a residual (or fitting deviation) is an observable estimate of the unobservable statistical error.

However, some data or observations may lie far from the regression line, thus leading to high values of residuals. Such points are called *outliers* and may come from:

- high fluctuations of a randomly developed phenomenon,
- erroneous data or mistakes at the recording processes,
- a regression line poorly fitted to the data.

5.9.2 Distribution of Residuals, Jarque–Bera Test, Skewness, and Kurtosis

It is essential to know whether residuals are distributed in a symmetrical and flat form. For this purpose, the histogram of residuals can be used to examine whether residuals are normally distributed. The Jarque–Bera test, a well-known test for normality, can determine whether residuals have the skewness and kurtosis matching a normal distribution. Skewness is a measure of the asymmetry of the probability distribution of a variable about its mean, whereas kurtosis is a measure of the flatness or the steepness of the tails of the probability distribution of a variable (Fig. 5.4).

Eqs. (5.32), (5.33), and (5.34) describe the skewness, the kurtosis, and the Jarque–Bera test [292], the latter named after the Mexican economist and politician Carlos Jarque and the American econometrician Anil Bera:

$$\text{Skewness} = \frac{\frac{1}{n} \cdot \sum_{i=1}^{n} (\varepsilon_i - \bar{\varepsilon})^3}{\left(\frac{1}{n} \cdot \sum_{i=1}^{n} (\varepsilon_i - \bar{\varepsilon})^2\right)^{3/2}} \tag{5.32}$$

$$\text{Kurtosis} = \frac{\frac{1}{n} \cdot \sum_{i=1}^{n} (\varepsilon_i - \bar{\varepsilon})^4}{\left(\frac{1}{n} \cdot \sum_{i=1}^{n} (\varepsilon_i - \bar{\varepsilon})^2\right)^2} \tag{5.33}$$

$$\text{Jarque–Bera test} = n \cdot \left(\frac{\text{Skewness}^2}{6} + \frac{(\text{Kurtosis} - 3)^2}{24}\right) \tag{5.34}$$

where ε_i (i = 1, 2, ..., n) are the residuals. For a normal distribution the skewness is 0 and the kurtosis is 3. The Jarque–Bera statistic follows the

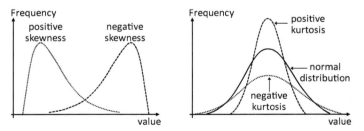

FIGURE 5.4 The skewness and the kurtosis of a probability distribution. *Source: Compiled by the authors.*

chi-square distribution (Table 5.5) with two degrees of freedom under the *null hypothesis of normally distributed residuals.*

5.9.3 Influence of Residuals—Determination of Outliers

In regression analysis, a common measure for the estimation of the influence of residuals and thus for the determination of outliers in a set of data of independent variables is Cook's distance (D_i). Cook's distance, named after the American statistician Dennis Cook, summarizes how much all the values in the regression model change when the i-th observation of the data set is removed.

Given a regression of the dependent variable Y on X_k (k denotes the number of regressors; in the case of simple linear regression the number k is equal to the number of independent variables, thus k = 1) by using a data set (y_j, x_{1j}, ..., x_{kj}) (j denotes the number of available observations for each variable, j = 1, 2, ..., n) the Cook's distance for the i-th observation is defined as:

$$D_i = \frac{\sum_{j=1}^{n}\left(\widehat{y}_j^{\,all} - \widehat{y}_j^{\,i-th}\right)}{\frac{(k+1)}{n} \cdot \sum_{j=1}^{n}\left(\widehat{y}_j^{\,all} - y_j\right)} \tag{5.35}$$

where

$\widehat{y}_j^{\,all}$ the fitted, by regression analysis, value of the dependent variable when using all available observations,

$\widehat{y}_j^{\,i-th}$ the fitted, by regression analysis, value of the dependent variable when the i-th observation is removed from the data set,

y_j the actual value of the dependent variable,

k   the number of independent variables.

A general guideline is that data points with $D_i > 1$ are possible outliers [293]. Other studies suggest that data points with $D_i > 4/(n - k - 1)$ could be characterized as highly influential points [294].

5.9.4 Serial Correlation (Autocorrelation) in the Residuals

As *serial correlation*, also known as *autocorrelation*, we describe the situation when data or observations of the same variable are related among them over specific periods of time. When dealing with residuals, the presence of serial correlation means that the residuals of a specific time period are correlated

TABLE 5.5: Critical values of the chi-square distribution.

This table gives the value χ_0^2 for which $P[\chi^2 > \chi_0^2] = \alpha$, for specific degrees of freedom (df) and for a given value of α.

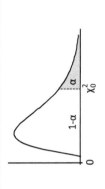

Values of α (probability of a larger value of χ^2)

df	0.99	0.95	0.90	0.75	0.50	0.25	0.10	0.05	0.01	0.005
1			0.016	0.102	0.455	1.323	2.706	3.841	6.635	7.879
2	0.020	0.103	0.211	0.575	1.386	2.773	4.605	5.991	9.210	10.60
3	0.115	0.352	0.584	1.213	2.366	4.108	6.251	7.815	11.34	12.84
4	0.297	0.711	1.064	1.923	3.357	5.385	7.779	9.488	13.28	14.86
5	0.554	1.145	1.610	2.675	4.351	6.626	9.236	11.07	15.09	16.75
6	0.872	1.635	2.204	3.455	5.348	7.841	10.64	12.59	16.81	18.55
7	1.239	2.167	2.833	4.255	6.346	9.037	12.02	14.07	18.48	20.28
8	1.646	2.733	3.490	5.071	7.344	10.22	13.36	15.51	20.09	21.95
9	2.088	3.325	4.168	5.899	8.343	11.39	14.68	16.92	21.67	23.59
10	2.558	3.940	4.865	6.737	9.342	12.55	15.99	18.31	23.21	25.19
11	3.053	4.575	5.578	7.584	10.34	13.70	17.28	19.68	24.72	26.76
12	3.571	5.226	6.304	8.438	11.34	14.85	18.55	21.03	26.22	28.30
13	4.107	5.892	7.042	9.299	12.34	15.98	19.81	22.36	27.69	29.82

14	4.660	6.571	7.790	10.17	13.34	17.12	21.06	23.68	29.14	31.32
15	5.229	7.261	8.547	11.04	14.34	18.25	22.31	25.00	30.58	32.80
16	5.812	7.962	9.312	11.91	15.34	19.37	23.54	26.30	32.00	34.27
17	6.408	8.672	10.09	12.79	16.34	20.49	24.77	27.59	33.41	35.72
18	7.015	9.390	10.86	13.68	17.34	21.60	25.99	28.87	34.81	37.16
19	7.633	10.12	11.65	14.56	18.34	22.72	27.20	30.14	36.19	38.58
20	8.260	10.85	12.44	15.45	19.34	23.83	28.41	31.41	37.57	40.00
21	8.897	11.59	13.24	16.34	20.34	24.93	29.62	32.67	38.93	41.40
22	9.542	12.34	14.04	17.24	21.34	26.04	30.81	33.92	40.29	42.80
23	10.20	13.09	14.85	18.14	22.34	27.14	32.01	35.17	41.64	44.18
24	10.86	13.85	15.66	19.04	23.34	28.24	33.20	36.42	42.98	45.56
25	11.52	14.61	16.47	19.94	24.34	29.34	34.38	37.65	44.31	46.93
30	14.95	18.49	20.60	24.48	29.34	34.80	40.26	43.77	50.89	53.67
40	22.16	26.51	29.05	33.66	39.34	45.62	51.81	55.76	63.69	66.77
50	29.71	34.76	37.69	42.94	49.33	56.33	63.17	67.50	76.15	79.49
60	37.48	43.19	46.46	52.29	59.33	66.98	74.40	79.08	88.38	91.95
80	53.54	60.39	64.28	71.14	79.33	88.13	96.58	101.88	112.33	116.32
100	70.06	77.93	82.36	90.13	99.33	109.14	118.50	124.34	135.81	140.17

Source: Compiled by the authors, based on the CHIINV function of Excel.

with the residuals of another time period. The presence of serial correlation causes significant problems in regression analysis, such as:

- violations of the ordinary least squares method basic assumption that the adjacent residuals should not be correlated with each other (serially uncorrelated),
- exaggerated goodness of fit (high values of the coefficient of determination),
- standard errors that are too small and consequently values of t-statistic that are too large. Thus, some regression coefficients appear to be statistically significant when in fact they are not.

The likely causes that may result in serial correlation in linear regression residuals are the following:

- the absence of one or more independent variables that ought to be included in a linear regression,
- misspecification of the functional form of the regression equation (e.g., when fitting a linear regression equation to data or observations that follow an exponential or polynomial pattern),
- errors of measurements in the dependent variable.

A visual check of residuals for evidence of serial correlation can be carried out through the plot of residuals. Fig. 5.5 presents the pattern of residuals when no serial correlation occurs (plot a), when residuals of a given sign tend to follow and to be followed by residuals of the same sign (plot b, positive serial correlation), and when residuals of a given sign tend to follow and to be followed by residuals of the opposite sign (plot c, negative serial correlation).

5.9.5 Testing Serial Correlation in the Residuals

5.9.5.1 The Durbin–Watson Test

The Durbin–Watson test examines whether there is a first-order serial correlation between the residuals $\hat{\varepsilon}$ of a calibrated regression equation. It is named

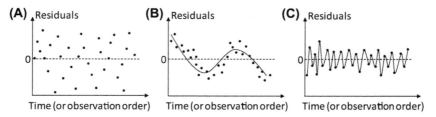

FIGURE 5.5 Visual examination for the existence of evidence of a serial correlation ((A) no serial correlation, (B) positive serial correlation, (C) negative serial correlation). *Source: Compiled by the authors.*

after the British statistician and econometrician James Durbin and the Australian statistician Geoffrey Watson. The statistic of the Durbin-Watson test, denoted as the DW-statistic, is calculated by the equation [295–297]:

$$\text{DW-statistic} = \frac{\sum_{i=2}^{n} \left(\hat{\varepsilon}_i - \hat{\varepsilon}_{i-1} \right)^2}{\sum_{i=1}^{n} \hat{\varepsilon}_i^2} \tag{5.36}$$

The null hypothesis H_0 for the Durbin-Watson test is that there is no first-order serial correlation in residuals and the alternative hypothesis H_1 is that a first-order correlation exists. Table 5.6 gives the lower (d_L) and the upper (d_U) critical values of the DW-statistic for k independent variables or regressors, in general, and n available data. We may distinguish the following cases [298]:

- DW-statistic $< d_L$: We should reject the null hypothesis in favor of the alternative,
- DW-statistic $> d_U$: We cannot reject the null hypothesis,
- $d_L <$ DW-statistic $< d_U$: The Durbin-Watson test is inconclusive concerning the presence or not of first-order serial correlation in the residuals. In such a case we proceed with another test.

If there is no serial correlation, then the DW-statistic will be around 2. The DW-statistic will fall below 2 if there is a positive serial correlation and in the worst case it will be near zero when the residuals are highly positively correlated. If there is a negative serial correlation, the DW-statistic will vary between 2 and 4 and in the worst case it will reach the value 4, which corresponds to highly negatively correlated residuals.

As a rule of thumb, it is considered that DW-statistic values in the range of 1.5–2.5 are acceptable, whereas values outside of this range (and especially values under 1 or greater than 3) are a definite indication of a model with serious serial correlation problems [299].

5.9.5.2 The Durbin's h-test

When studying the annual passenger demand of a transport mode, along with the independent variables that may affect the following year's demand (travel time, frequency of service, fares, income of users, variables related to competitors, etc.), the lagged-dependent variable, that is, the passenger demand of the previous year, may prove to be a useful and statistically significant variable, as it represents the habits of customers for using the specific transport mode and constraints on supply. Generally speaking, the use of a

TABLE 5.6: Critical values of the DW-statistic (α = 0.05).

n	k = 1		k = 2		k = 3		k = 4		k = 5	
	d_L	d_U	d_L	d_U	d_L	d_U	d_L	d_U	d_L	d_U
6	0.610	1.400	—	—	—	—	—	—	—	—
7	0.700	1.356	0.467	1.896	—	—	—	—	—	—
8	0.763	1.332	0.559	1.777	0.368	2.287	—	—	—	—
9	0.724	1.320	0.629	1.699	0.455	2.128	0.296	2.588	—	—
10	0.879	1.320	0.697	1.641	0.525	2.016	0.376	1.414	0.243	2.822
11	0.927	1.324	0.658	1.604	0.595	1.928	0.444	2.283	0.316	2.645
12	0.971	1.331	0.812	1.579	0.658	1.864	0.512	2.177	0.379	2.506
13	1.010	1.340	0.861	1.562	0.715	1.816	0.574	1.094	0.445	2.390
14	1.045	1.350	0.905	1.551	0.767	1.779	0.632	2.030	0.505	2.296
15	1.077	1.361	0.946	1.543	0.814	1.750	0.685	1.977	0.562	2.220
16	1.106	1.371	0.982	1.539	0.857	1.728	0.734	1.935	0.615	2.157
17	1.133	1.381	1.015	1.536	0.897	1.710	0.779	1.900	0.664	2.104
18	1.158	1.391	1.046	1.535	0.933	1.696	0.820	1.872	0.710	2.060
19	1.180	1.401	1.074	1.536	0.967	1.685	0.859	1.848	0.752	2.023
20	1.201	1.411	1.100	1.537	0.998	1.676	0.894	1.828	0.792	1.991

21	1.221	1.420	1.125	1.538	1.026	1.669	0.927	1.812	0.829	1.964
22	1.239	1.429	1.147	1.541	1.053	1.664	0.958	1.797	0.863	1.940
23	1.257	1.437	1.168	1.543	1.078	1.660	0.986	1.785	0.895	1.920
24	1.273	1.446	1.188	1.546	1.101	1.656	1.013	1.775	0.925	1.902
25	1.288	1.454	1.206	1.550	1.123	1.654	1.038	1.767	0.953	1.886
26	1.302	1.461	1.224	1.553	1.143	1.652	1.062	1.759	0.979	1.873
27	1.316	1.469	1.240	1.556	1.162	1.651	1.084	1.753	1.004	1.861
28	1.328	1.476	1.255	1.560	1.181	1.650	1.104	1.747	1.028	1.850
29	1.341	1.483	1.270	1.563	1.198	1.650	1.124	1.743	1.050	1.841
30	1.352	1.489	1.284	1.567	1.214	1.650	1.143	1.739	1.071	1.833
35	1.402	1.519	1.343	1.584	1.283	1.653	1.222	1.726	1.160	1.803
40	1.442	1.544	1.391	1.600	1.338	1.659	1.285	1.721	1.230	1.786
45	1.475	1.566	1.430	1.615	1.383	1.666	1.336	1.720	1.287	1.776
50	1.503	1.585	1.462	1.628	1.421	1.674	1.378	1.721	1.335	1.771
60	1.549	1.616	1.514	1.652	1.480	1.689	1.444	1.727	1.408	1.767
70	1.583	1.641	1.554	1.672	1.525	1.703	1.494	1.735	1.464	1.768
80	1.611	1.662	1.586	1.688	1.560	1.715	1.534	1.743	1.507	1.772
90	1.635	1.679	1.612	1.703	1.589	1.726	1.566	1.751	1.542	1.776
100	1.654	1.694	1.634	1.715	1.613	1.736	1.592	1.758	1.571	1.780

Continued

TABLE 5.6: Critical values of the DW-statistic ($\alpha = 0.05$).—cont'd

n	k = 1		k = 2		k = 3		k = 4		k = 5	
	d_L	d_U	d_L	d_U	d_L	d_U	d_L	d_U	d_L	d_U
150	1.720	1.746	1.706	1.760	1.693	1.774	1.679	1.788	1.665	1.802
200	1.758	1.778	1.748	1.789	1.738	1.799	1.728	1.810	1.718	1.820

n	k = 6		k = 7		k = 8		k = 9		k = 10	
	d_L	d_U	d_L	d_U	d_L	d_U	d_L	d_U	d_L	d_U
6	—	—	—	—	—	—	—	—	—	—
7	—	—	—	—	—	—	—	—	—	—
8	—	—	—	—	—	—	—	—	—	—
9	—	—	—	—	—	—	—	—	—	—
10	—	—	—	—	—	—	—	—	—	—
11	0.203	3.005	—	—	—	—	—	—	—	—
12	0.268	2.832	0.171	3.149	—	—	—	—	—	—
13	0.328	1.692	0.230	2.985	0.147	3.266	—	—	—	—
14	0.389	1.572	0.286	1.848	0.200	3.111	0.127	3.360	—	—
15	0.447	2.472	0.343	2.727	0.251	2.979	0.175	3.216	0.111	3.438
16	0.502	2.388	0.396	2.624	0.304	2.860	0.222	3.090	0.155	3.304

17	0.554	2.318	0.451	2.537	0.358	2.757	0.272	2.975	1.198	3.184
18	0.603	2.257	0.502	2.461	0.407	2.667	0.321	2.873	1.244	3.073
19	0.649	2.206	0.549	2.396	0.456	2.589	0.369	2.783	0.290	2.974
20	0.692	2.162	0.595	2.339	0.502	2.521	0.416	2.704	0.336	2.885
21	0.732	2.124	0.637	2.290	0.547	2.460	0.461	2.633	0.380	2.806
22	0.769	2.090	0.677	2.246	0.588	2.407	0.504	2.571	0.424	2.734
23	0.804	2.061	0.715	2.208	0.628	2.360	0.545	2.514	0.465	2.670
24	0.837	2.035	0.751	2.174	0.666	2.318	0.584	2.464	0.506	2.613
25	0.868	2.012	0.784	2.144	0.702	2.280	0.621	2.419	0.544	2.560
26	0.897	1.992	0.816	2.117	0.735	2.246	0.657	2.379	0.581	2.513
27	0.925	1.974	0.845	2.093	0.767	2.216	0.691	2.342	0.616	2.470
28	0.951	1.958	0.874	2.071	0.798	2.188	0.723	2.309	0.650	2.431
29	0.975	1.944	0.900	2.052	0.826	2.164	0.753	2.278	0.682	2.396
30	0.998	1.931	0.926	2.034	0.854	2.141	0.782	2.251	0.712	2.363
35	1.097	1.884	1.034	1.967	0.971	2.054	0.908	2.144	0.845	2.236
40	1.175	1.854	1.120	1.924	1.064	1.997	1.008	2.072	0.952	2.149
45	1.238	1.835	1.189	1.895	1.139	1.958	1.089	2.022	1.038	2.088
50	1.291	1.822	1.246	1.875	1.201	1.930	1.156	1.986	1.110	2.044
60	1.372	1.808	1.335	1.850	1.298	1.894	1.260	1.939	1.222	1.984

Continued

TABLE 5.6: Critical values of the DW-statistic ($\alpha = 0.05$).—cont'd

n	k = 6		k = 7		k = 8		k = 9		k = 10	
	d_L	d_U	d_L	d_U	d_L	d_U	d_L	d_U	d_L	d_U
70	1.433	1.802	1.401	1.837	1.369	1.873	1.337	1.910	1.305	1.948
80	1.480	1.801	1.453	1.831	1.425	1.861	1.397	1.893	1.369	1.925
90	1.518	1.801	1.494	1.827	1.469	1.854	1.445	1.881	1.420	1.909
100	1.550	1.803	1.528	1.826	1.506	1.850	1.484	1.874	1.462	1.898
150	1.651	1.817	1.637	1.832	1.622	1.847	1.608	1.862	1.594	1.977
200	1.707	1.831	1.697	1.841	1.686	1.852	1.675	1.863	1.685	1.874

Source: Compiled by the authors, based on data of Ref. [327].

lagged-dependent variable is a means for capturing *dynamic* effects and provides a statistical representation of theories of public behavior, in which an attitude at a time t is a function of the same attitude at time t−1 (modified by new information), rather than viewing an attitude at time t as a linear function of independent variables [301].

When the dependent variables are used as independent ones with time lag, Eq. (5.21) can be written as:

$$y_i = a + b_1 \cdot x_{i1} + b_2 \cdot x_{i2} + \cdots + b_k \cdot x_{ik} + b_{k+1} \cdot y_{i-1} + \varepsilon_i \tag{5.37}$$

The Durbin-Watson test is made for the purpose of testing for first-order serial correlation and it assumes that none of the independent variables is simultaneously a lagged dependent variable; thus, for the model of Eq. (5.37) the DW-statistic will present a tendency to be close to 2, even though the residuals are serially correlated. In such cases, for a considerable number of data or observations n, we can use the Durbin's h-test, for which the statistic is calculated by the following equation [302] (some computer software packages calculate the Durbin's h-statistic by using n − 1 instead of n, because of the time lag):

$$\text{Durbin's h-statistic} = \left(1 - \frac{\text{DW-statistic}}{2}\right) \cdot \sqrt{\frac{n}{1 - n \cdot \left(SE_{\hat{b}_{k+1}}\right)^2}} \tag{5.38}$$

The Durbin's h-statistic is standard normally distributed under the null hypothesis of no serial correlation. This means that the value of Durbin's h-statistic should be compared with a critical value from the one-tailed standard normal distribution (Table 4.6). By using the one-tailed test at the 5% significance level ($\alpha = 0.05$) we obtain a critical value for Durbin's h-statistic equal to 1.645. When the test value of Eq. (5.38) is smaller than this critical value, we accept the null hypothesis of no serial correlation, otherwise we reject it.

5.9.5.3 The Breusch–Godfrey Lagrange Multiplier Test

The Breusch–Godfrey Lagrange multiplier (LM)[5] test, named after the Australian econometrician Trevor Breusch and the British econometrician Leslie Godfrey, contrary to the previous tests for serial correlation, can be used for the detection not only of first- but also of second-, third-, etc., order serial correlation in residuals.

---

5. Lagrange multipliers (named after the Italian-French mathematician Joseph-Louis Lagrange) are used in multivariable calculus for finding the local maximum and minimum of a function subject to fixed conditions or constraints, without the need to explicitly solve the conditions.

After the calibration of a multiple linear regression model of the form of Eq. (5.27), we use the residuals $\widehat{\varepsilon}_i$ (i = 1, 2, ..., n) of the calibrated model as dependent variable(s) for the calibration of an auxiliary model of the form [303]:

$$\widehat{\varepsilon}_i = d_0 + d_1 \cdot x_{i1} + \cdots + d_k \cdot x_{ik} + \underbrace{\rho_1 \cdot \widehat{\varepsilon}_{i-1}}_{\substack{\text{first-order}\\\text{serial}\\\text{correlation}}} + \underbrace{\rho_2 \cdot \widehat{\varepsilon}_{i-2}}_{\substack{\text{second-order}\\\text{serial}\\\text{correlation}}} + \cdots + \underbrace{\rho_h \cdot \widehat{\varepsilon}_{i-h}}_{\substack{\text{h-th order}\\\text{serial}\\\text{correlation}}} + e$$

(5.39)

in which, in addition to the independent variables X_1, X_2, ..., X_k, we have included as independent variables the lagged residuals. For the detection of first-order serial correlation, the residuals will be included lagged once; for the detection of second-order serial correlation, the residuals will be included lagged once and lagged twice[6], and so on [303]. The auxiliary model of Eq. (5.39) will have after the calibration a coefficient of determination $R^2_{\widehat{\varepsilon}}$. The Breusch–Godfrey LM test is based on the calculation of the statistic:

$$LM = n \cdot R^2_{\widehat{\varepsilon}}$$

(5.40)

for which it is assumed that it is distributed asymptotically, following the chi-square distribution with h degrees of freedom. The *null hypothesis* H_0 for the Breusch–Godfrey LM test is *that there is no h-th order serial correlation* in residuals and the alternative hypothesis H_1 is that an h-th order serial correlation exists. From the chi-square distribution of Table 5.5, we calculate the value of α corresponding to the statistic LM. If this value of α is less than 0.05 (5%), then we have to reject the null hypothesis that there is no h-order serial correlation in the residuals.

5.9.5.4 The Ljung–Box Test

The Ljung–Box test, named after the Finnish statistician Greta Ljung and the British statistician George Box, is another test for the detection of (any order) serial correlation in residuals. The application of the Ljung–Box test requires the determination of the values for the autocorrelation function[7] of the time series of the calibrated multiple linear regression model's residuals $\widehat{\varepsilon}_i$ (i = 1, 2, ..., n). The Ljung–Box test is based on the calculation of the so-called Q-statistic, which is defined as [304]:

$$\text{Q-statistic} = n \cdot (n+2) \cdot \sum_{k=1}^{h} \frac{\widehat{\rho}_k^2}{n-k}$$

(5.41)

---

6. Some computer software set the missing values of lagged residuals equal to zero.
7. The methodology for the determination of the values of the autocorrelation function is presented in Chapter 6, §6.8.

where

n	the number of data or observations,
h	the number of lags being tested for the determination of the h-th order serial correlation,
$\widehat{\rho}_k^2$	the value of the autocorrelation function at lag k (k = 1, 2, …, h).

Concerning the selection of the number of lags being tested, it has been recommended that in general $h \leq 0.05$ or in more detail h = min (10, n/5) for nonseasonal data and h = min (2 m, n/5) for seasonal data, where m is the number of periods of seasonality (see §6.5) [305].

The Q-statistic follows the chi-square distribution with h degrees of freedom. The *null hypothesis* H_0 for the Ljung–Box test is *that the residuals are independently distributed and therefore there is no h-th order serial correlation*, and the alternative hypothesis H_1 is that the residuals exhibit an h-th order serial correlation. From the chi-square distribution of Table 5.5 we calculate the value of α corresponding to the Q-statistic. If this value of α is less than 0.05 (5%), then we have to reject the null hypothesis that there is no h-order serial correlation in the residuals.

5.10 HOMOSCEDASTICITY AND HETEROSCEDASTICITY

5.10.1 Definition

The ordinary least squares (OLS) method for the calibration of a linear regression equation assumes the existence of *homoscedasticity*, that is, the error term has a constant variance and does not depend on the values of the independent variable X (Fig. 5.6, plot A). Therefore, each probability distribution for the dependent variable Y should have the same standard deviation for all values of the independent variable X (Fig. 5.6, plot B). *Heteroscedasticity* is the absence of homoscedasticity (Fig. 5.6, plot C).

Heteroscedasticity is a situation which may be encountered very often in transport demand models, where the data and observations usually refer and describe the behavior or the decision made by individuals. So, there is no reason for the forecaster to believe or to expect that individuals will have

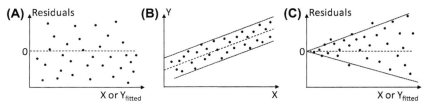

FIGURE 5.6 Visual examination for evidence of heteroscedasticity ((A and B) homoscedasticity, (C) heteroscedasticity). *Source: Compiled by the authors.*

similar behavior or preferences all the time. When performing a linear regression, what the forecaster is trying to do is to explain different person-alities and behaviors with one model. Therefore, he must be suspicious and ready to confront, if necessary, situations with heteroscedasticity.

The presence of heteroscedasticity does not cause OLS regression coef-ficient estimates to be biased, but it can cause OLS estimates of the variance, and thus of the standard errors and t-statistics (see §5.5.1), of the regression coefficients to be biased, possibly above or below the population variance. Consequently, regression analysis dealing with heteroscedastic data could provide an unbiased estimate for the relationship between the independent variable(s) and the dependent one; however, the biased standard errors and the resulting biased t-statistics will lead to biased values concerning the Student's t-test for the significance of the independent variable(s) and for the intercept.

Some authors underline that the heteroscedasticity by itself is not an adequate reason for the rejection of an otherwise sufficient (concerning other tests) model and that the unequal variance of residuals is worth correcting only when it causes severe problems for the calibration of the model. The most common and in most cases sufficient correction of heteroscedasticity is the use of logarithmized data (see §3.1.9 and §5.1.5) [300,306].

5.10.2 Testing for Homoscedasticity and Heteroscedasticity

5.10.2.1 The Breusch–Pagan Test

Consider the general form of the multiple linear regression described by Eq. (5.20). Since the application of the OLS method assumes homoscedasticity, the error term (ε) of Eq. (5.20) should present a constant variance σ^2 that does not depend on the values of independent variables X_j ($j = 1, 2, ..., k$). Thus, the multiple linear regression between ε^2 (as dependent variable) and X_j (as independent variables):

$$\varepsilon^2 = c_0 + c_1 \cdot X_1 + c_2 \cdot X_2 + \cdots + c_k \cdot X_k + e \tag{5.42}$$

should present, when homoscedasticity holds, equal partial regression co-efficients, that is, $c_1 = c_2 = \cdots = c_k$.

As we ignore the true population of the error term ε^2, we cannot use a sample to estimate it. However, we can use as estimator for the error term ε^2, the residuals $\widehat{\varepsilon}^2$ of the multiple linear regression model of Eq. (5.20), cali-brated with the use of OLS method. In such a way, we get the following auxiliary regression equation:

$$\widehat{\varepsilon}^2 = c_0 + c_1 \cdot X_1 + c_2 \cdot X_2 + \cdots + c_k \cdot X_k + e \tag{5.43}$$

which, after the calibration, will have a coefficient of determination $R^2_{\widehat{\varepsilon}^2}$.

The Breusch—Pagan test, named after the Australian econometrician Trevor Breusch and the Australian economist Adrian Pagan, is based on the calculation of the following statistic, which is based (like the Breusch—Godfrey LM test) on a Lagrange multiplier:

$$HT = n \cdot R_{\hat{\varepsilon}^2}^2 \tag{5.44}$$

for which it is assumed that it is distributed asymptotically, following the chi-square distribution with k degrees of freedom [307]. The *null hypothesis* for the Breusch—Pagan test is that *no heteroscedasticity* is present to residuals ($c_1 = c_2 = c_3 = \cdots = c_k = 0$). From the chi-square distribution of Table 5.5, we calculate the value of α corresponding to the statistic HT. If this value is less than 0.05 (5%), then we have to reject the null hypothesis of no heteroscedasticity in residuals.

5.10.2.2 The Glesjer Test

Named after the statistician Herbert Glejser, this test attempts to determine whether the variance of the dependent variable increases as a result of an increase of the magnitude of the values of independent variables. It is similar to the Breusch—Pagan test and is based on the regression between the absolute value of residuals of the calibrated model against the independent variables [308]. Thus, instead of the dependent variable $\hat{\varepsilon}^2$ of Eq. (5.43), in the Glesjer test we use the variable $|\hat{\varepsilon}|$ and we obtain the following auxiliary regression equation [309]:

$$|\hat{\varepsilon}| = c_0 + c_1 \cdot X_1 + c_2 \cdot X_2 + \cdots + c_k \cdot X_k + e \tag{5.45}$$

for which we calculate the coefficient of determination $R_{|\hat{\varepsilon}|}^2$. The next steps as well as the hypothesis test of the Glesjer test are exactly the same with the Breusch—Pagan test.

5.10.2.3 The Harvey—Godfrey Test

Named after the British econometricians Andrew Harvey and Leslie Godfrey, this test is similar to the Breusch—Pagan test and the Glesjer test since it follows the same reasoning. However, instead of the dependent variable $\hat{\varepsilon}^2$ of Eq. (5.43) or the dependent variable $|\hat{\varepsilon}|$ of Eq. (5.45), the Harvey—Godfrey test suggests the use of the variable $\ln\hat{\varepsilon}^2$ [310,311]. Thus, we get the following auxiliary multiple regression equation [309]:

$$\ln\hat{\varepsilon}^2 = c_0 + c_1 \cdot X_1 + c_2 \cdot X_2 + \cdots + c_k \cdot X_k + e \tag{5.46}$$

which, after the calibration, will have a coefficient of determination $R_{\ln\hat{\varepsilon}^2}^2$. The next steps of the Harvey—Godfrey test as well as the hypothesis test are the same with the Breusch—Pagan test.

5.10.2.4 The White Test

The White test, named after the American econometrician Halbert White, is similar to the Breusch–Pagan test since it makes use of the same statistic HT (see Eq. 5.44), for which it is also assumed that it is distributed asymptotically following the chi-square distribution (with a greater number of degrees of freedom, as we will see below), under the same null hypothesis for the absence of heteroscedasticity in the residuals. The only significant difference is that for the White test, the error term ε^2 is considered uncorrelated with the independent variables X_j (as in the Breusch–Pagan test), with the squares of the independent variables X_j^2 and with the cross products $X_j \cdot X_h$ ($j \neq h$, $j = 1, 2, ..., k$ and $h = 1, 2, ..., k$) of the independent variables, that is [312]:

$$\widehat{\varepsilon}^2 = d_0 + d_1 \cdot X_1 + \cdots + d_k \cdot X_k + d_{k+1} \cdot X_1^2 + d_{k+2} \cdot X_1 \cdot X_2 + \cdots + e \quad (5.47)$$

The inclusion in the White test of such a great number of auxiliary regressors is a weakness, since it uses too many degrees of freedom (as many as the number of the regressors X_j, X_j^2 and $X_j \cdot X_h$). For this reason, a variation of the White test permits the reduction of the degrees of freedom through the elimination of the cross products $X_j \cdot X_h$ and the level values X_j of independent variables. Thus, we will have:

$$\widehat{\varepsilon}^2 = d_0 + d_1 \cdot X_1^2 + d_2 \cdot X_2^2 + \cdots + d_k \cdot X_k^2 + e \quad (5.48)$$

5.10.2.5 The Autoregressive Conditional Heteroscedasticity Test

Autoregressive conditional heteroscedasticity (ARCH), a dynamic form of heteroscedasticity, is typical of time series models. A time series exhibiting conditional heteroscedasticity is said to have ARCH effects. The ARCH(p) test was brought about by the observation that in many time series the magnitude of the residuals appeared to be related to the magnitude of the recent residuals [313,314]. The test is based on the following auxiliary multiple regression model (p is the length of ARCH lags):

$$\widehat{\varepsilon}_i^2 = g_0 + g_1 \cdot \widehat{\varepsilon}_{i-1}^2 + g_2 \cdot \widehat{\varepsilon}_{i-2}^2 + \cdots + g_p \cdot g_1 \cdot \widehat{\varepsilon}_{i-p}^2 + e \quad (5.49)$$

which, after the calibration, has a coefficient of determination $R_{\widehat{\varepsilon}_p^2}^2$.

The ARCH(p) test, similar to the Breusch–Pagan test, is based on the calculation of the statistic:

$$\text{ARCH}(p) = (n - p) \cdot R_{\widehat{\varepsilon}_p^2}^2 \quad (5.50)$$

for which it is assumed that is distributed asymptotically following the chi-square distribution with p degrees of freedom. The *null hypothesis* H_0 for the ARCH(p) test is that there is no ARCH effect: this entails that all partial regression coefficients of Eq. (5.47) are equal to zero ($g_0 = g_1 = \dots = g_p = 0$). From the chi-square distribution (Table 5.5) we obtain the value of α corresponding to the statistic ARCH(p). If this value is less than 0.05 (5%), we reject the null hypothesis of no ARCH effect in the residuals.

5.10.2.6 Another Remedy to Confront Heteroscedasticity

As we have already mentioned, the presence of heteroscedasticity although does not affect the estimates of the regression coefficients, it can cause estimates of the variance, the standard error, and t-statistic of the regression coefficients to be biased. A well-known procedure for the remedy of heteroscedasticity is the application of the *generalized least squares* method, a procedure which results in a new set of estimates concerning the standard error and the t-statistic of the regression coefficients and the intercept of the calibrated model.

Let us consider the general form of a multiple linear regression model:

$$y_i = a + b_1 \cdot x_{i1} + b_2 \cdot x_{i2} + \cdots + b_k \cdot x_{ik} + \varepsilon_i \qquad (5.51)$$

where the variance of the error term ε_i, instead of being constant, is heteroscedastic, $\text{var}(\varepsilon_i) = \sigma_i^2$. By dividing each term of Eq. (5.51) by the standard deviation of the error term σ_i, we obtain the modified model [309]:

$$\frac{y_i}{\sigma_i} = a \cdot \frac{1}{\sigma_i} + b_1 \cdot \frac{x_{i1}}{\sigma_i} + b_2 \cdot \frac{x_{i2}}{\sigma_i} + \cdots + b_k \cdot \frac{x_{ik}}{\sigma_i} + \frac{\varepsilon_i}{\sigma_i} \qquad (5.52)$$

and by substituting

$$\frac{y_i}{\sigma_i} = y_i^*, \; \frac{1}{\sigma_i} = x_{i0}^*, \; \frac{x_{i1}}{\sigma_i} = x_{i1}^*, \; \frac{x_{i2}}{\sigma_i} = x_{i2}^*, \dots$$

we take

$$y_i^* = a \cdot x_{i0}^* + b_1 \cdot x_{i1}^* + b_2 \cdot x_{i2}^* + \cdots + b_k \cdot x_{ik}^* + \varepsilon_i' \qquad (5.53)$$

For the modified model of Eq. (5.53) it is valid that:

$$\text{var}(\varepsilon_i') = \frac{\text{var} \, \varepsilon_i}{\sigma_i^2} = 1 \text{ (constant)} \qquad (5.54)$$

In this way, the estimates obtained by the ordinary least squares of regressing y_i^* to $x_{i0}^*, \; x_{i1}^*, \; x_{i2}^*, \dots, x_{ik}^*$ constitute the so-called best linear unbiased estimators (BLUE) [309].

5.11 EVALUATION OF THE FORECASTING ACCURACY OF MODELS

5.11.1 A Plethora of Criteria

A fundamental issue in modeling is measuring the forecasting accuracy of a calibrated model for a given set of data or observations. Accuracy is defined as the goodness of fit or how well the forecasting model is able to reproduce data that are already known [315].

For the comparison of the forecasting accuracy of different regression models, some well-known statistics such as the mean absolute deviation, the mean squared error, and the mean absolute percentage error can be used as criteria. For these statistics, which are not informative by themselves but only when comparing different models, the smaller the values, the better the forecasting accuracy of the calibrated model is. On the contrary, Theil's inequality coefficient is a statistic that can evaluate both the fitting and the forecasting ability of each calibrated model, either in comparison among different models (all calibrated using the same set of data or observations) or for a specific model.

5.11.2 The Mean Absolute Deviation

The *mean absolute deviation* (MAD) is the sum of the absolute values of differences between the actual values y_i of available data or observations and the fitted by the regression model values $\widehat{y}_i$, divided by the number of available data or observations n:

$$\text{MAD} = \frac{1}{n} \cdot \sum_{i=1}^{n} \left| y_i - \widehat{y}_i \right| \tag{5.55}$$

5.11.3 The Mean Squared Error

The *mean squared error* (MSE), the most commonly used error metric, is the sum of squared errors (differences between the actual values y_i and the fitted by the regression model values $\widehat{y}_i$), divided by the number of available data or observations n:

$$\text{MSE} = \frac{1}{n} \cdot \sum_{i=1}^{n} \left(y_i - \widehat{y}_i \right)^2 \tag{5.56}$$

The MSE penalizes larger errors because squaring large numbers has a greater impact than squaring small numbers. Thus, the outliers have a greater effect on MSE than on MAD.

A variation of the MSE is the *root mean squared error* (RMSE), which is the square root of the MSE:

$$\text{RMSE} = \sqrt{\frac{1}{n} \cdot \sum_{i=1}^{n} \left(y_i - \widehat{y}_i \right)^2} \tag{5.57}$$

5.11.4 The Mean Absolute Percentage Error

The *mean absolute percentage error* (MAPE) is the average of the absolute errors (differences between the actual values y_i and the fitted by the regression model values $\widehat{y}_i$), divided by the actual values y_i of available data or observations:

$$\text{MAPE} = \frac{1}{n} \cdot \sum_{i=1}^{n} \left| \frac{y_i - \widehat{y}_i}{y_i} \right| \cdot 100 \tag{5.58}$$

5.11.5 Theil's Inequality Coefficient

Named after the Dutch econometrician Henri Theil, *Theil's inequality coefficient* (also known as Theil's U) between the actual values y_i and the fitted by a regression model values $\widehat{y}_i$ of n available data or observations is defined as [316]:

$$\text{Theil's U} = \frac{\sqrt{\frac{1}{n} \cdot \sum_{i=1}^{n} \left(y_i - \widehat{y}_i \right)^2}}{\sqrt{\frac{1}{n} \cdot \sum_{i=1}^{n} (y_i)^2} + \sqrt{\frac{1}{n} \cdot \sum_{i=1}^{n} \left(\widehat{y}_i \right)^2}}, \quad (i = 1, 2, \dots, n) \tag{5.59}$$

When Theil's U is calculated equal to zero for a model, then the model's forecasting ability is perfect, whereas when Theil's U is calculated equal to one, the model lacks any forecasting ability. In practice, values of Theil's U of 0.50 or less are considered to be good and values less than 0.10 are considered to be excellent [317,318].

Theil's U can be decomposed into the bias U^M, the variance U^S, and the covariance U^C proportions of U, respectively. The decomposition of Theil's U provides a powerful means of analyzing each component of the error in assessing the relative accuracy of the estimated demand by the calibrated model. The above proportions of Theil's U can be defined as [317,319]:

$$U^M = \frac{\left(\overline{y}_i - \overline{\widehat{y}}_i \right)^2}{\frac{1}{n} \cdot \sum_{i=1}^{n} \left(y_i - \widehat{y}_i \right)^2} \tag{5.60}$$

$$U^S = \frac{\left(\sigma_Y - \sigma_{\widehat{Y}} \right)^2}{\frac{1}{n} \cdot \sum_{i=1}^{n} \left(y_i - \widehat{y}_i \right)^2} \tag{5.61}$$

$$U^C = \frac{2 \cdot \left(1 - r_{Y\hat{Y}}\right) \cdot \sigma_Y \cdot \sigma_{\hat{Y}}}{\frac{1}{n} \cdot \sum_{i=1}^{n} \left(y_i - \hat{y}_i\right)^2} \tag{5.62}$$

where

$\sigma_{\hat{Y}}$	standard deviation of the fitted by the regression model values,
σ_Y	standard deviation of the actual values of data or observations,
$r_{Y\hat{Y}}$	Pearson correlation coefficient between the actual and the fitted values.

The bias proportion U^M is an indication of the systematic error, since it measures the extent to which the mean values of the fitted and actual time series deviate from each other. Whatever the value of the Theil's U, it is desirable for U^M to be close to zero. The variance proportion U^S indicates the ability of the model to replicate the degree of variability in the variable of interest. The covariance proportion U^C measures the nonsystematic (random) error of the model, which is very difficult to avoid, since it is unlikely to expect that predictions will be perfectly correlated with the actual data. Thus, this component of error is less worrisome than bias and variance [317,319].

Since bias, variance, and covariance are the three proportions of Theil's U, we will have:

$$U^M + U^S + U^C = 1 \tag{5.63}$$

5.12 AN APPLICATION OF MULTIPLE LINEAR REGRESSION ANALYSIS FOR TRANSPORT DEMAND

5.12.1 Multiple Linear Regression Analysis for the Calibration of an Econometric Model—Dependent and Independent Variables

We will illustrate a detailed step-by-step application of multiple linear regression for the analysis of rail passenger demand between 1960 and 2014 in Greece. The specific case presents some interesting characteristics, such as a great increase of rail fares (up to 50% in 2003), a significant reduction of frequency of services (route cuts and in some cases route cancellations), a serious economic and debt crisis (from 2009 upward), and the organization of a major event (the Olympic Games in 2004). According to the relevant bibliography [2,7,14,320−325], we selected the following independent variables for the modeling of rail passenger demand:

D_r rail trips per capita (dependent variable),
C_r unit cost of transport by rail (per passenger-km),
F_r frequency of services (vehicle-km),
I_{co} car ownership index,
GDP   gross domestic product per capita.

Variables referring to monetary units were adjusted in constant 2014 prices, according to the annual consumer price index. All variables incorporated in the model were indexed to a value of 100 for the year 1985 and then logarithmized. Fig. 5.7 presents the evolution between 1960 and 2014 for the dependent variable and the four independent variables.

5.12.2 Calibration of the Econometric Model

The calibrated econometric model will have the form:

$$\widehat{D}_r = \widehat{a} + \widehat{b}_1 \cdot C_r + \widehat{b}_2 \cdot F_r + \widehat{b}_3 \cdot I_{co} + \widehat{b}_4 \cdot GDP + \widehat{\varepsilon} \qquad (5.64)$$

The partial regression coefficients and the intercept of the model will be calculated with the use of a computer software (in this case: EViews); their values, with the corresponding standard errors (see §5.3.4) and t-statistic values (see §5.5.1 and §5.12.3 below) are given in Table 5.7. Thus, the final form of the calibrated model will be:

$$\widehat{D}_r = 5.1985 - 0.9865 \cdot C_r + 0.8104 \cdot F_r - 0.1989 \cdot I_{co} + 0.2494 \cdot GDP \quad (5.65)$$

Fig. 5.7 illustrates the econometric model's fitted values compared with the actual values of demand. A satisfactory model adjustment to real data can be observed, as well as the model's flexibility at transport demand curve inclination change points (turning points). Moreover, the signs of the regression coefficients of Eq. (5.65) are the expected ones, a negative sign for the relationship of rail demand to rail cost and private car ownership index, and a positive sign for the relationship of rail demand to per capita GDP, frequency of rail services, and the intercept.

5.12.3 Calculation of the t-statistic of the Regression Coefficients and of the Intercept of the Econometric Model

The t-statistic for each one of the independent variables (and the intercept) is calculated as the ratio of the regression coefficient of each independent variable to the standard error of that coefficient (see §5.3.4) (Table 5.7, last column).

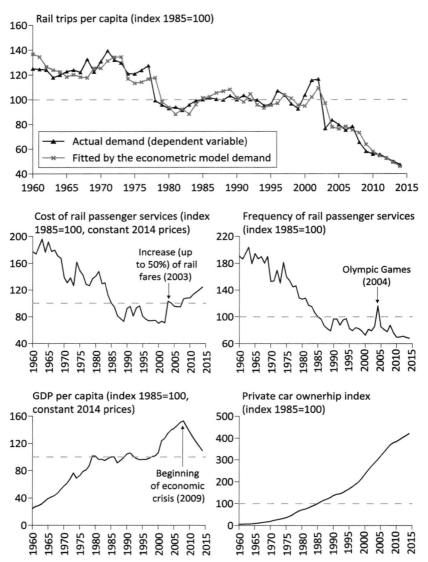

FIGURE 5.7 Evolution of the independent and the dependent variables for the calibration of an econometric model for the analysis and forecast of rail passenger demand—comparison between actual and fitted, by the econometric model, demand. *Source: Compiled by the authors, based on data of Ref. [326].*

The critical value for t-statistic is derived from the Student's t-distribution (Table 5.2) for $n-k-1$ degrees of freedom ($n = 55$ and $k = 4$) and for a confidence interval of 95%. All values of the t-statistic of Table 5.7 are much greater than the critical value ($t_c = 2.009$), permitting us to reject the null hypothesis

TABLE 5.7: Regression coefficients, standard errors, and t-statistic of the independent variables and the intercept.

Independent variable	Regression coefficient	Standard error	t-statistic
C_r	−0.9865	0.0584	−16.8921
F_r	0.8104	0.1140	7.1088
I_{co}	−0.1989	0.0526	−3.7814
GDP	0.2494	0.1028	2.4261
intercept	5.1985	0.4348	11.9561

Source: Compiled by the authors, based on data of EViews.

that the estimated regression parameters are equal to zero in favor of the alternative, that the parameters are different from zero. In conclusion, all parameters (independent variables and intercept) of the calibrated econometric model are statistically significant.

5.12.4 The F-test for the Overall Significance of the Econometric Model

The null hypothesis of the F-test is that all regression coefficients (except for the intercept) are jointly equal to zero and the alternative hypothesis is that they are nonequal to zero (see §5.5.2). The F-statistic is calculated from Eq. (5.26). For n = 55 and k = 4, it is calculated that F-statistic = 205.911.

From the F-distribution (Table 5.3) with 4 degrees of freedom for the numerator and 55 degrees of freedom for the denominator and probability $\alpha = 0.05$ (5%), we obtain, with linear interpolation[8], the critical value for F-statistic equal to 2.55. Thus, we can certainly reject the null hypothesis in favor of the alternative.

5.12.5 Coefficient of Determination and Adjusted Coefficient of Determination of the Econometric Model

The coefficient of determination R^2 for the calibrated econometric model of Eq. (5.64) is calculated from Eq. (5.29) as $R^2 = 0.943$. The coefficient of determination $\overline{R}^2$ adjusted to the degrees of freedom is calculated from Eq. (5.30), for n = 55 and k = 4, as $\overline{R}^2 = 0.938$. Both coefficients are almost

---

8. Linear interpolation is a method for the determination of unknown coordinates within the range of a set of known coordinates. It is based on the following equation, where X_1, X_2 = known abscissas, Y_1, Y_2 = known ordinates, X = target abscissa, and Y = interpolated ordinate: $Y = \frac{(X - X_1) \cdot (Y_2 - Y_1)}{X_2 - X_1} + Y_1$

equal to 0.94, which means that 94% of the variance in the dependent variable D_r is predictable from the independent variables C_r, F_r, I_{co}, and GDP.

5.12.6 Check of Residuals

5.12.6.1 Histogram and Normality Check

Fig. 5.8 illustrates the plot of residuals and the histogram of residuals of the econometric model; clearly the residuals are normally distributed. Reminding that for normally distributed residuals, the skewness is almost 0 and the kurtosis is close to 3, and by substituting in Eqs. (5.32), (5.33), and (5.34) the values of residuals of Fig. 5.8, we calculate the following values for the skewness, the kurtosis, and the Jarque—Bera test:

$$\text{skewness} = -0.553 \quad \text{kurtosis} = 3.615 \quad \text{Jarque—Bera test} = 3.674$$

For a value of the Jarque—Bera test = 3.674 and for two degrees of freedom, we can obtain (with linear interpolation) from the chi-square distribution (Table 5.5) the corresponding α-value, which is equal to 0.176. This value is greater than 0.05 (5%), meaning that we cannot reject the null hypothesis of normally distributed residuals; in other words there is a percentage of 17.6% (significantly greater from the threshold of 5%) of error when rejecting the null hypothesis. Thus, the residuals of the econometric model are normally distributed.

5.12.6.2 Determination of Possible Outliers

By using Eq. (5.35), we will examine the influence of residuals and possible outliers. Fig. 5.9 illustrates the Cook's distance D_i for the dependent variable for every year between 1960 and 2014. We can see the comparative high influence of the year 2003, which is compatible with the plot of residuals of Fig. 5.8. In any case, there is no indication for extreme outliers on the set of available data.

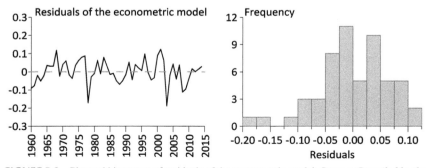

FIGURE 5.8 Plot and histogram of residuals of the econometric model. *Source: Compiled by the authors.*

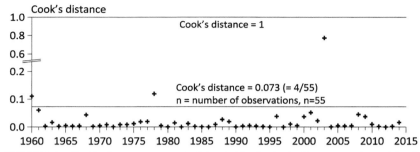

FIGURE 5.9 Cook's distance measure (and threshold values) of rail passenger demand for the determination of outliers. *Source: Compiled by the authors.*

5.12.7 Check for Serial Correlation

We will examine for the eventual presence of serial correlation in the residuals of the econometric model with the use of the Durbin-Watson test and the calculation of the DW-statistic (see §5.9.5.1). By applying the values of residuals of the econometric model to Eq. (5.36), we calculate that the DW-statistic is equal to 1.642. From Table 5.6, for $k = 4$ (number of independent variables) and $n = 55$ (number of available data), we obtain (with linear interpolation) the lower (d_L) and the upper (d_U) critical values of the DW-statistic to be equal to $d_L = 1.411$ and $d_U = 1.724$. Therefore, we have:

$$d_L = 1.411 < \text{DW-statistic} = 1.642 < d_U = 1.724$$

thus, the Durbin-Watson test is inconclusive concerning the presence or not of first-order serial correlation in the residuals. In such a case we proceed with the Breusch−Godfrey LM test (see §5.9.5.3) and the Ljung−Box test (see §5.9.5.4).

According to the Breusch−Godfrey LM test, by using Eq. (5.39) and for $h = 1$ we examine for an eventual presence of first-order serial correlation in residuals with the calibration of the following auxiliary model:

$$\widehat{\varepsilon}_i = d_0 + d_1 \cdot C_{r,i} + d_2 \cdot F_{r,i} + d_3 \cdot I_{co,i} + d_4 \cdot GDP_i + \underbrace{\rho_1 \cdot \widehat{\varepsilon}_{i-1}}_{\substack{\text{first-order} \\ \text{serial} \\ \text{correlation}}} + e$$

The coefficient of determination of the above model was calculated (with the use of a computer software) equal to $R^2_{\widehat{\varepsilon}} = 0.035$ and the LM statistic of Eq. (5.40) equal to LM = 1.923. For $h = 1$ degree of freedom, from the chi-square distribution of Table 5.5 we calculate the value of α corresponding to the statistic LM = 1.923. We obtain, with linear interpolation, $\alpha = 0.185$, a value which is greater than 0.05 (5%); this entails that we cannot reject the null hypothesis for no presence of first-order serial correlation in the residuals.

By applying one more time Eq. (5.39) for $h = 2$, we examine for the presence of second-order serial correlation in the residuals:

$$\widehat{\varepsilon}_i = d_0 + d_1 \cdot C_{r,i} + d_2 \cdot F_{r,i} + d_3 \cdot I_{co,i} + d_4 \cdot GDP_i + \underbrace{\rho_1 \cdot \widehat{\varepsilon}_{i-1}}_{\substack{\text{first-order} \\ \text{serial} \\ \text{correlation}}} + \underbrace{\rho_2 \cdot \widehat{\varepsilon}_{i-2}}_{\substack{\text{second-order} \\ \text{serial} \\ \text{correlation}}} + e$$

The coefficient of determination of the above auxiliary model becomes $R^2_{\widehat{\varepsilon}} = 0.048$ and the LM statistic equal to 2.665. For $h = 2$ degrees of freedom, from the chi-square distribution of Table 5.5 we obtain $\alpha = 0.269$, a value which is much greater than 0.05 (5%), meaning that again we cannot reject the null hypothesis for no presence of second-order serial correlation in the residuals. Therefore, the residuals of the econometric model are not serially correlated.

For the application of the Ljung—Box test, the determination of the values of the autocorrelation function for the residuals of the econometric model is required. Using a computer software package or applying Eq. (6.36), we calculate (Table 5.8) the values of the autocorrelation function for the examination of first-order ($h = 1$), second-order ($h = 2$), third-order ($h = 3$), and fourth-order ($h = 4$) serial correlation in the residuals. All values of probability α are greater than 0.05 (5%), thus we cannot reject the null hypothesis that the residuals are independently distributed and therefore there is no h-th order serial correlation. We confirm, in other words, the result of the Breusch—Godfrey LM test.

TABLE 5.8: Values of the autocorrelation function, of Q-statistic, and of the probability α corresponding to the Q-statistic (obtained from the chi-square distribution for h degrees of freedom).

Order of serial correlation h	Value ρ_h of the autocorrelation function	Q-statistic	Probability α
1	0.1591	1.4702	0.225
2	-0.1141	2.2408	0.326
3	-0.1356	3.3493	0.341
4	-0.0758	3.7021	0.448

Source: Compiled by the authors.

5.12.8 Check for Heteroscedasticity

5.12.8.1 The Informal Way: Visual Inspection of the Scatter Plot

A visual examination of the scatter plot between the values of rail passenger demand fitted by the econometric model and the residuals indicates evidence for the presence of heteroscedasticity (Fig. 5.10). As we mentioned in §5.10.1, heteroscedasticity is encountered in most transport demand models, which try to generalize and describe the behavior or the decisions made by individuals with heterogeneous characteristics.

Beyond the visual inspection of residuals, we will examine the presence of heteroscedasticity with the use of the appropriate statistical tests, such as the Breusch–Pagan test (see §5.10.2.1), the Glesjer test (see §5.10.2.2), the Harvey–Godfrey test (see §5.10.2.3), and the White test (see §5.10.2.4). The above tests provide (as we will see below) conflicting results for the specific problem.

5.12.8.2 The Bruce–Pagan Test

Based on the general form of Eq. (5.43), we will apply the Breusch–Pagan test by calculating the coefficient of determination $R^2_{\widehat{\varepsilon}^2}$ of the auxiliary model:

$$\widehat{\varepsilon}^2 = c_0 + c_1 \cdot C_r + c_2 \cdot F_r + c_3 \cdot I_{co} + c_4 \cdot GDP$$

where $\widehat{\varepsilon}^2$ are the squared residuals and C_r, F_r, I_{co}, and GDP are the independent variables of the calibrated econometric model of Eq. (5.60).

The coefficient of determination of the above model was calculated (with the use of a computer software package such as EViews, MATLAB, Microfit, Minitab, NumXL, PcGive, R, SPSS, Stata, XLSTAT, etc.) equal to $R^2_{\widehat{\varepsilon}^2} = 0.241$ and the HT statistic of Eq. (5.44) equal to HT = 13.255. For k = 4 (equal to the number of independent variables C_r, F_r, I_{co}, and GDP) degrees of freedom, from the chi-square distribution of Table 5.5 we calculate the value of α corresponding to the statistic HT = 13.288. We obtain $\alpha = 0.01$, a value which

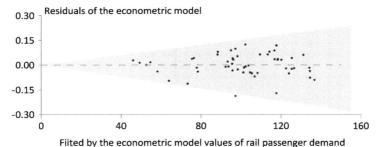

FIGURE 5.10 Visual examination for evidence of heteroscedasticity to the residuals of the econometric model. *Source: Compiled by the authors.*

is less than 0.05 (5%), meaning that we have to reject the null hypothesis of no heteroscedasticity in the residuals.

5.12.8.3 The Glesjer Test

The application of the Glesjer test will be based on the general form of Eq. (5.45) and the calculation of the coefficient of determination $R^2_{|\hat{\varepsilon}|}$ of the following auxiliary model:

$$|\hat{\varepsilon}| = c_0 + c_1 \cdot C_r + c_2 \cdot F_r + c_3 \cdot I_{co} + c_4 \cdot GDP$$

where $|\hat{\varepsilon}|$ are the absolute values of the residuals and C_r, F_r, I_{co}, and GDP are the independent variables of the calibrated econometric model of Eq. (5.65). The coefficient of determination of the auxiliary model was calculated equal to $R^2_{|\hat{\varepsilon}|} = 0.161$, and the HT statistic of Eq. (5.44) equal to HT = 8.855. For k = 4 (equal to the number of independent variables C_r, F_r, I_{co}, and GDP) degrees of freedom and HT = 8.855, from the chi-square distribution of Table 5.5 we obtain $\alpha = 0.06$, a value which is greater than 0.05 (5%); this entails that we cannot reject the null hypothesis of no heteroscedasticity in the residuals and thus the residuals are homoscedastic.

5.12.8.4 The Harvey–Godfrey Test

The application of the Harvey–Godfrey test will be based on the general form of Eq. (5.46) and on the calculation of the coefficient of determination $R^2_{\ln\hat{\varepsilon}^2}$ of the auxiliary model:

$$\ln\hat{\varepsilon}^2 = c_0 + c_1 \cdot C_r + c_2 \cdot F_r + c_3 \cdot I_{co} + c_4 \cdot GDP$$

where $\ln\hat{\varepsilon}^2$ is the natural logarithm of the squared residuals and C_r, F_r, I_{co}, and GDP are the independent variables of the calibrated econometric model of Eq. (5.65). The coefficient of determination of the above auxiliary model was calculated equal to $R^2_{\ln\hat{\varepsilon}^2} = 0.122$ and the HT statistic of Eq. (5.44) equal to HT = 6.710. As in Glesjer test, for k = 4 degrees of freedom and HT = 6.710, from the chi-square distribution of Table 5.5 we obtain $\alpha = 0.15$, a value which is greater than 0.05 (5%), meaning that we cannot reject the null hypothesis of no heteroscedasticity in the residuals and thus the residuals are homoscedastic.

5.12.8.5 The White Test

Based on the general form of Eq. (5.47), we will apply the White test by calculating the coefficient of determination $R^2_{\hat{\varepsilon}^2}$ of the auxiliary model:

$$\hat{\varepsilon}^2 = d_0 + d_1 \cdot C_r + d_2 \cdot F_r + d_3 \cdot I_{co} + d_4 \cdot GDP + d_5 \cdot C_r^2 + d_6 \cdot F_r^2 + d_7 \cdot I_{co}^2 +$$
$$+ d_8 \cdot GDP^2 + d_9 \cdot C_r \cdot F_r + d_{10} \cdot C_r \cdot I_{co} + d_{11} \cdot C_r \cdot GDP + d_{12} \cdot F_r \cdot I_{co} +$$
$$+ d_{13} \cdot F_r \cdot GDP + d_{14} \cdot I_{co} \cdot GDP$$

The coefficient of determination of the above model was calculated equal to $R^2_{\widehat{\varepsilon}^2} = 0.530$ and the HT statistic of Eq. (5.44) for the White test equal to $HT = 29.150$. For $k = 14$ (equal to the number of the regressors[9]) degrees of freedom, from the chi-square distribution of Table 5.5 we calculate the value of α corresponding to the statistic $HT = 29.150$. We obtain $\alpha = 0.01$, a value which is less than 0.05 (5%), meaning that we have to reject the null hypothesis of no heteroscedasticity in residuals.

We can come to the same conclusion by using the modified White test, without the level values and the cross products between independent variables. In this case, by using the general form of Eq. (5.48), we can apply the modified White test by calculating the coefficient of determination $R^2_{\widehat{\varepsilon}^2}$ of the auxiliary model:

$$\widehat{\varepsilon}^2 = d_0 + d_1 \cdot C_r^2 + d_2 \cdot F_r^2 + d_3 \cdot I_{co}^2 + d_4 \cdot GDP^2$$

The coefficient of determination of the above model was calculated equal to $R^2_{\widehat{\varepsilon}^2} = 0.324$ and the HT statistic of Eq. (5.43) for the modified White test equal to $HT = 17.826$. For $k = 4$ (equal to the number of the regressors C_r^2, F_r^2, I_{co}^2, and GDP^2), from the chi-square distribution of Table 5.5 we obtain $\alpha = 0.001$, which means that we have to reject the null hypothesis of no heteroscedasticity in the residuals.

It is obvious that there is no clear conclusion concerning the presence of heteroscedasticity or homoscedasticity. Two tests, the Breusch–Pagan test and the White test, suggest that we have to reject the null hypothesis of no heteroscedasticity in the residuals, and therefore the desired homoscedasticity does not exist in the residuals. However, two other tests, the Glesjer test and Harvey–Godfrey test, conclude that we cannot reject the null hypothesis of no heteroscedasticity in the residuals and therefore the desired homoscedasticity exists in the residuals. We explain in the next paragraph how such a situation can be confronted. In any case, as we have already underlined, heteroscedasticity by itself is not an adequate reason for the rejection of a sufficient (concerning other tests) model; on the other hand heteroscedasticity is in fact a situation which may be met very often in transport demand models which describe behavior or decisions made by individuals, and there is no reason for the forecaster to expect that individuals have always a similar and repeated behavior or preferences.

In any case, the application of the methodology described in §5.10.2.6 for the remedy of heteroscedasticity will permit a correction of the biased standard error and the t-statistic of the independent variables and the intercept. The new unbiased estimates of these parameters for the modified econometric model of

---

9. C_r, F_r, I_{co}, GDP, C_r^2, F_r^2, I_{co}^2, GDP^2, $C_r \times F_r$, $C_r \times I_{co}$, $C_r \times GDP$, $F_r \times I_{co}$, $F_r \times GDP$, $I_{co} \times GDP$

TABLE 5.9: Unbiased values for the standard error and the t-statistic for the independent variables and the intercept of the modified, free of heteroscedasticity, econometric model.

Independent variable	Regression coefficient	Standard error	t-statistic
C_r	−0.9865	0.0589	−16.7487
F_r	0.8104	0.1913	4.2363
I_{co}	−0.1989	0.0728	−2.7321
GDP	0.2494	0.1053	2.3685
intercept	5.1985	0.6841	7.5990

Source: Compiled by the authors, based on data of EViews.

Eq. (5.64) are presented in Table 5.9. The values of regression coefficients and of coefficient of determination R^2 remain, as it was expected, unchanged. All values of the t-statistic of Table 5.9 are much greater than the critical value ($t_c = 2.009$, see §5.5.1), thus we can conclude that all parameters (independent variables and intercept) of the calibrated econometric model of Eq. (5.65) remain statistically significant.

5.12.9 Forecasting Accuracy and Ability of the Econometric Model

We will calculate the mean absolute deviation (MAD), the mean squared error (MSE), the root mean squared error (RMSE), and the mean absolute percentage error (MAPE), although these statistics are not informative by themselves but only when we compare different models (which is not our case). From Eqs. (5.55)−(5.58) we have:

MAD = 0.050, MSE = 0.040, RMSE = 0.064, MAPE = 0.0111

On the other hand, Theil's U provides important information about the forecasting accuracy and the forecasting ability concerning the fitting of turning points of the calibrated econometric model. By using Eq. (5.59), we calculate Theil's U = 0.007, a value less than 0.10, which indicates an excellent model. We will proceed to the decomposition of Theil's U into its bias U^M, variance U^S, and covariance U^C proportions. From Eqs. (5.60)−(5.62), we calculate:

$$U^M \approx 0 \left(=1.306 \cdot 10^{-7} \right), \ U^S = 0.0145, \ U^C = 0.9855 \ \left(U^M + U^S + U^C = 1 \right)$$

Therefore, the 98.55% of the value of Theil's U comes from the covariance proportion U^C that measures the unavoidable and preferable (compared to the bias U^M and the variance U^S proportion) nonsystematic error of the calibrated econometric model.

Chapter 6

Trend Projection and Time Series Methods

Chapter Outline

6.1 THE ESSENCE OF TIME SERIES METHODS OF FORECAST: EXTEND THE PAST INTO THE FUTURE

6.1.1 Time as the Only Dependent Variable in Time Series Methods of Forecast

Time series methods are the most commonly used among quantitative methods for a quick estimation or forecast of future transport demand, when reliable data describing the evolution and tendency of past demand are available.

Modeling of Transport Demand. https://doi.org/10.1016/B978-0-12-811513-8.00006-6
Copyright © 2019 Elsevier Inc. All rights reserved.

Time series can be defined as a series of data recorded (by an observer or a recording unit) and analyzed in a time order, at equally spaced time periods (e.g., per year, month, day, hour). The only independent variable in time series methods is time. All other variables affecting transport supply and demand are considered in time series methods to pursue the same path in the future as in the past and to continue over the course of time to affect transport demand in the same manner and with the same degree of influence.

Time series methods are based on laws and techniques of the science of statistics, which can be defined as the branch of mathematics that deals with the collection, classification, analysis, and interpretation of numerical data describing a phenomenon. The purpose of the science of statistics is multifold; however, critical aspects of statistics focus on understanding, discovering, and interpreting the mechanisms that follow the data of the phenomenon under study, deriving forecasts and conclusions about its evolution in the future and suggesting methods and indices that can assure the validity of forecasts and conclusions. The various methods employed in statistics are based on solid and widely accepted mathematical foundations, and for this reason they are characterized by a high degree of objectivity.

Time series methods do not aim at explaining or researching the causal structure of the transport demand problem but simply at detecting its pattern and evolution over time.

6.1.2 Assumptions, Conditions of Use, and Suitability of Time Series Methods

Time series methods cannot establish any kind of cause and effect relationship between transport demand and the factors affecting it. They only give the possibility of understanding, recognizing, and describing in the form of an analytical equation the evolution over time of transport demand. Once such an equation is calibrated (that is, a relationship is established between the dependent variable [demand] on the one hand and the independent variable [time] on the other) and checked for its validity statistically (with the help of the appropriate statistical tests), then it can be used for forecasts within a rather limited future range of time.

The fundamental assumption that should be fulfilled before considering any time series method is that *all factors (such as costs, travel times, revenues of customers, elasticities, etc.) which affected transport demand in the past will remain the same in the future, with their degree of influence unchanged, while the characteristics of supply will also remain unchanged.* This fundamental assumption may be (more or less) close to the reality only for short-term or at the maximum for medium-term forecasts, with a forecasting time range going from some weeks to some years ahead. The shorter the period of forecast, the more likely it is to achieve statistically valid and accurate results.

6.1.3 Components of a Time Series: Trend, Seasonal, Cyclic, Random

Any time series is composed of one or more of the following components (Fig. 6.1):

- trend,
- seasonal,
- cyclical,
- random.

The *trend* component is nonstationary (see §5.1.5) and reflects and incorporates the general characteristics and the tendency (increasing, decreasing, etc.) of the time series.

The *seasonal* component is a data pattern that repeats itself after a period of days, weeks, months, or quarters. It is also a nonstationary component and represents fluctuations around the curve of the trend component. Typical seasonal fluctuations for some sectors of transport are increased air transport demand during the summer months, increased demand for metro and bus systems at the beginning and the end of a working day, increased road traffic to resorts during weekends, etc.

The *cyclical* component is also nonstationary and represents oscillations over long periods (usually some years) around the curve of trend component. These are similar to the cyclic variations of the economic cycle (recession, depression, recovery, prosperity). For instance, air transport manifests cyclical variations of a return period of around 10 years (see Fig. 2.5).

The *random* component (known also as *error term* or *disturbance* or *noise*; see also §5.3.1) is an irregular component and it does not exhibit any type of discernible pattern. The random component is inexplicable, unpredictable, should be stationary, and reflects the effects on demand of known or unknown variables or factors that we either ignore or are unable to measure and to consider (such as the effects of lifestyle in the choice of a transport mode).

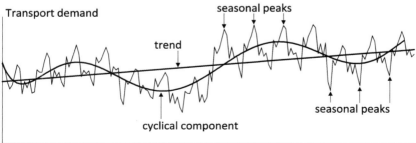

FIGURE 6.1 Time series components. *Source: Compiled by the authors.*

6.1.4 The Various Time Series Methods for the Forecast of Transport Demand

The following are the most frequently used time series methods for the forecast of transport demand:

- *Trend projection*: The available statistical data of demand are plotted in a scatter diagram, which has as abscissa time on constant intervals (e.g., per year, quarter, month, day, hour) and as ordinate values of demand. The forecaster should look for a curve or (preferably) for an equation relating demand to time, which best adjusts and fits to data already plotted. To establish the correlation between two variables (which in the case of trend projection are demand and time), many statistical methods are available, the most common among them being simple linear regression which is based on the ordinary least squares method (see §5.3). Trend projection can follow a linear pattern (§6.2.2) or a nonlinear one (§6.2.3).
- Autoregressive models or processes, denoted as AR(p): These specify that the current value of the dependent variable depends linearly on (and is generated by) the weighted average of its own previous p values and on a stochastic term[1]. Autoregressive models are analyzed in §6.7.4.
- Moving average models or processes, denoted as MA(q): These specify that the current value of the dependent variable depends linearly on (and is generated by) the current and the past q values of a stochastic term. The moving average models are analyzed in §6.7.5 and should not be confused with the moving average method (see §6.6.1).
- Autoregressive moving average models or processes, denoted as ARMA(p,q): these describe a mixed process that combines two polynomial terms, an autoregressive AR(p) and a moving average MA(q). Autoregressive moving average models are analyzed in §6.7.6.
- Panel data models: These refer to statistical data which may come from different observers or observation units. Time series is just a special and simple case of panel data which are collected by one observer or observation unit; thus another term for panel data is time series cross-sectional [328–330]. Panel data are categorized as balanced, if every panel member is observed for the same amount of time or unbalanced otherwise.
- Least median of squares models: While trying to fit a curve to statistical data of the past, it was observed that when some data are very distanced from the fitted curve, the least squares estimation is inefficient and can be biased. In such cases, a robust regression, known as least median of squares (LMS) regression, has been developed so as to achieve a forecast without the effect of extreme values (outliers, see §5.9.3, §5.12.6.2, and §6.3.5).

---

1. A stochastic term represents systems or phenomena which change in a random way, following a purely random process with zero mean and constant variance. A typical example of a stochastic term is the white noise (see §6.7.2) [2,285,298,300].

6.2 LINEAR AND NONLINEAR TREND PROJECTION METHODS FOR THE FORECAST OF FUTURE TRANSPORT DEMAND

6.2.1 Assumptions of Trend Projection Methods

Trend projection is a usual and common method of forecasting future transport demand: it entails the collection of statistical data of demand over some period of time and then the attempt to project them to the future. The fundamental assumption is that all factors which have affected demand in the past will continue to exert the same degree of influence in the future, and that the only independent variable affecting demand will be time. If statistical data are available, a trend projection forecast requires some hours of forecasting calculations.

6.2.2 Linear and Nonlinear Trend Projection

Linearity is a convenient assumption for any scientific problem, as it is very easy both to understand and to analyze a linear problem, which is graphically represented by a straight line. In such a case of a linear problem, the dependent variable has constant rates of evolution in relation to the independent one(s).

Linearity, however, is not encountered very often. Most problems have a nonlinear character, which means that the dependent variable is nonlinearly related to the independent one(s). The most typical method of analyzing nonlinear problems is to take natural logarithms (for which the base e of the logarithm is Euler's number, approximately equal to 2.718281, see §3.1.9) for both sides of a nonlinear equation, and thus transform the nonlinear problem into a linear one. As we have already mentioned in §3.1.9, it is preferable to use natural logarithms to stabilize the variance of the time series and in addition the coefficients on the natural-log scale are directly interpretable as approximate proportional differences [178].

6.2.3 Some Forms of Curves for Nonlinear Trend Projection

6.2.3.1 Exponential

An exponential correlation of the dependent variable Y in relation to the independent one T implies constant rates of increase (or decrease) among them. If for instance the independent variable T is time and the dependent one Y is transport demand, an exponential relationship between them implies constant annual percentage increases of demand in relation to time. This is a situation we often confront in new transport projects (e.g., a new airport, a new metro line, etc.) or in the first years of operation of a new transport service

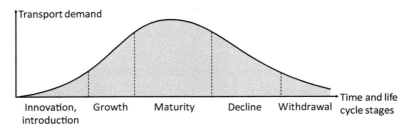

FIGURE 6.2 Life cycle of a transport product or a transport service. *Source: Compiled by the authors.*

or company. In such cases we encounter an upward constantly increasing demand curve as a result of the attractiveness of the new transport product or transport service (Fig. 6.2, left side). However, an exponential correlation may have negative rates (Fig. 6.2, right side), when the transport product or transport service has entered the negative and downward stage of its life cycle evolution.

The simplest form of an exponential relationship between the dependent variable Y and an independent one T (Fig. 6.3A, left) is:

$$Y = a \cdot (1 + b)^T \tag{6.1}$$

By taking logarithms on both sides of Eq. (6.1) we will have:

$$\ln Y = \ln \left[a \cdot (1 + b)^T \right] \Rightarrow \ln Y = \ln a + T \cdot \ln (1 + b) \tag{6.2}$$

Thus, by taking logarithms in an exponential correlation, we transform the exponential Eq. (6.1) into a linear logarithmic equation (Fig. 6.3A, right) and we can apply linear regression analysis (see §5.3 and §5.4).

6.2.3.2 Parabolic Second Degree

A parabolic correlation between variables Y and T (Fig. 6.3B) has the form:

$$Y = a + b \cdot T + c \cdot T^2 \tag{6.3}$$

The upward and downward cycles of a transport service in a parabolic evolution of demand are similar to those of an exponential evolution of demand. More particularly, if the independent variable is time and $c > 0$, a parabolic evolution of demand implies that the growth of demand in absolute terms per unit time increases linearly with time, while the rate of growth decreases with time.

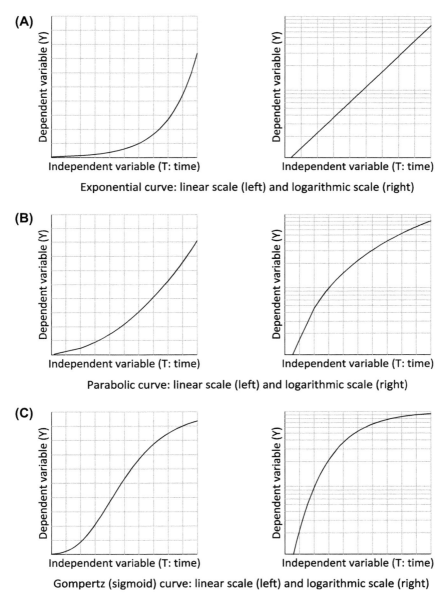

(A)

Exponential curve: linear scale (left) and logarithmic scale (right)

(B)

Parabolic curve: linear scale (left) and logarithmic scale (right)

(C)

Gompertz (sigmoid) curve: linear scale (left) and logarithmic scale (right)

FIGURE 6.3 Curves of exponential, parabolic, and Gompertz functions between an independent and a dependent variable in linear and logarithmic scale. *Source: Compiled by the authors, based on Ref. [351].*

6.2.3.3 Gompertz Sigmoid Curve

A Gompertz curve (or Gompertz function), named after the British mathematician Benjamin Gompertz, represents the evolution of demand over long periods of time in a sigmoid form, where growth is slower at the start and the end of a time period (Fig. 6.3C) [331,332].

A Gompertz correlation between Y and T is described by the equation:

$$Y = a \cdot e^{-b \cdot e^{-c \cdot T}} \qquad (6.4)$$

where a is the asymptote of demand curve at the saturation level, b sets the displacement along the x-axis, and c sets the growth rate of demand.

In all previous equations, coefficients a, b, and c are calculated by regression analysis (see §5.4).

6.3 METHODOLOGY, SUCCESSIVE STEPS, AND STATISTICAL METHODS FOR TREND PROJECTION FORECASTS—A TYPICAL EXAMPLE

6.3.1 Reliable Statistical Data as a Prerequisite for Trend Projection Methods

Trend projection cannot work unless reliable statistical data are available, which should cover at least 7—10 years [127]. In any case, the period covered by statistical data should give the forecaster a clear idea about whether demand is in its developing (upward), saturation, or declining (downward) stage (see Fig. 6.2).

Let us consider as an example the forecast of the annual number of passengers of Eurostar trains between London and Paris. Data can be accessed on the Internet site https://www.getlinkgroup.com/uk/home/ and can cover the years from 1995 to 2016 (22 years). The authority providing the data can be considered as reliable. However, any opportunity to cross-validate data provided by one authority with other independent sources is an additional factor that may strengthen the reliability of data.

6.3.2 Curves That Fit to Data

We plot the available data in a scatter diagram with abscissa the time (years 1995, 1996,…, 2016) and ordinate the annual number of passengers in Eurostar trains (Fig. 6.4, numerical data of Eurostar trains on Table 6.5, first column). The ordinates of the diagram clearly take the form of an upward curve of demand in the developing stage of the life cycle of a transport service. What is not evident from Fig. 6.4, however, is whether the phenomenon under study develops linearly or exponentially. For this

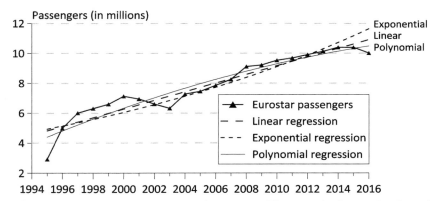

FIGURE 6.4 Data of the annual demand of passengers of Eurostar trains between London and Paris and plausible curves that fit to the data. *Source: Compiled by the authors based on data of Ref. [333].*

reason, we will attempt to adjust to the available data a linear, an exponential, and a polynomial regression.

6.3.3 Regression Analysis and Coefficient of Determination

We enter the data plotted in Fig. 6.4 in a computer software package[2], which incorporates many forms of regression analysis. We will try a linear, an exponential, and a polynomial regression analysis, and for each one of them we can calculate the regression equation and the coefficient of determination R^2 (see §5.7), the latter testifying whether the calibrated regression equation fits well with the data of the problem under study.

If we fit a linear regression, the computer software package in use provides us with the equation:

$$D_t = 290,086.47 \cdot t - 573,902,003.80 \qquad (6.5)$$

and a value of the coefficient of determination $R^2 = 0.904$, where:

D_t fitted, by regression analysis, demand for the year t,
t   successive years, 1995, 1996,..., 2016.

If we fit an exponential regression, the computer software provides us with the equation:

$$D_t = e^{0.04086 \cdot t} \cdot 1.961 \cdot 10^{-29} \qquad (6.6)$$

with a value of the coefficient of determination $R^2 = 0.785$.

---

2. Such as EViews, MATLAB, Microfit, Minitab, NumXL, PcGive, R, SPSS, Stata, XLSTAT, etc.

Finally, if we fit a second-degree polynomial regression, the computer software provides us with the equation:

$$D_t = -6,080.83 \cdot t^2 + 24,680,278.49 \cdot t - 2.503 \cdot 10^{10} \qquad (6.7)$$

with a value of the coefficient of determination $R^2 = 0.916$.

6.3.4 Choice of the Appropriate Regression Curve and Equation

The choice of the curve and equation that best fits with the data of the problem and consequently represents the problem in a mathematically correct way will be based on the value of the coefficient of determination R^2. The higher the value of R^2, the better the mathematical expression of the regression analysis fits with the data of the problem, thus assuring a satisfactory correlation of the dependent variable (demand) with the only independent variable (time).

In our case, both linear and second-degree polynomial regression provide high values for R^2, which are very close to 1. Indeed, the linear regression has a value of $R^2 = 0.904$, which means that 90.4% of the variance of the dependent variable (Eurostar passengers) around its mean is explained from the linear regression. Similarly, the polynomial regression has a value of $R^2 = 0.916$, which entails a plausible difference between fitted by the polynomial regression values and actual values of Eurostar trains demand of no more than 8.4% ($= 1.0 - 0.916$) on average. On the contrary, the exponential regression presents a weaker explanatory ability (in comparison with the linear and the polynomial regression) of the variation of the dependent variable ($R^2 = 0.785$).

However, when the values of R^2 of various regression equations are very close, the forecaster should consider very carefully which regression curve represents more satisfactorily the problem under study. Indeed, a linear evolution implies constant rates of annual increase of demand, which of course cannot continue for a long time. A second-degree polynomial evolution, on the other hand, which turns asymptotically, may be closer to the reality of transport demand problems. Therefore, in addition to a good statistical analysis, certain other features such as the experience and intuition of the forecaster are essential to put together a good forecast.

6.3.5 Check for Outliers

Before finalizing the form of the regression equation, a careful examination by the forecaster of the available statistical data can lead him or her to the observation that in the first year of full operation (1995) of the Channel Tunnel, demand (passenger services in operation since November 1994) had a very low value. Clearly, data for the year 1995 represent an outlier (Fig. 6.5) and could be either omitted (as it is the first year of operation) or analyzed by more robust regression methods, which are not sensitive to outliers or other violations of the assumptions of the usual regression methods, such as the least median of squares method [334].

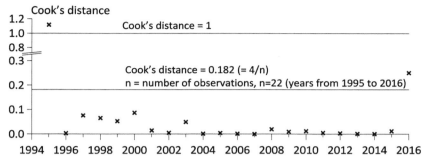

FIGURE 6.5 Cook's distance measure and threshold values (see §5.9.3) for the determination of outliers of the annual demand of passengers of Eurostar trains. *Source: Compiled by the authors based on data of Ref. [333].*

If we eliminate the value of year 1995 and proceed to the regression for the years 1996–2016, then the equations of the linear, exponential, and second-degree polynomial regression will be modified as follows:

$$D_t = 262,940.80 \cdot t - 519,357,310.20, \text{ with } R^2 = 0.936,$$
$$D_t = e^{0.03337 \cdot t} \cdot 6.757 \cdot 10^{-23}, \text{ with } R^2 = 0.921,$$
$$D_t = -537,46 \cdot t^2 + 2,419,175.95 \cdot t - 2,682,041,455, \text{ with } R^2 = 0.937.$$

We realize that a wiser use of the data of the problem may increase greatly the degree of correlation and the coefficient of determination R^2 for all three regression equations. Moreover, now the linear regression equation appears to have (together with the second-degree polynomial regression) the best value for R^2.

6.3.6 Ex Post Assessment

Any forecast should be assessed ex post by comparing the realized values of demand with the forecasted ones and thus validating (or invalidating) the forecast. Some form of ex post assessment can be undertaken even at the stage of choosing the appropriate regression equation. For instance, in our example, we could try all regression equations by using statistical data until the year 2014, calculate the forecasted demand for the years 2015 and 2016, and compare these values with the available statistical data of actual demand for the years 2015 and 2016. This would lead to a better understanding of which regression equation should be adopted to validate the statistical data in a more satisfactory way.

6.3.7 The Period of Forecast of a Trend Projection

After selecting the most appropriate regression equation, the question which arises is for how long this forecast can be used in the future. To achieve statistically accurate forecasts, the period of forecast of demand should not exceed half the period covered by the statistical data, and in any case no more than the period for which the supply can be considered unchanged [127]. Such a trend projection can provide reasonable forecasts as long as is still valid the fundamental assumption that all factors which affected demand in the past remain the same and with the same degree of influence, while the supply and demand characteristics remain unchanged.

6.4 SOME INDEXES USED FOR AN EXPLICIT EX POST ASSESSMENT OF A TREND PROJECTION FORECAST

When conducting any kind of forecast, the usual criterion for assessing its fitness to statistical data is the coefficient of determination R^2. Values of R^2 greater than 0.85 are considered as a satisfactory index that the realized values of the specific forecast will not exceed on average by more than $\pm 15\%$ the forecasted values.

Ex post assessment of a trend projection is based, in terms of systematic bias, on the degree of divergence DV_i between the realized and the forecasted values, which is given by the following equation:

$$DV_i = \frac{r_i - f_i}{r_i} \tag{6.8}$$

where

r_i realized value of demand for the year i (i=1, 2,..., n),
f_i forecasted value of demand for the year i.

An ex post assessment of any kind of calibration is based on the following criteria [335]:

- The maximum degree of divergence max $DV_i = \max \{DV_1, DV_2,..., DV_n\}$, where n is the number of observations for which we have available data for the forecasted and the realized values. In a good forecast, $DV_{max} < 15\%$.
- The mean divergence DV_{mean}, defined by the equation:

$$DV_{mean} = \frac{1}{n} \cdot \sum_{i=1}^{n} |DV_i| = \frac{1}{n} \cdot \sum_{i=1}^{n} \left| \frac{r_i - f_i}{f_i} \right| \tag{6.9}$$

In a perfect forecast, $DV_{mean} = 0$. Eq. (6.9) is another expression for the mean absolute percentage error, similar to Eq. (5.58).

- Whether there is a balance over time of errors with positive and negative sign. If we plot a diagram with axis of abscissas the time and axis of ordinates the positive and the negative values of the degree of divergence, then the values of the degree of divergence will form a band around the

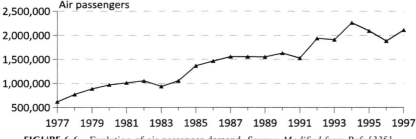

FIGURE 6.6 Evolution of air passenger demand. *Source: Modified from Ref. [335].*

axis of time. The better the balance between the area of positive and negative divergences, the more accurate to reality the forecast will be.

We will illustrate the above criteria in the case of the forecast of international passenger demand for the airport of Rhodes (southeastern Greece), which was conducted in 1997. Values of future demand for the years 1998–2010 were forecasted by projecting historical statistical data of demand of the period from 1977 to 1997 (Fig. 6.6). The period covered by the statistical data (21 years) is representative of the problem under study and gives a clear idea of the section of the life cycle to which the forecast refers. The period of forecast (1998–2010, 13 years) is a bit longer than the half of the period covered by statistical data (1977–97, 21 years).

In this forecast of the projection of statistical data, the forecaster had to choose between two models:

- a linear regression, based on the assumption that demand will continue for the period of forecast with constant growth rates, for which the calibrated equation was:

$$D_t = 75,309.5 \cdot t - 1.48364 \cdot 10^8, \quad R^2 = 0.931 \qquad (6.10)$$

where

t   successive years: 1998, 1999,…, 2010.

- a second-degree polynomial equation calibrated for the projection of demand in the future:

$$D_t = -454.729 \cdot t^2 + 1.88249 \cdot 10^6 \cdot t - 1.9437 \cdot 10^9, \quad R^2 = 0.932 \qquad (6.11)$$

which makes the appeal that, for an essentially tourist airport, demand will have an asymptotical tendency after an expansion period, as tourism reaches a saturation level, in part because of local infrastructure limitations in the area [335].

TABLE 6.1: Ex post assessment of a trend projection forecast—Realized and forecasted values of demand.

Year	Realized passenger demand	Forecasted values		Degree of divergence (%)	
		Linear regression (Eq. 6.10)	Second-degree polynomial regression (Eq. 6.11)	Linear regression (Eq. 6.10)	Second-degree polynomial regression (Eq. 6.11)
1998	2,137,028	2,104,381	2,235,033	1.53	−4.59
1999	2,653,129	2,179,690	2,299,971	17.84	13.31
2000	2,686,490	2,255,000	2,364,000	16.06	12.00
2001	2,745,706	2,330,309	2,427,119	15.13	11.60
2002	2,601,646	2,405,619	2,489,329	7.53	4.32
2003	2,476,755	2,480,928	2,550,629	−0.17	−2.98
2004	2,338,650	2,556,238	2,611,020	−9.30	−11.65
2005	2,457,038	2,631,547	2,670,502	−7.10	−8.69
2006	2,681,557	2,706,857	2,729,074	−0.94	−1.77
2007	2,786,636	2,782,166	2,786,736	0.16	0.00
2008	2,723,940	2,857,476	2,843,489	−4.90	−4.39
2009	2,643,434	2,932,785	2,899,333	−10.95	−9.68
2010	2,850,006	3,008,095	2,954,267	−5.55	−3.66

Source: Modified from Ref. [335].

The forecaster opted in 1997 for the polynomial second-degree calibration model of Eq. (6.11). Table 6.1 and Fig. 6.7 illustrate realized values of demand against forecasted values and the degree of divergence for each year for both models of forecast. We can remark that while the short-term forecast (year 1998) was very successful, medium-term forecasts were less accurate. Indeed, between 1999 and 2001 the forecasts underestimated demand, as there was a trend break due to an unanticipated tourist explosion. From 2002 to 2004 and from 2006 to 2008 the forecasts are highly accurate, very likely because this was a period broadly in line with historical trends. For 2009 and 2010 the forecasts overestimated demand, due to a failure to account for economic recession.

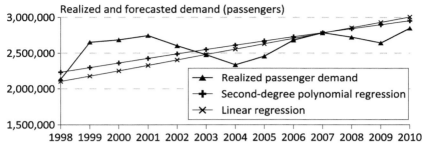

FIGURE 6.7 Forecasted values of demand (linear regression, second-degree polynomial regression) by projection of past data versus realized values. *Source: Modified from Ref. [335].*

The suggested second-degree polynomial equation of forecast results in the following values of the three criteria (described previously) of an ex post assessment of a forecast:

- maximum degree of divergence $D_{max} = 13.31\% < 15\%$,
- mean degree of divergence $D_{mean} = 6.82\%$,
- a balance of positive and negative errors, as the area of forecasted values above the forecast curve almost equals the area of forecasted values below the forecast curve.

6.5 SEASONALLY ADJUSTED TREND PROJECTION

A characteristic of transport demand is its seasonal variations, which cannot be taken into account by the trend projection analysis presented previously. When seasonal effects cannot be omitted, a seasonality adjustment should be conducted, to eliminate the effects of seasonal variations. The result of a seasonal adjustment is a deseasonalized time series.

Let us try to forecast the quarterly passenger (domestic + international) demand for the year 2017 for the airports of the United States. The available statistical data cover the period between 2009 and 2016 (Table 6.2, Fig. 6.8).

To take into account seasonal effects, we will pursue a methodology with the following steps:

1. calculation of the average historical demand of each quarter for the whole period of analysis (2009−16) by summing the demand of the same quarters in each year and dividing by the number of years of available data,
2. calculation of the average air transport passenger demand over all quarters of the period of analysis (2009−16) by summing the demand of all quarters and then dividing by the number of quarters,

TABLE 6.2: Quarterly air transport passenger demand (domestic+international) of US airports, seasonal index, and deseasonalized time series.

Sequence number of seasonal period of data	Year	Quarter	Air transport demand	Seasonal index	Seasonally adjusted air transport demand
1	2009	1st	177,037,011	0.922	191,930,970
2		2nd	198,733,043	1.038	191,380,408
3		3rd	205,730,373	1.063	193,509,288
4		4th	186,316,161	0.976	190,892,499
5	2010	1st	178,733,235	0.922	193,769,895
6		2nd	203,216,489	1.038	195,697,978
7		3rd	210,761,876	1.063	198,241,903
8		4th	194,766,456	0.976	199,550,352
9	2011	1st	182,699,324	0.922	198,069,648
10		2nd	208,906,368	1.038	201,177,345
11		3rd	214,294,569	1.063	201,564,742
12		4th	196,234,532	0.976	201,054,488
13	2012	1st	189,014,038	0.922	204,915,613
14		2nd	211,213,209	1.038	203,398,839
15		3rd	215,847,022	1.063	203,024,974
16		4th	197,049,096	0.976	201,889,059
17	2013	1st	191,116,291	0.922	207,194,726
18		2nd	213,840,776	1.038	205,929,192
19		3rd	217,864,028	1.063	204,922,163
20		4th	202,186,237	0.976	207,152,380
21	2014	1st	194,012,387	0.922	210,334,468
22		2nd	221,430,742	1.038	213,238,348
23		3rd	226,502,610	1.063	213,047,584
24		4th	209,667,784	0.976	214,817,690

TABLE 6.2: Quarterly air transport passenger demand (domestic+international) of US airports, seasonal index, and deseasonalized time series.—cont'd

Sequence number of seasonal period of data	Year	Quarter	Air transport demand	Seasonal index	Seasonally adjusted air transport demand
25		1st	201,585,033	0.922	218,544,194
26	2015	2nd	231,106,213	1.038	222,555,850
27		3rd	240,130,975	1.063	225,866,377
28		4th	223,791,383	0.976	229,288,196
29		1st	213,439,223	0.922	231,395,666
30	2016	2nd	240,267,391	1.038	231,378,087
31		3rd	247,478,330	1.063	232,777,274
32		4th	229,629,516	0.976	235,269,727

Source: Compiled by the authors based on data of Ref. [39].

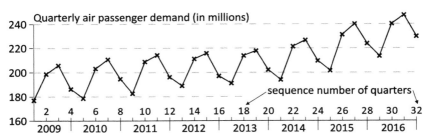

FIGURE 6.8 Evolution of the quarterly air transport passenger demand (domestic+international) at the US airports. *Source: Compiled by the authors based on data of Ref. [39].*

3. calculation of the *seasonal index* for each quarter, by dividing the average historical demand of this quarter (from step 1) by the average demand over all quarters (from step 2). In total, four seasonal indexes will be calculated, one for each quarter. The first three steps are presented in Table 6.3,
4. division of the actual demand of each quarter by the corresponding seasonal index. Thus, the seasonally adjusted time series of air passenger demand is determined (last column of Table 6.2),

TABLE 6.3: Calculation of the seasonal index.

Year	1st quarter (January −March)	2nd quarter (April −June)	3rd quarter (July −September)	4th quarter (October −December)
2009	177,037,011	198,733,043	205,730,373	186,316,161
2010	178,733,235	203,216,489	210,761,876	194,766,456
2011	182,699,324	208,906,368	214,294,569	196,234,532
2012	189,014,038	211,213,209	215,847,022	197,049,096
2013	191,116,291	213,840,776	217,864,028	202,186,237
2014	194,012,387	221,430,742	226,502,610	209,667,784
2015	201,585,033	231,106,213	240,130,975	223,791,383
2016	213,439,223	240,267,391	247,478,330	229,629,516
Average historical demand of the specific quarter	190,954,568	216,089,279	222,326,223	204,955,146
Average demand over all quarters	208,581,304			
Seasonal index	0.915	1.036	1.066	0.983

Source: Compiled by the authors based on data of Ref. [39].

5. conduction of a regression analysis of the seasonally adjusted time series (Fig. 6.9). We derive the following equation for this regression:

$$D_{quarter} = 1,354,279 \cdot Quarter + 186,235,701, \quad R^2 = 0.910 \quad (6.12)$$

where

$D_{quarter}$ seasonally adjusted demand for the specific quarter,
Quarter   successive quarters: 1, 2, 3, …, 32.

6. multiplication of the fitted or ex ante forecasted, by the regression analysis, seasonally adjusted data by the corresponding seasonal index. For the year 2017, the sequence numbers of the four quarters of the specific year will be 33, 34, 35, 36. By giving to the variable Quarter in Eq. (6.12) the numbers 33, 34, 35, 36, we can forecast the seasonally adjusted air transport demand

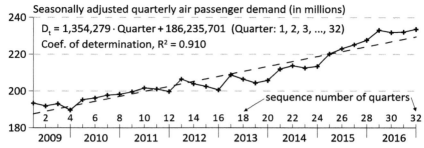

FIGURE 6.9 Regression analysis of the seasonally adjusted quarterly air transport passenger demand (domestic + international) at the US airports. *Source: Compiled by the authors based on data of Ref. [39].*

TABLE 6.4: Calculation of the forecasted for the year 2017 air transport demand.

Sequence number of seasonal period of data	Year	Quarter	Seasonally adjusted air transport demand	Seasonal index	Forecasted air transport demand
33		1st	230,926,908	0.915	211,411,795
34	2017	2nd	232,281,187	1.036	240,642,250
35		3rd	233,635,466	1.066	249,031,384
36		4th	234,989,745	0.983	230,904,480

Source: Compiled by the authors based on data of Ref. [39].

for the 1st, 2nd, 3rd, and 4th quarter of 2017 (Table 6.4). Finally, by multiplying the seasonal index with the seasonally adjusted air transport demand for the 1st, 2nd, 3rd, and 4th quarter of 2017, we can forecast the air transport demand of the year 2017 (Fig. 6.10).

6.6 OTHER STATISTICAL METHODS TO EXTEND DATA OF THE PAST INTO THE FUTURE

6.6.1 Methods Based on Average Values of Past Data

6.6.1.1 Average Values as a Good Predictor

Regression analysis is the most commonly used method to forecast future transport demand by extending past data into the future. However, future

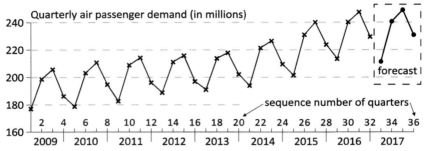

FIGURE 6.10 Evolution between 2009 and 2016 of the quarterly air transport (domestic + international) passenger demand at the US airports and forecast for the year 2017. *Source: Compiled by the authors based on data of Ref. [39].*

demand can be calculated on the basis of average values of demand made in the recent past. The basic assumption associated with such methods is that the average values of the recent past can be used as a good predictor for what will happen in the future.

6.6.1.2 Simple Moving Average

If we have available data of demand covering a time period t, the simple moving average method suggests that demand for the next time period $t+1$ will be a simple, equally weighted, running means of the previous values of demand data:

$$y_{t+1} = \frac{y_t + y_{t-1} + \cdots + y_{t-n+1}}{n} \tag{6.13}$$

where n is the number of successive periods for which demand data are available.

In the simple moving average method, older and more recent data are of equal importance, something that is not true for most transport demand problems.

Table 6.5 illustrates actual and forecasted annual passenger demand of Eurostar trains between London and Paris with the methods of 2-year and 3-year simple moving average (MA). Thus, the forecasted demand of Eurostar trains for the year 2016 is calculated as follows:

$$y_{2016}^{\text{2-year simple MA}} = \frac{y_{2014} + y_{2015}}{2} = 10,398,581$$

$$y_{2016}^{\text{3-year simple MA}} = \frac{y_{2013} + y_{2014} + y_{2015}}{3} = 10,309,951$$

For the year 2017, the 2-year simple moving average can be realized by using the actual values of demand of the years 2015 and 2016. The 2-year

TABLE 6.5: Actual and forecasted annual passenger demand of Eurostar trains with the methods of 2-year and 3-year simple and weighted moving average.

Year	Passengers transported by Eurostar trains	2-year simple moving average	3-year simple moving average	2-year weighted moving average	3-year weighted moving average
1995	2,920,309				
1996	4,995,010				
1997	6,004,268	3,957,660		4,476,335	
1998	6,307,849	5,499,639	4,639,862	5,751,954	5,443,558
1999	6,593,247	6,156,059	5,769,042	6,231,954	6,100,670
2000	7,130,417	6,450,548	6,301,788	6,521,898	6,463,000
2001	6,947,135	6,861,832	6,677,171	6,996,125	6,913,868
2002	6,602,817	7,038,776	6,890,266	6,992,956	6,957,567
2003	6,314,795	6,774,976	6,893,456	6,688,897	6,741,657
2004	7,276,675	6,458,806	6,621,582	6,386,801	6,450,035
2005	7,454,497	6,795,735	6,731,429	7,036,205	6,968,819
2006	7,858,337	7,365,586	7,015,322	7,410,042	7,296,071
2007	8,260,980	7,656,417	7,529,836	7,757,377	7,699,211
2008	9,113,371	8,059,659	7,857,938	8,160,319	8,079,671
2009	9,220,233	8,687,176	8,410,896	8,900,273	8,774,770
2010	9,528,558	9,166,802	8,864,861	9,193,518	9,097,592
2011	9,679,764	9,374,396	9,287,387	9,451,477	9,409,958
2012	9,911,649	9,604,161	9,476,185	9,641,963	9,596,009
2013	10,132,691	9,795,707	9,706,657	9,853,678	9,815,369
2014	10,397,894	10,022,170	9,908,035	10,077,431	10,032,138
2015	10,399,267	10,265,293	10,147,411	10,331,593	10,282,969
2016	10,011,337	10,398,581	10,309,951	10,398,924	10,372,266
2017	(forecast)	10,205,302	10,269,499	10,108,320	10,146,975
Pearson correlation coefficient (r)		0.952	0.947	0.965	0.966

Source: Compiled by the authors based on data of Ref. [333].

simple moving average for the year 2018, however, can be based on the actual value of demand of the year 2016 and the forecasted, right before, value of demand for the year 2017.

6.6.1.3 Weighted Moving Average

This method allows to allocate different weights to data regarding different time periods and thus emphasizes more on recent demand data. For n data covering a time period t, demand for the next time period t+1 will be:

$$y_{t+1} = w_1 \cdot y_t + w_2 \cdot y_{t-1} + \cdots + w_n y_{t-n+1} \tag{6.14}$$

where

w_1 the weight attributed to the more recent data referring at time t,
w_n the weight attributed to data referring at time $t - n + 1, w_1 > w_2 > \cdots > w_n$ and $w_1 + w_2 + \cdots + w_n = 1.0$.

Table 6.5 illustrates actual and forecasted annual passenger demand of Eurostar trains with the methods of 2-year and 3-year weighted moving average. Calculation of the 2-year weighted MA for the period t+1 was carried out by considering a percentage contribution of 75% for the period t and 25% for the period t−1, whereas for the 3-year weighted moving average the percentage contribution of the periods t, t−1, and t−2 were 65%, 25%, and 10%, respectively. The above percentages are selected more or less arbitrarily based on the assessment of the forecaster concerning the impact factor of demand for each one of the previous years. However, the forecaster should examine very carefully at which stage of its life cycle the transport service in consideration is situated (see Fig. 6.2). For instance, for a transport service in the growth or decline stage, data of the more recent period t should have a higher percentage contribution. For a transport service in the maturity stage, data of recent periods (t, t−1, t−2) should not have a very different percentage contribution.

For example, the forecasted annual demand of Eurostar trains for the year 2016 with the methods of 2-year and 3-year weighted moving average (MA) is calculated as follows:

$$y_{2016}^{\text{2-year weighted MA}} = \frac{0.25 \cdot y_{2014} + 0.75 \cdot y_{2015}}{2} = 10,398,924$$

$$y_{2016}^{\text{3-year weighted MA}} = \frac{0.10 \cdot y_{2013} + 0.25 \cdot y_{2014} + 0.65 \cdot y_{2015}}{3} = 10,372,266$$

6.6.2 Exponential Smoothing

Exponential smoothing methods are based on a combination of previous forecasts which are correlated with the more recent data. In relation to whether past trends are taken into account or not, these are classified into exponential smoothing with trend or simple exponential smoothing.

6.6.2.1 Simple Exponential Smoothing

This method is similar to the weighted moving average and can attribute more importance (weight) to recent data.

In its simplest form, the method can be used for the forecast of demand for the time period t as the sum of the weighted demand for that time and the exponential smoothing value for the time which proceeded:

$$y_t^{forecast} = y_{t-1}^{forecast} + \alpha \cdot \left(y_{t-1}^{actual} - y_{t-1}^{forecast} \right) \tag{6.15}$$

where

$y_t^{forecast}$	exponentially smoothed forecasted demand for the time t,
y_{t-1}^{actual}	actual (measured) demand for the time $t-1$,
$y_{t-1}^{forecast}$	exponentially smoothed forecasted demand for the time $t-1$ (if not defined otherwise, we set for the first period $y^{forecast} \equiv y^{actual}$, following the so-called naïve approach[3]),
α	the smoothing constant for the average, $0<\alpha<1$. The higher the value of α, the more weight is allocated to the more recent data and the smaller the level of smoothing. In other words, high values of α are chosen when the underlying average is likely to change, whereas low values of α are chosen when the underlying average is fairly stable [336].

Essentially, this method entails the consideration of the average of a previous forecast and of the more recent data of demand. The method assumes that there is no growth and no trend in the past data of demand.

Table 6.6 illustrates the forecasted passenger demand of Eurostar trains for the year 2017 with the simple exponential smoothing method for a smoothing constant for the average $\alpha=0.2$ and for a smoothing constant for the average $\alpha=0.8$.

6.6.2.2 Trend-Adjusted Exponential Smoothing

The trend-adjusted exponential smoothing includes the terms of simple exponential smoothing and in addition the trend component:

$$T_t = \beta \cdot \left(y_t^{forecast} - y_{t-1}^{forecast} \right) + (1 - \beta) \cdot T_{t-1} \tag{6.16}$$

---

3. Naïve approach is a simple way of forecast which assumes that transport demand in the next period will be equal to the transport demand in the most recent period, without trying to make any adjustment to the evolution of demand. Naïve approach provides a starting point against which more sophisticated methods, which follow, can be compared.

TABLE 6.6: Actual and forecasted annual passenger demand of Eurostar trains with the methods of simple exponential smoothing and trend-adjusted exponential smoothing.

Year	Passengers transported by Eurostar trains	Simple exponential smoothing ($\alpha = 0.2$)	Simple exponential smoothing ($\alpha = 0.8$)	Trend-adjusted exponential smoothing ($\alpha = 0.4$, $\beta = 0.3$)	Trend-adjusted exponential smoothing ($\alpha = 0.9$, $\beta = 0.1$)
1995	2,920,309	2,920,309	2,920,309	2,920,309	2,920,309
1996	4,995,010	2,920,309	2,920,309	2,920,309	2,920,309
1997	6,004,268	3,335,249	4,580,070	3,999,154	4,974,263
1998	6,307,849	3,869,053	5,719,428	5,290,777	6,180,691
1999	6,593,247	4,356,812	6,190,165	6,309,232	6,586,001
2000	7,130,417	4,804,099	6,512,631	7,068,546	6,884,042
2001	6,947,135	5,269,363	7,006,860	7,746,427	7,419,473
2002	6,602,817	5,604,917	6,959,080	7,983,928	7,265,552
2003	6,314,795	5,804,497	6,674,070	7,822,968	6,880,628
2004	7,276,675	5,906,557	6,386,650	7,430,202	6,531,990
2005	7,454,497	6,180,580	7,098,670	7,560,872	7,429,840
2006	7,858,337	6,435,364	7,383,332	7,697,637	7,681,884
2007	8,260,980	6,719,958	7,763,336	7,960,516	8,086,425
2008	9,113,371	7,028,163	8,161,451	8,315,357	8,504,968

2009	9,220,233	7,445,204	8,922,987	8,964,979	9,368,730
2010	9,528,558	7,800,210	9,160,784	9,428,128	9,537,918
2011	9,679,764	8,145,880	9,455,003	9,841,399	9,831,487
2012	9,911,649	8,452,657	9,634,812	10,130,447	9,983,274
2013	10,132,691	8,744,455	9,856,282	10,370,375	10,200,703
2014	10,397,894	9,022,102	10,077,409	10,574,226	10,415,262
2015	10,399,267	9,297,261	10,333,797	10,781,458	10,673,838
2016	10,011,337	9,517,662	10,386,173	10,860,484	10,676,220
2017	(forecast)	9,616,397	10,086,304	10,650,829	10,267,482
Pearson correlation coefficient (r)		0.949	0.968	0.934	0.968

Source: Compiled by the authors.

where

β the trend-smoothing constant $(0<\beta<1)$, which is similar to the constant α of Eq. (6.15). A high value of β better takes into account recent changes in the trend, whereas a low value of β gives less weight to the most recent trends and tends to smooth out the present trend [336].

Thus, exponentially smoothed transport demand for the time period t will be:

$$y_t^{forecast} = \alpha \cdot y_{t-1}^{actual} + (1-\alpha) \cdot \left(y_{t-1}^{forecast} + T_{t-1}\right) \qquad (6.17)$$

and the trend-adjusted exponential smoothed transport demand will be:

$$y_t^{forecast,\ including\ trend} = y_t^{forecast} + T_t \qquad (6.18)$$

Table 6.6 (last two columns) illustrates the forecasted passenger demand of Eurostar trains for the year 2017 with the trend-adjusted exponential smoothing for:

- a smoothing constant for the average $\alpha=0.4$ and a smoothing constant for the trend $\beta=0.3$,
- a smoothing constant for the average $\alpha=0.9$ and a smoothing constant for the trend $\beta=0.1$.

6.7 THE VARIOUS TIME SERIES PROCESSES: WHITE NOISE, RANDOM WALK, AUTOREGRESSIVE (AR), MOVING AVERAGE (MA), AUTOREGRESSIVE MOVING AVERAGE (ARMA), INTEGRATED ARMA (ARIMA), SEASONAL ARIMA (SARIMA)

6.7.1 The Need for Univariate Time Series Regression

The term *univariate* refers to equations or functions that consist of only one variable. Similarly, a univariate time series refers to a time series that consists of only one variable, whose data or observations are recorded sequentially, usually over equal time intervals. Although a univariate time series is usually considered as a series of observations, time is in fact an implicit variable, that is, a variable not explicitly, not plainly expressed. The need for univariate time series analysis is appropriate for situations where:

- there is no knowledge (or if any, this is not solid) of the mechanism that relates the under study dependent variable with other independent variables which affect it,
- though we know the mechanism relating the dependent variable to the independent ones, it is very difficult or it is cost- or/and time-consuming to obtain the entire set of data or observations for the independent variables.

6.7.2 The White Noise

A univariate time series is characterized as white noise (ε_t) process when it is purely random in nature, it has zero mean and constant variance, and its values are mutually uncorrelated. The diagram of a white noise process does not follow a specific form or pattern (Fig. 6.11 left). Therefore, the reliable forecast of future values of such a time series is practically not possible.

6.7.3 The Random Walk

In a random walk univariate time series, the current value of the variable y for the period t is equal to its value of the previous period $(t-1)$ plus a white noise component ε_t and the intercept (constant term) c:

$$y_t = c + y_{t-1} + \varepsilon_t \qquad (6.19)$$

Hence, the difference $y_t - y_{t-1}$ is equal to the white noise plus the intercept and therefore it is not predictable. The variance of a random walk process is not constant but varies with time t; consequently, a random walk is nonstationary. A random walk may present a drift (that is, a slow steady change) or not,

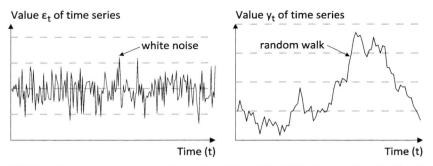

FIGURE 6.11   The white noise (left) and the random walk (right). *Source: Compiled by the authors.*

depending on whether the intercept (c) is equal to zero or not. For $c > 0$, the random walk presents an upward trend (Fig. 6.11, right).

6.7.4 The Autoregressive Process, AR(p)

An autoregressive process AR(p) specifies that the current value of the dependent variable y_t depends linearly on (and is generated by) a weighted average of its own previous p values ($y_{t-1}, y_{t-2}, \ldots, y_{t-p}$) and on a purely random process (i.e., a white noise ε_t) with zero mean and constant variance. Thus:

$$y_t = c + \phi_1 \cdot y_{t-1} + \phi_2 \cdot y_{t-2} + \cdots + \phi_p \cdot y_{t-p} + \varepsilon_t \qquad (6.20)$$

where

$\phi_1, \phi_2, \ldots, \phi_p$ parameters that are calculated with the use of a computer software,

c   the intercept, which is related to the mean (μ) of the time series and to the parameters $\phi_1, \phi_2, \ldots, \phi_p$ by the equation:

$$\mu = \frac{c}{1 - \phi_1 - \phi_2 - \cdots - \phi_p} \qquad (6.21)$$

The simplest autoregressive process is the AR(1) and is described by the equation:

$$y_t = c + \phi_1 \cdot y_{t-1} + \varepsilon_t \qquad (6.22)$$

In an AR(1) process, when $\phi = 1$ we have the case of a random walk process. In addition, values of $\phi > 1$ indicate a nonstationary time series; thus before any effort of calibration, we have to transform the time series to a stationary one by differencing (see §5.1.5, §6.9, and §6.12.1).

The number p of previous values of the dependent variable of an autoregressive process is called the order of the process. An indication for the order p of an AR(p) process could be the correlograms of the autocorrelation and the partial autocorrelation functions (see §6.8).

A common useful notation when dealing with the modeling of time series is the backshift (or lag) operator B, which is defined as [337]:

$$B^i y_t = y_{t-i} \qquad (6.23)$$

Thus, for example, $B^1 y_t = y_{t-1}$, $B^2 y_t = y_{t-2}$. When dealing with monthly data, to refer to the same month one year before we use the notation $B^{12} y_t = y_{t-12}$. By using the backshift operator B, Eq. (6.20) can be formulated as:

$$y_t = c + \sum_{i=1}^{p} \phi_i \cdot B^i y_t + \varepsilon_t \qquad (6.24)$$

The backshift operator B is also useful and convenient in the case of differencing. A first difference (that is, the change of the variable under study from a previous period to the next one) can be written with the use of the backshift operator B as:

$$y_t - y_{t-i} = y_t - By_t = (1 - B) \cdot y_t \qquad (6.25)$$

Similarly, a second difference can be written as:

$$(y_t - y_{t-1}) - (y_{t-1} - y_{t-2}) = y_t - 2 \cdot y_{t-1} + y_{t-2} = y_t - 2 \cdot By_t + B^2 y_t =$$
$$= (1 - 2 \cdot B + B^2) \cdot y_t = (1 - B)^2 \cdot y_t$$
$$(6.26)$$

In general, the d-th difference can be denoted with the use of the backshift operator B as:

$$(1 - B)^d \cdot y_t \qquad (6.27)$$

6.7.5 The Moving Average Process, MA(q)

In a moving average process MA(q), the current value of the dependent variable y_t depends linearly on and is generated by the current and the past q values of a random process (i.e., a white noise ε_t) with zero mean and constant variance. Thus:

$$y_t = \mu + \varepsilon_t - \theta_1 \cdot \varepsilon_{t-1} - \theta_2 \cdot \varepsilon_{t-2} - \cdots - \theta_q \cdot \varepsilon_{t-q} \qquad (6.28)$$

where

μ	the mean of the time series,
$\theta_1, \theta_2, \ldots$ and θ_q	parameters that are calculated with the use of a computer software.

By using the backshift operator B, Eq. (6.28) can be formulated as:

$$y_t = \mu - \sum_{i=1}^{q} \theta_i \cdot B^i \varepsilon_t + \varepsilon_t \qquad (6.29)$$

Contrary to an AR(q) process, an MA(q) process is always stationary; as with the case of an AR(q) process, the appropriate order q of an MA(q) process can be defined by the correlograms of the autocorrelation and the partial autocorrelation functions (see §6.8). The moving average process should not be confused with the moving average method, which was described previously (§6.6.1).

6.7.6 The Autoregressive Moving Average Process, ARMA(p,q)

This is a mixed process that exhibits the properties of both the autoregressive and moving average processes. The general form of such a time series model, which depends on its own p past values and on the q past values of white noise error terms, is the following:

$$y_t = c + \phi_1 \cdot y_{t-1} + \phi_2 \cdot y_{t-2} + \cdots + \phi_p \cdot y_{t-p} + \varepsilon_t - \theta_1 \cdot \varepsilon_{t-1} - \cdots - \theta_q \cdot \varepsilon_{t-q}$$

(6.30)

6.7.7 The Autoregressive Integrated Moving Average Process, ARIMA(p,d,q)

The AR(p) term of an ARMA(p,q) process should be stationary; thus the stationarity of the time series must be checked before calibration. If the AR(p) process is nonstationary, it must be differenced, once or twice or as many times as necessary to become stationary (see §6.9). The number of differences of the AR(p) term to become stationary denotes the order d of an ARIMA(p,d,q) process. In practice, d takes the values 1 or 2, since for most nonstationary time series one or two differencing operations are usually required to become stationary.

6.7.8 Seasonal Autoregressive Integrated Moving Average Process, SARIMA(p,d,q)(P,D,Q)m

As SARIMA are characterized the seasonal ARIMA processes. They are denoted as SARIMA(p,d,q)(P,D,Q)$_m$, where:

- m refers to the number of periods in each season (for example, when dealing with biannual data m=2, for quarterly data m=4, for monthly data m=12),
- the uppercase letters P,D,Q refer respectively to the autoregressive, differencing, and moving average terms for the seasonal part of the ARIMA process,
- the lowercase letters p,d,q refer to the nonseasonal ARIMA process, as explained previously in §6.7.7.

The difference between lowercase and uppercase letters is that in the nonseasonal ARIMA process the order p measures the autocorrelation between the successive values of the time series, whereas in the seasonal ARIMA the order P measures the autocorrelation between the successive periods s. Therefore, a seasonal AR(p) process will be described by Eq. (6.31) and a seasonal MA(q) process by Eq. (6.32):

$$\text{SAR(P)}: \quad y_t = \sum_{i=1}^{P} \Phi_i \cdot y_{t-s \cdot P} + \varepsilon_t$$

(6.31)

$$\text{SMA(Q)}: \quad y_t = \varepsilon_t - \sum_{i=1}^{Q} \Theta_i \cdot y_{t-s \cdot Q}$$

(6.32)

To take an example, a seasonal ARIMA$(0,1,1)(0,1,1)_{12}$ process will contain a nonseasonal MA(1) term (with the corresponding parameter θ) and a seasonal MA(1) term (with the corresponding parameter Θ). The equation of such a process will be:

$$y_t = y_{t-1} + y_{t-12} - y_{t-13} - \theta_1 \cdot \varepsilon_{t-1} - \Theta_1 \cdot \varepsilon_{t-12} + \theta_1 \cdot \Theta_1 \cdot \varepsilon_{t-13} \qquad (6.33)$$

By using the backshift operator B, the seasonal ARIMA $(1,1,1)(1,1,1)_{12}$ process can be written as:

$$(1 - \phi_1 B) \cdot (1 - \Phi_1 B^{12}) \cdot (1 - B) \cdot (1 - B^{12}) \cdot y_t =$$
$$= (1 + \theta_1 B) \cdot (1 + \Theta_1 B^{12}) \cdot \varepsilon_t \qquad (6.34)$$

where

$(1 - \phi_1 B)$	the nonseasonal AR(1) process,
$(1 - \Phi_1 B^{12})$	the seasonal AR(1) process,
$(1 - B)$	the nonseasonal difference for stationarity,
$(1 - B^{12})$	the seasonal difference for stationarity,
$(1 + \theta_1 B)$	the nonseasonal MA(1) process,
$(1 + \Theta_1 B^{12})$	the seasonal MA(1) process.

6.8 AUTOCORRELATION AND PARTIAL AUTOCORRELATION FUNCTIONS

The stationarity or not of an AR(p) process as well as the order p of an AR(p) and the order q of an MA(q) process can be defined by means of the autocorrelation function and the partial autocorrelation function.

For the observations y_t ($t = 1, 2, ..., n$) of a time series, the *autocovariance* γ_h is the covariance of the series with a time-shifted version of itself at a specific time lag h:

$$\gamma_h = \frac{1}{n} \cdot \sum_{t=1}^{n-h} (y_t - \bar{y}) \cdot (y_{t+h} - \bar{y}) \qquad (6.35)$$

The autocovariance (γ_h) of a series at time lag h divided by its variance (γ_0) is the *autocorrelation* ρ_h, and its values at $h = 0, 1, 2, ...$ constitute the *autocorrelation function (ACF)* for these time lags. Mathematically, the ACF is defined as:

$$\rho_h = \frac{\gamma_h}{\gamma_0} = \frac{\frac{1}{n} \cdot \sum_{t=1}^{n-h} (y_t - \bar{y}) \cdot (y_{t+h} - \bar{y})}{\sum_{t=1}^{n} (y_t - \bar{y})^2} \qquad (6.36)$$

The *partial autocorrelation function (PACF)* is a measure of the degree of association between y_t and y_{t-h}, when the effects of other time lags (1, 2, 3, ..., $h - 1$) are removed. Thus, the partial autocorrelation (denoted as π_h) of a time series y_t at time lag h is the autocorrelation between y_t and y_{t-h} after the linear dependence of y_{t-h} with y_t, y_{t+1}, ..., y_{t+h-1} has been removed.

The ACFs and the PACFs are dimensionless and they have values in the range $[-1, 1]$. Table 6.7 illustrates the theoretical (representative) forms of the ACFs and PACFs for the various values of the time lags of AR(p) and MA(q) processes. Thus, a comparison of the correlograms (plots of ACFs and PACFs) of a specific time series with the theoretical ACFs and PACFs helps the forecaster to the selection, for the time series under investigation, of the

TABLE 6.7: Plot of the correlograms of the autocorrelation function (ACF) and of the partial autocorrelation function (PACF) for the various time series models.

Model	ACF	PACF
AR(p)	Spikes exponentially decaying to zero, coefficients may oscillate	Spikes significant until p lags, they are cut off to zero afterward
MA(q)	Spikes significant until q lags, they are cut off to zero afterward	Spikes exponentially decaying to zero, coefficients may oscillate
ARMA(p,q)	Spikes decaying (either directly or oscillating) to zero	Spikes decaying (either directly or oscillating) to zero
Nonstationary time series	Spikes that do not decay to zero or decay very slowly	Not applicable

AR, autoregressive; ARMA, autoregressive moving average; MA, moving average.
Source: Compiled by the authors.

appropriate order p and order q for the autoregressive and moving average processes (if any), which better describe the time series.

The pattern of the correlograms of a seasonal AR(p) or a seasonal MA(q) is similar to those of nonseasonal AR(p) and MA(q), with the difference that in seasonal processes the pattern appears across multiples of time lags s. For example, a seasonal AR(1) process has spikes in the ACF at lags s, 2s, 3s, etc., while the PACF cuts off after lag s. A seasonal MA(1) process has spikes in the PACF at lags s, 2s, 3s, etc., while the ACF cuts off after lag s.

6.9 CHECK OF STATIONARITY OF A TIME SERIES

6.9.1 A Variety of Checks of Stationarity

Stationarity (see also §5.1.5) is a key issue for the analysis, calibration, and extension to the future of any time series. There exist a number of tests which are appropriate for checking the stationarity of a time series. The most commonly used among them are based on the so-called correlograms, that is, plots of the autocorrelation function (ACF) of a time series (§6.9.2). Another category of tests of stationarity is the unit root tests, the most popular among these being the Augmented Dickey−Fuller test (§6.9.3).

6.9.2 Correlogram of the Autocorrelation Function

One of the ways for identifying stationary time series is the autocorrelation function (ACF) correlogram. The ACF is a statistical tool for identifying repetitive patterns in a time series and represents the similarity between the time series data or observations as a function of the time lag between them. A nonstationary time series has an ACF correlogram that decreases slowly; on the contrary, an ACF correlogram quickly declining to zero is the case for a stationary time series (Table 6.7).

6.9.3 The Unit Root Tests

Another way for the identification of a time series stationarity is the unit root tests [338,339], which are statistical hypothesis tests of stationarity that are designed for determining whether differencing is required or not. A number of unit root tests are available (Dickey−Fuller, Phillips−Perron, Schmidt−Phillips, and others), the most popular among them being the Augmented Dickey−Fuller test, named after the American statisticians David Dickey and Wayne Fuller [340,341].

Let us take again the AR(1) process presented by Eq. (6.22). We will test whether ϕ_1 is equal to 1. By subtracting the term y_{t-1} from both sides of Eq. (6.22), we have:

$$\Delta(y_t) = y_t - y_{t-1} = \phi_1 \cdot y_{t-1} - y_{t-1} + \varepsilon_t = (\phi_1 - 1) \cdot y_{t-1} + \varepsilon_t \qquad (6.37)$$

We denote the term $\phi_1 - 1$ as ψ. We can test whether the term $\phi_1 - 1$ of Eq. (6.37) is equal to zero by means of the so-called *Dickey−Fuller test*, which is a typical Student's t-test examining if the parameter ψ of y_{t-1} is equal to zero. If an intercept or a trend is comprised in Eq. (6.37), then we can also use the Dickey−Fuller test adjusted for their impact on the distribution of the test statistic. We can distinguish three cases with the following equations for each one:

- no intercept, no trend: $\Delta(y_t) = \psi \cdot y_{t-1} + \varepsilon_t$ (6.38)

- intercept, no trend: $\Delta(y_t) = c + \psi \cdot y_{t-1} + \varepsilon_t$ (6.39)

- intercept and trend: $\Delta(y_t) = c + b \cdot t + \psi \cdot y_{t-1} + \varepsilon_t$ (6.40)

The Dickey−Fuller test described previously is referred to as the AR(1) process; it can be generalized to the *Augmented Dickey−Fuller test*, to include the case of a general ARIMA(p,d,q) process. The procedure for the Augmented Dickey−Fuller test is the same as with the Dickey−Fuller test, but it is applied to the model [342]:

$$\Delta(y_t) = c + b \cdot t + \psi \cdot y_{t-1} + \delta_1 \cdot \Delta y_{t-1} + \cdots + \delta_{p-1} \cdot \Delta y_{t-p+1} + \varepsilon_t =$$
$$= c + b \cdot t + \psi \cdot y_{t-1} + \sum_{i=1}^{p-1} \delta_i \cdot \Delta y_{t-i} + \varepsilon_t \qquad (6.41)$$

For the model of Eq. (6.41), the determination of the optimum lag length p can be carried out by examining information criteria such as the Akaike information criterion (AIC), the Bayesian information criterion (BIC), or the Hannan−Quinn information criterion (HQIC), which are analyzed in §6.10. As a rule of thumb for determining the maximum lag length p_{max}, the following ratio can be used [342]:

$$p_{max} = 12 \cdot \left(\frac{n}{100}\right)^{1/4} \qquad (6.42)$$

The *null hypothesis* H_0 for the Augmented Dickey−Fuller test is that the time series under examination *contains a unit root* (that is, $\psi = 0$), which means that it is *nonstationary* and the *alternative hypothesis* H_1 is that the time series *is stationary*. The Augmented Dickey−Fuller test statistic is calculated by the ratio:

$$\text{Augmented Dickey−Fuller test statistic} = \frac{\widehat{\psi}}{\text{standard error } \widehat{\psi}} \qquad (6.43)$$

which is always a negative number. The more negative the Augmented Dickey−Fuller test statistic is, the stronger the rejection of the null hypothesis that there is a unit root for a specified significance level. With the use of a computer software, we can calculate the Augmented Dickey−Fuller test statistic, its critical value for a specified significance level (usually 5%, $\alpha = 0.05$), and the corresponding p-value (Table 6.8).

TABLE 6.8: Critical values for the Augmented Dickey–Fuller test statistic.

n	No intercept, no trend			Intercept, no trend			Intercept and trend		
	$\alpha=0.001$	$\alpha=0.05$	$\alpha=0.10$	$\alpha=0.001$	$\alpha=0.05$	$\alpha=0.10$	$\alpha=0.001$	$\alpha=0.05$	$\alpha=0.10$
30	−2.647	−1.953	−1.610	−3.671	−2.968	−2.623	−4.310	−3.574	−3.223
40	−2.626	−1.950	−1.612	−3.609	−2.939	−2.608	−4.216	−3.530	−3.196
50	−2.616	−1.948	−1.612	−3.579	−2.927	−2.601	−4.171	−3.511	−3.186
100	−2.589	−1.944	−1.615	−3.515	−2.892	−2.583	−4.056	−3.457	−3.161
250	−2.574	−1.942	−1.616	−3.457	−2.873	−2.573	−3.996	−3.428	−3.137
500	−2.570	−1.942	−1.616	−3.412	−2.867	−2.570	−3.982	−3.419	−3.132
750	−2.568	−1.941	−1.616	−3.439	−2.865	−2.569	−3.973	−3.416	−3.130
1000	−2.567	−1.941	−1.616	−3.437	−2.864	−2.568	−3.967	−3.414	−3.129
∞	−2.565	−1.941	−1.616	−3.431	−2.862	−2.567	−3.960	−3.411	−3.126

Source: Compiled by the authors; critical values of the table are derived by simulation with the use of the programming language Python.

6.10 STATISTICAL TESTS AND MEASURES FOR THE SELECTION OF THE APPROPRIATE TIME SERIES MODEL

6.10.1 The Akaike Information Criterion

The Akaike information criterion (AIC) was developed by the Japanese statistician Hirotugu Akaike [343]. It is a statistical measure for the comparative evaluation among time series models (but econometric also, as we analyze in Chapter 7). However, given that the AIC is not based on a hypothesis test, it cannot ensure the quality of a model in relation to other models. Thus, in the case that all the models under evaluation fit poorly with respect to a given set of data or observations, the AIC will just indicate the model that fits a little bit better to the available data or observations than the other ones.

AIC provides an estimation of the information lost when a specific model is used to represent the process that generated the data. In such an approach, a model balances between the goodness of fit and the complexity [343,344]. Mathematically, the AIC is calculated by the following equation:

$$\text{AIC} = -2 \cdot \frac{\ell}{n} + 2 \cdot \frac{k}{n} \tag{6.44}$$

where

n	number of data or observations,
k	number of estimated parameters (regressors[4] + intercept),
ℓ	the log likelihood function (assuming normally distributed errors), which is computed by the equation:

$$\ell = -\frac{n}{2} \cdot \left(1 + \ln\left(2 \cdot \pi\right) + \ln\left(\frac{1}{n} \cdot \sum_{i=1}^{n}\left(y_i - \widehat{y}_i\right)^2\right) \right) \tag{6.45}$$

When comparing among many alternative models, the one with the minimum AIC value assures a good balance of goodness of fit and complexity.

6.10.2 The Bayesian Information Criterion

The Bayesian information criterion (BIC) (known also as Schwarz Criterion) is another statistical measure for the comparative evaluation among time series models [345]. It was developed by the statistician Gideon Schwarz and is

---

4. As defined in §3.1.4, we usually distinguish the variables of a transport model into independent and dependent ones. However, in time series models we often use the dependent variable with time lag as an independent one. For example, an AR(1) process has as dependent variable the demand D and as independent one the same variable with a time lag, D(−1). In such cases and for avoiding any confusion we can use the term regressors instead of independent variables.

closely related to the AIC. The difference between BIC and AIC is manifested when we add a number of k parameters (regressors or/and intercept), in order to increase the goodness of fit of the model. In such a case, the BIC penalizes more (in comparison to the AIC) such an increase of parameters.

Mathematically, the BIC is calculated by the equation:

$$\text{BIC} = -2 \cdot \frac{\ell}{n} + \frac{k \cdot \ln n}{n} \qquad (6.46)$$

Similarly to the AIC, among various alternative models, the model to be preferred is the one with the minimum BIC value.

6.10.3 The Hannan−Quinn Information Criterion

Introduced by the Australian statisticians Edward Hannan and Barry Quinn, the Hannan-Quinn information criterion (HQIC) employs yet another penalty function, very similar to the BIC, given by the equation [346]:

$$\text{HQIC} = -2 \cdot \frac{\ell}{n} + 2 \cdot \frac{k \cdot \ln(\ln n)}{n} \qquad (6.47)$$

It is obvious that the AIC, the BIC, and the HQIC present similarities, since they consist of a sum of two terms, the first term that evaluates the prediction error of the model, and the second term that evaluates the number of the regressors of the model. By minimizing both terms, we are seeking to identify an appropriate model that is parsimonious (it does not overfit the data with too many parameters), while at the same time fits well with the data or observations.

The forecaster can use one or more of the above mentioned criteria. The AIC is the most commonly used and the HQIC the less commonly used one. Computer software packages usually calculate all three of these.

6.10.4 Complementary Statistics

In addition to the AIC, the BIC, and the HQIC, the well-known statistics of the mean absolute deviation (MAD), the mean squared error (MSE) (as well as its variation, the root mean squared error [RMSE]), the mean absolute percentage error (MAPE), and Theil's inequality coefficient are all useful tools when comparing and evaluating different time series models (see §5.11).

6.11 THE BOX−JENKINS METHOD

Named after the British statisticians George Box and Gwilym Jenkins, the Box−Jenkins method consists of an iterative procedure of modeling a time series [347]. The method is based on three distinct phases:

1. *Model identification.* The original Box−Jenkins methodology was based on the plots of the autocorrelation and the partial autocorrelation functions

(correlograms) to identify the most suitable seasonal or nonseasonal ARIMA(p,d,q) process, which provides a good fit to the available data or observations. Later developments have enriched the existing model selection tools with statistical criteria such as the information criteria (AIC, BIC, HQIC) described previously. The phase of identification assumes the stability of a time series; therefore the stationarity check is a prerequisite. Some authors, however, consider the stationarity check as a separate phase, designated as *data preparation*, of the Box—Jenkins methodology.

2. *Model calibration.* There are many sophisticated computational algorithms and computer software packages designed to obtain the values of the various parameters of a seasonal or nonseasonal ARIMA(p,d,q) process, which can ensure *the best fit to the data or observations.*

3. *Model diagnostics.* The residuals of an adequately calibrated seasonal or nonseasonal ARIMA(p,d,q) process should have the characteristics of a white noise process, with constant variance and mutually uncorrelated values. The normality check which is based on the Jarque—Bera test (see §5.9.2) and the serial correlation check which is based on the Breusch—Godfrey LM test (see §5.9.5.3) are widely applied for checking whether the residuals are independently distributed or not. However, a similar evaluation for the residuals can also be carried out with the use of the Ljung—Box test (see §5.9.5.4); when this test is applied in an ARMA(p,q) process, the degrees of freedom should be set equal to h−p−q [348]. Concerning heteroscedasticity, the White test (see §5.10.2.4) and the autoregressive conditional heteroscedasticity (ARCH) test (see §5.10.2.5) are usually applied.

If the calibrated model is found to be adequate concerning the normality, the serial correlation, and the heteroscedasticity checks, then the various statistics for the evaluation of the forecasting accuracy of the calibrated time series model can be calculated (such as the MAD, the MSE, the RMSE, the MAPE, and Theil's inequality coefficient; see §5.11). Otherwise, the forecaster should identify a better model. Some authors consider the forecasts as a separate phase of the Box—Jenkins methodology, designated as *forecasting* phase.

A crucial issue in applications of the Box—Jenkins method is the number of data or observations that should be available. According to some forecasters, effective fitting of a seasonal or nonseasonal model with the Box—Jenkins method requires the time series to contain at least 50 data or observations; however, other forecasters recommend, especially for problems which exhibit seasonality, to have available at least 100 data or observations [349].

An extensive application of the Box—Jenkins method is presented in §6.12.

6.12 APPLICATION OF THE BOX—JENKINS METHOD FOR THE CALIBRATION OF AN ARIMA(p,d,q) MODEL

6.12.1 The Available Data—Check of Stationarity— Transforming a Nonstationary Time Series to a Stationary One

The time series under examination refers to the monthly vehicle traffic (VT) for a 10-year period at a new road section (Fig. 6.12). The first step is a careful examination of the stationarity of any time series. Visually, a time series may seem to be nonstationary, but this is a hypothesis that must be verified with the use of the appropriate statistical check of the correlogram of the autocorrelation function (ACF) and with the unit root tests.

Indeed, the values of the autocorrelation function (ACF) for the level and the first differences of the variable VT confirm that the time series is nonstationary, but it becomes stationary when the first differences of the values of data are used (Fig. 6.13).

Confirmation of the stationarity of the time series could also be achieved with the use of a unit root test. By applying the Augmented Dickey—Fuller test (see §6.9.3) to the level values and the first differences of the variable VT, we can deduce that when differencing once we can reject the null hypothesis of nonstationarity in favor of the alternative (Table 6.9).

Consequently, when differencing once the time series, it becomes stationary; thus the order d of the calibrated model is $d = 1$. Therefore it is an ARIMA(p,1,q) process.

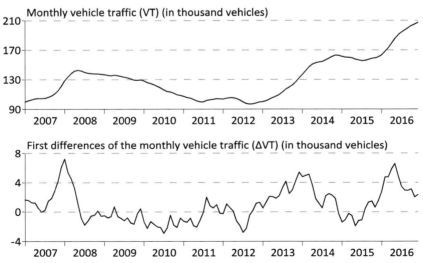

FIGURE 6.12   Monthly vehicle traffic on a new road section (level values and first differences).
Source: Compiled by the authors.

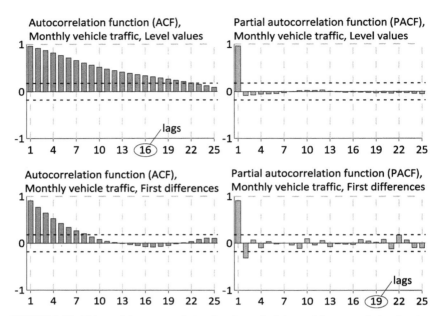

FIGURE 6.13 Values of the autocorrelation function and of the partial autocorrelation function for the level and the first differences of the variable representing the daily vehicle traffic. *Source: Compiled by the authors.*

TABLE 6.9: Identification of the stationarity (or not) of the time series with the use of the Augmented Dickey–Fuller test, including the test for the trend and the intercept.

	Augmented Dickey-Fuller test value	Test critical value for a 5% significance level	p-value[a]
Monthly vehicle traffic (VT)	−1.006	−3.448	0.938
First difference of VT (ΔVT)	−4.245		0.000

[a]*MacKinnon one-sided p-values [350].*
Source: Compiled by the authors, based on application of data on the EViews 7.2 software.

The pattern of the ACF and of the PACF functions are typical of an AR(1) process and of an MA(1) process, since the ACF function presents spikes, which decay exponentially to zero, and the PACF function presents spikes, which decay exponentially to zero with oscillating coefficients.

TABLE 6.10: Statistical criteria and measures for the selection of the appropriate time series model.

		Time series model		
		ARI(1,1)	IMA(1,1)	ARIMA(1,1,1)
Regressors (independent variables)	AR(1)			
	regression coefficient	0.923		0.869
	t-statistic	25.800		17.716
	p-value[a]	0.000		0.000
	MA(1)			
	regression coefficient		0.839	0.411
	t-statistic		16.128	4.555
	p-value[a]		0.000	0.000
Akaike information criterion (AIC)		2.772	3.638	2.664
Bayesian information criterion (BIC)		2.796	3.660	2.711
Hannan–Quinn inform. criterion (HQIC)		2.782	3.647	2.683
Coefficient of determination R^2		0.826	0.584	0.847
Adjusted $R^2 (\overline{R}^2)$		0.826	0.584	0.845

[a]*At 5% significance level.*
Source: Compiled by the authors, based on application of data on the EViews 7.2 software.

6.12.2 Identification and Calibration of the Best Fitted Model

The selection of the best fitted model will be done on the basis of the information criteria, the coefficient of determination, and the adjusted coefficient of determination.

Table 6.10 illustrates the estimated regression coefficients of the regressors (independent variables AR(1) and MA(1)) and the corresponding t-statistic and p-value (at 5% significance level) for the ARI(1,1)[5], the IMA(1,1), and the ARIMA(1,1,1) processes. Values of the Akaike information criterion, the Bayesian information criterion, and the Hannan-Quinn information criterion are also given. We remind the reader that these three criteria compare

---

5. A time series which became stationary after being differentiated d times is said to be integrated of order d and is denoted as I(d) (see §5.1.5). Thus, when the I(d) term is amended in an AR(p) or MA(q) process, it symbolizes that the process is based on an initially nonstationary time series, which became stationary after d differences [352].

alternative models among them, and the model with the lower values for the above three criteria is selected as the most suitable, compared with others. The coefficient of determination, and especially the adjusted one, is also taken into consideration as a measure of the ability of the regression to predict accurately, within the sample, the values of the daily vehicle traffic.

The *t-statistic* is calculated as the ratio of the estimated regression coefficients of the regressors AR(1) and MA(1) to their standard error. It is used to apply the hypothesis test for the significance of the regressors, based on the Student's t-distribution (Table 5.1). The null hypothesis of the test is that the estimated regression coefficient of the regressors is equal to zero (H_0: regression coefficient$=0$), whereas the alternative hypothesis is that the regression coefficient is different from zero (H_1: regression coefficient $\neq 0$). In all cases of Table 6.10, we reject the null hypothesis in favor of the alternative; thus we can conclude that the regression coefficients of the ARI(1,1) model, the IMA(1,1) model, and the ARIMA(1,1,1) model are all significant.

From the above analysis we can derive that the best fitted model to the data of the problem is the ARIMA(1,1,1), as it has the lower value of the Akaike information criterion, of the Bayesian information criterion, and of the Hannan-Quinn information criterion and at the same time the higher value of the coefficient of determination R^2 (simple and adjusted), whereas all regression coefficients are statistically significant. Fig. 6.14 illustrates the actual and the fitted values by the ARIMA(1,1,1) model of the first differences (ΔVT) of the monthly vehicle traffic; we can even visually confirm the satisfactory forecasting accuracy of the calibrated time series ARIMA(1,1,1) model.

6.12.3 Normality Test of the Residuals

Fig. 6.15 illustrates the plot of residuals, whereas Fig. 6.16 depicts the histogram of the residuals of the ARIMA(1,1,1) time series model. We can see in

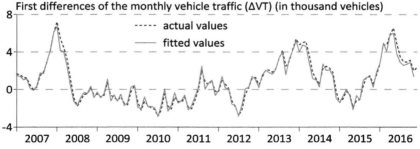

FIGURE 6.14 Comparison between the actual and the fitted, by the ARIMA(1,1,1) time series model, values of the first differences of the monthly vehicle traffic (ΔVT). *Source: Compiled by the authors.*

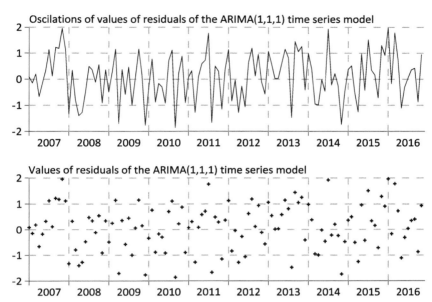

FIGURE 6.15   Plots of the residuals of the ARIMA(1,1,1) time series model. *Source: Compiled by the authors.*

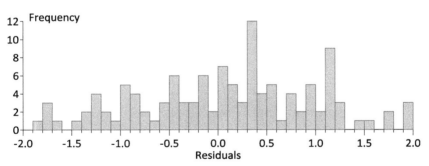

FIGURE 6.16   Histogram of the residuals of the ARIMA(1,1,1) time series model. *Source: Compiled by the authors.*

Fig. 6.15 that the residuals are normally distributed. Substituting into Eqs. (5.32) and (5.33) the values of the residuals of Fig. 6.15, we calculate the following values for the skewness, the kurtosis, and the Jarque–Bera test:

$$\text{skewness} = -0.128 \quad \text{kurtosis} = 2.407 \quad \text{Jarque–Bera test} = 2.068$$

In §5.9.2 we analyzed that for normally distributed residuals, the skewness is almost 0 and the kurtosis is close to 3, something that is verified by the above values for our case.

Finally, for a value of the Jarque—Bera test$=2.068$ and for two degrees of freedom, we can obtain from the chi-square distribution (Table 5.5) that the corresponding α-value is equal to 0.355, a value greater than 0.05 (5%), which means that we cannot reject the null hypothesis of normally distributed residuals.

6.12.4 Serial Correlation Test in the Residuals

We will examine the presence of serial correlation in the residuals with the help of the Ljung—Box test. For a number of time lags $h=10$ (since $n=119$, $h=\min(10, 119/5)$, see §5.9.5.4), Table 6.11 illustrates the values of the autocorrelation function of the residuals of the ARIMA(1,1,1) model, and the corresponding Q-statistic and the probability α values. For all the time lags that have been tested ($h=1, 2,..., 10$), the α values are greater than 0.05 (5%); thus we cannot reject the null hypothesis that *there is no* h-order serial correlation in the residuals.

6.12.5 Heteroscedasticity Test in the Residuals

Evidence for the existence of homoscedastic residuals may appear in a diagram with abscissa the fitted by the ARIMA(1,1,1) model values and

TABLE 6.11: Values of the autocorrelation function, of Q-statistic, and of the corresponding to the Q-statistic probability α (obtained from the chi-square distribution for h degrees of freedom, see Table 5.5) of the ARIMA(1,1,1) time series model.

Order of serial correlation h	Value of the autocorrelation function ρ_h		Q-statistic	Probability α
1		−0.0238	0.0693	
2		−0.0135	0.0918	
3		0.0618	0.5656	0.452
4		−0.0353	0.7213	0.697
5		−0.0303	0.8372	0.841
6		−0.0250	0.9172	0.922
7		−0.0661	1.4791	0.915
8		0.1323	3.7505	0.710
9		−0.1008	5.0796	0.650
10		−0.0209	5.1373	0.743

Source: Compiled by the authors.

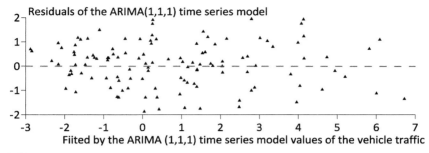

FIGURE 6.17 Visual check for heteroscedasticity to the residuals of the ARIMA(1,1,1) time series model of the first differences of the monthly vehicle traffic (DVT). *Source: Compiled by the authors.*

ordinates the residuals of the model (Fig. 6.17). However, beyond the visual inspection of residuals, we will examine the presence of heteroscedasticity with the use of the appropriate statistical tests, such as the Breusch—Pagan test (see §5.10.2.1), the Glejser test (see §5.10.2.2), the Harvey—Godfrey test (see §5.10.2.3), the White test (§5.10.2.4), and the autoregressive conditional heteroscedasticity (ARCH) test (§5.10.2.5). Table 6.12 illustrates the results of all heteroscedasticity tests, a common characteristic of which is that we cannot

TABLE 6.12: Heteroscedasticity tests of residuals of the ARIMA(1,1,1) time series model and the corresponding probability α (obtained from the chi-square distribution).

	Value of statistic	Degrees of freedom	Probability α
Breusch—Pagan test	HT=4.696	2	0.097
Glejser test	HT=4.349	2	0.114
Harvey—Godfrey test	HT=2.927	2	0.231
White test			
including cross terms	HT=6.157	3	0.104
without cross terms	HT=5.421	2	0.066
ARCH test			
p=1	ARCH(1)=0.270	1	0.604
p=2	ARCH(2)=1.222	2	0.543
p=3	ARCH(3)=2.568	3	0.463

Source: Compiled by the authors.

TABLE 6.13: Comparison of the forecasting accuracy of the various time series models.

Statistic	ARI(1,1)	IMA(1,1)	ARIMA(1,1,1)
Mean absolute deviation	0.797	1.123	0.740
Mean squared error	0.921	2.195	0.813
Root mean squared error	0.960	1.481	0.902
Mean absolute percentage error	1.160	0.773	0.937
Theil's inequality coefficient	0.202	0.399	0.189
bias proportion U^M	0.006	0.111	0.010
variance proportion U^S	0.035	0.588	0.027
covariance proportion U^C	0.959	0.301	0.963

Source: Compiled by the authors.

reject the null hypothesis of no heteroscedasticity in the residuals, since for all the above tests the probability α (obtained from the chi-square distribution) is greater than 0.05 (5%).

6.12.6 Comparative Forecasting Accuracy of the ARIMA(1,1,1) Time Series Model With Other Time Series Models

The forecasting accuracy of the ARIMA(1,1,1) time series model, in comparison with the ARI(1,1) and the IMA(1,1) models, will be evaluated with application of the various statistics described in §5.11. Table 6.13 gives the values of the various statistics, from which we can assess the superiority of the ARIMA(1,1,1) model, since it presents the lower values for almost all statistics describing errors of the forecast (except for the mean absolute percentage error) and the greater value for the covariance proportion U^C, which measures the avoidable nonsystematic error of the model.

Chapter 7

Econometric, Gravity, and the 4-Step Methods

Chapter Outline

7.1 METHODOLOGY AND SUCCESSIVE STEPS FOR THE CONSTRUCTION OF AN ECONOMETRIC MODEL

7.1.1 Causal Relationships and Econometric Models

Causality has always been a central topic in human thinking and in its various undertakings and activities. It entails that when we know the causes and factors that affect a particular problem, then it is to our interest to study and quantify the interactions and relationships of these factors to their outcome. Thus, if some of these factors change, it will be possible to predict (with the use of the established relationship between causes and effect) the quantitative changes and the effects on their outcome. Such a relationship of causality may have the same form with no (or small) changes in relation to time for physics or biology. Nevertheless, in economic and social sciences, causality has a changing form. Transport demand serves the satisfaction of economic or societal needs, which are constantly changing and in some cases are even unpredictable. However, most individuals, when facing a specific need for the

Modeling of Transport Demand. https://doi.org/10.1016/B978-0-12-811513-8.00007-8
Copyright © 2019 Elsevier Inc. All rights reserved.

use of a particular transport mode, exhibit similar behavior, a fact that reveals an inherent character of rationality in choices or decisions related to transport. This means that the same causes under similar conditions will produce similar effects. If this pattern is expressed mathematically, it constitutes what we call an econometric model for transport and allows us to calculate transport demand even if some of its generating causes (often called driving forces or drivers) change. This trivial ascertainment is the foundation of causality for transport demand: knowledge of the evolution of some variables of the problem can lead to the calculation and prediction of future values of transport demand with the help of a mathematical equation, the econometric model, which relates causes (the driving forces) to their effect (transport demand).

The driving forces of transport demand are the variables of an econometric model. These variables may be independent, when there is no correlation between all possible pairs among them, or, more generally, explanatory when they contribute to the explanation of the evolution of the dependent variable (transport demand) (see also §3.1.4). However, an independent variable always has an explanatory character, but an explanatory variable may well be non-independent, if it is correlated with another explanatory variable. The econometric methods that will be analyzed in this chapter will be based principally on independent variables and not on explanatory ones. The reason is that a great number of explanatory variables (many of them may be inter-related) might give the misperception of a global analysis of the problem, whereas fewer variables could lead to the same (or even better) result of a successful forecast; in addition, it is easier to have a trustworthy forecast for the evolution of a small number of independent variables (which will be introduced as inputs in the econometric model) than for a larger one. The experience of many researchers suggests that a strong econometric model with a high forecasting ability and long-range applicability may be built on a small number of independent variables [18,353].

7.1.2 Necessary Conditions Before Trying an Econometric Model

Crafting an econometric model is always a fascinating challenge for any researcher. However, an econometric model is a powerful tool for forecasting, if and only if the following three necessary conditions apply simultaneously:

1. A strong relationship exists between any of the independent variables and the dependent variable, that is, any change in an independent variable has substantial effects in the dependent variable.
2. It is possible to establish a functional form between the dependent variable and the independent ones. The most convenient functional form is of course linearity. However, many problems present strong nonlinearities. Some of the nonlinear problems can be transformed to linear ones by

taking logarithms on both sides of the econometric equation. In linear econometric equations, the coefficients of the various variables have a natural meaning and represent elasticities (see §1.9.2 and §3.1.9).
3. Future values of each one of the independent variables can be forecasted accurately.

If one or more of the above conditions are not satisfied, the forecaster had better use another method of forecast.

7.1.3 Transport Problems That Require an Econometric Model

Econometric models take time to be constructed, validated, checked, and applied. They require specialized staff with a high expertise. Accurate statistical data for the dependent and the independent variables over a long period of time should be collected, and in addition trustworthy forecasts for the evolution of the independent variables should be either available or easy to conduct. For these reasons, econometric models have a high cost of realization and therefore should be used for problems for which other methods cannot provide satisfactory forecasts. Such typical problems for which an econometric model is necessary to assess future transport demand are the following:

1. Construction of new transport infrastructure, such as a new highway, airport, railway line, metro line, and terminal and logistics facilities. The construction of any transport infrastructure is a costly undertaking with an economic life cycle of many decades. A prerequisite for feasibility studies, master plans, employment of staff, revenue estimation, and any strategic or tactical managerial decision related to an infrastructure is the most accurate assessment of the number of customers. Most time series methods (such as trend projection, moving average, etc.) have a short or medium time range of forecasting ability (from some weeks to some years), as they are based on the assumption that the only factor that affects demand is time, while all other factors (such as economic output, costs of transport services, revenues of customers, travel times, quality of services, etc.) will remain the same in the future with their degree of influence on demand unchanged, whereas supply of transport services will also remain unchanged. Thus, the forecast of demand for a new transport infrastructure for a long time ahead requires a causal relationship, which assesses the effects on transport demand of the various factors affecting it. This causal relationship is most often ensured by econometric models.
2. Procurement, buying, or leasing of a number of vehicles (busses, aircrafts, trains, private cars, ships, metro vehicles, etc.) of a transport company. As with the case of infrastructure, increasing the number of vehicles of a transport company is a long-range engagement, which should be based on the most accurate forecast of future customers; econometric models are a

suitable tool, as they correlate causally for a number of years ahead the number of customers to the various factors of demand.

3. Master plans, business plans of transport companies (both operation and infrastructure) describe future policies, organization, management, and investment and depend greatly on the number of future customers (for many years ahead). An econometric model is necessary for any seriously structured business or master plan, as it provides forecasts of transport demand in relation to the various alternatives and for a number of years (up to $10-15$ years) (see also §1.6.2).

4. Creation of a new transport company, extension, or shrinkage of activities of an existing company. As in any economic activity, the crucial issue is the number of potential customers, that is, future demand.

5. Long-term pricing policy and estimation of revenues, which require the most accurate possible assessment of effects of various pricing measures (changes in fares, offers, upgrading of services, etc.) on the number of customers.

6. Short-term changes in the pricing policy, offer or withdrawal of new transport products, changes in the offer, timetables, frequency, etc., which require a clear assessment of effects of each one of these measures on transport demand.

7.1.4 Successive Steps for the Construction of an Econometric Model

The general methodology and flow chart of successive steps for any effort of forecast of transport demand which were presented in Chapter 3 (Fig. 3.1) are also valid for econometric models, as long as some necessary adaptations are made. Fig. 7.1 illustrates a step-by-step methodology for the construction of an econometric model for transport demand. We can distinguish the following *levels* of work:

- Description of the *general form* of the model, which includes a clear statement of the problem under study (e.g., number of passengers for the month x of year z or number of tonnes of oil between origin i and destination j for the winter of year z, etc.), of the forecast horizon (e.g., how long in the future), and of the level of detail (e.g., is it sufficient a forecast of demand of an airport for a whole year or detailed forecasts are required for some months, days or even hours). At this level, the general assumptions, on which the model will be based, are formulated. These assumptions refer to factors that are not considered as the independent variables of the problem and to the general economic conditions (e.g., competition, regulation, etc.), within which transport demand is expected to develop.

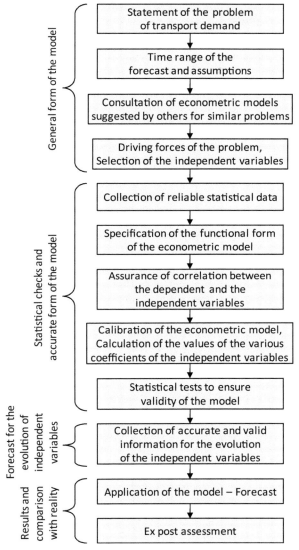

FIGURE 7.1 Methodology and successive steps for the construction of an econometric model for transport demand. *Source: Compiled by the authors.*

The forecaster has strong interest not to depart his or her analysis from zero but to collect any available information about econometric models that have been suggested and (even more) used by others to solve similar problems. There is no reason to reinvent the wheel all over again; others have already done this job. Econometric models which were suggested and used by others will make clear the driving forces of the problem, the likely independent variables, and the functional form (linear, exponential, etc.) between the dependent and the independent variables. Of course, the forecaster will decide, in relation to the nature of the problem, if other driving forces should be included as variables in his or her model. When there is any doubt whether a factor should be considered as an independent variable or not, it is better at this stage not to omit it and leave the decision to remove it at a later stage, if the analysis illustrates a low degree of correlation (between the specific independent variable and the dependent one) or some form of multicollinearity (that is, the specific independent variable is strongly interrelated with another independent variable).

- Collection of the necessary and appropriate *statistical data* (which are related to the problem) and conduct of a number of *statistical checks*, which can ensure the validity of the model and its capacity to represent accurately the problem under study. The statistical checks have been analyzed extensively in Chapters 5 and 6 and will be summarized in §7.2 as well. At the end of this level, the forecaster must conclude what we often call a measurement or explanatory model; this is *an equation* which, in relation to the values of the independent variables (that were recorded or observed in the past), can provide for the dependent variable values which are very close to the recorded or measured ones.

- *Forecast* for the evolution of the *independent variables*, which can be either conducted by the forecaster or based on forecasts made by others. In this latter case, the forecaster should examine carefully the assumptions and the statistical checks related to forecasts made by others. Before using the measurement or explanatory model as a forecasting model, the fore-caster should examine whether coefficients in his or her measurement or explanatory model should be adjusted to represent the conditions expected over the forecast period.

- *Application* of the model and *calculation* of values for the dependent variable. The validity of an econometric model should never be taken for granted; for this reason, the forecaster should conduct constantly *ex post assessment*, that is, compare the forecasted values of his or her model with the actual values that will be recorded [335].

7.2 STATISTICAL TESTS OF AN ECONOMETRIC MODEL

7.2.1 Explore Statistical Validity of Similar Econometric Models

After stating the transport demand problem under study (the dependent variable) and before trying his or her own econometric model, the forecaster is urged to consult in the literature or special studies the econometric models suggested and used by others in the case of similar problems. Thus, he or she can form a basic idea of the eventual plausible independent variables and of the functional form of the relationship between the dependent and the independent variables (linear, exponential, etc.).

However, he or she must be careful and examine whether the appropriate statistical tests have been conducted for the suggested models, look for the values of the various statistical tests (according to what was analyzed in Chapter 5, §5.5, §5.7, §5.8, §5.9, §5.10 and is summarized below), and have a first assessment of how valid a previous model for the current problem can be. If such information about values of statistical tests cannot be found, previous models can be used as a form of knowledge that should be checked and verified.

7.2.2 Selection of the Independent Variables of the Model

Econometric models which were used to solve similar problems in the past will lead the forecaster to assess the likely plausible independent variables of the problem. If such models are not available, then the forecaster must consider carefully the driving forces of his or her problem and decide which can be considered as the independent variables that affect substantially the dependent variable. The forecaster should always have in mind that a small number of independent variables can yield better results than a larger number of variables, which are selected principally for statistical reasons.

Take for instance an effort to construct an econometric model for the forecast of passenger demand with private cars within a specific country. By giving some key words, the forecaster can gather general information in the Internet or look for specialized and documented information in specific scientific journals, relevant reports of international institutions, etc. The second approach is more serious and reliable compared with the first one, which may suffer from low validity and inaccurate information originating from unreliable sources. Based on a number of previous studies, the forecaster can select the following variables [14]:

- car ownership index (I_{CO}),
- cost of fuel (C_{fuel}).

Some researchers suggest to consider the per capita gross domestic product (GDP) instead of (or in addition to) the variable I_{CO}, as the former incorporates the economic, demographic, and income factors of the country. A more careful examination, however, will make clear that there may exist a form of correlation (see §5.6) between I_{CO} and per capita GDP, and consequently these two variables cannot be considered as independent, as they reflect the same or similar economic and societal characteristics and attitudes. If the forecaster aims to construct a model with only independent variables, then he or she can choose one variable (between per capita GDP and I_{CO}) or both and then finalize (with the use of the appropriate statistical tests [see §5.5]) the one that assures stronger association with the dependent variable. But if the forecaster aims at a model with only explanatory variables (see §3.1.4), then he or she can consider both variables until the end of his or her analysis, while being aware that the considered variables may express and reflect the same economic or societal factor.

7.2.3 Statistical Data and Functional Form of the Econometric Model

Once the plausible variables of the problem are identified, the next step is to look for the appropriate statistical data, which should provide an accurate description and overall assessment of the problem under study. Essential characteristics of statistical data are validity, consistency, objectivity, accuracy, continuity, confidentiality, low cost.

Statistical data may be *historical*, when the variable under study is recorded successively by one institution, a record device, or an observer, or *experimental*, when it is the outcome of an experiment, such as a questionnaire survey, in which the investigator poses statements to experimental units (the sample in a questionnaire survey) and then he or she records and assesses the effects of these statements. As experimental data are expensive, they are used principally when no valid historical data are available.

Historical statistical data are easily collected and they should be based on the same or comparable measurement process over time and for all the measurement organizations or recorders. If the last condition is not fulfilled, historical data are not fully representative of the problem under study, cannot be used as reliable inputs in an econometric model, and they simply provide a rather qualitative assessment of the problem.

Historical statistical data can have the following forms [300]:

- *time* series, when they are provided in time order as a sequence of successive points in time (e.g., per year, per month, etc.), which are equally spaced,
- *cross-sectional* data, when they refer either to many variables at the same point of time or to the same variable, whose statistical data are not ordered in a temporal sequence and are randomly presented,
- *panel* (or *longitudinal*) data, which combine both cross-sectional and time series data, and consider how variables change over time.

As econometric models are trying to establish a causal relationship between the dependent and the independent variables in the course of time, they are usually based on time series and panel data.

A crucial question is the period of time which should be covered by statistical data. The general principle is that it should represent as accurately as possible the problem under study. Thus, for data covering successive years, a period of 7−10 years is the minimum [127] (see also §6.3.1).

After having gathered the available statistical data for the dependent and all the plausible independent variables of the econometric model, we can plot the available data for each variable in a scatter diagram, which will illustrate how the problem under study is evolving (linearly, exponentially, etc.). Thus, we can have a *first estimation of the functional form* for the evolution of both the dependent and the independent variables.

7.2.4 Statistical Checks for Stationarity

The first statistical check of a time series of data refers to *stationarity*, that is, whether the beginning time point of the time series affects its pattern and evolution over time. An econometric model should be based on stationary time series data. If data are nonstationary, then they can be transformed to stationary ones as follows (see §5.1.5):

- by taking the first or second differences between consecutive data or observations,
- by taking natural logarithms for the data or observations.

An indication as to whether a time series is stationary or not can be drawn by means of the correlograms, which are the plots of the autocorrelation function (ACF) and the partial autocorrelation function (PACF) (see §6.8 and §6.9). The correlogram of the ACF is a statistical tool for identifying repetitive patterns in a time series: a nonstationary time series has an ACF correlogram which decreases slowly, whereas a stationary time series has an ACF correlogram which declines quickly to zero (see §6.8, Table 6.7).

Instead of examining the ACF correlogram, an alternative and stricter way for identifying stationarity of a time series is to conduct the so-called unit root tests, the most popular among them being the Augmented Dickey–Fuller test (see §6.9.3).

7.2.5 Statistical Test of the Correlation of the Dependent Variable to Each One of the (Considered as) Independent Ones

A fundamental characteristic of an econometric model is that the dependent variable should be strongly correlated with each one of the independent ones. Such a correlation can be tested for a linear regression by means of the Pearson correlation coefficient r_{XY}, which is applied for the various pairs of the dependent variable Y with each one of the independent ones X_j. Values of $r_{XY} > 0.85$ testify a strong correlation between X and Y, values between 0.6 and 0.8 a moderate correlation, whereas values of $r_{XY} < 0.30$ testify a weak correlation. If at this stage of construction of the econometric model the Pearson correlation coefficient between an independent variable X and the dependent variable Y is smaller than 0.30, the forecaster had better to drop out the specific variable X from the independent variables.

The forecaster should always have in mind that the existence of some form of correlation between an independent variable and the dependent one (as it can be testified from values of the Pearson correlation coefficient approaching the value 1.0) does not mean any kind of cause and effect between the specific independent variable and the dependent one (see §7.3).

After calculating the Pearson correlation coefficient for all the independent variables with the dependent one, the forecaster can identify the plausible independent variables of a problem. These are strongly correlated with the dependent one.

7.2.6 Calculation of the Various Coefficients of the Econometric Model and of the Coefficient of Determination

Up to this step we have identified the functional form of the model, as well as the independent variables which are correlated with the dependent one, and we have available a series of statistical data for all the variables of the problem. The statistical tool typically used to accurately calculate the equation relating the dependent variable to the independent ones is linear regression analysis (see §5.2, §5.3, and §5.4). This permits us to calculate the various coefficients (known also under the name regression coefficients or parameters) of the econometric model. Indeed, the econometric model under construction can take the form of a regression equation of the form:

$$Y = a + b_1 \cdot X_1 + b_2 \cdot X_2 + \cdots + b_k \cdot X_k + \varepsilon \qquad (7.1)$$

where

Y	the dependent variable,
$X_j \ (j = 1, 2, ..., k)$	the various independent variables $(j = 1, 2, ..., k)$,
$a, b_1, b_2, ..., b_k$	the various regression coefficients; they are calculated with the ordinary least squares method, which minimizes the sum of squared errors between the actual and the fitted (by the regression equation) values of the dependent variable,
ε	the error term, which is the random component of the regression (see §5.3.1).

When some driving forces are not taken into account as independent variables or when the transport demand problem under study exhibits effects of exceptional events of the past (wars, general strikes, epidemics, etc.), then it is necessary to add to Eq. (7.1) an additional variable to incorporate effects of omitted factors or exceptional events. This additional variable is called a dummy variable (see also §3.1.7) and in such a case Eq. (7.1) takes the form:

$$Y = a + b_1 \cdot X_1 + b_2 \cdot X_2 + \cdots + b_k \cdot X_k + \text{dummy variable} + \varepsilon \qquad (7.2)$$

Now the forecaster can introduce his or her available statistical data to one computer software package (such as EViews, MATLAB, Microfit, Minitab, NumXL, PcGive, R, SPSS, Stata, XLSTAT, etc.), which will provide him or her with the accurate values of the various regression coefficients. This process is often known as the calibration of the model.

A measure of how well the regression equation represents and simulates the problem under study is the coefficient of determination R^2 (see §5.7.1 and §5.7.2) and the adjusted coefficient of determination $\overline{R}^2$ (see §5.7.4). The closer to 1.0 the values of R^2 and $\overline{R}^2$, the better the regression equation simulates the problem under study. If the coefficient of determination does not have a satisfactory value, then the forecaster can increase the number of independent variables and calculate the adjusted coefficient of determination.

7.2.7 Statistical Tests That Testify the Significance of Independent Variables (Student's t-statistic and F-statistic)

The statistical test that can testify how strongly each one of the independent variables of the regression equation is associated with the dependent variable is the Student's t-statistic (see §5.5), given by Eq. (5.25). The t-statistic will be calculated for each one of the independent variables and it should be greater than its critical value, which is a function of the degrees of freedom and of the confidence interval (see §5.5.1 and §5.12.3).

The F-statistic goes further than Student's t-test and permits us to simultaneously evaluate the effects on the dependent variable of all the regression coefficients of all the independent variables. The F-statistic is given by Eq. (5.26) and should be greater than its critical value, which is a function of the degrees of freedom and of the confidence interval (see §5.5.2 and §5.12.4).

7.2.8 Dependence Between Independent Variables—Multicollinearity

A basic assumption of linear regression analysis is that the various independent variables are not correlated with each other. Multicollinearity is the existence of a high correlation between two or more variables which were considered, a priori, as independent. The presence of multicollinearity violates the principle that each coefficient of the linear regression should indicate the expected change in the dependent variable for a unit change in the independent variable under consideration. An indication of multicollinearity is the Pearson correlation coefficient between the various pairs of independent variables. If it takes values greater than 0.4, this is a sign of existence of multicollinearity between the two independent variables under consideration (see Table 5.4).

When the forecaster depicts multicollinearity, he or she must decide which independent variable to eliminate. This is not an easy task and he or she can use either the variance inflation factor (see §5.8), which can clarify which of the collinear variables is less important, or consult previous studies and experience of other researchers.

7.2.9 Residuals and Outliers of the Econometric Model

It is very rare (and only for simple deterministic problems, see §3.2) that the regression equation of an econometric model provides just the same values with the data of the problem. The usual case is that the values $\widehat{y}_i{}^1$ of the dependent variable Y, as they are calculated by the regression equation, are different from the actual values y_i and the difference $y_i - \widehat{y}_i$ is the residual of the regression equation. The reader is reminded not to confuse residuals with errors: a residual is an observable estimate of the unobservable error (see also §5.3.1 and §5.9).

Residuals of a good econometric model should be normally distributed, which is assured if skewness (see §5.9.2) is close to 0 and kurtosis (see §5.9.2) is close to 3. Whether residuals are normally distributed or not is checked by the Jarque—Bera test (see §5.9.2 and §5.12.6.1).

The values of the most distanced data from the regression line are called outliers and represent extreme values of residuals. A good econometric model should contain as few outliers as possible. A great number of outliers may result from a poor fitness of the regression equation to the data of the problem, from erroneous data, or from high fluctuations of data.

The statistical test which can measure effects of outliers on the regression equation is known as Cook's distance (see §5.9.3) and identifies extreme outliers on the set of statistical data, on which the regression equation is based (see §5.12.6.2).

When outliers are the effect of exogenous causes or exceptional events (such as wars, general strikes, epidemics, etc.), the use of dummy variables (see §3.1.7) as independent variables can reduce them.

---

1. We remind that the symbol ˆ above a variable $\widehat{Y}$ denotes the fitted (i.e., calculated) form of the dependent variable Y that results from linear regression and for specific statistical data of the past for the dependent and the independent variables (see §5.3.1).

7.2.10 Serial Correlation (Autocorrelation) in the Residuals of an Econometric Model

Regression analysis is based on the fundamental assumption of the least squares method that residuals of adjacent time periods should not be correlated with each other. Serial correlation (or autocorrelation) is just the opposite and characterizes the situation when the residuals of a specific time period are correlated with the residuals of another time period (see §5.9.4). Serial correlation is observed when some essential variables of the problem are omitted or the functional form of the econometric equation is not the right one or measurement errors occurred in the statistical data.

Serial correlation can be checked visually in the plot of residuals (see Fig. 5.5), when residuals of a given sign tend to be followed by residuals of the same sign. However, the accurate testing of serial correlation is conducted by means of the Durbin—Watson test. The statistic of the Durbin—Watson test, denoted as the DW-statistic, is calculated by the Eq. (5.36). Values of the DW-statistic outside of the range 1.5—2.5 and particularly values greater than 3.0 or smaller than 1.0 are an indication of the presence of serial correlation in the econometric model. In such a case, a plausible solution is to consider the model in terms of first differences, which means that changes in the dependent variable are correlated with changes in the independent variables.

A serial correlation may also occur in the first (or higher) order of residuals. The first-order serial correlation can be tested by means of the Durbin's h-statistic, which is defined by the Eq. (5.38). Another test for the check of any order serial correlation is the Breusch—Godfrey LM test, which is defined by Eqs. (5.39) and (5.40) and the Ljung—Box test, which is defined by Eq. (5.41).

7.2.11 Heteroscedasticity

Another assumption of the least squares method is that the error term has a constant variance and does not depend on the values of the independent variables of the model. When this assumption does not hold, then we have the case of heteroscedasticity, which does not cause any bias to the regression coefficients but can cause bias to the variance and the standard error of the regression coefficients and consequently to the Student's t-test for the significance of the independent variables (see §5.10.1). The usual remedies for heteroscedasticity are the use of logarithmized data or application of the generalized least squares method. Some authors consider that heteroscedasticity is not a problem in an econometric model and should be corrected only when it causes severe problems to the calculation of the regression coefficients [108,300].

The presence of heteroscedasticity in an econometric model can be checked by means of the Breusch—Pagan test (see §5.10.2.1), the Glejser test (see §5.10.2.2), the Harvey–Godfrey test (see §5.10.2.3), the White test (see §5.10.2.4), or the autoregressive conditional heteroscedasticity test (see §5.10.2.5).

7.3 DISTINCTION OF CAUSALITY FROM CORRELATION IN ECONOMETRIC MODELS

We should once again distinguish between correlation and causality. Correlation is the existence of a mutual relationship or connection between two or more processes or phenomena that tend to vary, be associated, or occur together in a way not expected on the basis of chance alone. Causality (referred to also as cause and effect) is the rational relationship between two processes, the first of which (the cause) is partially or totally responsible for the second, while the second is partially or totally dependent on the first. A process can have many causes, which beginning from the past can determine quantitatively the evolution of effects in the future. Causality cannot exist without a form of correlation; however, any correlation does not mean the existence of causality. In addition, causality cannot exist unless the cause happens prior to its effect and moreover it provides statistically significant information about its effect [354,355].

Causality between two variables X and Y can be proved with the use of the so-called *Granger causality test*, named after the British econometrician Sir Clive Granger. This test makes use of Student's t-statistic and F-statistic tests and testifies when values of the variable X provide statistically significant information about the evolution of the future values of the variable Y. Let us assume that Y and X are two variables having stationary time series of data or observations. To test the null hypothesis that X does not Granger-cause Y, we first find the appropriate p lagged values of Y (the order p of the AR(p) process) to include in an AR process of Y (see also §6.7.4) [354,355]:

$$y_t = c + \phi_1 \cdot y_{t-1} + \phi_2 \cdot y_{t-2} + \cdots + \phi_p \cdot y_{t-p} + \varepsilon_t \qquad (7.3)$$

where

$\phi_1, \phi_2, \ldots, \phi_p$ parameters that are calculated with the use of a computer software,

c   the intercept of the AR(p) process.

Next, the Eq. (7.3) is augmented by including lagged values of the variable X:

$$y_t = c + \phi_1 \cdot y_{t-1} + \phi_2 \cdot y_{t-2} + \cdots + \phi_p \cdot y_{t-p} + \omega_m \cdot x_{t-1} + \cdots + \omega_n \cdot x_{t-n} + \varepsilon_t$$
$$(7.4)$$

where

n   the longest lag length for which the lagged value of the variable X has been proved statistically significant.

We retain in Eq. (7.4) all lagged values of the variable X that are statistically significant (according to their t-statistic test), provided that jointly all of them contribute to the explanatory ability of Eq. (7.4) according to the F-statistic test.

The null hypothesis that variable X does not Granger-cause variable Y is accepted when no lagged values of the variable X are retained, after the application of t-statistic and F-statistic tests, in Eq. (7.4). Otherwise, we reject the null hypothesis in favor of the alternative, and we conclude that variable X Granger-cause variable Y and thus the future values of variable Y are depended on the present values of variable X [354,355].

Take for instance a search whether the length of railway lines in operation in China (variable Y) is causally correlated with the life expectancy at birth in China (variable X). We illustrate statistical data of X and Y in Fig. 7.2, and we calculate the Pearson correlation coefficient r_{XY}, for which we find an extremely high value of 0.994. From a statistical point of view, variables X and Y are perfectly correlated. However, could anybody argue that there is a causal correlation between X and Y? The answer is evidently no. Why then these two variables are so closely correlated? The most plausible reason is that both X and Y are related to the level of economic growth in China. As the economy is boosting, revenues are increasing and health conditions are improving. At the same time, more investments are oriented to railway infrastructure. Thus, high economic growth affects in a parallel and similar way both the length of railway lines and the life expectancy at birth.

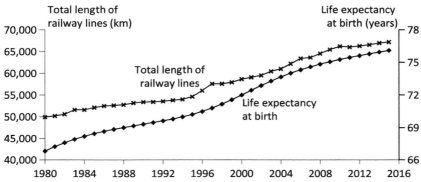

FIGURE 7.2 Evolution of the total length of railway lines and of the life expectancy at birth in China. *Source: Compiled by the authors, based on data of Ref. [38].*

7.4 ECONOMETRIC MODELS FOR AIR TRANSPORT DEMAND

7.4.1 The Driving Forces for Air Transport and the Plausible Independent Variables

7.4.1.1 A Variety of Driving Forces in Relation to the Level of Analysis

Each passenger in an aircraft has his or her own reasons and driving forces for traveling by air; some travel for leisure, others for business, some for health issues, and a few for reasons that may occur once in their life. Thus, the air transport forecaster should take into account all these and some other categories of passengers.

One way to deal with the heterogeneity of the air market is to split it into specific homogeneous categories, such as leisure or business, for which it is easier to identify the driving forces. This split could have clear characteristics in the past, before low-cost air companies had entered the market. It is less meaningful today, with most of the air market being deregulated and in many areas (USA, European Union) fully liberalized; as a consequence, both the leisure and the business traveler are looking for lower cost and are coexisting in the same aircraft in economy class seats [356]. Thus, most air traffic forecasts are conducted at an aggregate level and more particularly at the level of:

- a country (e.g., how many passengers will travel by air to China for the year 2023) or a region (such as Europe or North America),
- an airport, which has a specific catchment area with known economic, demographic, and social characteristics,
- a specific air route (e.g., London–New York), in which many companies are competing,
- an air route of a specific company (e.g., London–New York, United Airlines).

Some of the driving forces for air transport demand are predominant and will be selected as plausible independent variables. Other driving forces are reflected or incorporated in driving forces already selected as independent variables. As mentioned earlier, the analysis of this book focuses on independent variables and not on explanatory ones in general (see §3.1.4 and §7.2.2).

7.4.1.2 A Detailed Analysis of the Various Driving Forces for Air Transport

The first family of driving forces for air transport is related to the economic situation of the passenger as well as of the area (or the country) where the airport is located or from where the passenger is originating. Such economic driving forces are [28,357−359]:

- *disposal income* of an individual or a household, which is the amount of money for spending and saving after income taxes have been accounted for. The disposable income, which is left after more essential needs, such as food, bills (electricity, telephone, etc.), shelter, etc., have been paid, equals the *discretionary income*,
- *purchasing power*, which is the money and credit available for an individual or a household for spending and consumption of goods and services,
- *consumer expenditure*, which is the monetary value of goods and services purchased by individuals or households,
- *trade*, which includes all the activities of buying, selling, or exchanging goods and services related to the location of an airport or an air route,
- *industrial production*, which measures the output of the industrial sector and comprises mining (like the extraction of oil), manufacturing, utilities, and in some cases construction,
- *tourism*, which includes a variety of businesses that provide transport (in most of the cases air transport), hotels, restaurants, entertainment, etc., for people who are traveling,
- *relocation* of companies, which includes all businesses related to transfer the departments, employees, and their families of an economic activity to a new location.

All the above economic indicators have a degree of influence on air transport demand. However, most of them are interrelated. Surprisingly, they can be incorporated and included in a *global economic indicator*, the *GDP per capita*, which is the monetary value of all final goods and services produced within the geographic boundaries of a country during a specified period of time, normally a year, divided by the population. If instead of a country we refer to the economic output of a *region*, then we have the *gross regional product*.

Gross domestic or regional product per capita is the essential independent variable of the great majority of econometric models for air transport demand.

The second essential driving force for air transport is the *cost for the traveler*, the basic component of which is the *air fare*. To the cost of air fare should be added the access cost to the airport, which may be low (compared with the air fare) if access is assured by metro or bus systems but may be as high (and even higher) for remote airports, which serve low-cost airlines. As airlines practice many types of fares, to maximize their revenues, a measure of the medium fare is the revenue per passenger-kilometer (or mile), which is called also unit revenue or *yield*. Mean unit air revenue (yield) per passenger-kilometer was at world level 8.7 US$ cents in 2016 and 8.3 US$ cents in mid-2017 against 16.2 US$ cents (in 2017 prices) in 1975 [126].

Another evident essential factor for air transport demand models is *population*, urban structure, and population concentrations in major poles. The catchment area of an airport includes population with an access time (by trains, private cars, or busses) of no more than 90−120 min [28]. Population does not appear as a separate independent variable to most air transport demand models but is incorporated in the variable GDP per capita [9,28,360,361].

Fuel costs are a substantial part of total air transport costs. They represent 15%−35% of air passenger costs and 35%−45% of air freight costs (see also §1.8.4.2) in relation to variations of oil prices. Fuel costs are not a separate variable in air transport demand models but are usually incorporated in the variable yield per passenger-kilometer.

Technology (with new aircrafts, easy procurement of ticket through the Internet, etc.) is another essential factor of air transport demand, which, however, is also reflected and incorporated in air yields.

Exchange rates of the currency of the host country of a traveler in relation to the currencies of origin countries of passengers may be considered either important (e.g., for a tourist airport) and are introduced as an independent variable or marginal (e.g., for business travelers) and are incorporated in the variable GDP per capita.

The *institutional framework* (regulation, liberalization, open skies, competition, see §1.8.4.7) affects also air transport demand [362,363] but is usually reflected and incorporated in air yields. The same applies with political risks and problems and with the forms of organization of flights between origin and destination, which may eventually include hubbing [364,365]. However, in the case of hubbing with long waiting times at the transfer airport, the factor time is introduced as an independent variable.

For distances beyond 700−1000 km, air transport has practically no competitor. But for lower distances, and particularly for distances around 500 km, air transport faces intense competition from high-speed trains, busses, and private cars. In such a case, the fare of the substitute mode or the ratio of the air fare to the fare of the substitute mode should be included in the model as independent variable.

Air transport causes high levels of *environmental problems*. Environmental agreements at the world level [such as the Paris Agreement (2016) or the Kyoto Protocol (1997)] exempt air transport from their field of application. However, some countries impose an environmental tax in relation to the level of noise pollution, CO_2 emissions, etc. Such environmental factors are incorporated in the variable air yield [366].

7.4.2 Availability of Valid Forecasts for the Evolution of Independent Variables

Before finalizing the choice of the independent variables of an econometric model, the forecaster should carefully examine whether he or she can conduct valid forecasts for the evolution of each independent variable or trust forecasts conducted by others (international institutions, national authorities, individual scientifically documented analyses). If any of these alternatives is not feasible at a reasonable cost, forecasts will be based on questionable data for the evolution of the independent variables and should be evaluated with major reservations.

7.4.3 Econometric Models With Gross Domestic Product as the Only Independent Variable

Econometric models for air transport demand with GDP as the only independent variable are suitable when the effects on demand of all other variables are low compared with the effect of GDP.

For instance, in the United Kingdom in 2012, rising economic activity contributed more than 80% to air transport demand, while declining air fares contributed less than 20% [367]. However, in 2008 (in the middle of the financial and economic crisis for the United Kingdom), rising economic activity contributed less than 50% to air transport demand, while declining air fares contributed more than 50% [367]. In light of these findings, an econometric model for the United Kingdom which will be constructed on the basis of data of 2012 can have GDP as the only independent variable, whereas if it is constructed on the basis of data of 2008 it must have two independent variables, GDP and air fares.

A simple econometric model based on GDP with a high explanatory and forecasting ability has the following form [9]:

$$\ln AT = a \cdot \ln GDP + b + \varepsilon \tag{7.5}$$

where

AT   air trips per 1000 inhabitants,
GDP   gross domestic product per capita expressed in purchasing power parity (PPP),
a, b   coefficients calculated by linear regression analysis,
ε   the error term.

Eq. (7.5) has been calibrated in the year 2014 for the various geographical areas of the world, according to the classification of the World Bank: North

America, Europe and Central Asia, East Asia and Pacific, South Asia, Latin America and the Caribbean, Middle East and North Africa, Sub-Saharan Africa (Figs. 7.3–7.5). For each geographical area, data of GDP were collected for the period from 1980 to 2013, which is representative for the

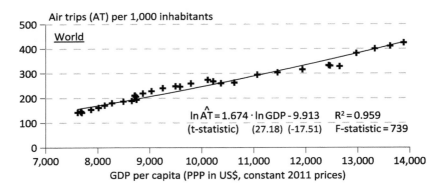

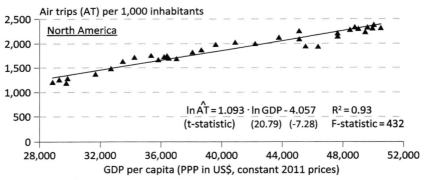

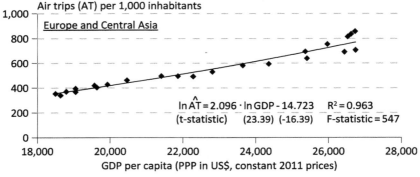

FIGURE 7.3 Econometric models relating air transport demand with gross domestic product (GDP) worldwide and for the regions of North America and Europe and Central Asia. *Source: Compiled by the authors, based on Ref. [9].*

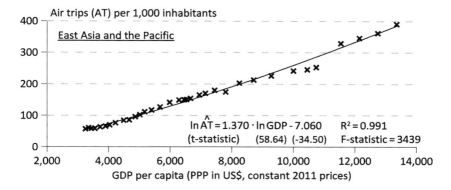

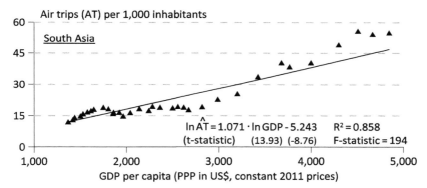

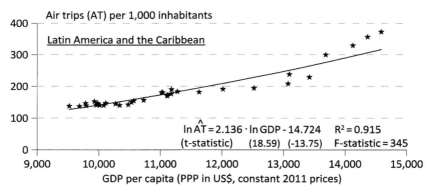

FIGURE 7.4 Econometric models relating air transport demand with gross domestic product (GDP) for the regions of East Asia and Pacific, South Asia, Latin America, and the Caribbean. *Source: Compiled by the authors, based on Ref. [9].*

evolution of the problem under study. These data were introduced to a computer software package (such as EViews, MATLAB, Microfit, Minitab, NumXL, PcGive, R, SPSS, Stata, XLSTAT, etc.), which provided for each geographical area values of the coefficients a and b of Eq. (7.5), the accurate

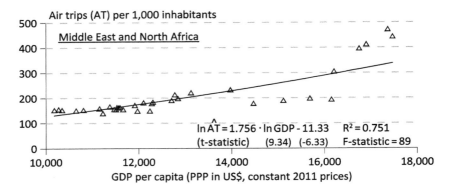

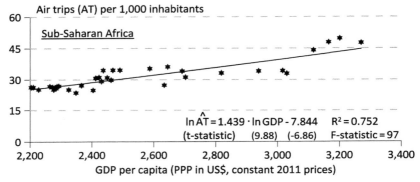

FIGURE 7.5 Econometric models relating air transport demand with gross domestic product (GDP) for the regions of Middle East and North Africa, Sub-Saharan Africa. *Source: Compiled by the authors, based on Ref. [9].*

form of the calibrated linear regression equation and the coefficient of determination R^2 which testifies the degree of correlation of the dependent variable (AT) with the independent one (GDP). The coefficient of determination R^2 has high and very satisfactory values for all air markets which are in the development or the maturity stage (e.g., $R^2 = 0.931$ for North America, $R^2 = 0.963$ for Europe and Central Asia, $R^2 = 0.991$ for East Asia and the Pacific, $R^2 = 0.915$ for Latin America and the Caribbean, $R^2 = 0.858$ for South Asia). Only air markets in the beginning stage (such as Sub-Saharan Africa, Middle East, and North Africa) have lower values of R^2 at the level of $R^2 = 0.75$, which, however, can be considered also as satisfactory. The coefficient of determination at world level is $R^2 = 0.959$.

The high values of the coefficient of determination R^2, the t-statistic test (all values significantly greater than the critical value $t_c \approx 2.03$ derived from the Student's t distribution table [see Table 5.1] for a confidence interval of 95%), and F-statistic test (all values significantly greater than the critical value

$F_c \approx 4.17$ derived from the F-distribution table [see Table 5.2] for a confidence interval of 95%) assure a robust regression of the dependent variable to the independent one.

Now we can use the calibrated equations illustrated in Figs. 7.3–7.5 for the forecast of air transport demand for all geographical areas of the world. This step requires the introduction of the estimated future values for the GDP and the population for each geographical area in the calibrated equations. The forecaster can conduct his own forecasts (which is preferable) or use forecasts of others. Thus, the forecaster will have all the necessary inputs for the calculation of future air transport demand, under the assumption that GDP will be in the future the principal essential factor which affects air transport demand and will keep the same degree of influence as in the past. Table 7.1 gives forecasts of the future air transport demand for a predicting horizon of 15 years.

TABLE 7.1: Air trips per 1,000 inhabitants—Evolution between 1980 and 2013 and application of the econometric model for the forecast of future air transport demand.

| Geographical area | Year | | | Forecast | | Forecast of the annual growth rate (%) of air passenger transport between 2013 and 2030 |
	1980	2000	2013	2020	2030	
North America	1262	2259	2319	2569	2836	1.19
Europe and Central Asia	166	497	859	1079	1567	3.60
East Asia and Pacific	57	165	391	549	884	4.92
South Asia	12	19	55	68	94	3.20
Latin America and Caribbean	143	185	373	424	678	3.58
Middle East and North Africa	150	191	472	494	754	2.79
Sub-Saharan Africa	34	27	48	67	81	3.19
World	145	274	424	560	812	3.90

Source: Compiled by the authors, based on Ref. [9].

Econometric models based only on GDP (or on gross regional product) are used for the forecast of future air transport demand at the level of a *region*, a *state*, or an *airport*.

7.4.4 Econometric Models With Gross Domestic Product and Yield as the Independent Variables

A number of econometric models of air transport demand are based on two independent variables, GDP and yield, and have the following form:

$$\ln AT = c + a \cdot \ln GDP + b \cdot \ln Yield + \varepsilon \qquad (7.6)$$

These models are used for the forecast of future air demand on specific air routes (e.g., London—New York) or on a specific air route for a specific airline (e.g., London—New York, United Airlines), for which it is practically feasible to calculate mean values of yield. They are also sometimes used for forecasts at the level of a region, a state, or an airport. They require accurate knowledge of the evolution over a number of years, and a forecast for the coming years not only of GDP but also of the mean value of yields of the various airlines for each one of their air routes. Many airlines do not publish data concerning the evolution of their yields. Even more, no airline can forecast accurately and reliably the evolution of its yields for a long period ahead. Thus, use of Eq. (7.6) is based in most cases on assumptions related to the values of yields in the past and on their evolution in the future.

The International Civil Aviation Organization (ICAO) calibrated Eq. (7.6) at world level, which is modified by the authors and is suggested as follows [351]:

$$\ln \widehat{AT} = -2.23 + 2.31 \cdot \ln GDP - 0.35 \cdot \ln Yield \qquad (7.7)$$

Eq. (7.7) was found to have an extremely high value for the coefficient of determination $R^2 = 0.992$ and very satisfactory values for the Student's t-statistic, which were t-statistic$_{GDP} = 29.5$ for the variable GDP and t-statistic$_{Yield} = 4.1$ for the variable Yield.

If there are connecting flights with long waiting times at the transfer airport in relation to the total air travel time between the origin and the destination airport, then the air transport total travel time T should be introduced as a third independent variable, and thus Eq. (7.6) takes the form:

$$\ln AT = c + a \cdot \ln GDP + b \cdot \ln Yield + d \cdot \ln T + \varepsilon \qquad (7.8)$$

The International Air Transport Association (IATA) applies for the forecast of air transport demand econometric models of a logarithmic form with a number of explanatory variables (and not independent ones), the principal one of which is the mean value of air fares.

7.4.5 Econometric Models With Independent Variable the Economic Output of a Region

Some econometric models for air transport demand have the economic output of a region as the only independent variable. Such is the case of the model for the forecast of demand for the airport of Riyadh in Saudi Arabia. This model has the following forms for the domestic and international traffic [351]:

$$\widehat{AT}_{domestic} = 0.00206 \cdot IMP^{0.833}, \; R^2 = 0.99 \tag{7.9}$$

$$\widehat{AT}_{international} = 0.000185 \cdot IMP^{0.828}, \; R^2 = 0.93 \tag{7.10}$$

where IMP is the monetary value of imports of the country.

7.4.6 Econometric Models With Independent Variable the Exchange Rate of the National Currency to Currencies of Origin Countries

When analyzing the evolution of demand of some airports or airlines with primarily tourist traffic, it was noticed that air transport demand follows the exchange rates of the currency of the host country in relation to the currencies of origin countries. In such an analysis for the evolution of international passengers at the island of Rhodes (southeastern Greece), it was noticed (Fig. 7.6) that the international traffic of the airport can be calculated by an

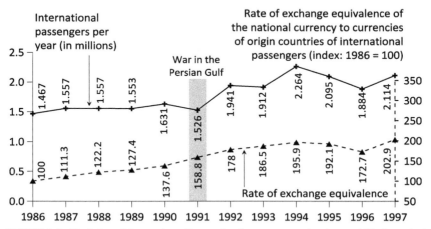

FIGURE 7.6 Evolution of the number of international passengers at the airport of Rhodes and of the rate of exchange equivalence of the national currency in relation to currencies of origin countries of international passengers. *Source: Compiled by the authors, based on Ref. [18].*

econometric equation with only one independent variable, the exchange rate EXR of the national currency of Greece at that time in relation to the currencies of origin countries of passengers of the airport. After calibration, the accurate form of this econometric model (with a high value for the coefficient of determination $R^2 = 0.87$) was [18]:

$$\widehat{D}_{airport} = 1/2 \cdot \left[e^{0.004 \cdot EXR} \cdot 925,332 + EXR \cdot (0.175 \cdot EXR^2 - \right. $$
$$\left. - 43.212 \cdot EXR + 7,548) + 906,696 \right] \tag{7.11}$$

where

$\widehat{D}_{airport}$ annual international passenger demand (dependent variable),

EXR   the exchange rate of the national currency per year in relation to the currencies of origin countries of passengers of the airport. In the calculation of the variable EXR, the currency of each origin country was multiplied by a weight factor which is the percentage of passengers of the specific country in relation to the total number of international passengers.

7.4.7 Econometric Models With Independent Variables the Gross Domestic Product, Exchange Rate, and Tourist Arrivals

For airports combining both business and leisure traffic, econometric models have three independent variables: GDP, exchange rate, and number of tourist arrivals. In such a model for the demand D of the airport of Singapore, the following econometric equation has been suggested, with an extremely high value for the coefficient of determination ($R^2 = 0.999$) [368]:

$$D_{airport} = c + a \cdot GDP - b \cdot EXR + d \cdot TRA + \varepsilon \tag{7.12}$$

where

EXR   the exchange rate of the Singapore dollar to the Chinese yuan,

TRA   tourists' arrivals in Singapore.

7.4.8 Transformation of Aggregate Forecasts at Annual Level to Peak Month, Busy Day, and Typical Peak Hour Traffic

As analyzed in §7.1.3, forecasts of air transport demand are conducted to be used for the planning of facilities and staff of an airport and of the number of aircrafts that will be required to respond to the expected demand, which is not constant over a whole year but manifests variations for the various months, days, and hours during a day. Thus, it is necessary to transform aggregate forecasts at annual level to the traffic that should be expected for the busy day or the busy hour. International institutions such as the ICAO and the IATA and national ones such as the FAA (Federal Aviation Administration) have detailed methodologies, regulations, and software packages to calculate the hourly traffic on which planning of facilities of the airport and aircraft movements will be conducted. However, nobody in the world plans and designs in relation to the busiest hour traffic over the year; such an approach would be economically inefficient, as facilities would be fully used just for 1 hour over the year, whereas they would be underutilized the rest of the time.

The FAA calculates the typical peak hour traffic for the design of facilities of an airport as a percentage of annual traffic, which differs in relation to the volume of annual traffic (Table 7.2).

The ICAO calculates the typical peak hour traffic for the design of facilities of an airport as the traffic of the 30th or 40th busiest hour of the year. The method consists to calculate for the previous years the ratio of the 30th or 40th busiest hour traffic to the annual traffic, to consider that this pattern will continue in the future, and then multiply this ratio with the forecasted future annual traffic [369,370].

The IATA calculates the typical peak hour traffic for the design of facilities of an airport as the traffic of the peak hour of the second busiest day in an

TABLE 7.2: Coefficient for the calculation of peak hour traffic for the design of facilities of an airport in relation to the volume of annual traffic according to the Federal Aviation Administration (values apply separately to domestic and international passengers).

Number of passengers per year	Percentage (%) for the calculation of the typical peak hour traffic
Up to 100,000	0.200
100,000 to 499,999	0.130
500,000 to 999,999	0.080
1,000,000 to 9,999,999	0.050
10,000,000 to 19,999,999	0.045
20,000,000 to 29,999,999	0.040
30,000,000 and over	0.035

Source: Compiled by the authors, based on Refs. [369,371,372].

average week during the peak month. As in the case of ICAO, it is assumed that previous patterns of the evolution of hourly, daily, and monthly traffic will continue unchanged [369].

Many computer software packages (such as the ArcPort and the CAST Simulation) can facilitate calculation of the facilities of an airport (e.g., number of gates, waiting areas for the passengers, etc.) in relation to the previously calculated peak hour traffic.

The number of aircraft required for the satisfaction of the forecasted future demand will be calculated in relation to the expected number of passengers, the load factor, and the aircraft size:

$$\text{number N of aircrafts} = \frac{\text{number of passengers}}{\text{load factor} \times \text{aircraft size}}$$

7.4.9 Econometric Models for Air Freight Transport Demand

7.4.9.1 Air Freight Demand: A Derived Demand for High-Value Products

Freight transport demand is a derived demand, which is a function of the volumes of goods that are produced and consumed and of the location of the various suppliers and the numerous consumers around the world. In contrast to road, sea, and rail transport, air freight transport does not serve the major types of freight, and particularly bulk and general merchandise freight (see §7.11.2), but only specific freight of high value. Air freight is a high-value industry which is sensitive in time and in the safeguarding of quality of the products transported, demanding speed, reliability, and just-in-time delivery. Air freight transport is less than 1% of total world freight transport, but the value of the transported products by air counts for 35% of the total world trade [373]. In 2015, 10.8 million tonnes were transported by air, against 52.2 billion tonnes by sea. Transporting freight by air costs 10−20 times more compared with transporting it by sea. The average air shipment weight was 6.8 kg in 2015, against only 2.7 kg in 1999 [373].

Fig. 7.7 illustrates the evolution of air freight traffic at world level for the period 1970−2015. Growth rates of air freight declined from 7.10% for the period 1970−85 and 8.04% for the period 1985−2000 to 3.12% for the period 2000−15. Not only the financial and economic crisis of 2008 count for this slowdown. Other factors, such as the expansion of use of e-mail and the electronic transmission of documents, have a degree of contribution to the slowing of the growth rate of air freight, whereas factors such as the online purchase of goods have a positive effect on air transport. A rough estimation at world level (which should be considered with great caution due to uncertainties) suggests that air freight traffic for 2035 will be more than double, compared with the traffic of the year 2015 [373].

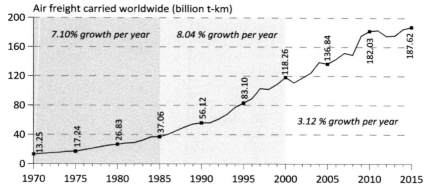

FIGURE 7.7 Evolution of the volume and of the growth rate of air freight traffic at world level. *Source: Compiled by the authors, based on data of Ref. [38].*

7.4.9.2 The Driving Forces for Air Freight Transport and the Plausible Independent Variables

The driving forces for freight transport in general have been analyzed in §1.5.2 and can be specified for air freight transport as follows:

- *Economic output* (gross or regional) in the importing country or region, which can be measured by the GDP/capita or the RDP/capita. In the case of an airport, the economic output refers to the catchment area of the airport, which is perceived as the area and population from which business is attracted. Fig. 7.8 illustrates growth rates of real GDP and air freight transport at world level for the period 1970—2015. Rough estimates for the period 2015—35 suggest at world level an average growth rate for air freight of 2.9% [373]. All econometric models for air freight transport demand suggest a high degree of correlation between air freight traffic and GDP.

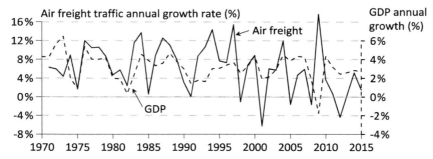

FIGURE 7.8 Evolution of the growth rate of air freight traffic and of gross domestic product (GDP) at world level. *Source: Compiled by the authors, based on data of Ref. [38].*

- *Purchasing power* or *disposal income* of individuals, which is usually reflected and incorporated in the factor GDP/capita.
- *Population* (see also §1.5), an increase of which has direct effects on the increase in consumption (and therefore demand) of the various products, a part of which is transported by air.
- *Air freight costs*, reflected in the values of air freight yields, which have declined on average by 2.7% per year for the period 2005—16 (−2.1% for the period 1995—2015), due principally to productivity gains, technical improvements, and an increasing competition between air careers. Fig. 7.9 illustrates the evolution of rates of yields of air freight transport between 2005 and 2016. The average air shipment charge was 1.80 US$ per kg in 2015, against 4.61 US$ per kg in 1995 [373].
- *Fuel prices*, as fuel costs count for almost 40% of air freight costs. In most econometric models, fuel prices are incorporated in the variable yield.
- *Competition* from substitute transport modes, such as sea transport for long distances and rail and road transport for medium distances. The factor of competition is introduced in an econometric air freight model, when this is required, as the ratio of the fare of air transport to the fare of the substitute transport mode.
- *Exchange rates*, a change of which can affect substantially the prices of products and thus the conditions of demand.

Other factors, such as the institutional framework, various constraints (environmental and economical), and technological evolutions beyond the control of airlines (such as the explosion of electronic purchase of products), are usually not included in air freight econometric models, as it is supposed that these will exert the same influence in the future. All econometric models have as an inherent assumption that adequate capacity will be in place to satisfy demand.

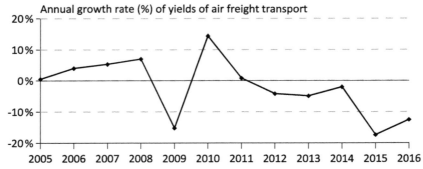

FIGURE 7.9   Evolution of rates of yields of air freight transport at world level. *Source: Compiled by the authors, based on data of Ref. [373].*

7.4.9.3 Some Forms of Econometric Models for Air Freight Transport Demand

Once the driving forces for air freight transport are identified and are transformed to quantifiable plausible independent variables, the forecaster should look for forms of models and equations that have been suggested and used in the past by other specialists in relevant fields. Some typical forms of air freight transport demand models are the following:

- Linear: Air freight transport demand Y is a linear function of the various independent variables X_j:

$$Y = a + b_1 \cdot X_1 + b_2 \cdot X_2 + \cdots + b_k \cdot X_k + \varepsilon \qquad (7.13)$$

where a, b_1, b_2, ..., b_k are the various regression coefficients which are calculated, on the basis of statistical data, with the application of linear regression analysis.

- Log−log: Both sides of the econometric equation are in logarithmic form:

$$\ln Y = a + b_1 \cdot \ln X_1 + b_2 \cdot \ln X_2 + \cdots + b_k \cdot \ln X_k + \varepsilon \qquad (7.14)$$

- Linear−log: The one side of the econometric equation (demand) is in linear form, whereas the other side (which includes the independent variables and the regression coefficients) is in logarithmic form:

$$Y = a + b_1 \cdot \ln X_1 + b_2 \cdot \ln X_2 + \cdots + b_k \cdot \ln X_k + \varepsilon \qquad (7.15)$$

Two typical forms of econometric equations for the forecast of air freight transport demand Y between two regions are the following [351]:

i. $\ln Y = a + b_1 \cdot \ln(\text{EXP}) + b_2 \cdot \ln(\text{Yield}) + \varepsilon$ (7.16)

where

EXP   the monetary value of exports between the regions under study,
Yield   the average air freight fare per tonne-kilometer between the regions under study.

Eq. (7.16) has been used by ICAO for many years.

ii. $\ln Y = a + b_1 \cdot \ln(\text{GDP}) + b_2 \cdot \ln(\text{EXR}) + b_3 \cdot \ln(\text{Freight rates}) + \varepsilon$ (7.17)

where

GDP   the per capita GDP at the arrival region,
EXR   the exchange rate of currencies of the regions under study,
Freight rates   rates of evolution of freight.

Eq. (7.17) is in use by some airports and airlines.

7.5 ECONOMETRIC MODELS FOR RAIL TRANSPORT DEMAND

7.5.1 Classification of the Principal Types of Rail Transport Demand

In contrast to air trips, rail trips present a greater variety of types, which are related to the distance traveled and the principal competitors of railways. As analyzed previously, air transport has no competitor for very long distances, whereas for medium and long distances it faces competition mostly from high-speed railways [137,374,375]. Therefore, rail transport for long distances faces competition from air transport, whereas for short and medium distances it faces competition from busses and private cars [2,137,374,376]. Rail services at urban level are principally used for commuting; the resulting rail demand is a function not only of the competition from busses and private cars but also of the length and density of the road network, the offer of parking facilities and their availability and cost, the existence of urban road toll schemes, etc.

In a train, passengers who travel for business coexist with those who travel for leisure or other reasons. Most econometric models do not calculate rail transport demand in relation to the reason of trip, but in relation to the various types of the rail services, which are classified as follows [7,14]:

1. long-distance (d > 500 km) rail passenger transport, for which the principal competitor of railways is the airplane,
2. interurban rail passenger transport for distances in the range 50–500 km, for which the principal competitors of railways are busses and private cars,
3. urban rail transport for short (d < 50 km) distances, for which railways are used for commuting and face competition from busses and private cars,
4. rail freight demand.

7.5.2 The Driving Forces for the Various Types of Rail Transport Demand

7.5.2.1 Long-Distance Rail Passenger Transport

The driving forces for long-distance rail passenger demand are similar to air transport of short distance and can be summarized as follows [7,14,377,378,519].

- Rail *fares*, a representative and common measure of which is the average rail revenue per passenger-kilometer, and fares of the principal *competitor* (air transport), a measure of which is the average air revenue per passenger-kilometer. Instead of introducing rail and air unit revenues, some models use the following ratio:

$$\frac{\text{rail revenue per passenger} - \text{kilometer}}{\text{air revenue per passenger} - \text{kilometer}}$$

- Total *travel time* (door to door) and *quality of service* (punctuality, reliability, comfort, etc.) for rail transport and its principal competitor (air transport).
- *Socioeconomic* factors, such as the *GDP per capita*, the *household revenue*, the *population*, the *employment*, etc.

7.5.2.2 Interurban Rail Passenger Transport

What differentiates this type of rail passenger transport demand from the previous one is the factors related to competition. To take into account competition from private cars and busses, factors such as the cost of fuel, the private car ownership index, and the cost of bus services are taken into account.

7.5.2.3 Urban Rail Passenger Transport

Factors affecting urban rail transport for commuting are the following: total rail travel times and those of competing modes, mean return journey cost of rail and of competitors, household revenue, perceived (by customers) quality of services provided by railways and other modes, and the access time to the railway station.

7.5.3 Some Forms of Econometric Models for the Forecast of Rail Passenger Demand

For the forecast of interurban rail passenger demand, for which competitors of the railways are private cars, the following econometric model has been suggested (and already analyzed in detail in §5.12):

$$D_r = a + b_1 \cdot C_r + b_2 \cdot F_r + b_3 \cdot I_{co} + b_4 \cdot GDP + \varepsilon \qquad (7.18)$$

where

D_r	rail trips per capita,
C_r	unit cost of transport by rail (per passenger-km),
F_r	frequency of rail services (number of vehicle-km),
I_{co}	car ownership index,
GDP	gross domestic product per capita.

The period of analysis was between 1960 and 2014, and the variables referring to monetary units (C_r, GDP) were adjusted in constant 2014 prices, according to the annual consumer price index. All variables incorporated in the model were indexed to a value of 100 for the year 1985 and then logarithmized. Fig. 5.7 (see §5.12.2) illustrates the results of the econometric model as well as the actual values of the statistical data. We can observe that the econometric model represented by Eq. (7.18) gives values very close to the statistical data; thus it can be used for the forecast of future rail passenger demand, provided that reliable forecasts are available (or can be produced by the forecaster) for the evolution of the various independent variables. It must be outlined for the problem under study that until 1999 travel times of rail and bus services were similar. This fact is not the case for the years after 2000, when the completion of major infrastructure projects in the country decreased the rail travel time; meanwhile the offer to customers of nonstop rail services between major population concentrations rendered the private car as the only competitor of the railways. There are many similar cases in the world, such as the Paris—Brussels route, etc.

However, when the analysis focuses on the period 1960—2000, the econometric model takes a different form:

$$D_r = a + b_1 \cdot C_r + b_2 \cdot C_{b,r} + b_3 \cdot I_{co} + b_4 \cdot GDP + b_5 \cdot D_r(-1) + \varepsilon \qquad (7.19)$$

where

$C_{b,r}$ ratio of cost (per passenger-km) for the use of bus to the cost for the use of railway,

$D_r(-1)$ the time lag dependent variable D_r. The use of a lagged dependent variable may represent factors related to habitual inertia and constraints of supply of rail services (service frequency, rail capacity, services in stations and on trains, etc.) [14]. However, the use of a lagged dependent variable must be considered very carefully and should always be checked whether it covers up the effects of other independent variables [379].

For the forecast of rail passenger demand in the United Kingdom, a number of econometric models of the following form have been suggested [321,380].

$$\ln D_{ij,t} = a + \sum_{k=1}^{n} b_k \cdot \ln X_{ij,t}^k \qquad (7.20)$$

where

$D_{ij,t}$ rail passenger demand between stations i and j for the time t,

$X_{ij,t}^k$ number of k variables describing behavior and choices of travelers when using railways from station i to station j for the time t,

a, b_k the various regression coefficients.

Variables of Eq. (7.20) were selected in relation to the distance of trip, the purpose of trip (leisure, work, other), whether the trip has a commuting or noncommuting character, etc. Such variables were the total rail travel time, the unit revenue of the rail company per trip, the estimated average annual revenue of passengers of each category, the population in the area, the number of employees of the area, the proportion of working age population in the area who are in employment, car fuel costs, bus costs, car journey times, bus travel times, time access to the station, and proportion of households in the area with no car [321,380,381].

For the forecast of rail passenger demand in the Melbourne metropolitan area, the following econometric model has been suggested [382]:

$$D_r = a + b_1 \cdot C_r + b_2 \cdot C_f + b_3 \cdot P + \varepsilon \qquad (7.21)$$

where

D_r annual rail passengers,
C_r average unit cost of transport by rail,
C_f average annual price of fuel per liter,
P estimated population of the area.

For the forecast of rail freight demand, econometric models of the following form have been suggested [380,381,383]:

$$\ln D_{r,freight} = a + b_1 \cdot \ln(freight) + b_2 \cdot \ln(EXR) + b_3 \cdot \ln(GDP) + \varepsilon \qquad (7.22)$$

where

$D_{r,freight}$ rail freight demand,
freight   the freight rate or the volume (in monetary values) of the specific product to be transported,
EXR   the exchange rate, which reflects financial conditions,
GDP   gross domestic product.

7.6 ECONOMETRIC MODELS FOR PUBLIC TRANSPORT DEMAND

7.6.1 The Driving Forces for Public Transport

Public transport includes busses, metros, and tramways and is an old-fashioned term from the time that all the above transport systems belonged to the state. However, the private sector has an increasing participation in many cities in the world for the above systems. Instead of the term public transport, the term mass transit systems has been suggested [384,385,386].

Public transport is an alternative to the use of private cars and presents a number of advantages: high capacity, lower cost for the user, reliable travel times not affected by congestion (for metro, tramways, and busses on reserved lanes), integrated services, and access to central and densely populated urban areas. Major disadvantages of public transport are the inability to provide for every user a direct link from origin to destination and a quality of service with less convenience and easiness compared with the private car, which is an extension for many individuals of their private space [387,388].

Demand of public transport depends on attributes such as speed, travel time, convenience, accessibility of embarkation and debarkation points, lifestyle considerations, and price of ticket which is greatly affected by the degree of subsidies of public or local authorities to the public transport system under consideration.

The driving forces for public transport demand are the following [12,115,387−396]:

- population,
- average cost of a trip when using a specific public transport system (e.g., metro) or another competing public transport system (e.g., bus) or a private car. Instead of using average values of costs for the user, many models use the ratio of the cost for the user of a specific public transport system to the cost of the competing mode,
- travel time of a specific public transport system, of other competing public transport systems, and of private car. As with costs, many models use the ratio of travel time of a public transport system to the travel time of the competing mode,
- average speed of a specific public transport system, of other competing public transport systems, and of private car. As with costs, many models use the ratio of the average speed of a public transport system to the average speed of the competing mode,
- other operational characteristics of public transport, such as frequency, load factor, and number of seats,
- price of fuel (either per liter or per km of trip),
- car ownership index (see also §2.5.1),
- number of daily trips per capita,
- part of the household income which is spent for transport in general (see Table 1.2, §1.5.1) and for public transport more specifically. As analyzed in §1.9.3, income elasticities of busses and other public transport systems are lower than 1.0,
- average daily distance traveled, average trip distance, average distance from home to work,
- supply of road infrastructure per capita: length of road network, density of road network, number of parking places,

- supply of public transport infrastructure per capita, total length of public transport routes and of public transport vehicle-kilometers, or seat-kilometers,
- employment: number of jobs and jobs density,
- local GDP per capita,
- city profile, radial or other pattern of trips, land uses, major poles of attraction of trips.

The forecaster of a public transport demand problem will select some of the above variables as independent variables for his or her problem in relation to the specific characteristics of the problem and the available data.

7.6.2 Some Forms of Econometric Models for the Forecast of Public Transport Demand

There are many authorities worldwide dealing with public transport issues, among them is the International Association of Public Transport (UITP, from its French initials Union Internationale des Transports Publics), which publishes detailed data of public transport systems all over the world. Based on the analysis and data of UITP for more than 100 cities around the world with public transport systems, the following econometric model with explanatory variables and a coefficient of determination $R^2 = 0.74$ has been suggested:

$$\ln PT = a + b_1 \cdot \ln GDP + b_2 \cdot SR + b_3 \cdot F + b_4 \cdot PS + b_5 \cdot CR + \varepsilon \qquad (7.23)$$

where

PT	public transport demand,
GDP	percentage (%) of gross domestic product spent on investment for public transport,
SR	ratio of the average speed of public transport to the average speed of private cars,
F	price of fuel,
PS	number of parking places per 1000 jobs,
CR	ratio of cost for the use of public transport to the cost for the use of private car.

Another econometric model suggested the following econometric equation for the ratio of the demand D_{PT} of a public transport system to the demand D_{car} of private cars [397]:

$$\frac{D_{PT}}{D_{car}} = a \cdot \left(\frac{\text{travel time}_{PT}}{\text{travel time}_{car}}\right)^{b_1} \cdot \left(\frac{\text{cost of use of public transport}}{\text{cost of use of private car}}\right)^{b_2} \qquad (7.24)$$

where a, b_1, b_2 are the various regression coefficients.

7.7 ECONOMETRIC MODELS FOR ROAD TRANSPORT DEMAND

7.7.1 The Driving Forces for Road Transport

Road transport is the prevailing mode of mobility in urban areas and for interurban trips for distances up to 500 km. However, there are a number of upcoming reasons that may affect the use of private cars in the future to assure mobility, such as:

- cost of use of a private car for a specific trip and cost of alternative modes,
- alternative ways to assure mobility (metros, urban railways, busses, bicycles, walking) are more and more available by public authorities to safeguard sustainable mobility,
- economic reasons limit the number of cars per household and the number of kilometers run by private cars,
- people realize that carpooling and car sharing (see §1.7.3.4) are efficient, comfortable, and lower-cost alternatives to the possession of a private car,
- environmental considerations encourage individuals to reduce the use of their private cars. An eventual internalization of external costs (see §1.8.4.5) will make the use of a private car even more costly [71,520].

The driving forces for road transport are some of the following [14,185]:

- population: number of individuals, age distribution, number of members of a household,
- economic factors: GDP per capita, disposable income, purchasing power, consumer expenditure,
- supply of road infrastructure: length and characteristics (freeway, arterial, collector and distributor, local) of the road network, average speeds in roads, number of parking places, etc.,
- private car ownership index, cost of fuel, cost of purchase of a car,
- employment, number of jobs,
- lifestyle, sociocultural factors, level of education, recreation and leisure habits,
- land-use patterns, densities of population, major poles of attraction of trips.

Percentages of use of road transport to assure mobility of individuals are very diversified in the various parts of the world (see §2.2.1 and §2.5.1) and are reflected in the car ownership index (see §2.5.1) and the share of road transport to the total number of trips (see Table 2.1, §2.2.1). For each specific case, the forecaster should consider the above driving forces and select among them the independent variables that will be introduced in an econometric equation, which will permit to relate causally road transport demand with the selected as independent variables.

7.7.2 An Econometric Model for the Forecast of Road Transport Demand

An econometric model for the forecast of road transport demand with private cars D_{car} had only two independent variables: the private car ownership index I_{CO} and the cost of fuel C_{fuel}. The econometric equation of the model was as follows [14]:

$$\ln D_{car} = a + b_1 \cdot \ln I_{CO} + b_2 \cdot \ln C_{fuel} + \varepsilon \qquad (7.25)$$

The model was calibrated for the case of Greece for the period 1980–2000 with a high value for the coefficient of determination $R^2 = 0.99$ and very satisfactory values for the Student's t-statistic, which are illustrated between parentheses just beneath the following calibrated Eq. (7.26):

$$\underset{(\text{t-statistic})}{\ln \widehat{D}_{car}} = \underset{(8.03)}{1.723} + \underset{(34.61)}{0.691 \cdot \ln I_{CO}} - \underset{(-2.40)}{0.066 \cdot \ln C_{fuel}} \qquad (7.26)$$

We remind that t-statistic values must be greater than the critical values, given in Table 5.2 (§5.5.1), which for a confidence interval of 95% are usually within the range -2.00 to $+2.00$.

7.8 ECONOMETRIC MODELS FOR THE FORECAST OF DEMAND FOR TAXI SERVICES

7.8.1 The Driving Forces for Taxi Services

Taxis are vehicles which are licensed from a public authority to transport passengers who pay for the taxi services rendered to them a fare usually computed and indicated by a taximeter; they are private vehicles which are used for public transport services and provide door-to-door personal transport. Therefore, they are a substitute of private cars (in some cases of public transport) and respond to specific transport needs of individuals, who either do not own a private car, or who own a private car but have difficulties in finding a parking place at a reasonable cost or do not want to use it (for cost or other reasons). Taxi services are classified into three categories [398]:

- taxi stands (or taxi ranks), where taxis are waiting for passengers and vice versa,
- cruising taxis on the streets, looking for a client,
- prebooked taxi services by clients who can contact a dispatching center with the use of telephone, e-mail, or SMS either for an immediate service or for a service which will be provided later.

The driving forces for taxi services, some of which will be the independent variables of an econometric model for taxi demand, are the following [398,399]:

- price of taxi services,
- purchasing power or disposable income of customers,

- cost of parking and availability of parking places,
- cost of substitute or alternative transport modes (bus, metro, tram),
- quality of service of substitute modes: travel time, convenience, distance to access a bus stop or a metro station,
- number of taxi licenses or taxis in service for specific time intervals (e.g., midnight taxi demand),
- form of the taxi market: regulated (specified costs for picking a passenger and per kilometer of traveling), competitive (the fare is freely negotiated between the passenger and the taxi driver).

7.8.2 Some Econometric Models for the Demand of Taxi Services

Demand for taxi services is a case of demand at urban level for a specific transport mode (taxi). Thus, a first approach to model taxi demand is to use the 4-step model (see §3.9.7 and §7.10) with the appropriate modifications, which can lead to the reduction of the four steps of the model to two. The first step is known as trip generation. The total number of trips originating at the study area is calculated as in the classic 4-step model with the help of an econometric equation, which can be calibrated with a number of independent (or explanatory) variables. The second step consists in calculating the percentage of total trips which will be realized by taxis. The selection of mode is based on the generalized cost of the alternative transport modes and depends greatly on the value of travel time for the various categories of passengers. For instance, it was suggested in the United Kingdom, in the early 2010s, a value of travel time per hour that was £48 for taxi passengers against £40 for railway passengers [400]. The calibration of the model is based, both for the first and the second step, on data collected from traditional sources (such as official statistics) but also on big data collected with the help of GPS technologies [400].

Another approach is to use a direct demand econometric model. It has been suggested that taxi demand is a function which incorporates the following variables: flag drop charge, unit cost of taxi per km, average distance traveled by taxi, waiting time of taxi customers, value of time of taxi customers, perceived (by taxi customers) quality of taxi services [401].

Another econometric model, derived from the analysis of taxis in the city of Hong Kong, suggested the following econometric equation for the demand of taxi services, with a satisfactory value of the coefficient of determination ($R^2 = 0.83$) [402]:

$$\ln \widehat{D}_{taxi} = 15.684 - 0.5867 \cdot \ln(W + T) - 0.0444 \cdot \ln\left(\frac{F}{I_d}\right) \qquad (7.27)$$

where

D_{taxi}	average number of daily taxi trips (dependent variable),
W	average waiting time of taxi passengers,
T	average travel time of taxi passengers,
F	unit taxi fare (per 200 meters),
I_d	average annual personal disposable income.

A controversial issue is very often the required number of taxis to be licensed in an area. An analysis of the number of taxis in 118 US cities (New York City included) calculated, with an extremely high value for the coefficient of determination ($R^2 = 0.99$), the number of taxis of a city [403]:

$$\widehat{N}_{taxi} = 31.42 + 21.81 \cdot S + 5.14 \cdot NC + 0.64 \cdot A + 129.95 \cdot DM \qquad (7.28)$$
$$\text{(t-statistic)} \quad (0.6) \quad (12.7) \quad (4.0) \quad (7.2) \quad (1.4)$$

where

N_{taxi}	number of licensed taxis (dependent variable),
S	number of workers commuting by metro,
NC	number of households with no private car available,
A	number of travelers commuting from airports by taxi,
DM	dummy variable (see §3.1.7), which takes the value 1 when a city has more than 19,000 households without a private car and the value 0 otherwise.

New York City was considered as an extreme case among the sample of 118 US cities, since it presented five to nine times as many taxis, no-car households, and metro commuters as any other city of the sample. When the model was calibrated without New York City, it presented the following more representative for the majority of US cities form, with a less satisfactory value for the coefficient of determination ($R^2 = 0.86$) [403]:

$$\widehat{N}_{taxi} = 36.10 + 19.72 \cdot S + 4.47 \cdot NC + 0.70 \cdot A + 145.79 \cdot DM \qquad (7.29)$$
$$\text{(t-statistic)} \quad (0.7) \quad (8.0) \quad (3.2) \quad (6.7) \quad (1.6)$$

7.9 ECONOMETRIC MODELS FOR THE SIMULATION OF ROAD SAFETY

7.9.1 Factors Related to Road Accidents

Road safety continues to be a major problem for every society, particularly for low- and medium-income countries (see §2.5.4). Surprisingly, most individuals consider road accidents (and accidents in general) to be other people's concern, until they themselves are involved in a road accident.

Factors that can be related to road accidents and therefore can be selected as independent variables of a road safety model are the following [147,404−410]:

- tendency of an individual to be exposed to risks,
- age of the driver,
- population and its characteristics,
- previous record and history of the driver related to road safety,
- car ownership index,
- geometrical characteristics of the road (radius of curvature, longitudinal gradient, transverse slopes, roughness of the pavement),
- level of maintenance of the road,
- level of saturation of the road network,
- speed and conditions of flow of vehicles,
- weight of the vehicle (light, heavy),
- characteristics of the vehicle (power, systems preventing the driver for an imminent failure, control systems of speed and braking),
- age of the vehicle,
- level of maintenance of the vehicle,
- visibility conditions,
- lighting conditions,
- weather conditions (rain, snow, wind, temperature),
- level of fines and penalties,
- level of alcohol in the blood of the driver,
- information of the driver about the risks and dangerous points in the road,
- social culture, which affects the degree of aggressiveness of drivers,
- conditions of fatigue of the driver (total hours in driving, eventual pause and stop for relaxing),
- use of seat belt.

The dependent variable in a road safety model can be one of the following [408,410]:

- number of accidents (in general, all accidents),
- number of accidents with fatalities,
- number of accidents with injuries,
- number of victims (fatalities, injuries),
- number of victims per category (car occupants, pedestrians, bicyclists, motorcyclists),
- severity of the accident.

7.9.2 Econometric Equations for Road Safety Issues

Based on data of various European countries for the year 2015 (Fig. 7.10), the following econometric Eq. (7.30) was compiled by the authors and can be suggested for the correlation of the number of fatalities (RF) from road accidents in these countries with the GDP per capita, with a high and satisfactory value of the coefficient of determination ($R^2 = 0.86$):

$$\widehat{\ln RF} = \underset{(12.69)}{7.583} - \underset{(-13.08)}{0.741 \cdot \ln GDP} \qquad (7.30)$$
$$\text{(t-statistic)}$$

Fig. 7.11 illustrates the actual number of fatalities (RF) from road accidents in the various European countries and the estimated number of fatalities derived from Eq. (7.30).

A crucial issue in road safety is the impact of the radius of horizontal curves on the frequency of road accidents. Based on data of a number of road accidents in Norway (Fig. 7.12) [405], the following equation can be suggested for the forecast of the frequency (FA) of road accidents with injuries per million vehicle-kilometers run, with a relatively satisfactory value for the coefficient of determination ($R^2 = 0.77$):

$$\widehat{\ln FA} = \underset{(3.09)}{0.811} - \underset{(-8.29)}{0.412 \cdot \ln R} \qquad (7.31)$$
$$\text{(t-statistic)}$$

where R is the radius (in meters) of the horizontal curve.

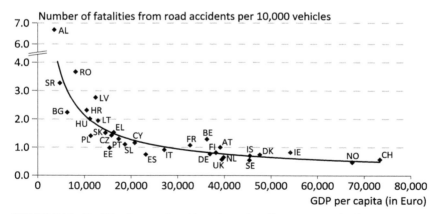

FIGURE 7.10   Fatalities from road accidents for various European countries in relation to the gross domestic product (GDP) per capita (for the abbreviations of the countries see Fig. 7.11). *Source: Compiled by the authors, based on data of Ref. [4].*

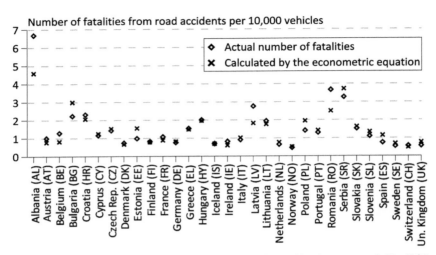

FIGURE 7.11 Comparison between the actual and the calculated by the econometric Eq. (7.31) number of fatalities from road accidents in various European countries. *Source: Compiled by the authors.*

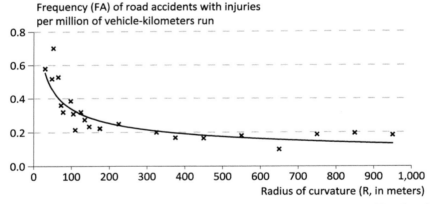

FIGURE 7.12 Correlation of the radius R of horizontal curves to the frequency (FA) of road accidents with injuries. *Source: Compiled by the authors, based on data of Ref. [405].*

7.10 FORECAST OF TRANSPORT DEMAND AT URBAN LEVEL—THE 4-STEP MODEL

7.10.1 A Choice Among Many Alternatives Through Maximization of Utility of Individuals

A traveler at urban level has many alternative (but mutually exclusive) options: car (driving alone or carpooling or car sharing), bus, metro, tramway, walking, and bicycle. It has been proven that before deciding on making a trip, a traveler evaluates the various attributes of each alternative in his or her attempt to maximize the utility he or she will obtain from a specific choice (see §3.3.2). Attributes of each alternative transport mode may include the following: travel cost, total travel time, in-vehicle travel time, out-of-vehicle travel time, number of travelers, number of transfers and waiting times at transfers, walk distance, reliability of on time arrival, convenience of travel. In his or her evaluation of the attributes of a transport mode, a traveler is affected by its personal characteristics: revenue, age, gender, lifestyle preferences, number of private cars in a household, and number of the adults of the household.

As it has been analyzed in §3.3.2 (Eqs. 3.2 and 3.3), the utility of an individual when using a specific alternative transport mode can be calculated as the sum of four partial components: a utility component associated with the characteristics of the individual, a utility component associated with the attributes of the transport mode chosen, a utility component resulting from interactions of the above two components, and a utility component resulting from measurement errors.

At urban level, a great number of individuals with largely different socioeconomic, employment, demographic, and land-use characteristics make a number of trips for various reasons (work, leisure, etc.) by exploiting the technical and economic advantages of the existing infrastructures and transport modes. Thus, transport demand at urban level will result from the interaction of the characteristics of the various individuals, of the capacity offered by the various existing infrastructures, and of the attributes of the alternative transport modes. This interaction is studied by a number of processes, the most popular of which is the (known as) 4-step process or 4-step model.

7.10.2 Principles, Assumptions, and Successive Steps of the 4-Step Model

The 4-step model permits the calculation of transport demand for a specific mode at urban level through a composite process which includes, in principle, four steps: trip generation (first step), trip distribution and allocation to origin—destination pairs (second step), choice of mode of transport and modal split (third step), assignment and determination of route for the various trips (fourth step) [411—415].

The 4-step model was first applied in the early 1950s for the study of transport demand for the Greater Chicago Area in the United States and just afterward it was imposed by the legislation in the United States as a required analysis and prerequisite for any continuous, comprehensive, and cooperative urban transportation planning [416]. Other countries of the world (Japan, the United Kingdom, France, Germany, etc.) have also introduced the 4-step model as part of a comprehensive urban transportation planning, hence the popularity of the method.

The 4-step model has a number of assumptions at each step, which are detailed in the following paragraphs. Some general characteristics and assumptions of the 4-step model (for which a serious criticism has been addressed) are the following [417]:

- The model does not account for the variable time, as behavioral theories of maximization of individual utility, on which it is based, suppose that individual behavior and choices are not affected in any way in the course of time. Thus, congestion conditions in any infrastructure cannot be considered by the 4-step model.
- It supposes that each trip at urban level is independent of all other trips, an assumption which is contrary to the reality of urban trips interrelated among them; thus the 4-step model cannot take into account the impact of eventual travel demand management measures (such as the introduction of urban road toll schemes).
- Any error at each step is reflected in the successive steps.
- Any changes in the supply side of transport demand (construction or improvement of infrastructure) cannot be taken into account in the 4-step model.

In spite of its popularity, the 4-step model is not a method in itself. It is a complex process, which is based on both quantitative and qualitative methods. The first step (trip generation) employs time series and econometric methods, the second step (trip distribution) questionnaire surveys and gravity methods, the third step (choice of mode) probabilistic methods (such as the Logit and Probit models, see §7.10.5), and the fourth step (trip assignment) probabilistic and mathematical minimization methods.

A large amount of data are necessary for the 4-step model as well as a number of specialists with a knowledge and expertise in statistical and econometric methods.

Some specialists suggest a 2-step method for transport demand at urban level. According to this method, the first step includes trip generation and distribution and the second step encompasses choice of mode and assignment of route.

7.10.3 Trip Generation

7.10.3.1 The Various Classifications of Trip Generation Models

The first step of the 4-step model is trip generation and aims at the calculation of the total number of trips which are originating or destined within the study area, being partitioned in homogeneous zones based on socioeconomic, demographic, employment, and land-use characteristics. Generated trips are classified into two categories:

- *home-based* trips, for which the home refers either to the origin or to the destination of the trip,

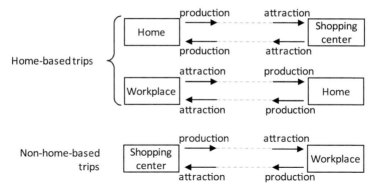

FIGURE 7.13 Attraction and production of home-based and non-home-based trips. *Source: Compiled by the authors.*

- *non-home-based* trips, for which neither the origin nor the destination of the trip is the home of the traveler (e.g., trip from the work place to a shopping center or vice versa).

Trip production and trip attraction differ from the origin and destination of a trip. The origin refers to the start point of a trip, whereas the destination refers to the end point of a trip. Trip production, however, is defined as the origin of a non-home-based trip or as the home end of a home-based trip, whereas trip attraction is defined as the destination of a non-home-based trip or the nonhome end of a home-based trip (Fig. 7.13). Thus, trips are produced by travelers even when they are returning home (that is, when the home is the destination). Therefore, household areas are the primary producers of trips, while employment areas are the primary attractors of trips.

The zones in which the study area is partitioned must be of a similar size, with an easy determination of their centroids[2], as homogeneous as possible in terms of size and land use, compatible with the administrative segregation of the study area.

Models of trip generation are classified, whether they face and calculate originating and destined trips as a whole or per household, as:

- *aggregate* models, mainly based on zonal aggregation approaches considering the travelers as a whole,
- *disaggregate* models, mainly based on travelers' behavior and individual characteristics (gender, age, car ownership index, disposable income, etc.).

---

2. A centroid is an imaginary point within a zone, from which departing trips are assumed to originate and at which arriving trips are assumed to terminate.

Trip generation models are further classified into *growth factor models*, *cross-classification models* (sometimes referred to as *category analysis models*), and *regression models*.

7.10.3.2 Growth Factor Models

If there exist a number of data of trips per zone, a simple method is to project these data into the future by multiplying trip data of the past by a growth factor F, which is a relation of the changes of population and other zonal economic characteristics (car ownership index, employment, disposable income, land use, building density, etc.) of the various zones. The estimation of the growth factor F can be based either on trends of trip data or on forecasts of future economic characteristics. Thus, according to this simplistic method, trips T_i^N generated from zone i for the future year N will be calculated in relation to trips T_i^0 generated for the base year, as follows:

$$T_i^N = F_i \cdot T_i^0 \tag{7.32}$$

where F_i is the growth factor for the zone i.

The model assumes that all other factors (such as cost and travel times), which affect passenger transport demand and are not taken into account in the growth factor F, will remain the same in the future with their degree of influence unchanged (see also §6.1.2). It is evident that this method can be used for short- or at the maximum for medium-term forecasts.

Therefore, if some kind of origin—destination study was conducted in the past and resulted in the calculation of the number of trips, then trip generation in the future can be calculated by multiplying previously calculated transport demand by a growth factor, which is a relation of population, income, car ownership index, and land-use patterns [413,418].

Let us consider an origin zone i which includes 1000 households, 100 out of which do not possess a private car and generate 1.5 trips per day and per household, 600 households possess one private car/household and generate 3.5 trips/day/household, and 300 households possess two private cars/household and generate 4.5 trips/day/household. The total number of trips generated by the specific zone i for the base year is:

$$T_i^0 = 100 \cdot 1.5 + 600 \cdot 3.5 + 300 \cdot 4.5 = 3600 \text{ trips}$$

The average private car ownership index (I_{CO}) for the base year is:

$$I_{CO}^0 = \frac{100 \cdot 0 + 600 \cdot 1 + 300 \cdot 2}{1000} = 1.20 \text{ private cars/household}$$

If we study the trend for the variable I_{CO}, we can forecast its value for the year N to be $I_{CO}^N = 1.50$ private cars/household; then the growth factor F_i for the specific zone i will be the ratio of the two values of I_{CO}:

$$F_i = \frac{I_{CO}^N}{I_{CO}^0} = \frac{1.50}{1.20} = 1.25$$

and the total number of trips which will be generated by the specific zone i for the future year N will be:

$$T_i^N = F_i \cdot T_i^0 = 1.25 \cdot 3600 = 4500 \text{ trips}$$

7.10.3.3 Cross-Classification (or Category Analysis) Models

Trip generation is calculated in relation to the characteristics of a household, such as the household size, household income, car ownership, etc. The various households are classified into categories on the basis of one or more characteristics of the household, and a questionnaire survey is conducted to record the number of trips per household of each category for the base year. The number of trips for the future year N will be calculated from the equation:

$$T_i^N = \sum_{k,l,m,n} H_{i_{k,l,m,n}}^N \cdot t_{k,l,m,n}^0 \tag{7.33}$$

where

T_i^N	number of trips originating from zone i for the future year N,
k, l, m, n	characteristics for the classification of households in categories (e.g., k: income, l: size, m: car ownership index, n: number of employees),
$H_{i_{k,l,m,n}}^N$	estimated, for the future year N, number of households of category k, l, m, and n,
$t_{k,l,m,n}^0$	base year trips per household of category k, l, m, and n.

Fig. 7.14 illustrates an example of category analysis of the households of a zone in order to calculate rates of trip generation per household category. We consider the case of a middle-income household nonpossessing a private car with three members, two of which are working. A questionnaire survey for the base year recorded a number of 2.3 trips/day for this household category. If the future year N the zone i includes 400 middle-income households nonpossessing a private car and two out of the three members of these households are working, then the number of generated trips for the specific household category will be for the year N:

$$400 \text{ households} \cdot 2.3 \text{ trips/day} = 920 \text{ trips/day}$$

A basic assumption of the cross-classification models is that trip generation per category remains stable during the period of analysis.

7.10.3.4 Regression Models

A more rational way consists in calculating the number of trips as a function of the various attributes of individuals within the study area. The total

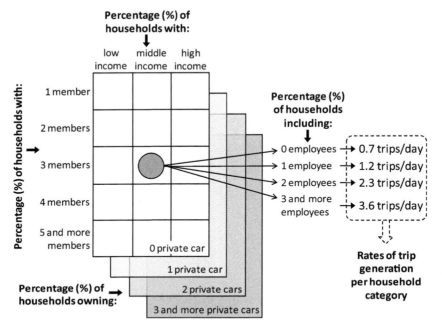

FIGURE 7.14 An example of category analysis of the households of a zone for the calculation of trip generation. *Source: Compiled by the authors.*

number Y of trips originating at zone i or terminating at zone j can be calculated by a linear regression equation of the form:

$$Y = a + \sum_{\ell=1}^{n} b_\ell \cdot X_\ell \qquad (7.34)$$

where

b_ℓ the various regression coefficients,

X_ℓ the various independent variables which refer to socioeconomic and employment characteristics in the study area,

a   the intercept.

7.10.3.5 The Principle of Conservation

Trips at urban level are usually classified into two categories, home-based and non-home-based. For each category, trip generation is a function of a number of variables such as the number of members of the household, the income of the household, and the car ownership index. Thus, Eq. (7.34) can be specified for the number $Y_{i,p}$ of trips originating at zone i with purpose p as follows:

$$Y_{i,p} = a + b_1 \cdot X_1 + b_2 \cdot X_2 + b_3 \cdot X_3 \qquad (7.35)$$

where

X_1 the number of households at zone i,

X_2 the rate of production of trips for households included in a margin of income level (e.g., 30,000−40,000 €/year),

X_3 the percentage (out of the total number) of trips generated at zone i with purpose p,

a   the intercept.

The principle of conservation implies that the total number of trips T_i generated from all origin zones must be equal to the total number of trips T_j destined to all zones j:

$$\sum_{i=1}^{n} T_i = \sum_{j=1}^{n} T_j \qquad (7.36)$$

Eq. (7.34) approaches the nonlinear problem of trip generation as a linear one. An inevitable effect of this approach is that trips calculated according to Eq. (7.34) cannot satisfy Eq. (7.36). Thus, the forecaster is in front of the dilemma of basing his or her analysis either on originating or on destined trips. It is argued that we can have more confidence in the trip origination process, as it is based on more solid socioeconomic characteristics, than in the trip destined process. In light of the previous statement, the total number of destined trips (T_j) should be normalized by using the following Eq. (7.37) [411,413]:

$$T_j' = T_j \cdot \frac{\sum_{i=1}^{n} T_i}{\sum_{j=1}^{n} T_j} \qquad (7.37)$$

where T_j' are the normalized trips destined to zone j.

7.10.4 Trip Distribution

7.10.4.1 The Various Models of Trip Distribution

Trip distribution is the second step of the 4-step model. In this step the number of trips is allocated to origin−destination pairs in relation to the attractiveness of a zone and to the total number of trips originating in the specific zone (Table 7.3).

Models of trip distribution use *growth factor*, or *gravity*, or *probability theory* techniques.

TABLE 7.3: Allocation of trips at origin-destination pairs.

Origin zone i	Destination zone j						$O_i = \sum_{j=1}^{n} T_{ij}$
	1	2	$\cdots$	j	$\cdots$	n	
1	T_{11}	T_{12}	$\cdots$	T_{1j}	$\cdots$	T_{1n}	O_1
2	T_{21}	T_{22}	$\cdots$	T_{2j}	$\cdots$	T_{2n}	O_2
$\vdots$	$\vdots$	$\vdots$		$\vdots$		$\vdots$	
I	T_{i1}	T_{i2}	$\cdots$	T_{ij}	$\cdots$	T_{in}	O_i
$\vdots$	$\vdots$	$\vdots$		$\vdots$		$\vdots$	
n	T_{n1}	T_{n2}	$\cdots$	T_{nj}	$\cdots$	T_{nn}	O_n
$D_j = \sum_{i=1}^{n} T_{ij}$	D_1	D_2	$\cdots$	D_j	$\cdots$	D_n	$T = \sum_{i=1}^{n}\sum_{j=1}^{n} T_{ij}$

Source: Compiled by the authors.

7.10.4.2 Trip Distribution With the Use of Constrained Growth Factor Models

We consider an area for which a trip distribution T_{ij}^0 between the various zones i and j, to which the area is partitioned, has been calculated for the base year; therefore all values of Table 7.3 are available for the base year. For the future year N we calculate, according to one of the models of trip generation, the number O_i^N of trips originating from each zone and the number D_j^N of trips destined to each zone. We can then calculate the trip distribution T_{ij}^N for the future year N by using the trip distribution T_{ij}^0 for the base year with application of the constrained growth factor model from the following equation [419]:

$$T_{ij}^N = T_{ij}^0 \cdot F_O \cdot F_D \qquad (7.38)$$

where F_O and F_D are two balancing factors, calculated according to an empirical methodology described below.

7.10.4.3 A Detailed Example of a Constrained Growth Factor Model

As an example, let us consider a study area with an existing, for the base year, trip distribution between the various origin–destination pairs as illustrated in Table 7.4A. For the future year N we have forecasted, with application of the trip generation step, the total number of trips originating from each zone and

TABLE 7.4: The necessary input data of trip distribution when using constrained growth factor models. (A) The origin—destination matrix of the area under study for the base year and (B) the total number of trips originating and destined to the various zones of the area under study for the future year N.

A. *Present situation for the base year*

Origin zone i	Destination zone j				Total number of trips originating from zone i **Base year**
	1	2	3	4	
1	500	1200	1350	1800	4850
2	1300	600	1050	1050	4000
3	1600	1300	950	1450	5300
4	1550	1450	1150	1700	5850
Total number of trips destined to zone j **Base year**	4950	4550	4500	6000	20,000

B. *Future situation for the year N*

Origin zone i	Destination zone j				Total number of trips originating from zone i **Future year N**
	1	2	3	4	
1	?	?	?	?	6500
2	?	?	?	?	5800
3	?	?	?	?	7100
4	?	?	?	?	7600
Total number of trips destined to zone j **Future year N**	6900	6600	6200	7300	27,000

Source: Compiled by the authors.

destined to each zone. What we need now is to allocate the forecasted trips to the various origin—destination pairs, to calculate, in other words, the unknown values of Table 7.4B.

The procedure of trip distribution by using the constrained growth factor models is as follows:

1. We construct the origin—destination matrix of trips for the area under study for the base year (Table 7.5). We also give the total number of trips

TABLE 7.5: The origin–destination matrix of the area under study and the future (in Italics) total number of trips originating from and destined to the various zones.

Origin zone i		Destination zone j				Total number of trips originating from zone i	
		1	2	3	4	Base year	Future year N
1		500	1200	1350	1800	4850	6500
2		1300	600	1050	1050	4000	5800
3		1600	1300	950	1450	5300	7100
4		1550	1450	1150	1700	5850	7600
Total number of trips destined to zone j	Base year	4950	4550	4500	6000	20,000	
	Future year N	6900	6600	6200	7300		27,000

originating from and destined to each zone, i.e., the recorded values for the base year and forecasts for the future year N (the last two columns and the last two rows of Table 7.5).

2. We calculate (Table 7.6, bold figures) the intermediate values of the balancing factor F_O by dividing the number of trips originating from each zone for the future year N with the number of trips originating from each zone for the base year (e.g., $6500/4850 = 1.3402$, Table 7.6).

3. By multiplying the intermediate values of the balancing factor F_O with the initial values of trips of the various origin–destination pairs of Table 7.5, we calculate (Table 7.7, bold figures) the intermediate values of trips of the various origin–destination pairs.

4. We calculate (Table 7.8, bold figures) the intermediate values of the balancing factor F_D by dividing the number of trips destined to each zone for the future year N with the estimated (from the previous stage 3) number of trips (e.g., $6900/6713 = 1.0279$, Table 7.8).

5. By multiplying the intermediate values of the balancing factor F_D (as calculated at stage 4) with the intermediate values of trips of the various origin–destination pairs of Table 7.7, we update (Table 7.9, bold figures) the intermediate values of trips of the various origin–destination pairs. Thus, the first iteration of the procedure is completed.

TABLE 7.6: Distribution of future trips—first iteration: balancing to satisfy the originating trips constraint (calculation of the values of the balancing factor F_O).

Origin zone i		Destination zone j				Total number of trips originating from zone i		Balancing factor F_O
		1	2	3	4	Base year	Future year N	
1		500	1200	1350	1800	4850	6500	**1.3402**
2		1300	600	1050	1050	4000	5800	**1.4500**
3		1600	1300	950	1450	5300	7100	**1.3396**
4		1550	1450	1150	1700	5850	7600	**1.2991**
Total number of trips destined to zone j	Base year	4950	4550	4500	6000	20,000		
	Future year N	6900	6600	6200	7300		27,000	

TABLE 7.7: Distribution of future trips—first iteration: estimation of the adjusted to the balancing factor F_O originating and destined trips.

Origin zone i		Destination zone j				Total number of trips originating from zone i	
		1	2	3	4	Estimates from the first iteration	Forecasted for the future year N
1		**670**	**1608**	**1809**	**2413**	**6500**	6500
2		**1886**	**870**	**1522**	**1522**	**5800**	5800
3		**2143**	**1742**	**1273**	**1942**	**7100**	7100
4		**2014**	**1884**	**1494**	**2208**	**7600**	7600
Total number of trips destined to zone j	Estimates from the first iteration	**6713**	**6104**	**6098**	**8085**		
	Forecasted for the future year N	6900	6600	6200	7300		27,000

TABLE 7.8: Distribution of future trips—first iteration: balancing to satisfy the destined trips constraint (calculation of the values of the balancing factor F_D).

Origin zone i		Destination zone j				Total number of trips originating from zone i	
		1	2	3	4	Estimates from the first iteration	Forecasted for the future year N
	1	670	1608	1809	2413	6500	6500
	2	1886	870	1522	1522	5800	5800
	3	2143	1742	1273	1942	7100	7100
	4	2014	1884	1494	2208	7600	7600
Total number of trips destined to zone j	Estimates from the first iteration	6713	6104	6098	8085		
	Forecasted for the future year N	6900	6600	6200	7300		27,000
Balancing factor F_D		1,0279	1,0813	1,0167	0,9029		

TABLE 7.9: Distribution of future trips—first iteration: estimation of the adjusted to the balancing factor F_D originating and destined trips.

Origin zone i		Destination zone j				Total number of trips originating from zone i	
		1	2	3	4	Estimates from the first iteration	Forecasted for the future year N
	1	689	1739	1839	2179	6446	6500
	2	1938	941	1548	1374	5801	5800
	3	2203	1883	1294	1753	7133	7100
	4	2070	2037	1519	1994	7620	7600
Total number of trips destined to zone j	Estimates from the first iteration	6900	6600	6200	7300		
	Forecasted for the future year N	6900	6600	6200	7300		27,000

TABLE 7.10: Distribution of future trips—second iteration: balancing to satisfy the originating trips constraint (calculation of the values of the balancing factor F_O).

		Destination zone j				Total number of trips originating from zone i		
Origin zone i		1	2	3	4	Estimates from the first iteration	Forecasted for the future year N	Balancing factor F_O
	1	689	1739	1839	2179	6446	6500	**1.0084**
	2	1938	941	1548	1374	5801	5800	**0.9998**
	3	2203	1883	1294	1753	7133	7100	**0.9954**
	4	2070	2037	1519	1994	7620	7600	**0.9974**
Total number of trips destined to zone j	Estimates from the first iteration	6900	6600	6200	7300			
	Forecasted for the future year N	6900	6600	6200	7300		27,000	

6. We check whether the calculated values of the balancing factors F_O (Table 7.6, last column) and F_D (Table 7.8, last row) are close to the value 1.0. If not, we proceed to the second iteration of the process and repeat stage 2 (Table 7.10), stage 3 (Table 7.11), stage 4 (Table 7.12), and stage 5 (Table 7.13) until the values of all intermediate factors F_O and F_D converge to the value 1. When this occurs, the trip distribution to the various origin—destination pairs for the future year N is completed.

From Table 7.10 (last column) we can deduce the convergence to 1.0 of values of the balancing factor F_O and from Table 7.12 (last row) the convergence to 1.0 of values of the balancing factor F_D. Thus, the resulting estimates of the second iteration (Table 7.13, bold figures) can be considered as the values of trips originating from each zone and destined to each zone for the future year N.

7.10.4.4 Trip Distribution With the Use of Gravity Models

The gravity model for trip distribution calculates the number of trips $T_{ij,p}$ for a specific purpose p (work, leisure, etc.) from origin i to destination j as the product of the total number of trips O_i originating at i multiplied by the total number of trips D_j destined to j, and by an impedance (or friction) factor c_{ij}

TABLE 7.11: Distribution of future trips—second iteration: estimation of the adjusted to the balancing factor F_O originating and destined trips.

Origin zone i		Destination zone j				Total number of trips originating from zone i	
		1	2	3	4	Estimates from the second iteration	Forecasted for the future year N
	1	695	1754	1854	2197	6500	6500
	2	1937	941	1548	1374	5800	5800
	3	2193	1874	1288	1745	7100	7100
	4	2064	2032	1515	1989	7600	7600
Total number of trips destined to zone j	Estimates from the second iteration	6889	6601	6205	7305		
	Forecasted for the future year N	6900	6600	6200	7300		27,000

TABLE 7.12: Distribution of future trips—second iteration: balancing to satisfy the destined trips constraint (calculation of the values of the balancing factor F_D).

Origin zone i		Destination zone j				Total number of trips originating from zone i	
		1	2	3	4	Estimates from the second iteration	Forecasted for the future year N
	1	695	1754	1854	2197	6500	6500
	2	1937	941	1548	1374	5800	5800
	3	2193	1874	1288	1745	7100	7100
	4	2064	2032	1515	1989	7600	7600
Total number of trips destined to zone j	Estimates from the second iteration	6889	6601	6205	7305		
	Forecasted for the future year N	6900	6600	6200	7300		27,000
Balancing factor F_D		1,0016	0,9998	0,9992	0,9993		

TABLE 7.13: Distribution of future trips—second iteration: estimation of the adjusted to the balancing factor F_D originating and destined trips.

Origin zone i		Destination zone j				Total number of trips originating from zone i	
		1	2	3	4	Estimates from the second iteration	Forecasted for the future year N
	1	696	1754	1852	2195	6497	6500
	2	1940	941	1547	1373	5801	5800
	3	2197	1874	1287	1744	7102	7100
	4	2067	2031	1514	1988	7600	7600
Total number of trips destined to zone j	Estimates from the second iteration	6900	6600	6200	7300		
	Forecasted for the future year N	6900	6600	6200	7300		27,000

between i and j, which is calculated as a function (called deterrence function) of the distance or of the travel time or of the generalized cost between i and j [413, 420−422]:

$$T_{ij,p} = a_i \cdot O_{i,p} \cdot b_j \cdot D_{j,p} \cdot f(c_{ij}) \qquad (7.39)$$

where

a_i balancing factor, so that $\sum_j T_{ij,p} = O_{i,p}, \quad a_i = \dfrac{1}{\sum_j b_j \cdot D_{j,p} \cdot f(c_{ij})}$ (7.40)

b_j balancing factor, so that $\sum_i T_{ij,p} = D_{i,p}, \quad b_j = \dfrac{1}{\sum_i a_i \cdot O_{i,p} \cdot f(c_{ij})}$ (7.41)

Both balancing factors a_i and b_j are interdependent; therefore some iteration procedure, similar to the method described previously in §7.10.4.3, will be applied for their calculation,

$f(c_{ij})$ the deterrence function, which in general represents the disincentive to travel (or to transport in the case of freight), as long as distance or travel time or generalized cost increases. Some forms of the deterrence function are the following [423]:

i.   exponential function: $f(c_{ij}) = e^{-\beta \cdot c_{ij}}$ (7.42)

ii.   power function: $f(c_{ij}) = c_{ij}^{-\alpha}$ (7.43)

iii.   combined exponential and power function, known as Tanner (or Gamma) function: $f(c_{ij}) = e^{-\beta \cdot c_{ij}} \cdot c_{ij}^{-\alpha}$ (7.44)

Let us consider again the example described previously in §7.10.4.3. We will distribute the forecasted trips for the future year N (illustrated in Table 7.4B) between the various origin–destination pairs. The gravity model methodology does not need any information concerning the total number of trips originating from and destined to each zone; the same applies to the trip distribution during the base year (data of Table 7.4A). What we need is to estimate the deterrence function. We choose a deterrence function as it appears in Eq. (7.43) and we set for the coefficient α the value 1.2. Table 7.14 gives the average traveled distance and the corresponding values of the deterrence function within (intrazonal trips) and between (interzonal trips) the various origin–destination pairs. Intrazonal trips are not always included in trip distribution models, and in this case it is presumed that their exclusion does not affect the results of the gravity model. However, it has been reported that omitting intrazonal trips should be avoided, since it results in biased results [424].

TABLE 7.14: Average traveled distance c_{ij} within and between various zones and values of the deterrence function of the form $f(c_{ij}) = c_{ij}^{-1.2}$.

Average traveled distance c_{ij}					Values of deterrence function $f(c_{ij})$				
	Destination zone j					Destination zone j			
Origin zone i	1	2	3	4	Origin zone i	1	2	3	4
1	1.90	2.45	3.80	2.75	1	0.463	0.341	0.201	0.297
2	2.70	1.85	2.65	3.10	2	0.304	0.478	0.311	0.257
3	3.45	2.40	1.95	2.40	3	0.226	0.350	0.449	0.350
4	3.00	3.20	2.50	1.90	4	0.268	0.248	0.333	0.463

Source: Compiled by the authors.

The iterative procedure for the determination of the number of trips originating from and destined to the various zones is the following:

1. We set for the balancing factor b_j the value 1 ($b_j = 1$) and we calculate, by using Eq. (7.40), an intermediate value for the balancing factor a_j (Table 7.15).
2. We update, by using Eq. (7.41), the initial value for b_j of previous stage 1, and we estimate by using Eq. (7.39) the number of trips originating from and destined to the various origin−destination pairs (Table 7.16).
3. We calculate the error at the specific iteration, defined as the difference between the total number of the forecasted trips originating from and destined to each zone with the estimated number of trips from the previous stage 2 (Table 7.16). If that difference is significant (the forecaster needs to evaluate the significance or not of that difference), we continue to the next stage 4.
4. We set for the balancing factor b_j the values calculated at stage 2 and we recalculate, with the use of Eq. (7.40), a new intermediate value for the balancing factor a_j (Table 7.17, next page) and a new estimation for the number of trips originating from and destined to the various origin−destination pairs (Table 7.18).
5. We repeat stages 3 and 4 until a convergence of the forecasted and the estimated values for the total trips originating from and destined to each pair is achieved.

Table 7.19 illustrates the trip distribution after four iterations. The difference between estimates from the fourth iteration and forecasted values for the future year N is 0.02% (Table 7.19) and can be considered as satisfactory.

7.10.4.5 Trip Distribution With the Use of Probability Theory

Another model for trip distribution is the probability model, which is based on the maximization of the utility of a traveler and more particularly on the Logit model (which is analyzed in detail in §7.10.5). If we denote with u_{ij} the real (or perceived or observed) utility of individuals T_{ij} who choose to travel from zone i to zone j, then:

$$T_{ij} = T_i \cdot \frac{e^{u_{ij}}}{\sum\limits_{j=1}^{n} e^{u_{ij}}} \tag{7.45}$$

In Eq. (7.45), T_i denotes the total number of trips originating at zone i, whereas the ratio of the second term denotes the ratio of probability to choose the origin−destination pair i−j to the probability of choosing all other alternative origin−destination pairs (n in total).

TABLE 7.15: Calculation of the balancing factors a_i and b_j of Eqs. (7.40) and (7.41) for the distribution of trips originating from and destined to various zones—first iteration.

Origin zone i	Destination zone j	Balancing factor b_j	Number D_j of trips destined to zone j	Deterrence function $f(c_{ij})$	$b_j \cdot D_j \cdot f(c_{ij})$	$\sum b_j \cdot D_j \cdot f(c_{ij})$	Balancing factor a_i
1	1	1	6900	0.463	3194.70	8859.60	0.00011
	2	1	6600	0.341	2250.60		
	3	1	6200	0.201	1246.20		
	4	1	7300	0.297	2168.10		
2	1	1	6900	0.304	2097.60	9056.70	0.00011
	2	1	6600	0.478	3154.80		
	3	1	6200	0.311	1928.20		
	4	1	7300	0.257	1876.10		
3	1	1	6900	0.226	1559.40	9208.20	0.00011
	2	1	6600	0.350	2310.00		
	3	1	6200	0.449	2783.80		
	4	1	7300	0.350	2555.00		
4	1	1	6900	0.268	1849.20	8930.50	0.00011
	2	1	6600	0.248	1636.80		
	3	1	6200	0.333	2064.60		
	4	1	7300	0.463	3379.90		

Destination zone j	Origin zone i	Balancing factor a_i	Number O_i of trips originating from zone i	Deterrence function $f(c_{ij})$	$a_i \cdot O_i \cdot f(c_{ij})$	$\sum a_i \cdot O_i \cdot f(c_{ij})$	Balancing factor b_j
1	1	0.00011	6500	0.463	0.3397	0.9368	1.0675
	2		5800	0.341	0.1947		
	3		7100	0.201	0.1743		
	4		7600	0.297	0.2281		
2	1	0.00011	6500	0.304	0.2502	1.0372	0.9641
	2		5800	0.478	0.3061		
	3		7100	0.311	0.2699		
	4		7600	0.257	0.2111		
3	1	0.00011	6500	0.226	0.1475	0.9762	1.0244
	2		5800	0.350	0.1992		
	3		7100	0.449	0.3462		
	4		7600	0.350	0.2834		
4	1	0.00011	6500	0.268	0.2179	1.0464	0.9557
	2		5800	0.248	0.1646		
	3		7100	0.333	0.2699		
	4		7600	0.463	0.3940		

Source: Compiled by the authors.

TABLE 7.16: Distribution of trips originating from and destined to various zones and calculation of the difference between the estimated and the forecasted number of trips—first iteration.

Origin zone i		Destination zone j				Total number of trips originating from zone i	
		1	2	3	4	Estimates from the first iteration	Forecasted for the future year N
1		2438	1551	913	1482	6384	6500
2		1429	1941	1260	1144	5774	5800
3		1300	1739	2227	1907	7173	7100
4		1650	1319	1968	2700	7637	7600
Total number of trips destined to zone j	Estimates from the first iteration	4950	4550	4500	6000	26,968	
	Forecasted for the future year N	6900	6600	6200	7300		27,000

Difference = |6500 − 6384| + |5800 − 5774| + |7100 − 7173| + |7600 − 7637| = |6900−6817| + |6600 − 6550| + |6200 − 6368| + |7300 − 7233| = 252 + 368 = 620 (or 2.30% on the forecasted number of 27,000 trips)
Source: Compiled by the authors.

7.10.5 Choice of Mode of Transport—the Logit and Probit Models

Choice of mode of transport is the third step of the 4-step model. In this step, the total number of trips is split into the various transport modes: car, taxi, metro, bus, bicycle, walking. Models of mode choice refer essentially to utility theory techniques: when people make a choice to solve a problem, they make use of critical thinking, of their previous experiences (as recorded in their memory), but also of psychological aspects. Mode choice models permit the comparison of two or more alternatives and can take into account the various attributes of each alternative. Mode choice models use probability techniques based on utility theories and more particularly on the real (or perceived or observed) utility $u_{q,m}$ by an individual q associated with the alternative transport mode m, which is the sum of the deterministic (or systematic or

TABLE 7.17: Calculation of the balancing factors a_i and b_j of Eqs. (7.40) and (7.41) for the distribution of trips originating from and destined to various zones—second iteration.

Origin zone i	Destination zone j	Balancing factor b_j	Number D_j of trips destined to zone j	Deterrence function $f(c_{ij})$	$b_j \cdot D_j \cdot f(c_{ij})$	$\sum b_j \cdot D_j \cdot f(c_{ij})$	Balancing factor a_i
1	1	1.0675	6900	0.463	3410.34	8928.80	0.00011
	2	0.9641	6600	0.341	2169.80		
	3	1.0244	6200	0.201	1276.61		
	4	0.9557	7300	0.297	2072.05		
2	1	1.0675	6900	0.304	2239.19	9048.97	0.00011
	2	0.9641	6600	0.478	3041.54		
	3	1.0244	6200	0.311	1975.25		
	4	0.9557	7300	0.257	1792.99		
3	1	1.0675	6900	0.226	1664.66	9185.26	0.00011
	2	0.9641	6600	0.350	2227.07		
	3	1.0244	6200	0.449	2851.72		
	4	0.9557	7300	0.350	2441.81		
4	1	1.0675	6900	0.268	1974.02	8897.21	0.00011
	2	0.9641	6600	0.248	1578.04		
	3	1.0244	6200	0.333	2114.98		
	4	0.9557	7300	0.463	3230.17		

Destination zone j	Origin zone i	Balancing factor a_i	Number O_i of trips originating from zone i	Deterrence function $f(c_{ij})$	$a_i \cdot O_i \cdot f(c_{ij})$	$\sum a_i \cdot O_i \cdot f(c_{ij})$	Balancing factor b_j
1	1	0.00011	6500	0.463	0.3310	0.9255	1.0805
	2		5800	0.341	0.1940		
	3		7100	0.201	0.1765		
	4		7600	0.297	0.2240		
2	1	0.00011	6500	0.304	0.2438	1.0295	0.9713
	2		5800	0.478	0.3050		
	3		7100	0.311	0.2734		
	4		7600	0.257	0.2073		
3	1	0.00011	6500	0.226	0.1437	0.9712	1.0297
	2		5800	0.350	0.1984		
	3		7100	0.449	0.3507		
	4		7600	0.350	0.2784		
4	1	0.00011	6500	0.268	0.2124	1.0369	0.9644
	2		5800	0.248	0.1640		
	3		7100	0.333	0.2734		
	4		7600	0.463	0.3871		

Source: Compiled by the authors.

TABLE 7.18: Distribution of trips originating from and destined to various zones and calculation of the difference between the estimated and the forecasted number of trips—second iteration.

Origin zone i		Destination zone j				Total number of trips originating from zone i	
		1	2	3	4	Estimates from the second iteration	Forecasted for the future year N
1		2468	1563	917	1495	6443	6500
2		1446	1955	1267	1154	5822	5800
3		1316	1752	2239	1924	7231	7100
4		1670	1329	1777	2725	7501	7600
Total number of trips destined to zone j	Estimates from the second iteration	6900	6599	6200	7298	26,997	
	Forecasted for the future year N	6900	6600	6200	7300		27,000

Difference = |6500 − 6443| + |5800 − 5822| + |7100 − 7231| + |7600 − 7501| = |6900 − 6900| + |6600 − 6559| + |6200 − 6200| + |7300 − 7298| = 309 + 3 = 312 (or 1.16% on the forecasted number of 27,000 trips)
Source: Compiled by the authors.

mean) utility $v_{q,m}$ and of the error term $\varepsilon_{q,m}$, which reflects the uncertainty of the random variable $u_{q,m}$ [425,426]:

$$u_{q,m} = v_{q,m} + \varepsilon_{q,m} \qquad (7.46)$$

A linear function of the deterministic utility $v_{q,m}$ can be written as:

$$v_{q,m} = a + \sum_{n=1} b_n \cdot x_{q,m,n} \qquad (7.47)$$

where

$x_{q,m,n}$ the n independent variables (n = 1, 2, ...,) which refer to the characteristics of the quality and level of service of the alternative mode m and the socioeconomic characteristics of the individual q,

b_n the various regression coefficients,

a the intercept.

TABLE 7.19: Distribution of trips originating from and destined to various zones and calculation of the difference between the estimated and the forecasted number of trips—fourth iteration.

Origin zone i		Destination zone j				Total number of trips originating from zone i	
		1	2	3	4	Estimates from the fourth iteration	Forecasted for the future year N
1		2485	1579	928	1506	6498	6500
2		1438	1950	1265	1149	5800	5800
3		1289	1723	2202	1887	7101	7100
4		1688	1348	1805	2758	7599	7600
Total number of trips destined to zone j	Estimates from the fourth iteration	6900	6600	6200	7300	26,997	
	Forecasted for the future year N	6900	6600	6200	7300		27,000

Difference $= |6500 - 6498| + |5800 - 5800| + |7100 - 7101| + |7600 - 7599| = |6900 - 6900| + |6600 - 6600| + |6200 - 6200| + |7300 - 7300| = 6 + 0 = 6$ (or 0.02% on the forecasted number of 27,000 trips)
Source: Compiled by the authors.

If in Eq. (7.46) we assume that the errors are independently and identically distributed following the Gumbel distribution (Fig. 7.15), then we have the case of the Logit model, which, when considering two alternative transport modes 1 and 2, calculates the probability $P_{q,1}$ that a given individual q will choose the transport mode 1 instead of the transport mode 2:

$$P_{q,1} = \frac{e^{\beta \cdot v_{q,1}}}{e^{\beta \cdot v_{q,1}} + e^{\beta \cdot v_{q,2}}} \tag{7.48}$$

where β is the scale parameter of Gumbel distribution (Fig. 7.15) and usually takes the value $\beta = 1$. It is evident that the greater the utility, the greater the number of customers of a mode [425].

The Gumbel distribution (named after the German mathematician Emil Gumbel), also known as the extreme value type I distribution, is an asymmetric

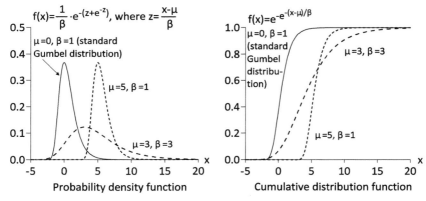

FIGURE 7.15 The probability density function (left) and the cumulative distribution function (right) of the Gumbel distribution (μ and β are, respectively, the location and scale parameters of the distribution). *Source: Compiled by the authors.*

extreme value distribution, which is used to model maximums and minimums of a problem [427]. It is used to predict the chance that an (extreme) event can occur. Thus, a Logit model is based on extreme value type errors.

In the Logit model, it is assumed that each member of a zone is making his or her travel decisions independently of others, based on his or her personal needs and perceptions. The Logit model makes the assumption that individual utility deviations from mean utility in a homogeneous market segment are statistically independent for the various alternatives. Thus, the Logit model is based on (hypothetical) stable patterns of human conduct and behavior.

The utility of alternative m can be written as a function of both observed and unobserved attributes of the specific transport mode and of socioeconomic characteristics of individuals. If we restrict the problem to the choice of an individual between only two alternative modes, e.g., car (A) and public transport (T), when traveling from zone i to zone j, then the deterministic utility for modes A and T can be written as:

$$v_A = a_A + b_1 \cdot c_A + b_2 \cdot t_A + b_3 \cdot w_A \qquad (7.49)$$

$$v_T = a_T + b_1 \cdot c_T + b_2 \cdot t_T + b_3 \cdot w_T \qquad (7.50)$$

where

c_A, c_T total cost (including parking cost) for car (A) and public transport (T),

t_A, t_T in-vehicle travel time for car (A) and public transport (T). In the case of car, the in-vehicle time includes the parking time,

w_A, w_T out-of-vehicle time (time for walking, waiting, etc.) for car (A) and public transport (T),

a_A, a_T the intercept, which represents comfort and convenience characteristics of car (A) and public transport (T).

The probability of an individual to choose the mode A (car) is calculated by Eq. (7.48), and can be written as:

$$P_A = \frac{e^{v_A}}{e^{v_A} + e^{v_T}} \Rightarrow P_A = \frac{1}{1 + e^{v_T - v_A}} \Rightarrow \frac{1}{P_A} = 1 + e^{v_T - v_A} \Rightarrow \frac{1 - P_A}{P_A} =$$

$$= e^{v_T - v_A} \Rightarrow \ln\left(\frac{1 - P_A}{P_A}\right) = v_T - v_A \qquad (7.51)$$

and by replacing in Eq. (7.51) the Eqs. (7.49) and (7.50) we will have:

$$\ln\left(\frac{1 - P_A}{P_A}\right) = (a_T - a_A) + b_1 \cdot (c_T - c_A) + b_2 \cdot (t_T - t_A) + b_3 \cdot (w_T - w_A)$$

$$(7.52)$$

which is similar to a regression equation of the form:

$$Y = \ell_0 + \ell_1 \cdot X_c + \ell_2 \cdot X_t + \ell_3 \cdot X_w \qquad (7.53)$$

where Y is the probability of an individual to choose the transport mode A (car); X_c ($= c_T - c_A$), X_t ($= t_T - t_A$), and x_w ($= w_T - w_A$) are the relative differences in the characteristics among the two alternative transport modes (car and public transport); and $\ell_0, \ell_1, \ell_2, \ell_3$ are the intercept and the regression coefficients.

Again, Eq. (7.52) is based on a number of unrealistic assumptions, and more specifically:

- behavior of individuals is of a deterministic character, that is, under the same alternatives they will always make the same choice,
- all involved in both the supply and demand side have a perfect knowledge of all attributes of modes and infrastructures in the transport market.

When the Logit model is applied for the forecast of choice of a traveler among more than two transport modes, this is referred to as the multinomial Logit model (MNL). However, some transport choices may have similar characteristics and attributes, e.g., tramway—metro, carpool—car share, and therefore they have a high correlation between them. Such a situation leads to a violation of the fundamental principle of the multinomial Logit model that the error terms of the utility function are independent with each other and are identically distributed. A remedy to such a situation is the partitioning of similar options into nests, hence the nested Logit models.

All forms of Logit models are based on the assumption that the error terms of the utility function are independently distributed. When this is not the case and the error terms (ε) follow a normal distribution (see §5.9.2), then we have the case of Probit models.

Both Logit and Probit models try to solve the problem of choice, as experienced by a traveler, among mutually exclusive transport modes by fitting to the data of the problem a function, which, however, in the case of the Logit model is a cumulative distribution function of the logistic distribution, whereas in the case of the Probit model is a cumulative function of the standard normal distribution (Fig. 7.16). Both yield similar but not identical results.

Let us consider again the two transport modes A (car) and T (public transport) and suppose that the deterministic utility functions, based on the generalized cost of the two modes, are as follows:

$$v_A = 17 - 0.7 \cdot c_A - 0.2 \cdot t_A - 0.1 \cdot w_A \qquad (7.54)$$

$$v_T = 12 - 0.7 \cdot c_T - 0.2 \cdot t_T - 0.1 \cdot w_T \qquad (7.55)$$

We will calculate the probability P_A of an individual to choose the use of his or her car instead of public transport, for the three cases illustrated in Table 7.20. The values of the deterministic utility of transport modes A and T for each one of the three cases under study (Table 7.20, last row) are calculated by using the Eqs. (7.54) and (7.55).

By using the Eq. (7.51), we can calculate the corresponding probability P_A for each one of the three cases under study. Thus, we will have:

$$P_A^{1^{st} \ case} = 0.969 \quad P_A^{2^{nd} \ case} = 0.815 \quad P_A^{3^{rd} \ case} = 0.416$$

It can be deduced that in the first two cases of Table 7.20 the probability of choosing the car is 96.9% in the first case and 81.5% in the second case, whereas the probability of choosing the car when considering the third case is much lower, 41.6%; thus for the third case it is more likely the choice of public transport instead of car. Fig. 7.17 gives the evolution of the probability P_A for various values of the deterministic utility functions v_A and v_T.

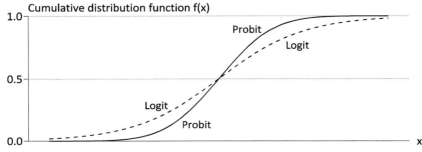

FIGURE 7.16 The cumulative distribution function in the Probit and Logit models. *Source: Compiled by the authors.*

TABLE 7.20: Total cost, in-vehicle travel time, and out-of-vehicle travel time for car and public transport and values of the deterministic utility for each case.

	First case		Second case		Third case	
	Car (A)	Public transport (T)	Car (A)	Public transport (T)	Car (A)	Public transport (T)
Total cost c (in €)	7	1.2	10	1.4	13	1.8
In-vehicle travel time t (in min)	15	20	20	25	25	30
Out-of-vehicle travel time w (in min)	5	10	10	15	15	20
Deterministic utility v	8.60	5.16	5.00	3.52	1.40	1.74

Source: Compiled by the authors.

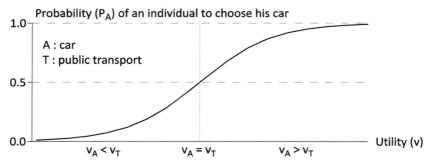

FIGURE 7.17 The probability of an individual to choose the use of car (A) instead of public transport (T) in relation to the values of utility (v) of the transport modes under study. *Source: Compiled by the authors.*

7.10.6 Trip Assignment

7.10.6.1 The Two Principles of Wardrop

Trip assignment is the fourth step of the 4-step model. It aims at determining which route will be followed to go from one zone to another. Again in this step, as in the previous ones of the 4-step model, utility theories are the basic technique and tool for trip assignment.

Among the various trip assignment methods (all-or-nothing, incremental, capacity restraint, user equilibrium, system optimum) the most widespread is the user equilibrium assignment method, which is based on the first principle of Wardrop, named after the British mathematician John Glen Wardrop.

The *first principle of Wardrop*, also known as *user equilibrium*, establishes a rule on how a traveler chooses an origin–destination route in a network which approaches congestion conditions: in an equilibrium condition of a transport network, choice of a route is made by the traveler so as to obtain the minimum travel time or travel cost, while all unused routes have greater travel times or more travel costs [428]. According to the *second principle of Wardrop*, also known as *system optimum*, in an equilibrium condition of a transport network, the average (or total) travel times or costs are minimized [428]. Wardrop's first principle is more realistic to modeling travelers' behavior, since the second principle implies that all travelers cooperate with each other in their route choice to ensure the most efficient use of the system (e.g., road network).

The second principle of Wardrop is more likely to be used as the basis for software which will rule self-driven vehicles in the future. Indeed, in such a case, vehicles interact among themselves and with the traffic management center.

7.10.6.2 Trip Assignment on the Principle All-or-Nothing

Trip assignment on the all-or-nothing principle assumes that there are no congestion effects and that all drivers consider the same attributes when choosing their routes, while perceiving all attributes in the same way and with the same degree of importance. The all-or-nothing principle is based on empirical evidence: experience and personal assessment of a driver lead him or her to choose a specific route, without examining carefully all the other alternative routes, eventual congestion conditions, etc. The all-or-nothing principle assumes that between an origin and a destination point only a specific route is utilized, even if other routes have similar travel costs or travel times. This principle is closer to reality for low-density areas and networks for which there are few alternative routes with large differences (concerning travel times and costs) among them.

Let us consider the road network of Fig. 7.18. The network has four nodes (the centroids of the zones) and six routes ($1 \leftrightarrow 2$, $1 \leftrightarrow 3$, $1 \leftrightarrow 4$, $2 \leftrightarrow 3$, $2 \leftrightarrow 4$, $3 \leftrightarrow 4$) that connect the nodes. Fig. 7.18 illustrates the traffic volume between the various zones (Matrix I) and the average travel time for the various routes (Matrix II). The assignment of the traffic volume to the various

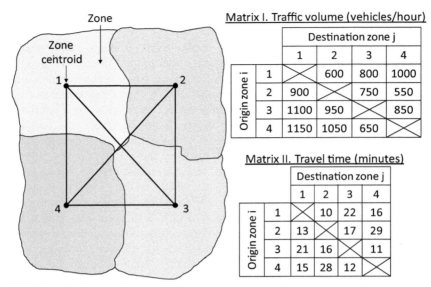

Zone

Matrix I. Traffic volume (vehicles/hour)

		Destination zone j			
		1	2	3	4
Origin zone i	1		600	800	1000
	2	900		750	550
	3	1100	950		850
	4	1150	1050	650	

Matrix II. Travel time (minutes)

		Destination zone j			
		1	2	3	4
Origin zone i	1		10	22	16
	2	13		17	29
	3	21	16		11
	4	15	28	12	

FIGURE 7.18 The road network of a trip assignment problem and the origin—destination matrixes of traffic volume and travel time between origin—destination pairs. *Source: Compiled by the authors.*

routes of the road network can be done on the basis of the all-or-nothing principle as follows:

1. Determination of the shortest route between the zones: departing from the centroid of each zone, we calculate the shortest (in terms of distance or travel time) route to each centroid that can be reached directly or via another centroid. Thus, departing from zone 1 (Fig. 7.18), someone can reach zone 2 directly in 10 min, whereas any other route presents longer travel time; in the same way, departing from zone 2, the shortest way for someone to reach zone 4 is via zone 3 with a total travel time of 28 min (17 min +11 min), whereas the direct route from zone 2 to zone 4 presents longer travel time (29 min). Fig. 7.19 illustrates the shortest routes for every trip departing from each one of the four zones of the area under study.
2. Assignment of trips (expressed as the traffic volumes illustrated in the Matrix I of Fig. 7.18) to the shortest routes: by taking into account the shortest routes when departing from each zone (Fig. 7.19), the assigned traffic is illustrated in Fig. 7.20.
3. Summation of the trips which are assigned to the shortest routes (Fig. 7.21).

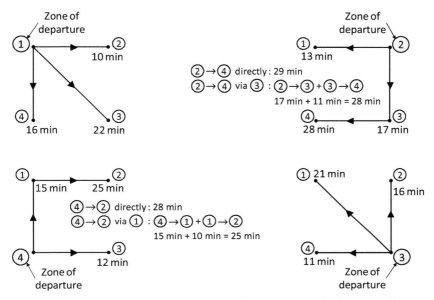

FIGURE 7.19 The shortest routes (in terms of travel time) when departing from a specific zone. *Source: Compiled by the authors.*

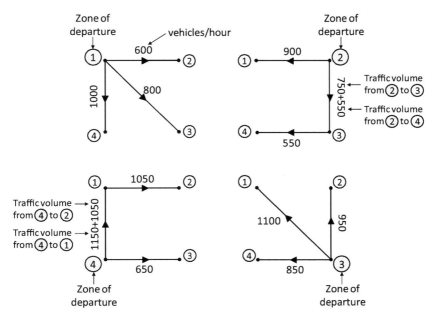

FIGURE 7.20 Trip assignment (when departing from a specific zone) to the shortest routes of the road network. *Source: Compiled by the authors.*

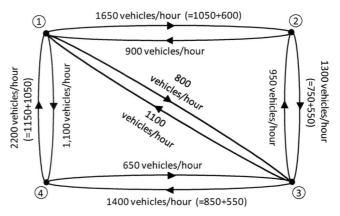

FIGURE 7.21 Trip assignment to the routes of a road network. *Source: Compiled by the authors.*

7.11 MODELING OF FREIGHT TRANSPORT DEMAND

7.11.1 Freight Transport Demand and Its Complexities

Freight transport demand satisfies human needs for a variety of products and goods, which are produced and consumed at very distant points between them by an extremely great number of consumers in the different parts of the world. Freight transport is more closely related to the economic activity than passenger transport. It is also a derived demand which relates a great number of production centers to numerous final consumers (as much as the population on earth) across the world. Thus, a dense network of freight lines connect production and consumption points to provide in time and with the lowest cost the quantities of a large variety of commodities, which are required and ordered, by using any available transport mode (road, rail, sea, air, inland waterways, pipelines, or combined transport).

Freight transport demand is more complex than passenger demand; however, it is related to and depends on more countable and measurable characteristics, such as the quantities of the various commodities produced and consumed, the locations of production points, suppliers, distribution points, and final consumers, the availability of a transport mode, the total transport (called also transit) time from origin to destination and particularly the delivery time, the transport cost, and the logistics costs (see §1.5.2). Logistics costs comprise, in addition to transport costs (see Fig. 1.8), costs of ordering, loading and uploading, transshipment (for combined transport), storage, eventual assembling, damages, losses, delays, etc. [429–431].

7.11.2 The Principal Types of Freight and the Suitability of the Various Transport Modes for Each Type of Freight

Each transport mode has its specific characteristics that make it more or less suitable for the transport of the various categories of freight. Thus, sea transport is suitable when production and consumption points are very distant or land access is not possible or costly, railways and inland navigation are suitable for the transport of bulk products or specialized freight, such as cars and chemicals, trucks are suitable for the flexible, direct and fast transport from origin to destination, and air transport is suitable for express transport of high-value products.

The various types of freight are usually classified into four principal categories:

- *Bulk* freight: grains, minerals, stones, gravel, steel, coal, cements, wood, coal, oil, gas. They are cheap products, for which the transport cost is an important component of the final cost of the product. Railways and inland waterways for land transport and ships for sea transport are the most suitable modes, provided that there are appropriate connections or terminal facilities. For the transport of fluids, pipelines are also a suitable mode. For short and medium distances of land transport, trucks are also a suitable and (principally) efficient mode.
- *Specialized* freight: cars, chemicals, containers. These are products of high value which are transported in large volumes between a small number of senders and receivers. Railways and sea transport are the most suitable transport modes for this type of freight, which has higher requirements than bulk freight for on-time delivery and for eventual losses and damages during transport, loading, uploading, eventual transshipment, etc.
- *General* merchandise, which comprises the great variety of products sold in supermarkets. Due to its flexibility, truck is the most suitable mode for short and medium distances for this type of freight.
- *Express* freight, small packages, mail. Transported products are of a very high value and usually logistics costs are more important than transport costs. For this type of freight, air transport is the most suitable (but also the most expensive) mode (see §7.4.9.1).

A general guidance, when considering the economic conditions of the USA, suggests that [432]:

- for products of a value $0.01—$0.02 per kg, sea transport and inland waterways are the most suitable modes,
- for products of a value $0.06—$0.20 per kg, railways and trucks are the most suitable modes,
- for products of a value higher than $1 per kg, air transport is the most suitable mode, as these products are highly sensitive in time.

7.11.3 Freight as a Part of the Logistics Chain

Freight transport is not an isolated activity but only a part and a component of the logistics chain which, as we analyzed in §1.5.2, includes the following, in addition to the transport activity (see Fig. 1.8) [2,7,433−435]:

- all the flow of information between the production and consumption centers, which specifies what product is needed, where is supposed to be delivered, and at what time,
- the collection of freight from the production centers to the departing point of transport. To reduce transport costs, all transport modes aim at full load transport. This entails that a transport unit, such as a truck or a railway vehicle, comprises products coming from various production centers or points and directed to various consumption centers or points,
- the distribution and delivery of freight to the final point of consumption, which usually does not coincide with the arriving point of freight under full load conditions,
- depending on the nature of the product and its sensitivity over time, products may be stored in great quantities in warehouses both at the departing and the arriving point of freight transport,
- with the exception of trucks for which loading takes place at the origin point and uploading at the destination point, all other categories of freight transport include one or more transshipments from one mode to another,
- a number of loadings and unloadings of the freight take place in the collection, transport, transshipment, storage, and distribution process described above. Even with the best equipment, qualified staff, and managerial and operational procedures, a number of losses, alterations, or damages of transported products are inevitable to occur.

7.11.4 Successive Steps for the Modeling of Freight Transport Demand

With the exception of air transport of products of high value, all other ways of forwarding of freight from origin to destination entail the possibility of choice among various transport modes and for each transport mode among various alternative routes from origin to destination. Thus, modeling of freight transport demand usually includes the following successive steps:

- calculation of the volume of products which are produced and consumed at the two ends of a plausible freight transport,
- calculation of the volumes and rates of flows of the various products between the production and the consumption points,
- possibility of some products to be stored in relation to their nature (e.g., strawberries cannot be stored) and the existence and the size of warehouses at both ends,

- choice of the appropriate transport mode (or modes for the case of combined transport),
- calculation of the origin—destination pairs for the various products,
- determination of the final route for each origin—destination pair.

It is clear that the 4-step model analyzed previously for passenger transport can also be applied for the simulation and modeling of freight transport demand.

7.11.5 Projection of Past Freight Demand in the Future

If data about the flows of freight by mode are available, one simple method is to project these data in the future by multiplying past freight data by a growth factor F, which is a relation of the changes of supply S_i at the origin point and demand D_j at the destination point. The estimation of the growth factor F can be based either on trends of historical freight supply and demand data or on forecasts of future economic activity. Thus, according to this simplistic method, freight demand T_{ij}^n, between i and j for the year n, will be calculated in relation to demand T_{ij}^0, for the base year, as follows:

$$T_{ij}^n = F \cdot T_{ij}^0, \quad \sum_j T_{ij} = S_i \text{ and } \sum_i T_{ij} = D_j \tag{7.56}$$

With the exception of changes in the supply and demand sides (that are taken into account), this method assumes that all other factors (such as cost and travel times) that affect freight transport demand are not taken into account in the growth factor F and will remain the same in the future with their degree of influence unchanged (see also §6.1.2 and §6.3). It is evident that the method of projection into the future of past freight data can be used for short- or at the maximum for medium-term forecasts.

7.11.6 The Driving Forces for Freight Transport

The following driving forces, some of which can constitute the independent variables of a freight transport demand model (see also §1.5.2), can be considered [436–445]: freight transport costs, transport (transit[3]) times, quality of freight transport (reliability, safety, eventual losses and damages, etc.), purchasing power of consumers, technological innovations, (re)location of companies, rates of growth of the considered industries. The most critical among them seem to be the freight transport cost, the total transport time, and the location of suppliers and consumers.

---

3. The transit time usually refers to the planned traveling time from terminal to terminal, which may vary considerably when the destination point is not reached directly but via intermediate transshipment points.

7.11.7 Application of the 4-Step Model for the Forecast of Freight Transport Demand

The 4-step freight model follows the same steps as the 4-step passenger model (see §7.10.2) and more specifically:

1. *Generation.* The area under study is partitioned into zones. For each zone, the demand of freight is calculated at the production and consumption areas. To account for and deal with the great variety of products produced and consumed, it is suggested, before zoning the area under study, to classify the various products according to the classification used by the statistical authority of the specific country and by the authorities of the various alternative transport modes. Freight demand at the origin or destination is calculated either by the projection of past freight demand into the future (see §7.11.5) or by an econometric equation, with the use of regression analysis and independent variables such as the population (which represents the consumer market), the economic growth rate, and the employment.

2. *Distribution.* Freight demand, as calculated at the previous step for the production and consumption areas, is distributed to origin–destination pairs with the use of the gravity model of Eq. (7.39), in which:

    $T_{ij,p}$ freight traffic for the product (or category of products) p from origin zone i to destination zone j,

    $O_{i,p}$ freight traffic for the product p originating at zone i,

    $D_{j,p}$ freight traffic for the product p destined to zone j.

3. *Choice of mode of transport.* In the choice of mode for freight transport, a company or an individual q tries to maximize the real (or perceived or observed) utility $u_{q,m}$ which will result from the specific choice of transport mode m (see Eq. 7.46). The utility $u_{q,m}$ of Eq. (7.46) for freight is usually calculated as a function of the various attributes of the specific transport mode, such as transport cost or logistics cost (see §7.11.1), total transport (or transit) time, service frequency, carrying capacity, punctuality and eventuality of damages. Once the utility of each freight transport mode is calculated, freight demand distributed at step 2 between origin and destination pairs is allocated to the various alternative transport modes with the use of the Logit or the Probit model (or multinomial Logit or multinomial Probit in the case of more than two transport modes).

    The freight demand calculated at this step can be converted to number of trucks, railway vehicles, ships, and aircrafts by taking into account the payload capacity of the above transport modes.

4. *Route choice and assignment.* If the selected transport mode is railway, determination of route results from consideration of the few (in some cases only one) alternative routes, by taking into account the capacity of the track, the travel time aimed, and other constraints such as the coexistence in mixed tracks of freight trains with passenger trains and delivery time.

If the selected transport mode is truck, there are more alternative routes than in the case of railways and the optimum route is selected by the application either of the all-or-nothing technique or of the equilibrium technique (see §7.10.6), by taking into account traffic conditions (and particularly congestion), the travel time aimed, labor law restrictions about the maximum time of driving, etc.

Chapter 8

Artificial Intelligence—Neural Network Methods

Chapter Outline

8.1 REASONS FOR CHOOSING ARTIFICIAL INTELLIGENCE METHODS FOR MODELING TRANSPORT DEMAND

Forecasting transport demand is both a science and (to a certain degree) an art. It permits to estimate in real-time unknown variables of demand with a certain degree of rationality and reliability. Time series and econometric methods,

Modeling of Transport Demand. https://doi.org/10.1016/B978-0-12-811513-8.00008-X
Copyright © 2019 Elsevier Inc. All rights reserved.

in spite of their apparent complexity, can nevertheless be overly simplistic. They possess a number of inherent flaws, for example:

- transport demand is often considered as a linear problem; in most cases, however, it exhibits *nonlinear* characteristics,
- while trying to establish a causal relationship, trend projection and moving average methods have only one independent variable (time), and time series and econometric methods have a limited number of independent variables (the more important ones) but *omit a number of less important variables*. Even if a dummy variable is introduced, omitting any other variables in a causal relationship introduces unreliability and inaccuracy,
- both time series and econometric methods are based on a set of assumptions, which *limit the degrees of freedom and flexibility* exhibited in real problems of transport demand,
- time series and econometric methods use a limited data set and can hardly incorporate the *large amounts of data* (like big data, see §2.1.5 and §3.1.3) which are available today from many sources,
- once a time series or econometric relationship is established, it is used unchanged for months or years; as transport reflects a human behavior, in most of the cases it has a *dynamic* character and it *changes* during the course of time.

Many of the above drawbacks can be dealt with the use of methods based on *artificial intelligence* (AI), which can be defined as the science of making machines or systems do things that would require human intelligence [446,447]. There are many types of AI systems, which, however, share some fundamental characteristics in common, as they are programmed to think like people, to act like people, and to think rationally and reasonably.

Incorporating AI in transport systems requires a number of prerequisites: powerful computer systems (speedy processors, high-capacity memory devices), suitable algorithms (though necessarily simplistic) simulating human cognitive processes, and data that permit the machine to analyze the phenomenon under study. Thus, the cornerstone of AI is machine learning (ML) techniques.

The method of artificial neural networks (ANNs), called also neural network method or simply neural method, is one of the techniques of AI. Other such techniques include genetic algorithms, case-based reasoning, rule-based systems, fuzzy models, multiagent systems, swarm intelligence, reinforcement learning and hybrid systems, etc. [446,448]. ANN is a machine learning method which is inspired and tries to imitate (in a very simplistic manner) the way that biological neuronal systems, such as the human brain, work and process information. Though there is still a great deal that is unknown about how the human brain works, approximately 100 million neurons of the brain allow human beings to understand, remember, think, and apply previous experiences. An artificial neuron simulates these fundamental functions of a natural neuron and thus imitates the basic operations of the human neuron network.

Although ANNs are inspired by the operation of biological neurons, their purpose is not a direct replication of the way that biological neurons function (this is strictly impossible), but rather to imitate the operation of biological neurons in order to construct AI algorithms which are able to solve a great variety of specific problems.

8.2 STRUCTURE AND ELEMENTS OF A BIOLOGICAL NEURON

A biological neuron is the basic structural component of the neuron system. A simplified representation (Fig. 8.1) of a biological neuron makes clear three fundamental functional units [449]:

- the cell body (called *soma*),
- the *dendrites*, which receive signals from other neurons and pass them over the cell body,
- the *axon*, which receives signals of the cell body and transmits them to dendrites of neighboring neurons.

The primary impulse to a neuron is a form of electric signal which travels through a dendrite and before reaching the cell body goes through a small gap, called *synapse* or *synaptic joint*. This gap is full of substances that act as

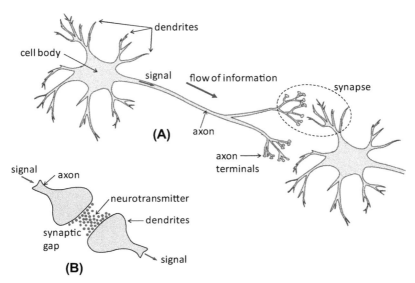

FIGURE 8.1 Constituent elements of a biological neuron (A) and mechanism of signal transfer between two biological neurons (B). *Source: Compiled by the authors.*

neurotransmitters, which either accelerate or decelerate the flow of electric signals. Each neuron has a *threshold* value of electric signals, below which the signal is not transmitted to the cell body and over which the signal is transmitted. In the latter case, the newly generated signal passes through the following neuron. Thus, electrochemical processes are part and parcel of cognitive processes, which in turn affect neurophysiology. Through such processes, the human brain records, stores, and learns from the various sources of information of his environment.

In conclusion, a biological neuron receives external inputs, combines them, and finally processes an output, usually in a nonlinear way. The basic characteristics of a biological system composed of many neurons are [450,451]:

- nonlinearity, which permits adaptation to external inputs,
- fault and failure tolerance,
- ability to take into account even partial or imprecise information,
- learning capability,
- capacity to generalize,
- noise insensitivity, understood as the capacity to reach accurate conclusions from nonaccurate data and measurement errors.

8.3 STRUCTURE OF AN ARTIFICIAL NEURON AND ACTIVATION FUNCTION

8.3.1 The Conception of an Artificial Neuron

The idea of a synthetic (artificial) neuron, which imitates in a very simplistic way the behavior of a biological neuron, was first presented in 1943 [452]. In this conception of artificial neuron (Fig. 8.2B), a number of inputs x_i are each multiplied by a weight w_i. The product $\xi = \sum w_i \cdot x_i$ is compared with the neuron's threshold value for activation b and thus it is determined whether the neuron is activated or not. If it is activated, the result is an output y_i ($y = f(\xi)$).

8.3.2 Analogies Between an Artificial and a Biological Neuron

A clear analogy exists between a biological neuron (Fig. 8.2A) and an artificial one (Fig. 8.2B). A biological neuron receives various signals of intensity x_i and synaptic strength w_i, and has a threshold value for activation b (Fig. 8.2A). In an artificial neuron, the connections between nodes simulate the axon and dendrites, the connection weights simulate the synapses, and the threshold value for activation has a similar operation (Fig. 8.2B) [449,453].

The artificial neuron receives many inputs x_i of a relative importance (weight) w_i, which result in a total input $\xi = \sum w_i \cdot x_i$. If this total input ξ is greater than the neuron's threshold limit value for activation b, then the artificial neuron will be activated and the output y_i, a function of ξ ($y = f(\xi)$), will be transmitted to another neuron or to the environment. In successive

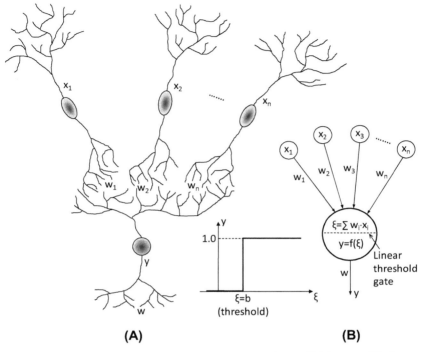

(A) **(B)**

FIGURE 8.2 Analogies between a biological neuron (A) and an artificial neuron (B). *Source: Compiled by the authors, modified from Ref. [449].*

calculations, an artificial neuron modifies the weights w_i in such a way that the calculated output y_i approaches the targeted output Y, if this is known. If Y is not known, successive calculations are terminated when values of y_i (calculated successively) are very close and the error is small compared with some fixed value. Thus, the key element of an artificial neuron consists in adjusting, during successive calculations, each weight w_i until the difference between the desired or expected output Y and the calculated actual output y_i is below a predetermined value. In such an approach, there is a clear dependence on the choice of initial parameters.

8.3.3 Artificial Neurons and Artificial Neural Networks

Many artificial neurons interconnected among them form an artificial neural network (ANN), which has become a strong computational tool that can take into account large amounts of data, perform massively parallel computations based on these data, assign the appropriate weights to the more important (usually the more recent) data, discover the linear or nonlinear relationship of the phenomenon under study, recognize patterns of operation and performance,

Input   Processing element   Output

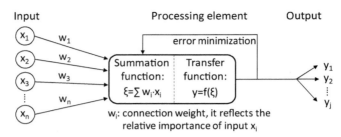

FIGURE 8.3 Fundamental operations in an artificial neuron. *Source: Compiled by the authors.*

generalize such relationships or patterns, and provide accurate and reliable evolutions and predictions. ANNs are not based on specific rules; they are developed through a trial and error procedure across successive calculations.

8.3.4 The Four Functions of an Artificial Neural Network

All kinds of artificial neurons (Fig. 8.3) simulate the four basic functions of a biological neuron:

- reception of information from the external environment (the dendrites of a biological neuron),
- decision whether this information will be activated and be taken into account or will be ignored as nonimportant (the synapses of a biological neuron),
- processing of the information (the soma of a biological neuron),
- the output of the whole procedure (the axon of a biological neuron).

Thus, the first step in an artificial neuron is the summation of the various inputs x_i multiplied by their respective connection weights w_i. Then, the products $w_i \cdot x_i$ are fed into the summation function $\xi = \sum w_i \cdot x_i$ (Fig. 8.3). However, many types of operators can be selected, which could produce a number of different values, such as the average, the largest, the smallest, the ORed (bitwise disjunction[1]) values, the ANDed (bitwise conjunction[2]) values, or other values for ξ.

---

1. The bitwise disjunction (denoted as ∨) compares one by one the bits in two operands and when the two corresponding bits are both 0 (or false, in a binary Boolean variable), the result is 0. If either or both bits are 1 (or true, in a binary Boolean variable), then the result is 1. For example, the bitwise disjunction of the operands 010010, 001011 is 010010 ∨ 001011 = 011011. The Boolean variables represent an algebraic system of logic and they have only two values, denoted *true* and *false*.
2. The bitwise conjunction (denoted as ∧) compares one by one the bits in two operands; when two corresponding bits are both 1 (or true, in a binary Boolean variable), the result is 1; when either or both bits are 0 (or false, in a binary Boolean variable), the result is 0. For example, the bitwise disjunction of the operands 010010 and 001011 is 010010 ∧ 001011 = 000010.

8.3.5 The Transfer or Activation Function of an Artificial Neural Network

Whatever way computed, the value $\xi = \sum w_i \cdot x_i$ is then used for the calculation of the *transfer* (or activation) function, which determines whether the input x_i will be taken into account and an activation of the neuron will take place. The most commonly used transfer functions are (Fig. 8.4):

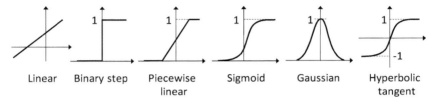

| Linear | Binary step | Piecewise linear | Sigmoid | Gaussian | Hyperbolic tangent |

FIGURE 8.4   The common types of transfer (or activation) functions. *Source: Compiled by the authors.*

- a linear function, $f(\xi) = a \cdot \xi + b$,
- a binary step (threshold) function:
  - if $\xi \geq 0$, then $f(\xi) = 1$,
  - if $\xi < 0$, then $f(\xi) = 0$,
- a piecewise linear function:
  - if $\xi \geq \xi_{max}$, then $f(\xi) = 1$,
  - if $\xi_{min} > \xi > \xi_{max}$, then $f(\xi) = a \cdot \xi + b$,
  - if $\xi \leq \xi_{min}$, then $f(\xi) = 0$,
- a sigmoid function, $f(\xi) = \frac{1}{1+e^{-b \cdot \xi}}$, interval $(0,1)$,
- a Gaussian function, $f(\xi) = e^{-\xi^2}$, interval $(0,1]$,
- a hyperbolic tangent function, $f(\xi) = \frac{2}{1+e^{-2 \cdot \xi}} - 1$, interval $[-1,1]$.

8.4 TYPES OF ARTIFICIAL NEURAL NETWORKS, ALGORITHMS, AND SOFTWARE

8.4.1 Input Layers, Output Layers, and Hidden Layers

Each unit of an ANN is connected with the other units through a model of connections which is called the *topology* (or *architecture*) of the network and describes which unit (or group of units) is connected with another specific unit. Let w_{ij} be the connection weight between units i and j. For an ANN with n units, its topology can be represented by a matrix W of dimensions n × n. Thus, the line i of W includes all the weights received by unit i from other units of the network, that is, the input weights of unit i. The column j includes all the weights sent from the specific unit to the other units of the network, that is, the output weights of unit j. Matrix W represents the codified knowledge of an ANN, often called the *long-term memory*. The connection weights of an ANN are the *equivalent* of the *coefficients* in a *regression* model.

Layer 1: input layer (i),   Layer 2:   Layer 3: output layer (k),
Independent variables   hidden layer (j)   Dependent variable

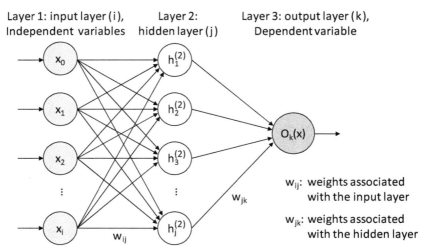

FIGURE 8.5   Input layer, output layer, and hidden layer of an artificial neural network. *Source: Compiled by the authors.*

Units of an ANN that receive signals from the external environment are called *input* units, whereas units that send signals to the external environment are called *output* units. Units that are not connected to the external environment and are neither input nor output are called *hidden* units. The various units can be grouped, according to some properties, in *layers*. Each layer is composed of many units. Thus, an ANN has an *input layer*, an *output layer*, and one or more *hidden layers* (Fig. 8.5).

8.4.2 Feedforward and Recurrent Artificial Neural Networks

Each unit of an ANN can send its output to other units and can receive as inputs the outputs of other units. The topology or architecture of an ANN describes the way the various dependent variable(s) of the output layer are associated with independent variables of the input layer and can be:

- *Feedforward*: The various units send their outputs to other units, from which they do not receive any input, either directly or indirectly (that is, through other units) [454,455].
- *Recurrent:* Information is propagated both forward and backward as outputs of some neurons are fed back to the same neurons or to neurons in preceding layers. In a recurrent network (Fig. 8.6), there exists at least one path that, following the connections, leads back to the starting neuron. Such a path is called a cycle and may cause a delay of specific time units (which may be zero) [455,456].

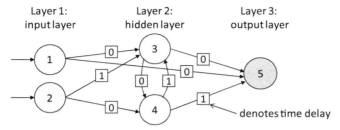

Layer 1: input layer
Layer 2: hidden layer
Layer 3: output layer

denotes time delay

FIGURE 8.6 A two-input recurrent artificial neural network. *Source: Compiled by the authors.*

8.4.3 Classification of Artificial Neural Networks

There is a great number of ANNs in use today, which can be classified in relation to their structure and features.

8.4.3.1 Supervised Learning, Reinforcement Learning, Nonsupervised Learning

According to the method of supervision of learning, we can classify ANNs into the following two categories:

- *Supervised*, when the external environment affords the desirable outputs for each one of the inputs received and operates as a kind of teacher. In supervised learning, the network has, during successive iterations, a methodology so that the computed output converges to the desired one. Popular algorithms with a supervised learning technique are the Perceptron (which uses continuous data), the Adaline (which uses binary data), the Madaline (developed from the Adaline), and others [451,457,458].

  A special case of supervised learning is *reinforcement* learning, when the external environment only affords information as to whether the output is acceptable or unacceptable, instead of indicating the right output. In reinforcement learning, the strength of the most active input connections to neurons which performed well is increased over successive iterations. This is often done following an all-or-nothing technique, wherein only the connections related to the strongest input are improved across successive iterations. Popular algorithms with a reinforcement learning technique are the learning vector quantization (known after the name of Kohonen), Hopfield networks, and the Boltzmann machine [457,459,460],

- *Nonsupervised*, when the external environment affords neither the desirable output nor any information as to whether the output is acceptable or unacceptable. The various weights are grouped in *clusters* in such a way that similar input vectors (belonging to the same group) result in similar outputs. Nonsupervised learning is based only on input data, and updating of weights during successive iterations is done internally within the ANN.

If during one iteration a new pattern is detected, then it is classified as a new cluster. A popular algorithm using nonsupervised learning is the algebraic reconstruction technique (ART), which exploits information and data without any kind of intervention. This algorithm provides a set of patterns and classifies them into clusters. If a new pattern is presented which cannot be classified to the existing ones, but at the same time it is sufficiently different from the closest one, then it is classified as a new cluster. ART algorithms resemble time series algorithms and are used for pattern recognition, completion, and classification [449,457,461].

8.4.3.2 The Backpropagation Algorithm

A popular algorithm for the fitting of connection weights is the back-propagation: the error computed at any step can be sent from the output layer backward to the hidden layer and next to the input layer [462]. Many applications of ANNs in transport use this backpropagation algorithm.

8.4.3.3 The Learning Rule

The *learning rule* reflects how exactly the network weights should be adjusted between successive iterations. There are five types of learning rules [449,463,464]:

1. *Error-correction* learning: At any iteration, weights are modified in relation to the error recovered, that is, the difference between the fitted (calculated) and actual (measured) values. This method is used in supervised learning and consists in modifying the connection weights at each iteration so as to reduce the overall error.
2. *Boltzmann* learning: This method is similar to error-correction learning; however, the output at each successive iteration is based on a Boltzmann statistical distribution.
3. Learning according to the rule of *Hebb*: This method is based on the principle that if neurons on both sides of a synapse are activated synchronously and repeatedly, then the synapse's strength is selectively increased. Connection weights during successive iterations are modified on the activities and performances of neurons locally. A simple application of Hebb's rule is the Linear Associative Matrix algorithm, in which the output is a linear function of inputs (Fig. 8.7A). The algorithm can only model linear relationships, but can do so in real time, and is able to forecast evolutions of the problem under study.
4. *Competing* learning: Neurons compete among them and the model is based on the strongest neuron. In an iteration, only one neuron is activated and all the weights are adjusted to it [449].
5. *Perceptron* learning: The weights in each iteration are modified in relation to the difference between the targeted value and the calculated value by

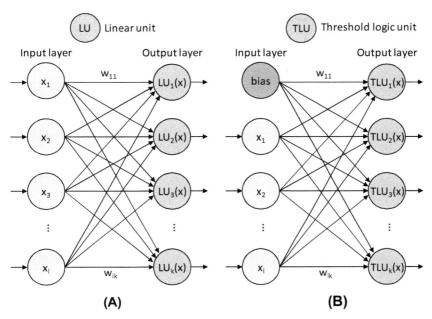

FIGURE 8.7 The Linear Association Matrix model (A) and the one-layer Perceptron model (B). *Source: Compiled by the authors.*

the model. This difference is the equivalent of the residual in time series and econometric models. Regardless of the initial values given to the weights, the model can optimize weights after a number of iterations. Such an approach is feasible with linearly separable classes. Fig. 8.7B illustrates a Perceptron one-layer model, which can be efficient for linear problems. Nonlinear systems will require the introduction of intermediate (hidden) layers, described previously in §8.4.1.

8.5 A COMPARATIVE ANALYSIS OF ARTIFICIAL NEURAL NETWORKS WITH OTHER FORECASTING METHODS

8.5.1 Features of Artificial Neural Networks and Applications for Transport

ANN is a recently developed method which has a high degree of complexity and provides applications in various scientific areas (and in transportation more particularly). All these features of ANN impress and attract many scientists in the forecasting field. It is necessary, therefore, to highlight the ways in which ANNs differ from other quantitative forecasting methods (time series, econometric, etc.), as well as under what conditions and for which problems ANNs should be applied, instead of other more traditional quantitative methods.

Let us summarize some fundamental characteristics that are associated with ANNs and are essential for their application in the transport sector:

- ANNs can take easily into account great amounts of data, which, however, may present high fluctuations,
- ANNs can simulate nonlinearities and complex situations,
- ANNs provide real-time results and they have a high degree of flexibility, adaptability, and generalization,
- ANNs operate empirically and do not provide any kind of interpretability or understanding of the mechanism and processes which govern the problem under study.

8.5.2 Terms and Methods Associated With Artificial Neural Networks and Equivalence With Statistical Methods

Many terms used in ANNs have their origin in biological sciences; however, they are totally equivalent with terms used in statistical methods, which were analyzed in Chapters 5 and 6 of this book. Statistical methods (among them the regression analysis) are used as the basic tool in all traditional quantitative methods, such as time series, econometric, etc.

Thus, inputs and outputs of ANNs are just the equivalent of independent and dependent variables in statistical methods. Synaptic (connection) weights of ANNs are the equivalent of the coefficients of the independent variables of statistical methods, whereas the errors of ANNs are the equivalent of residuals in statistical methods.

8.5.3 The Inherent Mechanism and Process of the Problem Under Study and the Predictability of the Method

ANNs do not take into account either the mechanism or the process governing the problems under study, which, however, are simulated with the help of the hidden layer. In contrast, statistical methods cannot provide meaningful, accurate, and reliable results, unless they simulate and describe mechanisms and processes of the problem. As a result of taking into account the inherent characteristics of the problem, statistical methods can interpret the problem, including its variations and characteristics, whereas ANNs cannot do so.

8.5.4 Assumptions

As analyzed in Chapters 5 and 6, statistical methods are based on a set of assumptions that restrict many degrees of freedom of the problem under study. In contrast, ANNs have few assumptions (particularly in the process of improving the initial solution) and in many cases none.

8.5.5 Nonlinearities

ANNs can take easily into account nonlinearities, something that is difficult with statistical methods, which either deal with a linear problem or transform a nonlinear problem to a linear one.

8.5.6 Collinearities

ANNs are not affected by eventual collinearities among inputs, whereas eventual collinearities among variables considered as independent can result in erroneous values of coefficients of statistical methods.

8.5.7 Missing Data or Small Sample Size

ANNs can provide reasonable results even when the size of the sample is small or a number of data are missing [465]. In contrast, statistical methods either fail or give poor results in such cases.

8.5.8 Huge Amounts of Data

Modern technology in everyday use (mobile telephone, internet, social media, etc.) can provide huge amounts of data, all of which can be easily incorporated in ANN models. A similar procedure with statistical methods is more difficult.

8.5.9 Fluctuations of Data

ANNs can easily and efficiently simulate fluctuations of data; for this reason they are suitable for the study of problems such as traffic flow, road accidents, seasonal freight demand, demand for taxi services, exceptional events (athletic games, etc.), etc. In contrast, statistical methods are usually based on mean values and cannot simulate phenomena with high fluctuations.

8.5.10 Value of Error Accepted

Both ANNs and statistical methods are based on a number of iterative calculations, which, however, is much greater in ANNs than in statistical methods. They both terminate when a predetermined value of error (for ANNs) or residual (for statistical methods) is reached.

8.5.11 Apparent Differences and Hidden Similarities

ANNs and statistical methods give the impression of totally different methods. However, a careful in-depth survey in both can reveal that a simple ANN model with one hidden layer and a linear output is just the equivalent of a polynomial regression [190].

8.5.12 Problems for Which Artificial Neural Networks or Statistical Methods Are More Suitable

The study of a great number of applications of ANNs in transport problems and the previous comparative analysis can highlight the nature of problems for which ANNs are more suitable, specifically when:

- we do not know or (even more so) we are not interested in the mechanisms and processes that follow the data of the problem,
- there is no need to interpret the specific phenomenon,
- assumptions and restrictions of statistical methods are not valid,
- huge amounts of data (which may present fluctuations) should be taken into account.

On the other hand, statistical methods are suitable when:

- we know the mechanism and process of the problem, the variables that affect it, and the way and the degree of the effect of each variable,
- we need to interpret the results,
- assumptions and restrictions do not transform the problem under study to a different problem, compared to the examined one,
- there are no missing data, which in addition do not present high fluctuations,
- statistical methods in similar problems provided satisfactory results.

8.5.13 Choice of the Appropriate Model

The principles presented in Chapter 3 (§3.12) for the choice of the appropriate model of forecast are valid for the choice of an ANN model.

Forecasters should not be impressed or attracted by complex, highly nonlinear ANN methods, when statistical methods are simpler and can provide reasonable results with a satisfactory degree of accuracy.

ANN may be an efficient tool of forecasting a transport problem when we are not interested in the mechanism and process of the problem, large amounts of data with fluctuations are available, the problem has nonlinear characteristics, and the assumptions and restrictions of statistical methods are not valid.

In any case, when opting for an ANN (or any other) method, the following should be considered: accuracy, simplicity and suitability of the method, adaptability to changing conditions, and the required skills, time, and effort of the forecaster [190].

8.5.14 Types of Artificial Neural Networks Mostly Used

The vast majority of applications of ANNs use the multilayer Perceptron (see §8.4.3.3) model with the backpropagation learning algorithm, which is the most popular learning rule [466].

8.6 ANALYTICAL EXAMPLE OF AN APPLICATION OF ARTIFICIAL NEURAL NETWORKS FOR TRANSPORT: A LONG-TERM FORECAST OF AIR TRANSPORT DEMAND

8.6.1 The Problem, the Dependent (Output), and Independent (Input) Variables

We will illustrate an application of ANNs for the forecast of the number of air trips per inhabitant, which will be the dependent variable of the problem. We will examine a mature market (North America, including the United States and Canada, population: 0.357 billion inhabitants in 2015) and a developing market (South Asia, including, among others, India, Pakistan, Afghanistan, Bangladesh, etc., population: 1.744 billion inhabitants in 2015). As it has been already analyzed in Chapter 7 (see §7.4.2), demand for air transport is principally affected by the GDP per capita of the considered area, which will be the single or one of the independent (input) variables of the problem. However, air transport is more and more affected by a number of other variables, such as [467]:

- Percentage of population with easy access to the internet. An increasing number of customers of airlines (both low-cost and full-service airlines) collect information (about tariffs, departure and arrival times, etc.), buy their tickets, and check in for their flight with the use of the internet.
- Concentrations of populations in urban areas. In 2013, 20% of air trips worldwide had either as origin or destination 26 megacities, each one with a population of more than 10 million inhabitants, whereas another 40% of air trips worldwide were between urban agglomerations with populations of 5 million or more. Fig. 8.8 illustrates how airlines increased the number of available seat-kilometers for city-pairs with a major hub city (the 26 megacities plus the next 6 largest urban agglomerations of the world) at one or both ends.
- Population in the largest city.

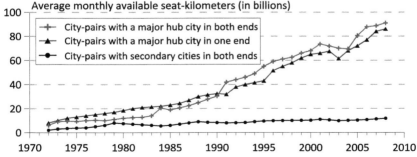

FIGURE 8.8   Evolution of the average monthly available seat-kilometers offered by airlines worldwide in relation to the population of departure (origin) and arrival (destination) city. *Source: Modified from Ref. [468].*

TABLE 8.1: Pearson correlation coefficient (r) between the dependent (output) variable and each one of the independent (input) variables.

Dependent variable (output variable to ANN)	Independent variables (input variables to ANN)	Pearson correlation coefficient (r)	
		North America	South Asia
Air trips per 1000 inhabitants	Per capita GDP (in PPP)	0.97	0.95
	Users of internet	0.87	0.95
	Degree of urbanization	0.95	0.86
	% of population living in the largest city[a]	−0.95	0.82

[a]The analysis illustrates an almost perfect negative correlation between the percentage of the population living in the largest city and air transport demand in a mature market (North America) and a strong positive correlation in a developing market (South Asia). The reason is that in developed countries the megacities present an almost stable population, and thus when the population of the country increases the percentage of population living in megacities decreases, a situation which is the opposite in developing countries.
Source: Compiled by the authors, based on data of Ref. [38].

Thus, the ANN model under study will have one output variable (annual number of air trips per 1000 inhabitants) and one (per capita GDP in purchasing power parity, PPP) or four input variables (per capita GDP in purchasing power parity, users of internet as percentage of the whole population, degree of urbanization as percentage of the population living in urban areas, and percentage of the whole population living in the largest city).

Each of these four independent variables has a high value of Pearson correlation coefficient (r) in relation to the dependent variable (Table 8.1), a fact that testifies that each independent variable has a high correlation with the dependent one.

8.6.2 Architecture of the Artificial Neural Network Model

We will try two well-known architectures of ANNs: feedforward and recurrent (see §8.4.2). ANN models using the recurrent technique can be trained in two phases, open loop and closed loop (see below §8.6.9).

8.6.3 Single and Multiple Inputs

For ANN applications using the feedforward method, we will study two cases:

- single input (per capita GDP in purchasing power parity, PPP)—single output (annual number of air trips per 1000 inhabitants),
- multiple inputs (four independent variables, see §8.6.1)—single output (annual number of air trips per 1000 inhabitants).

8.6.4 Architecture of the Four Artificial Neural Network Models Under Study

Fig. 8.9 recapitulates the architecture of the four ANN models under study:

Fig. 8.9A: feedforward single input—single output model,
Fig. 8.9B: feedforward multiple input—single output model,
Fig. 8.10A: recurrent (open-loop phase) double input—single output model,
Fig. 8.10B: recurrent (closed-loop phase) double input—single output model.

All ANN models under study will include one hidden layer of 10 neurons, a choice that minimizes the forecast error.

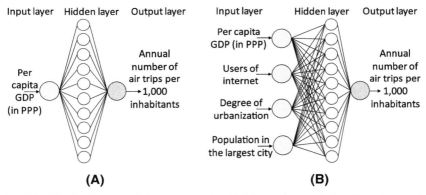

FIGURE 8.9 Architecture of the feedforward artificial neural network (ANN) models used. (A). Feedforward single input—single output ANN, (B). Feedforward multiple input—single output ANN. *Source: Compiled by the authors.*

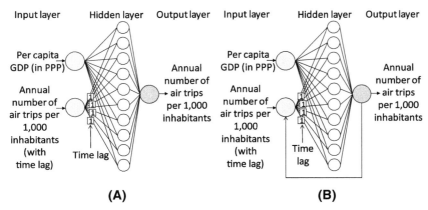

FIGURE 8.10 Architecture of the recurrent artificial neural network model used. (A) Open-loop phase. (B) Closed-loop phase. *Source: Compiled by the authors.*

8.6.5 Data and Software

Data will be collected from the database of the World Bank (2017), which can be considered among the most reliable in the world. The sample data will be randomly split into three sets, the training set, the validation set, and the testing set, with the respective percentages of 70%, 15%, 15%. The training set, as indicated by the name, will be used to train the ANN, the validation set will be used to inform the network when training will be stopped (when the estimated values of the dependent variable between successive iterations have no significant differences), and finally the test set will provide a completely independent measure of the accuracy of the ANN. For the training procedure, the Levenberg—Marquardt algorithm will be used, since it is appropriate for solving nonlinear least squares problems (further details concerning this algorithm in [469]). The software that will be used is MATLAB, a platform which is used for machine learning, signal and image processing, etc.

8.6.6 Activation Function—Check of the Forecasting Ability

The activation function in the hidden layer is a sigmoid function and in the output layer is a linear function (see §8.3.5).

The forecasting ability of the ANN models was checked on the basis of the values of the following statistical measures (see §5.7 and §5.11):

- mean squared error (MSE),
- mean absolute percentage error (MAPE),
- mean absolute deviation (MAD),
- coefficient of determination (R^2).

8.6.7 Results of the Feedforward Single Input—Single Output Artificial Neural Network Model

Fig. 8.11 illustrates results of the feedforward single input—single output ANN model and comparison with values of statistical data. The model has a high value of the coefficient of determination (R^2) and follows well the turning points of statistical data.

8.6.8 Results of the Feedforward Multiple Input—Single Output Artificial Neural Network Model

Fig. 8.12 illustrates results of the feedforward multiple input—single output ANN model and a comparison with the values of statistical data. As in the case of the previous ANN model, the calculated values of the multiple input—single output model fit well with the actual (measured) values of air transport demand.

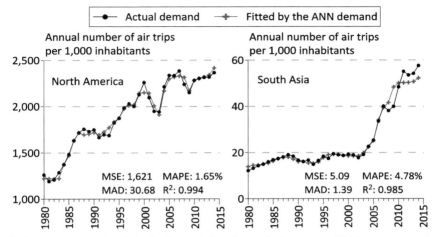

FIGURE 8.11 Results of the feedforward singe input—single output artificial neural network (ANN) model and comparison with the actual values of air transport demand. *Source: Compiled by the authors.*

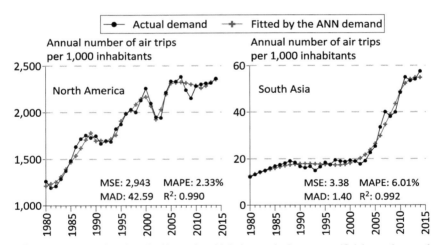

FIGURE 8.12 Results of the feedforward multiple input—single output artificial neural network (ANN) model and comparison with the actual values of air transport demand. *Source: Compiled by the authors.*

In the case of North America, however, the single input ANN model has a better forecasting ability compared with the multiple input ANN model (with four independent variables). Apparently, adding more independent variables (four instead of one) does not increase the ANN's forecasting ability or accuracy, as the new three additional variables do not affect air transport demand, probably because they have similar values for all the customers doing an air trip in North America. Another reason could be that North America has a mature air market, whereas urbanization has already attained high levels.

In contrast, for South Asia the multiple input ANN model gives slightly better results (compared with the single input ANN model). Thus, in that region of the world, some of the three additional input variables contribute to the increase of its forecasting ability.

8.6.9 Results of the Recurrent Artificial Neural Network Model

In a recurrent ANN model, the output variable (annual number of air trips per 1000 inhabitants) is also an input lagged variable, in order to incorporate feedback over time. The model has the ability to use as input in successive steps the previously calculated values of output. Thus, we will have two input variables (per capita GDP in purchasing power parity, lagged annual number of air trips per 1000 inhabitants) and one output variable (annual number of air trips per 1000 inhabitants). Recurrent ANNs are particularly suitable for systems with a highly dynamic behavior, strong fluctuations, and unpredictable changes in the course of time [456].

We will train the recurrent ANN model in two phases (see Fig. 8.10):

- Phase of open-loop training: It permits the training of the model with the actual targeted values, thus minimizing the forecast error.
- Phase of recurrent closed-loop feedback training: After the open-loop training phase, the output of an iteration becomes input for the next iteration, thus providing the possibility for out of sample forecasting.

The selection of time lags is similar to the selection of the optimal subset of independent variables in the calibration process of a statistical model. In an optimal subset selection, it is desired that the model includes as many independent variables as possible, so that the information contained in these independent variables will influence the predicted value of the dependent variable. However, it is also desired that the model include as few independent variables as possible, since the variance of the predictions of the model increases along with the increasing number of independent variables [470].

The appropriate time lags for the recurrent ANN can be estimated with the use of the correlograms of the autocorrelation function (ACF) and of the partial autocorrelation function (PACF) (see §6.8). The ACF and the PACF of the output variable (annual number of air trips per 1000 inhabitants), which is also an input lagged variable, are illustrated in Fig. 8.13. The plots of the correlograms of ACF and PACF are typical of a first-order autoregressive process: an exponentially declining ACF and statistically significant spikes in the first lag of the PACF, the latter indicating the order of the autoregression.

Fig. 8.14 illustrates results of the recurrent ANN model for the 5 years ahead forecast of air transport demand. We can observe a high value of the

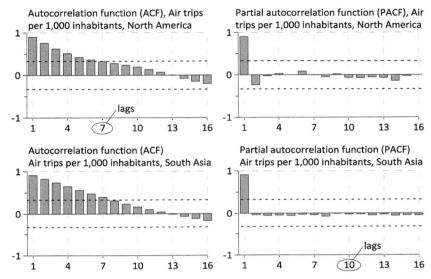

FIGURE 8.13   Values of the autocorrelation function (ACF) and of the partial autocorrelation function (PACF) for the selection of the appropriate time lags of the recurrent artificial neural network model. *Source: Compiled by the authors.*

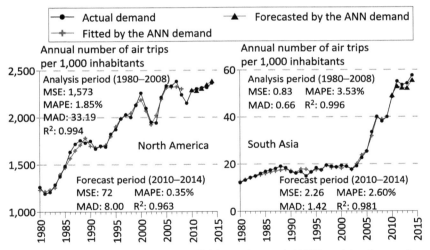

FIGURE 8.14   Results of the recurrent artificial neural network (ANN) model and comparison with the actual values of air transport demand. *Source: Compiled by the authors.*

coefficient of determination, which testifies the high forecasting ability of the model. The recurrent model is suitable for the forecast of future air transport demand, whereas the feedforward model is suitable for analyzing the evolution of demand in the past.

8.7 APPLICATION OF ARTIFICIAL NEURAL NETWORKS FOR SHORT-TERM FORECASTS OF AIR TRANSPORT DEMAND

Medium- and long-term forecasts of air transport demand are essential for airlines, as these are the basis for planning the use of aircrafts, the employment of staff (pilots, cabin crew), the estimation of future revenues and costs, etc.

However, short-term forecasts (one to several weeks ahead) are also essential, as they can be used for the calculation of the best tariffs that an airline can offer to customers, as well as for the optimization of the employment of staff and of the use of aircrafts.

In addition to traditional statistical forecasting methods, such as the moving average (see §6.6.1), exponential smoothing (see §6.6.2), or regression analysis, applications of ANNs have been also reported. In their simplest form, they utilized single-layer neural networks, which, however, can solve only linearly separable problems. Ex post assessment of forecasted and realized values of demand illustrated a much better performance of ANNs compared to traditional statistical methods. The reason for this may be the capacity of ANNs to take into account multiple input data, while allocating a higher importance to more recent data (by allocating higher synaptic weights to more recent data) [471].

8.8 APPLICATION OF ARTIFICIAL NEURAL NETWORKS FOR THE FORECAST OF RAIL TRANSPORT DEMAND

Railways (as any other transport mode) present high fluctuations of demand during the day, the week, the month, and successive years. Nowadays, a great number of input data are available. The above characteristics can be taken into account in forecasting methods which use ANNs.

A number of applications of ANNs for the forecast of rail demand have been reported [472,473]. We will refer first to an application of ANNs for the forecast of the annual demand of a rail company and will use statistical data that have been presented and analyzed previously (see §5.12 and §7.5.3). The analysis period covers the years from 1960 to 2010 and takes into account data of annual demand. The dependent (D_r) and the five selected independent variables that were investigated are as follows:

D_r rail trips per capita (dependent variable),
C_r unit cost of transport by rail (per passenger-km),
I_{co} car ownership index,
$C_{b,r}$ ratio of cost (per passenger-km) for the use of bus to the cost for the use of railway,
GDP   gross domestic product per capita,
$D_r(-1)$ lagged variable, which represents factors related to habitual inertia and constraints of supply of rail services [see §7.5.3, Eq. (7.18)].

Variables referring to monetary units were adjusted according to the annual consumer price index. All values incorporated into the model were indexed to a value of 100 for the year 1985.

Among the many available ANN models, a multilayer feedforward ANN was used. The model consisted of one input, one hidden, and one output layer. The sigmoid function was used as a transfer function. The backpropagation algorithm was used for the propagation rule, in an effort to minimize the mean squared error between the actual (measured) output y_i and the fitted (calculated) output $\hat{y}_i$. In successive calculations, the values of weights w_i were modified so as to reach an optimal output value. The network had the above mentioned five input (independent) variables, one hidden layer, and one output (dependent) variable.

The training process included the following steps:

- choice of the architecture of the network (particularly the number of hidden nodes),
- randomly chosen weights for the first iteration of the various layers of the network,
- choice of the training parameters (learning rate and momentum) and number of iterations,
- calculation of the difference between the actual and the fitted (calculated by the ANN model) value of the dependent variable for each step,
- optimization of the values of the weights of the ANN model (by applying the fmincon[3] solver in MATLAB) in order to minimize the error function,
- based on the obtained values of weights, calculation of the mean squared error of the test data,
- if the value of the error is within the predetermined values, the training is stopped.

The network architecture was selected after a trial and error procedure and consisted of one input layer (comprising five input neurons), one hidden layer (comprising two neurons), and one output layer (comprising one neuron). The number of iterations to attain the desired result was 150. Fig. 8.15 illustrates how close to actual values are the calculated values with the above application of ANNs. The forecasting ability of the ANN model was tested against Theil's inequality coefficient (see §5.11.5). The calculated value of this coefficient was 0.0063, very close to zero, which is the ideal value.

In *another* application of ANNs for the forecast of future trends of reservations and cancellations (and indirectly of the number of passenger demand, which is equal to reservations minus cancellations) of a rail company [474], the architecture of the system consisted of one input layer (comprising seven

---

3. A solver which permits to obtain the minimum of a constrained nonlinear multivariable function.

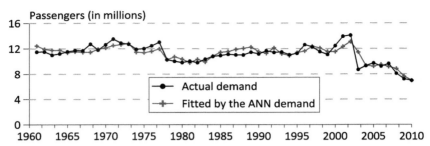

FIGURE 8.15 Comparison between actual and fitted values of an artificial neural network (ANN) for the forecast of rail passenger demand. *Source: Compiled by the authors.*

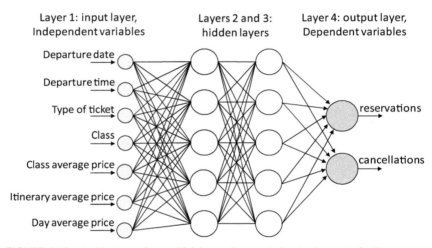

FIGURE 8.16 Architecture of an artificial neural network for the forecast of rail passenger demand with seven input variables, two hidden layers, and two output variables. *Source: Modified from Ref. [474].*

neurons), two hidden layers (each comprising five neurons), and one output layer (comprising two neurons) (Fig. 8.16). However, it is important to remember that a large number of hidden layers can mimic the phenomenon under study without, however, understanding the actual underlying processes.

The initial weights of the model were selected randomly, and for the iterative process the backpropagation algorithm with 300 iterations was used. The process stops when a local minimum is achieved. 80% of the data were used to train the ANN and 20% of the data were used to test the accuracy of the ANN. Again, the sigmoid function as the transfer function was used. The performance of the ANN model has been assessed by averaging the squared error under validation over all the trials of the process (Fig. 8.17) [474].

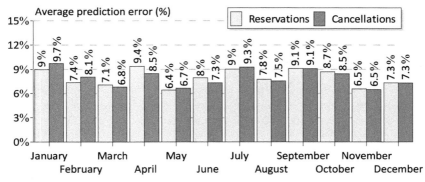

FIGURE 8.17 Average prediction error between actual and fitted values of an artificial neural network for the forecast of the monthly passenger reservations and cancellations of a rail company. *Source: Compiled by the authors, based on data of Ref. [474].*

8.9 APPLICATION OF ARTIFICIAL NEURAL NETWORKS FOR THE FORECAST OF ROAD TRAFFIC DEMAND

Intelligence transport systems (ITS) have become powerful tools for many cities to increase safety and combat traffic congestion and air pollution. Though their principal targets are the optimization of traffic signal times and of the capacity of the road network, many of the recorded data can be used for the short-term prediction of traffic flows, particularly during peak hours. Such data are usually:

- speed,
- volume (vehicles/hour),
- occupancy rates.

A traffic forecast with traditional statistical methods is usually based on average values for the above data; however, such a forecast cannot predict accurately what happens during peak hours, as it cannot take into account exceptional or abnormal factors. In such cases, ANN methods can be an efficient tool for more accurate short-time forecasts of road traffic demand, e.g., for the next half an hour in 5-min intervals [476].

Among the many applications, we will refer to the application of a back-propagation ANN model with one hidden layer of 10 neurons which was trained using a learning rate (a training parameter that controls the size of weight and bias changes in the learning process, $0 \leq$ learning rate ≤ 1 [477,478]) of 0.3 and a momentum (a training parameter which is used to prevent the system from converging to a local minimum or saddle point, $0 \leq$ momentum ≤ 1 [477,478]) of 0.4 [479]. As input variables the following were introduced: traffic volume (time t), traffic volume (time t—15 min), average (during the analysis period) traffic volume (time t), average (during the analysis period) traffic volume (time t + 15 min), average speed (time t), and condition of pavement (binary variable: wet or dry). In addition to the ANN application, the same problem was studied with the use of the ARIMA(2,1,0) time series model (ARIMA: Autoregressive Integrated Moving Average, see §6.7.7) and with a trend projection model [479].

The predicted traffic volume for a particular hour at a specific day is calculated on the basis of the average value of the traffic volumes that were recorded during the same hours of the same days in the past. The analysis examined congestion periods, for which traffic volumes exceed capacity, and average values during all periods of the day [479].

Table 8.2 gives a comparative performance concerning the average forecast error of the three methods. For peak periods, the ANN method provided better results, as it had a lower forecasting error, but if the period of a whole day was taken into account, the trend projection of average data proved to be more accurate than the ANN method.

In another application of ANNs, traffic flows for the coming 15 min with the use of the recorded data of the past 45 min and the application of the multilayer Perceptron model were calculated [475]. ANN was selected for this problem, as it does not set any a priori assumptions, takes into account nonlinearities, has a self-adaptive nature and capacity to be trained, and permits the consideration of a great number of input variables. Indeed, 19 input variables were taken into account, among them: day of week, time of day, type of vehicle, average speed for each type of vehicles, traffic density, etc. 60% of the data set was used for training, 15% for validation, and the remaining 25% for testing.

TABLE 8.2: A comparison of forecast errors of artificial neural network (ANN), time series, and trend projection methods for short-term road traffic volume forecasts.

Model	Average (%) forecast error, congestion period	Average (%) forecast error, whole period of analysis
Trend projection of historical average	5.0	6.4
ARIMA(2,1,0) time series model	10.8	9.0
ANN backpropagation model	4.3	7.5

Source: Modified from Ref. [479].

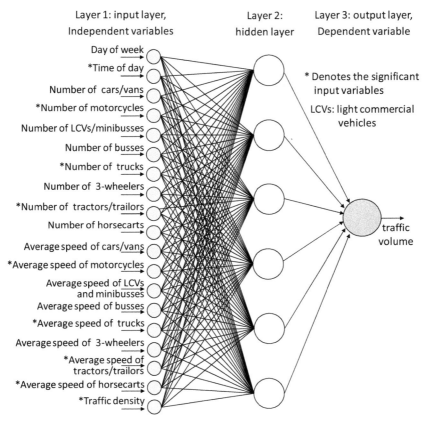

| Layer 1: input layer, Independent variables | Layer 2: hidden layer | Layer 3: output layer, Dependent variable |

Day of week
*Time of day
Number of cars/vans
*Number of motorcycles
Number of LCVs/minibusses
Number of busses
*Number of trucks
Number of 3-wheelers
*Number of tractors/trailors
Number of horsecarts
Average speed of cars/vans
*Average speed of motorcycles
Average speed of LCVs and minibusses
Average speed of busses
*Average speed of trucks
Average speed of 3-wheelers
*Average speed of tractors/trailors
*Average speed of horsecarts
*Traffic density

* Denotes the significant input variables

LCVs: light commercial vehicles

traffic volume

FIGURE 8.18 Architecture of an artificial neural network for the forecast of road traffic with 19 input variables and one hidden layer. *Source: Modified from Ref. [475].*

Ten ANN models were constructed with one hidden layer, a varying number of hidden neurons (from 3 to 6), and with a transfer function of either sigmoid or hyperbolic tangent form (see §8.3.5 and Fig. 8.4). Techniques of learning were either momentum or the Levenberg—Marquardt algorithm (further details concerning the algorithms in [469]), both of which are ways to adjust the weights among the neurons and improve the backpropagation ANN model performance. Performances of the calibrated models were checked and evaluated according to the values of the following statistical measures: mean squared error, mean absolute error, and coefficient of correlation.

Fig. 8.18 illustrates the architecture of the network selected as the best and Fig. 8.19 a comparison between actual (measured) and fitted (calculated) values. A sensitivity analysis, in addition, permitted the identification of the most important input variables [475].

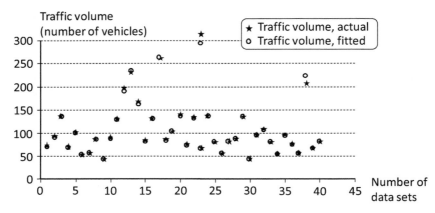

FIGURE 8.19 Comparison between actual and fitted values of an artificial neural network for the forecast of road traffic. *Source: Modified from Ref. [475].*

8.10 APPLICATION OF ARTIFICIAL NEURAL NETWORKS IN PROBLEMS OF ROAD SAFETY, DRIVER BEHAVIOR, AND SELF-DRIVEN VEHICLES

Road safety results from the interaction among road infrastructure, the vehicle, and the driver. After all, it is principally an issue of travel behavior. Self-driven vehicles apply methods similar to those used by humans when driving. Intelligent transport systems (ITS) can provide huge amounts of information which may be used to simulate behavior of drivers and vehicles and increase road safety.

ANNs are particularly suitable to simulate traffic and road safety problems, as they can take into account in real time numerous input data, adapt to changing situations, and consider nonlinearities.

Route choice by a driver can be simulated by ANNs. In this way, we may have ex ante knowledge about a driver's choices, calculate whether some roads will be saturated, and orient drivers to safer routes and itineraries. The learning method is usually the all-or-nothing method: the driver either makes a specific choice of route or not.

ANNs also permit the assessment of the importance placed by travelers on a piece of information given to them. If drivers did not consider or were not given sufficient information, then their decisions may be characterized by a certain degree of irrationality.

Researchers have reported many applications of ANNs for the optimization of routes of self-driven vehicles. Input data concerning geographical position, traffic flow (speed, density, etc.), and the origin and destination of the itinerary are introduced in real time to an ANN, which optimizes these data and selects the best route [480].

ANN applications for ITS utilize data that have the form of an irregular distribution or are not suitable for statistical methods. They usually employ feedforward backpropagation techniques with a number of inputs, one single output, and a number of hidden layers. Input data that feed the ANN for the calculation of the suggested route, estimated travel times, and (eventually) energy consumption include speed and acceleration of vehicles and traffic volume of the route under study and the neighboring routes.

One major task of self-driven vehicles is traffic sign recognition. Detecting and recognizing traffic signs can be accomplished with the use of convolutional neural networks, a specific type of ANN, which is a feedforward ANN, possessing a nonlinear activation function. The connectivity pattern between neurons of this ANN was designed on the basis of the organization of the animal visual cortex, the part of the brain that allows vision [481,482].

8.11 APPLICATION OF ARTIFICIAL NEURAL NETWORKS FOR ROUTING AND SCHEDULING OF FREIGHT TRANSPORT

Optimizing the routing and scheduling of freight transport in both urban and nonurban environments is a nonlinear problem, the features and critical parameters of which may change from one case to another. ANNs can contribute to the study of such problems and provide practical solutions in real time and for real-world simulation scenarios.

Applications of ANNs for the optimization of routing of freight transport give a better performance (by around 50%) compared with heuristic algorithms [483]. The latter can be applied to solving a problem or improving an existing solution by employing a practical method, which does not guarantee to be optimal or perfect, but is sufficient for the specific goals of the study. One example of a heuristic algorithm is the nearest neighbor algorithm [484].

8.12 APPLICATION OF ARTIFICIAL NEURAL NETWORKS FOR THE FORECAST OF MAINTENANCE NEEDS OF VEHICLES AND TRANSPORT INFRASTRUCTURE

Many problems of progressive deterioration and damage of transport infrastructure give, at a certain stage of their evolution, clear signs on the surface. Thus, for example, rail defects are apparent on the surface of the rail [7]. The pavements of roads and airports give also signs on the surface after a threshold of degradation. ANNs can help for an efficient scheduling of maintenance works by image processing of road and airport pavement and rail surface [485,486]. This allows the in-time detection of points of the infrastructure that will require maintenance. However, the degree of deterioration is just one element when scheduling the maintenance of infrastructure. It should be combined with other parameters of the problem, such as safety levels and margins of quality of service, level of traffic, and budget available.

ANNs can also be applied for the optimization of a vehicle's design self-diagnostic safety systems. Information from various nodes, such as the assembly units and subsystems of the vehicle, are introduced as inputs, while the efficiency of the maintenance and repair techniques employed are the outputs [487].

8.13 APPLICATION OF ARTIFICIAL NEURAL NETWORKS TO ASSESS PERFORMANCE OF TRANSPORT SYSTEMS AND EFFECTS OF UNPREDICTED EVENTS

Transport economics and policy need a trustworthy assessment of the relative performance of different transport modes (travel times, costs, etc.). ANNs can be used for such situations, as they can exploit more efficiently a greater amount of data. However, it is essential to take into account the service quality assessment made by passengers of a transport system, as well as the weight or relative importance assigned to each one of the attributes considered, in order to assess strengths and weaknesses. The following are fed into the ANN as inputs: fare, speed, frequency, information, punctuality, safety, driver courtesy, interior cleanliness and temperature, space available, accessibility, and proximity to/from origin/destination. The output of the ANN is typically customer satisfaction [466].

ANNs are particularly suitable for the study of travel times and delays resulting from effects of incidents and unpredicted events, such as accidents, strikes, closure of roads or crossroads, all of which are of a random nature [488].

Chapter 9

Fuzzy Methods

Chapter Outline

9.1 THE DETERMINISTIC, STOCHASTIC, AND FUZZY WAYS OF THINKING

9.1.1 The Limits of the Deterministic and Stochastic Way of Thinking

Transport demand aims at calculating the number of users of a transport company, a transport mode, or a transport infrastructure. In Chapters 3, 5, and 6, we emphasized the importance of accurate data, measurements, or observations that will permit us to analyze and forecast the evolution of a transport phenomenon or problem. We presented a number of methods which can make use of the existing data and give us the possibility of constructing a model that provides a mathematical simulation of a specific problem (disaggregate model) or of a number of problems (aggregate model). These methods are either deterministic (i.e., the conclusions and results have a character of certainty in

Modeling of Transport Demand. https://doi.org/10.1016/B978-0-12-811513-8.00009-1
Copyright © 2019 Elsevier Inc. All rights reserved.

relation to the assumptions made) or probabilistic—stochastic (i.e., the results have a degree of probability in relation to the assumptions related to the problem) (see also §3.2). Both deterministic and probabilistic methods are based on the *measurability* of the problem under study.

However, there is never certainty regarding the accuracy and validity of the available data; there may also be some periods of time for which the data are missing. Thus, a fundamental question associated with any model of transport demand is how representative of reality a mathematical simulation might be. Thus, the objectivity of quantitative methods (both deterministic and probabilistic) is rather relative.

If the data are totally missing or nonexisting, then any demand analysis and forecast is based on qualitative methods (see Chapter 4), which have an inherent character of subjectivity.

Whether quantitative or qualitative, the choice of a traveler for a given transport mode is based on a totally personal assessment which is the result of his or her evaluation of the various attributes related to his or her choice. Such an assessment is never constant over time, even in similar situations, as any individual tries to maximize his or her utility by using the specific transport mode (see §3.3.2 and §7.10.5). Moreover, it seems there are limits in the cognitive ability of an individual to properly assess all the attributes of a complex phenomenon such as transport, and in addition in many cases human reasoning is based on imprecise, vague, or partial access to true knowledge.

In spite of technological advances, inaccuracy continues to be a problem of measuring or recording systems of passengers and freight.

9.1.2 The Fuzzy Way of Thinking and Its Characteristics

Limits in the ability of human mind and eventual deficiencies of technological systems, which record data, led transportation science to exploit another way of thinking, known as fuzzy thinking. Indeed, our logic of understanding and interpreting a phenomenon is based on the principle of Aristotle (ancient Greek philosopher and scientist [384—322 BC]) that a statement may be only either true or false[1]. This principle is expressed in computers by the binary system (which follows the Boolean logic in mathematics) with only two alternatives, 1 and 0. In contrast, in the fuzzy way of thinking there may be many truths between 1 (a statement is completely true) and 0 (a statement is completely false). Thus, under the fuzzy way of reasoning, Boolean logic is a special case of fuzzy logic and more particularly it coincides with the two

---

1. In his Laws of Thought, Aristotle excluded the case of middle states between true and false, which were (according to him) the only two (though extreme) real situations of logic and thought. Not all Greek philosophers shared this view. Heraclitus proposed that things could be simultaneously true and not true, whereas Plato argued for a third region between true and false, where these opposites tumble out.

(A)   **(B)**

FIGURE 9.1 From absolutely true or false statements (A) to partially true or false statements (fuzzy) (B). *Source: Compiled by the authors.*

extreme cases of fuzzy logic (1: absolute or completely true, 0: absolutely or completely false) (Fig. 9.1).

Some argue that the fuzzy way of thinking reflects the way our mental apparatus conceives of and understands the world. Indeed, the human brain makes a number of observations and then combines partial truths to a more general truth, until it reaches the highest possible truth. In a similar way, fuzzy logic tries to progressively reduce ambiguity and fuzziness related to a phenomenon and concludes with a small margin of bounds, within which many eventual realities (that is, many plausible values of the problem under study) can exist.

The fuzzy way of thinking combines subjective (based on numbers) and objective (based on personal assessment) knowledge of quantitative and qualitative methods by taking into account inherent characteristics of the transport problem such as uncertainty, imprecision, and ambiguity and permits us, while departing from vague data, to make a range of rational conclusions and decisions. It employs for some problems linguistic variables (see §3.1.8), that is, variables which appear in the form of words rather than numbers, and can combine numerical information obtained from measurements with linguistic information [489−491].

9.1.3 The Pioneers of the Fuzzy Way of Thinking

The idea to approach the fuzzy character of phenomena is very recent; it was first conceived by the Azerbaijani-American mathematician−electrical engineer Lotfi Zadeh in 1965, and ever since it has spread over all domains of science, permitting the creation of algorithms, which can lead from vague data to conclusions and results close to reality [492].

Before Zadeh, in 1920 the Polish logician and philosopher Jan Łukasiewicz thought innovatively about multivalued logic and expressed the necessity of intermediate situations between 0 (false statement) and 1 (true statement), whereas in 1921 the American mathematician Emil Post also introduced the formulation of additional truth degrees.

The innovative works of Zadeh were further developed by a number of scientists, among them the Japanese instrumentation−electrical engineer Hideo Tanaka, who developed fuzzy modeling and its applications.

9.1.4 Transport Demand and the Fuzzy Way of Thinking

An example of how close to the reality of transport demand is the fuzzy way of thinking and understanding of the world is the following: the choice of a traveler between a low-cost airline and a high-speed rail company is based on his or her assessment of a number of attributes, such as cost, travel times, and convenience. However, when stating his or her decision, he or she very seldom declares that he or she will definitely take the airplane or the train. In most cases, his or her decision is followed by a statement, which includes expressions such as for sure yes, usually, quite possible, may be, in some cases, and for sure not. Such a statement can be modeled either with a quantitative probabilistic approach or with a qualitative survey (with the use, preferably, of the Likert scale, see §4.4.6.4). The fuzzy way of thinking gives us the ability to model such a problem in a different way: transform the linguistic variable related to the degree of certainty of his or her decision into a quantitative analysis and calculate the upper and lower limits of a bound within which the decision of the traveler is shifting (see §9.2.2).

9.2 FUNDAMENTAL CHARACTERISTICS, PROPERTIES, AND DEFINITIONS OF THE FUZZY METHOD

9.2.1 Fuzzy Numbers

Fuzzy means not clear enough, not well-known. A fuzzy number is a generalization of a regular real number, a quantity whose value is imprecise, rather than exact as is the case with usual ordinary numbers, such as, e.g., 2.34. Whereas real numbers reflect a certainty and no ambiguity, a fuzzy number should be conceptualized rather as a function, whose domain is specified and within which a fuzzy number can take a multitude of usual ordinary numbers. Thus, a *fuzzy number does not refer to one single numerical value* (as an ordinary number) *but to a set of plausible numerical values within a specified domain.*

Fuzzy numbers are suitable for representing phenomena which show variations or oscillations around a numerical value, as is the case of transport demand. Take for instance a highway, for which we calculate demand so as to avoid saturation [e.g., 2000 passenger car equivalents (PCE)/h/lane, for the definition of PCE see §1.3.1.5]. In real terms, it is not possible to have (even for some seconds) a value of traffic constant and equal to 2000 PCE/h/lane, but rather a set of values with variations and oscillations around the value of 2000. This is what a fuzzy number can represent, *a set of plausible values around a central value.*

9.2.2 Fuzzy Sets

In the *classic* theory of sets, a set A has precise boundaries, and an element x is situated either within the boundary and belongs to the set A or outside the

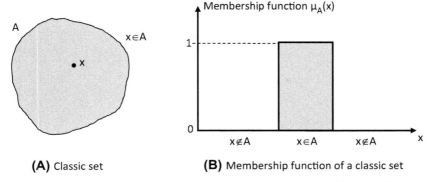

(A) Classic set

(B) Membership function of a classic set

FIGURE 9.2 Classic set and membership function. *Source: Compiled by the authors.*

boundary and does not belong to the set A. Membership (or not) of x within the set A is described by a membership function $\mu_A(x)$ as follows (Fig. 9.2):

$$\mu_A(x) = \begin{array}{l} 1, \text{ if and only if x is a member of the set A} \\ 0, \text{ if and only if x is not a member of the set A} \end{array}$$

Thus, in a classic set, the membership function of an element takes crisp values, either 1 or 0. The process of converting a crisp value to a fuzzy value is called *fuzzification*.

In contrast to a classic set, a fuzzy set has vague boundaries, which are neither precisely nor sharply defined. The membership function $\mu_A(x)$ in a fuzzy set can take any value from 0 to 1 in the closed interval [0, 1]. The greater the value of $\mu_A(x)$, the greater the possibility that the element x belongs to the fuzzy set A [493].

If we reconsider the various alternative statements of a traveler (see §9.1.4) before choosing between an airplane and a high-speed train (with comparable characteristics of transport services), the membership function $\mu_A(x)$ for each alternative could have the values presented in Table 9.1.

Thus, a fuzzy set is a collection of elements that might belong to the set to a certain degree, which varies from 1 (= full belongingness) to 0 (= full nonbelongingness), through all intermediate values between 0 and 1. The membership function in a fuzzy set indicates the intensity of belongingness. In this way, fuzzy sets can convert into numbers the vagueness and inaccuracy of our perception of the world.

A representative example of the difference between crisp values and fuzzy values as well as of the degree of membership can be illustrated by studying variations of traffic volume. A traffic volume between 500 PCE/h/lane and 1000 PCE/h/lane is usually considered as medium and is represented as a crisp set (Fig. 9.3A). The membership degree of this crisp set in the classic set theory is 1, whatever the traffic volume between 500 PCE/h/lane and 1000 PCE/h/lane

TABLE 9.1: Values of the membership function in a fuzzy analysis of alternative statements of a traveler when choosing between two alternative transport modes.

Statement of the traveler	Value of the membership function $\mu_A(x)$ (or degree of membership)
for sure yes	1.0
usually	0.9
quite possible	0.7–0.8
may be	0.5
in some cases (or sometimes)	0.2–0.3
for sure not	0.0

Source: Compiled by the authors.

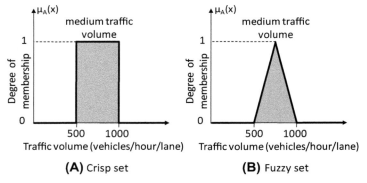

FIGURE 9.3 Medium traffic volume (500–1000 PCE/hour/lane) and its representation as a crisp set and as a fuzzy set. *PCE*, passenger car equivalents. *Source: Compiled by the authors.*

(e.g., 501 PCE/h/lane or 999 PCE/h/lane) and is characterized by the linguistic variable "medium traffic volume."

If now we represent the same traffic volume with a fuzzy set (Fig. 9.3B), the membership degree will vary from 0 to 1 and the value 1 for the membership degree corresponds to the mean value of the traffic volume, i.e., 750 PCE/h/lane.

9.2.3 Fuzzy Logic, Its Elements, and Methodology of Approaching a Problem

Fuzzy logic is an approach in computing which is based on degrees of truth (represented by the degree of membership in a fuzzy set) rather than the usual

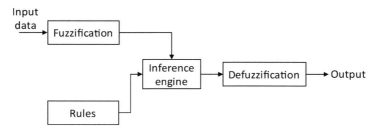

FIGURE 9.4 Elements of a fuzzy logic system. *Source: Compiled by the authors.*

true or false (1 or 0) Boolean logic on which modern computers are based. In fuzzy logic, the transition from the membership of an element of a fuzzy set to nonmembership is gradual and not abrupt. Thus, in fuzzy logic, *membership represents similarities of objects to imprecisely defined properties.* Fuzzy logic can quantify linguistic variables and efficiently combine subjective and objective knowledge.

The basic elements of a fuzzy logic system are (Fig. 9.4):

- *rules*: calculation of the membership function and decision of whether an element belongs to the fuzzy set or not,
- *fuzzification*: as input data are most usually crisp values, the process of fuzzification is to map real scale values into fuzzy values,
- *inference engine*: it maps fuzzy numbers into fuzzy sets,
- *defuzzification*: it aims to choose the one (and appropriate) value for the output variable.

A number of computer software packages (among them the commercial software MATLAB, Mathematica, etc., and various open source software packages, such as FisPro, etc.) can contribute to an easy application of the fuzzy logic. What is needed from the transport researcher is very simple: to define the rules of his or her problem and to provide the appropriate data to the computing machine.

9.2.4 The Fuzzy Logic and the Artificial Neural Network Method

If we compare the internal structure of a fuzzy logic system with artificial neural networks (ANNs) (see Chapter 8), we note that both methods can solve the same kinds of problems, by departing from available numerical data, but in a different way.

Thus, ANN can generate input—output models from a number of training data without being interested in the mechanism and the understanding of what happens between inputs and outputs. Fuzzy logic also departs from the same or similar data but relies on the experience of people who already understand the mechanism and the rules of the system under study.

9.2.5 The Fundamental Properties of the Fuzzy Logic

Fuzzy logic has a number of characteristics, such as:

- tolerance on imprecise, vague, or inaccurate data,
- flexibility,
- ability to consider previous experience,
- ability to consider nonlinearities of the problem.

A fundamental prerequisite of the fuzzy logic is that the set of input data can be mapped to an output set.

9.2.6 Some Forms of Fuzzy Numbers

Depending on whether the center value of a fuzzy number occurs only once or a number of times (within an interval of time), there are many forms of fuzzy numbers. The most commonly used fuzzy numbers are the following (Fig. 9.5):

- triangular. It is mostly used in the case of transport demand problems, as the center value is changing quickly in relation to time. Triangular fuzzy numbers may be symmetric (the usual case) or nonsymmetric,
- trapezoidal,
- Gaussian.

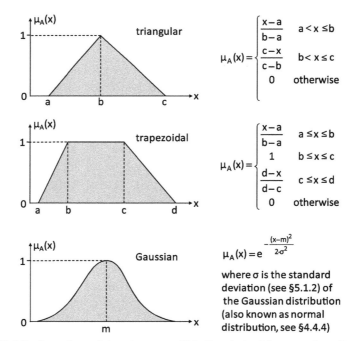

$$\mu_A(x) = \begin{cases} \dfrac{x-a}{b-a} & a < x \leq b \\ \dfrac{c-x}{c-b} & b < x \leq c \\ 0 & \text{otherwise} \end{cases}$$

$$\mu_A(x) = \begin{cases} \dfrac{x-a}{b-a} & a \leq x \leq b \\ 1 & b \leq x \leq c \\ \dfrac{d-x}{d-c} & c \leq x \leq d \\ 0 & \text{otherwise} \end{cases}$$

$$\mu_A(x) = e^{-\frac{(x-m)^2}{2\sigma^2}}$$

where σ is the standard deviation (see §5.1.2) of the Gaussian distribution (also known as normal distribution, see §4.4.4)

FIGURE 9.5 Some forms (triangular, trapezoidal, Gaussian) of fuzzy numbers A and their membership function $\mu_A(x)$. *Source: Compiled by the authors.*

9.3 DEFINITION AND MATHEMATICAL DESCRIPTION OF A SYMMETRIC TRIANGULAR FUZZY NUMBER

9.3.1 The Symmetric Triangular Fuzzy Number in Transport Problems

As explained in §9.2.1, a fuzzy number is a generalization of a regular real number, in the sense that it does not refer to one single real value but rather to a connected set of possible values, where each possible value has its own degree of membership (also called *membership grade* or *degree of truth*) with values varying from 0 to 1. Among the various forms of fuzzy numbers (triangular, trapezoidal, Gaussian, see §9.2.6), the triangular symmetric fuzzy number is the most commonly used for transport demand problems, as it simulates better than the other forms the varying and changing character of transport demand at any moment or observation [473,494].

9.3.2 Mathematical Description of a Symmetric Triangular Fuzzy Number—The Membership Function

A symmetric triangular fuzzy number A is specified as $A = (r, c)_L$ (Fig. 9.6), where [18,494,495]:

r   the center value of the fuzzy number A; this center value has a degree of membership equal to 1,

c   the spread of the fuzzy number A, that is, the difference of the upper and lower value from its center value. Within the spread of a fuzzy number, the degree of membership takes values from 0 to 1, $0 \leq \mu < 1$,

$\mu_A(x)$ the membership function, which describes the boundaries of the fuzzy number A. In our case of a symmetric triangular fuzzy number, the membership function is an increasing or decreasing linear function of the two sides of the symmetric triangle and is described by the following equation:

$$\mu_A(x) = L\left(\frac{x - r}{c}\right), \quad c > 0 \tag{9.1}$$

in which L(x) is given by the formula:

$$L(x) = \max(0, 1 - |x|)$$

and satisfies the following conditions [473,494,496,497]:

1. $L(x) = L(-x)$,
2. $L(0) = 1$,
3. $L(x)$ is a strictly decreasing function in the interval $[0, \infty)$.

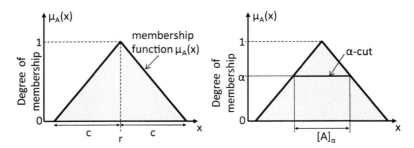

FIGURE 9.6 Characteristics of a symmetric triangular fuzzy number and α-cut values. *Source: Compiled by the authors.*

The various values of the membership function $\mu_A(x)$ express the degree to which an element x verifies the characteristic properties of the fuzzy number A. Thus, the closer to 1 are the values $\mu_A(x)$, the higher the membership degree of x is in A [498].

9.3.3 Fuzzy Numbers and Crisp Numbers

In contrast to a fuzzy number, which is imprecise and has a plausible range of values, a *crisp* number has a specific and precise value. The fuzzy logic uses crisp values which are mapped into fuzzy numbers (or sets) in the fuzzification process. Inversely, in the defuzzification process, among the various output values, the most appropriate crisp values are chosen.

Let us consider the case of a fuzzy number A and a value α of the membership function $\mu_A(x)$ (Fig. 9.6 right). The value of A which corresponds to the value α of $\mu_A(x)$ is called α-cut. If we take into account all the values $\mu_A(x) \geq \alpha$, then the various crisp α-cut values constitute the crisp set $[A]_\alpha = \{x \in A: \mu_A(x) \geq \alpha\}$. Thus, a fuzzy number can be represented by the various α-cut values, which correspond to the various values α of the membership function $\mu_A(x)$.

9.4 LINEAR REGRESSION ANALYSIS WITH THE USE OF FUZZY NUMBERS (LINEAR FUZZY REGRESSION ANALYSIS)

9.4.1 Classic and Fuzzy Regression Analysis

In Chapter 5 (§5.2–§5.4), we analyzed that regression analysis is the basic tool when trying to correlate transport demand with one or more of the variables that affect it and thus construct any kind of transport demand model. Among the various forms of equations of regression analysis, the simplest but also the most commonly used is linear regression. As we explained in Chapter 5 (§5.4.1) and Chapter 6 (§6.2.3), if a specific problem does not have linear form, it is transformed (e.g., by taking logarithms) to a linear one. A linear regression equation of the dependent variable Y in relation to the independent variables X_i ($i = 1, 2,..., n$) has the form:

$$Y = a_0 + a_1 \cdot X_1 + a_2 \cdot X_2 + \cdots + a_n \cdot X_n \qquad (9.2)$$

The parameters $a_0, a_1, a_2,..., a_n$ of Eq. (9.2) are real numbers, are called *regression coefficients* (or *partial regression coefficients*), and are calculated with the ordinary least squares method, which aims at minimizing the sum of squared errors between the calculated (fitted) by the regression analysis values of the dependent variable Y and its actual values which are recorded or observed.

If we use fuzzy numbers for the various parameters of Eq. (9.2) instead of real numbers, then we have the case of a *fuzzy linear regression* equation of the form:

$$Y = A_0 + A_1 \cdot X_1 + A_2 \cdot X_2 + \cdots + A_n \cdot X_n \qquad (9.3)$$

where $A_i = (r_i, c_i)_L$, $i = 0, 1, 2,..., n$ are symmetric triangular fuzzy numbers [496,499−503]. For other kinds of problems (economic, hydrological, etc.), other forms of fuzzy numbers (trapezoidal, Gaussian, etc.) could be used.

9.4.2 Calculation of the Fuzzy Regression Coefficients

We indicate with x_{ij} and y_j ($i = 1, 2,..., n$ and $j = 1, 2, ..., m$) the various real values that the variables X_i and Y can take. Table 9.2 illustrates these various real values (numerical data) of the variables X_i and Y, in the form of a time series.

Table 9.2 constitutes a system of fuzzy equations of the form:

$$Y_j = A_0 + A_1 \cdot x_{1j} + A_2 \cdot x_{2j} + \cdots + A_n \cdot x_{nj} \quad (j = 1, 2, ..., m) \qquad (9.4)$$

TABLE 9.2: Real values x_{ij} and y_j in the form of time series of the variables X_i and Y on which the fuzzy equations will be calculated.

Independent variables					Dependent variable Y
X_1	X_2	X_3	$\cdots$	X_n	
x_{11}	x_{21}	x_{31}	$\cdots$	x_{n1}	y_1
x_{12}	x_{22}	x_{32}	$\cdots$	x_{n2}	y_2
$\vdots$	$\vdots$	$\vdots$	$\vdots$	$\vdots$	$\vdots$
x_{1m}	x_{2m}	x_{3m}	$\cdots$	x_{nm}	y_m

Source: Compiled by the authors.

Thus, we will have [496, 500]:

$$
\begin{aligned}
Y_1 &= A_0 + A_1 \cdot x_{11} + A_2 \cdot x_{21} + \cdots + A_n \cdot x_{n1} \\
Y_2 &= A_0 + A_1 \cdot x_{12} + A_2 \cdot x_{22} + \cdots + A_n \cdot x_{n2} \\
&\vdots \\
Y_m &= A_0 + A_1 \cdot x_{1m} + A_2 \cdot x_{2m} + \cdots + A_n \cdot x_{nm}
\end{aligned}
\tag{9.5}
$$

The next step is to choose the degree h of the membership function ($0 \leq h < 1$) in such a way that the available data or observations $((x_{1j}, x_{2j},..., x_{nj}), y_j)$ related to both the independent variables X_i and the dependent one Y will be included in the inferred fuzzy number Y_j. The situation of $h = 0$ is generally selected in the case of perfect uncertainty, which allows fuzzy regression analysis to predict the most extensive boundaries for Y_j. In fact, higher values of h lead to smaller prediction boundaries and to higher certainties for the inferred (predicted) values. Thus the following inequality should be valid [496]:

$$
\mu_{Y_j}(y_j) \geq h \quad (j = 1, 2, ..., m) \tag{9.6}
$$

When there is a sufficient number of available data or observations ($m > 10$, see Table 9.2), we can take $h = 0$, a value that maximizes the regression's ambiguity [473]. In any case, the chosen value for h must be greater than or equal to 0 but smaller than 1, since for $h = 1$ the fuzzy linear regression turns into a classic linear regression [504].

It has been found that for the case of symmetric triangular fuzzy numbers, the various parameters of a linear fuzzy regression analysis have the following membership function [505]:

$$
\mu_{A_i}(x) = \begin{cases}
\dfrac{1}{c_i} \cdot x + \dfrac{c_i - r_i}{c_i}, & r_i - c_i \leq x \leq r_i \\[2mm]
-\dfrac{1}{c_i} \cdot x + \dfrac{c_i + r_i}{c_i}, & r_i \leq x \leq r_i + c_i \\[2mm]
0 & \text{otherwise}
\end{cases}
\tag{9.7}
$$

Their α-cuts are determined from Eq. (9.7) [505]:

$$
\alpha = \frac{1}{c_i} \cdot x + \frac{c_i - r_i}{c_i} \Leftrightarrow x = \alpha \cdot c_i - (c_i - r_i) \tag{9.8}
$$

$$
\alpha = -\frac{1}{c_i} \cdot x + \frac{c_i + r_i}{c_i} \Leftrightarrow x = -\alpha \cdot c_i + (c_i + r_i) \tag{9.9}
$$

Consequently, the α-cuts of the fuzzy numbers A_i ($i = 1, 2,..., n$) are the closed intervals [505]:

$$
[A_i]_\alpha = [\alpha \cdot c_i - (c_i - r_i), -\alpha \cdot c_i + (c_i + r_i)], \quad \alpha \in [0, 1] \tag{9.10}
$$

What we are looking for is to determine the membership function of any symmetric triangular fuzzy number Y_j ($j = 1, 2,..., m$) of the form of Eq. (9.4) or equivalently its α-cuts. The center, the spread, and the membership function of this symmetric triangular fuzzy number will be, respectively [496,506,507]:

$$r_0 + \sum_{i=1}^{n} r_i \cdot x_{ij}, \quad c_0 + \sum_{i=1}^{n} c_i \cdot |x_{ij}|, \quad \mu_{Y_j}(y) = L\left(\frac{y - r_0 - \sum_{i=1}^{n} r_i \cdot x_{ij}}{c_0 + \sum_{i=1}^{n} c_i \cdot |x_{ij}|}\right)$$

$$\text{center} \qquad\qquad \text{spread} \qquad\qquad \text{membership function}$$

$$(9.11)$$

By combining Eqs. (9.6) and (9.11) we can take [406,506,507]:

$$\mu_{Y_j}(y_j) = L\left(\frac{y - r_0 - \sum_{i=1}^{n} r_i \cdot x_{ij}}{c_0 + \sum_{i=1}^{n} c_i \cdot |x_{ij}|}\right) \geq h \quad (j = 1, 2, ..., m) \qquad (9.12)$$

It is clear that the smaller the fuzziness of a fuzzy number, the better the approximation of reality. Thus, we require the total spread of the fuzzy numbers Y_j to be as small as possible. Then, we should minimize the function [496,500,506,507]:

$$J = \sum_{j=1}^{m}\left(c_0 + \sum_{i=1}^{n} c_i \cdot |x_{ij}|\right) = m \cdot c_0 + \sum_{j=1}^{m}\sum_{i=1}^{n} c_i \cdot |x_{ij}| \qquad (9.13)$$

The following equations are derived from Eqs. (9.11) and (9.12) [496,500,506,507]:

$$y_j + c_0 - r_0 + \sum_{i=1}^{n} c_i \cdot |x_{ij}| - \sum_{i=1}^{n} r_i \cdot |x_{ij}| \geq h \cdot c_0 + h \cdot \sum_{i=1}^{n} c_j \cdot |x_{ij}| \qquad (9.14)$$

Thus, for $j = 1, 2,..., m$, we have

$$y_j \geq r_0 + \sum_{i=1}^{n} r_i \cdot x_{ij} - (1 - h) \cdot \left(c_0 + \sum_{i=1}^{n} c_i \cdot |x_{ij}|\right) \qquad (9.15)$$

and

$$-y_j + c_0 + r_0 + \sum_{i=1}^{n} c_i \cdot |x_{ij}| + \sum_{i=1}^{n} r_i \cdot |x_{ij}| \geq h \cdot c_0 + h \cdot \sum_{i=1}^{n} c_i \cdot |x_{ij}| \qquad (9.16)$$

from which it follows that

$$y_j \leq r_0 + \sum_{i=1}^{n} r_i \cdot x_{ij} + (1 - h) \cdot \left(c_0 + \sum_{i=1}^{n} c_i \cdot |x_{ij}|\right) \qquad (9.17)$$

9.4.3 Transforming a Linear Fuzzy Regression Analysis Into a Linear Programming Problem

The inequalities (9.15) and (9.17) form constraints of a linear programming problem, which is a mathematical technique for maximizing or minimizing a linear function of several variables, also called an *objective* function. The objective function is subject to a number of constraints, which can be expressed in the form of linear equalities or inequalities. In the case of symmetric triangular fuzzy numbers, the objective function is given by Eq. (9.13). An additional constraint is that the spread c_i can take only positive values, since it represents the fuzziness of a model, thus:

$$c_i \geq 0 \quad (i = 0, 1, ..., n) \tag{9.18}$$

It has been proven [496] that the linear programming problem composed of Eq. (9.13) and of inequalities (9.15), (9.17), and (9.18) has an optimal solution, which permits us to obtain the h-level coefficients $A_i^h = \left(r_i^h, c_i^h\right)_L$ $(0 \leq h < 1)$ of the fuzzy linear regression.

9.5 A DETAILED APPLICATION OF FUZZY LINEAR REGRESSION ANALYSIS FOR A TRANSPORT DEMAND PROBLEM

9.5.1 Statement and Data of the Problem

We will illustrate a detailed step-by-step application of fuzzy linear regression, based on symmetric triangular fuzzy numbers, for the analysis and forecast of rail passenger demand between two nearby cities. According to the relevant literature [7,14,320−322,325], the rail passenger demand between these cities depends, among other factors, on the level of economic development of their regions, expressed satisfactorily by the regional per capita domestic product, the unit cost of transport by rail, the unit cost of transport by competitive transport modes (for distances up to 400 km the main competitors of railways are private cars and busses), as well as other factors such as the quality of transport services, the frequency of services, eventual exogenous to the problem events such as strikes, extremely cold weather conditions, etc.

Table 9.3 presents the evolution between 2003 and 2017 of the dependent variable (rail passengers) and of the independent variables (per capita gross regional product [GRP], cost of transport by rail, fuel prices), which are necessary for the calibration of the fuzzy linear regression. All monetary values were adjusted in constant 2017 prices, according to the annual consumer price index. The model additionally takes into account an exceptional event which occurred in 2011, a strike of air companies for many days, which resulted in an unusual shift of air traffic to the railways for that year. This event will be introduced in the model as a dummy variable.

TABLE 9.3: Values of the dependent and the independent variables of the problem.

Observation	Year	Rail passengers (actual demand) Y	Per capita gross regional product (€) X_1	Cost of transport by rail (€) X_2	Fuel prices (€/liter) X_3	Dummy variable X_4
1	2003	165,560	11,029	17	1.52	0
2	2004	168,871	12,230	17	1.55	0
3	2005	172,182	13,601	19	1.58	0
4	2006	165,560	14,542	21	1.61	0
5	2007	162,249	15,551	23	1.71	0
6	2008	173,838	17,302	23	1.75	0
7	2009	185,427	18,743	23	1.77	0
8	2010	163,904	17,551	23	1.75	0
9	2011	193,365	19,019	23	1.81	1
10	2012	160,593	20,888	26	1.79	0
11	2013	157,282	21,079	26	1.80	0
12	2014	153,971	21,419	26	1.72	0
13	2015	145,693	21,700	29	1.69	0
14	2016	144,587	20,260	29	1.58	0
15	2017	139,527	20,302	29	1.53	1
	Sum $\sum x_{ij}$:	265,216	354	25.16		

Source: Compiled by the authors.

9.5.2 Equations and Constraints of the Problem

The problem of calibration of a linear fuzzy regression model with a number of independent variables (in our example: 4) can be represented by the following equation:

$$Y = A_0 + A_1 \cdot X_1 + A_2 \cdot X_2 + A_3 \cdot X_3 + A_4 \cdot X_4 \qquad (9.19)$$

where

Y	rail passengers (dependent variable),
X_1	per capita GRP (in €),
X_2	cost of transport by rail (in €),
X_3	fuel prices (in €/liter),
X_4	dummy variable for the year 2011,
$A_0, ..., A_4$	symmetric triangular fuzzy numbers.

The available data of the problem (Table 9.3) correspond to a number q of 15 observations, $q > 10$. From Eqs. (9.15) and (9.17) and for $h = 0$ (since $q > 10$), we can obtain a number of 30 ($= 2 \cdot q = 2 \cdot 15$) inequalities, which formulate the transformation of our fuzzy problem to a linear programming problem as follows:

For the year 2003:

$165560 \geq r_0 + 11029 \cdot r_1 + 17 \cdot r_2 + 1.52 \cdot r_3 - c_0 - 11029 \cdot c_1 - 17 \cdot c_2 - 1.52 \cdot c_3 - 0 \cdot c_4$

$165560 \leq r_0 + 11029 \cdot r_1 + 17 \cdot r_2 + 1.52 \cdot r_3 + c_0 + 11029 \cdot c_1 + 17 \cdot c_2 + 1.52 \cdot c_3 + 0 \cdot c_4$

For the year 2004:

$168871 \geq r_0 + 12230 \cdot r_1 + 17 \cdot r_2 + 1.55 \cdot r_3 - c_0 - 12230 \cdot c_1 - 17 \cdot c_2 - 1.55 \cdot c_3 - 0 \cdot c_4$

$168871 \leq r_0 + 12230 \cdot r_1 + 17 \cdot r_2 + 1.55 \cdot r_3 + c_0 + 12230 \cdot c_1 + 17 \cdot c_2 + 1.55 \cdot c_3 + 0 \cdot c_4$

For the year 2005:

$172182 \geq r_0 + 13601 \cdot r_1 + 19 \cdot r_2 + 1.58 \cdot r_3 - c_0 - 13601 \cdot c_1 - 19 \cdot c_2 - 1.58 \cdot c_3 - 0 \cdot c_4$

$172182 \leq r_0 + 13601 \cdot r_1 + 19 \cdot r_2 + 1.58 \cdot r_3 + c_0 + 13601 \cdot c_1 + 19 \cdot c_2 + 1.58 \cdot c_3 + 0 \cdot c_4$

For the year 2006:

$165560 \geq r_0 + 14542 \cdot r_1 + 21 \cdot r_2 + 1.61 \cdot r_3 - c_0 - 14542 \cdot c_1 - 21 \cdot c_2 - 1.61 \cdot c_3 - 0 \cdot c_4$

$165560 \leq r_0 + 14542 \cdot r_1 + 21 \cdot r_2 + 1.61 \cdot r_3 + c_0 + 14542 \cdot c_1 + 21 \cdot c_2 + 1.61 \cdot c_3 + 0 \cdot c_4$

For the year 2007:

$162249 \geq r_0 + 15551 \cdot r_1 + 23 \cdot r_2 + 1.71 \cdot r_3 - c_0 - 15551 \cdot c_1 - 23 \cdot c_2 - 1.71 \cdot c_3 - 0 \cdot c_4$

$162249 \leq r_0 + 15551 \cdot r_1 + 23 \cdot r_2 + 1.71 \cdot r_3 + c_0 + 15551 \cdot c_1 + 23 \cdot c_2 + 1.71 \cdot c_3 + 0 \cdot c_4$

For the year 2008:

$173838 \geq r_0 + 17302 \cdot r_1 + 23 \cdot r_2 + 1.75 \cdot r_3 - c_0 - 17302 \cdot c_1 - 23 \cdot c_2 - 1.75 \cdot c_3 - 0 \cdot c_4$

$173838 \leq r_0 + 17302 \cdot r_1 + 23 \cdot r_2 + 1.75 \cdot r_3 + c_0 + 17302 \cdot c_1 + 23 \cdot c_2 + 1.75 \cdot c_3 + 0 \cdot c_4$

For the year 2009:

$193365 \geq r_0 + 18743 \cdot r_1 + 23 \cdot r_2 + 1.77 \cdot r_3 - c_0 - 18743 \cdot c_1 - 23 \cdot c_2 - 1.77 \cdot c_3 - 1 \cdot c_4$

$193365 \leq r_0 + 18743 \cdot r_1 + 23 \cdot r_2 + 1.77 \cdot r_3 + c_0 + 18743 \cdot c_1 + 23 \cdot c_2 + 1.77 \cdot c_3 + 1 \cdot c_4$

For the year 2010:

$163904 \geq r_0 + 17551 \cdot r_1 + 23 \cdot r_2 + 1.75 \cdot r_3 - c_0 - 17551 \cdot c_1 - 23 \cdot c_2 - 1.75 \cdot c_3 - 0 \cdot c_4$

$163904 \leq r_0 + 17551 \cdot r_1 + 23 \cdot r_2 + 1.75 \cdot r_3 + c_0 + 17551 \cdot c_1 + 23 \cdot c_2 + 1.75 \cdot c_3 + 0 \cdot c_4$

For the year 2011:

$193365 \geq r_0 + 19019 \cdot r_1 + 23 \cdot r_2 + 1.81 \cdot r_3 - c_0 - 19019 \cdot c_1 - 23 \cdot c_2 - 1.81 \cdot c_3 - 0 \cdot c_4$

$193365 \leq r_0 + 19019 \cdot r_1 + 23 \cdot r_2 + 1.81 \cdot r_3 + c_0 + 19019 \cdot c_1 + 23 \cdot c_2 + 1.81 \cdot c_3 + 0 \cdot c_4$

For the year 2012:

$160593 \geq r_0 + 20888 \cdot r_1 + 26 \cdot r_2 + 1.79 \cdot r_3 - c_0 - 20888 \cdot c_1 - 26 \cdot c_2 - 1.79 \cdot c_3 - 0 \cdot c_4$

$160593 \leq r_0 + 20888 \cdot r_1 + 26 \cdot r_2 + 1.79 \cdot r_3 + c_0 + 20888 \cdot c_1 + 26 \cdot c_2 + 1.79 \cdot c_3 + 0 \cdot c_4$

For the year 2013:

$157282 \geq r_0 + 21079 \cdot r_1 + 26 \cdot r_2 + 1.80 \cdot r_3 - c_0 - 21079 \cdot c_1 - 26 \cdot c_2 - 1.80 \cdot c_3 - 0 \cdot c_4$

$157282 \leq r_0 + 21079 \cdot r_1 + 26 \cdot r_2 + 1.80 \cdot r_3 + c_0 + 21079 \cdot c_1 + 26 \cdot c_2 + 1.80 \cdot c_3 + 0 \cdot c_4$

For the year 2014:

$153971 \geq r_0 + 21419 \cdot r_1 + 26 \cdot r_2 + 1.72 \cdot r_3 - c_0 - 21419 \cdot c_1 - 26 \cdot c_2 - 1.72 \cdot c_3 - 0 \cdot c_4$

$153971 \leq r_0 + 21419 \cdot r_1 + 26 \cdot r_2 + 1.72 \cdot r_3 + c_0 + 21419 \cdot c_1 + 26 \cdot c_2 + 1.72 \cdot c_3 + 0 \cdot c_4$

For the year 2015:

$145693 \geq r_0 + 21700 \cdot r_1 + 29 \cdot r_2 + 1.69 \cdot r_3 - c_0 - 21700 \cdot c_1 - 29 \cdot c_2 - 1.69 \cdot c_3 - 0 \cdot c_4$

$145693 \leq r_0 + 21700 \cdot r_1 + 29 \cdot r_2 + 1.69 \cdot r_3 + c_0 + 21700 \cdot c_1 + 29 \cdot c_2 + 1.69 \cdot c_3 + 0 \cdot c_4$

For the year 2016:

$144587 \geq r_0 + 20260 \cdot r_1 + 29 \cdot r_2 + 1.58 \cdot r_3 - c_0 - 20260 \cdot c_1 - 29 \cdot c_2 - 1.58 \cdot c_3 - 0 \cdot c_4$

$144587 \leq r_0 + 20260 \cdot r_1 + 29 \cdot r_2 + 1.58 \cdot r_3 + c_0 + 20260 \cdot c_1 + 29 \cdot c_2 + 1.58 \cdot c_3 + 0 \cdot c_4$

For the year 2017:

$139527 \geq r_0 + 20302 \cdot r_1 + 29 \cdot r_2 + 1.53 \cdot r_3 - c_0 - 20302 \cdot c_1 - 29 \cdot c_2 - 1.53 \cdot c_3 - 0 \cdot c_4$

$139527 \leq r_0 + 20302 \cdot r_1 + 29 \cdot r_2 + 1.53 \cdot r_3 + c_0 + 20302 \cdot c_1 + 29 \cdot c_2 + 1.53 \cdot c_3 + 0 \cdot c_4$

9.5.3 Calculation of the Fuzzy Numbers and Calibration of the Fuzzy Model

From Table 9.4 we can calculate the various sums $\sum x_{ij}$ ($i = 1, 2, 3, 4$, and $j = 1, 2,\dots 15$) as follows:

$$\sum_{j=1}^{15} x_{1j} = 265216, \quad \sum_{j=1}^{15} x_{2j} = 354, \quad \sum_{j=1}^{15} x_{3j} = 25.16, \quad \sum_{j=1}^{15} x_{4j} = 1$$

The objective function of the linear programming problem stems from Eq. (9.13) as follows:

$$J = \min\left\{ m \cdot c_0 + \sum_{j=1}^{m} \sum_{i=1}^{n} |x_{ij}| \cdot c_i \right\} =$$

$$= \min\{15 \cdot c_0 + 265216 \cdot c_1 + 354 \cdot c_2 + 25.16 \cdot c_3 + 1 \cdot c_4\}$$

The solution of the problem must also respect the constraints of a linear programming problem (see §9.4.3), that is:

$$c_0 \geq 0, \ c_1 \geq 0, \ c_2 \geq 0, \ c_3 \geq 0, \ c_4 \geq 0$$

There are a number of computer software packages (among them Maple, Mathematica, etc.) that can accommodate the solution of the system of the above equations and inequalities, provide accurate values for r_i, c_i ($i = 1, 2, 3, 4$), and thus describe the various fuzzy numbers $A_i = (r_i, c_i)$ as follows:

$$
\begin{aligned}
A_0 &= (r_0, c_0) &=& \quad (94641.46, 0) \\
A_1 &= (r_1, c_1) &=& \quad (0.996, 0.510) \\
A_2 &= (r_2, c_2) &=& \quad (-4299.305, 0) \\
A_3 &= (r_3, c_3) &=& \quad (91206.84, 0) \\
A_4 &= (r_4, c_4) &=& \quad (3873.975, 0)
\end{aligned}
$$

TABLE 9.4: Estimated future values for the independent variables of the problem.

Year	Rail passengers $\hat{Y}$	Per capita GRP (€) X_1	Cost of transport by rail (€) X_2	Fuel prices (€/liter) X_3
2018	?	20,505	30	1.55
2019	?	20,915	31	1.60
2020	?	21,542	31	1.65
2021	?	22,296	33	1.70

Source: Compiled by the authors.

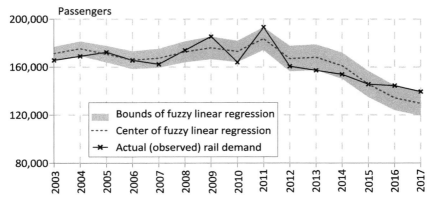

FIGURE 9.7 Results of the fuzzy linear regression model (center and bounds) and comparison with actual values. *Source: Compiled by the authors.*

From the above fuzzy numbers we can note that only the independent variable X_1 (per capita regional domestic product) contributes to the ambiguity of the fuzzy linear regression (since $c_1 \neq 0$), whereas all other values of spread c_i ($i \neq 1$) are equal to zero. In the rare case where all values of the spread c_i are equal to 0, the fuzzy linear regression model does not contain any ambiguity and thus it is transformed into a classic linear regression model.

Thus, the estimation of demand $\widehat{Y}$ with application of fuzzy linear regression analysis will result from the equation:

$$
\begin{aligned}
\widehat{Y} = 94641.46 + 0.996 \cdot X_1 - 4299.305 \cdot X_2 + \\
+ 91206.84 \cdot X_3 + 3873.975 \cdot X_4 \pm 0.510 \cdot X_1
\end{aligned}
\tag{9.20}
$$

Fig. 9.7 illustrates graphically the results of the fuzzy linear regression model and more specifically its center and its bounds (that is, the part $\pm 0.510 \cdot X_1$ of Eq. 9.20).

9.5.4 Macroscopic Assessment of the Values of Fuzzy Regression Coefficients

In any calibration of a model, a first assessment of its validity may come from a macroscopic assessment of the values and signs of the regression coefficients. The regression coefficient of the independent variable X_2 has a negative sign, as it was expected, since it expresses the cost of transport by rail; consequently an eventual increase of the cost should result in the reduction of the rail demand (the dependent variable of the linear regression). Therefore, an increase by 1€ of the rail transport cost will lead to a reduction of demand of approximately 4299 passengers (see Eq. 9.20). In addition and due to the nature of the dependent variable (passenger demand), the intercept of the fuzzy linear regression (94,641.46) is expected to be a positive number, since a negative value for the intercept means a negative number of passengers.

9.5.5 Values of the Degree of Membership

Fig. 9.8 illustrates (for each year) the membership degree $\mu_A(y_i)$ of the actual rail demand (Y) on the estimated (fitted) demand ($\widehat{Y}$), as calculated by the equation:

$$\mu_A(y_i) = 1 - \frac{|y_i - r|}{c} \tag{9.21}$$

Recall that the membership degree $\mu_A(y_i)$ takes values in the continuous closed interval [0, 1]. The closer the actual demand is to the center of the fuzzy linear regression, the greater the value of the membership degree. When $\mu_A(y_i) = 1$, then the value of actual demand coincides with the center value of the fuzzy linear regression and when $\mu_A(y_i) = 0$, the value of actual demand is exactly on the bound (upper or lower) of the fuzzy linear regression (Fig. 9.7).

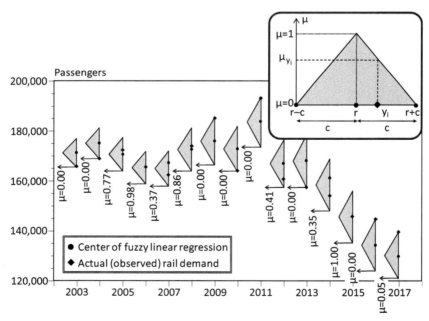

FIGURE 9.8 Membership degree, bounds, and center of the fuzzy linear regression model. *Source: Compiled by the authors.*

9.5.6 Forecast of Future Transport Demand With Application of the Calibrated Fuzzy Linear Regression Model

Now we can use the calibrated fuzzy linear regression model for the forecast of future transport demand. To achieve this stage of the modeling process, we will need the most accurate forecasts for the evolution of the independent variables of the problem. Table 9.4 illustrates plausible values provided by the central bank for the per capita regional domestic product, by the railway authority for rail fares, and by the energy authority for fuel prices.

By substituting values of Table 9.4 in the calibrated fuzzy Eq. (9.20), we can forecast future demand as follows (Fig. 9.9):

- Year 2018: forecast (center value r_{2018}) 127,462 ± 5,229 passengers,
- Year 2019: forecast (center value r_{2019}) 128,131 ± 5,334 passengers,
- Year 2020: forecast (center value r_{2020}) 133,317 ± 5,494 passengers,
- Year 2021: forecast (center value r_{2021}) 130,030 ± 5,686 passengers.

9.5.7 Statistical Indexes for the Comparison of the Forecasting Accuracy and Ability of the Fuzzy Linear Regression With the Classic Linear Regression

A crucial issue in modeling is to evaluate the forecasting accuracy and ability of a calibrated model for a given set of data or observations. For the comparison of the forecasting accuracy and ability of different regression models, some well-known statistics, such as the mean absolute deviation, the mean squared error, and the mean absolute percentage error, can be used as criteria (see §5.11). For these statistics, which are not informative by themselves but only when comparing different models, the smaller the values, the better the forecasting accuracy of the calibrated model. On the contrary,

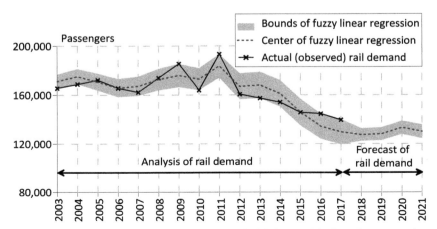

FIGURE 9.9 Forecast of future rail passenger demand with the use of the fuzzy linear regression. *Source: Compiled by the authors.*

Theil's inequality coefficient is a statistic that can evaluate both the fitting and the forecasting ability of each calibrated model, either in comparison among different models (all calibrated using the same set of data or observations) or for a specific model.

As explained previously, however, a fundamental characteristic of the fuzzy linear regression is the presence of patches (the bounds of the fuzzy linear regression, see Figs. 9.7 and 9.9) that include all the actual values of the dependent variable. Consequently, in the fuzzy linear regression there are no residuals (the measured differences between the actual and the estimated values of the dependent variable). However, by taking into account only the center value of the fuzzy numbers and hence the center of the fuzzy linear regression of Fig. 9.7, we can consider as residuals the differences between the actual values of the dependent variable and the estimated values, which are derived from the center of the fuzzy regression.

9.6 APPLICATION OF FUZZY LINEAR REGRESSION ANALYSIS FOR THE FORECAST OF RAIL PASSENGER DEMAND

9.6.1 Independent Variables of the Problem and the Calibrated Econometric Model

In Chapter 5, §5.12, we constructed a classic econometric model for the forecast of rail passenger demand at the level of a country or a region. This econometric model has as independent variables (with no collinearity among them) the following:

D_r rail demand (rail trips per capita of a country or a region),
C_r unit cost of transport by rail (per passenger-km),
F_r frequency of rail services (modeled through the number of total vehicle-kms per year),
I_{co} car ownership index,
GDP   gross domestic product per capita.

Variables referring to monetary units were adjusted in constant 2014 prices, according to the annual consumer price index. All variables incorporated in the model were indexed to a value of 100 for the year 1985 and then logarithmized.

The calibrated econometric model was given by the following equation:

$$\widehat{D}_r = 5.1985 - 0.9865 \cdot C_r + 0.8104 \cdot F_r - 0.1989 \cdot I_{co} + 0.2494 \cdot GDP \quad (9.22)$$

9.6.2 Calibration of a Fuzzy Model and Calculation of the Fuzzy Numbers

Now we will try to use fuzzy numbers instead of real numbers for the various regression coefficients of the econometric model of Eq. (9.22). The fuzzy linear regression model will have the form:

$$\widehat{D}_r = A_0 + A_1 \cdot C_r + A_2 \cdot F_r + A_3 \cdot I_{co} + A_4 \cdot GDP$$

or equivalently

$$\widehat{D}_{r, j} = \left(r_0 + r_1 \cdot C_{r, j} + r_2 \cdot F_{r, j} + r_3 \cdot I_{co, j} + r_4 \cdot GDP_j\right) \pm$$
$$\pm \left(c_0 + c_1 \cdot C_{r, j} + c_2 \cdot F_{r, j} + c_3 \cdot I_{co, j} + c_4 \cdot GDP_j\right) \qquad (9.23)$$

where

$\widehat{D}_r$	estimated demand with the use of fuzzy linear regression,
$A_i = (r_i, c_i)$	symmetric triangular fuzzy numbers (see §9.3.2),
r_i	center of the fuzzy number A_i,
c_i	spread of the fuzzy number A_i,
$i = 0, 1, 2, 3, 4$	number of independent variables,
$j = 1, 2,\ldots, 55$	number of annual data for the years from 1960 to 2014.

Since we have more than 10 data for each variable (in our case 55), it will be $h = 0$ (see §9.4.2). By using Eqs. (9.13), (9.15), (9.17), and (9.18), we can calculate the center r_i and the spread c_i for each one of the five fuzzy numbers (A_0, A_1, A_2, A_3, A_4) of our problem. Indeed, the system of the above equations can be transformed into a linear programming problem. Among the many available computer software packages we will use Maple, which provides the following values for the fuzzy numbers:

$$
\begin{aligned}
A_0 &= (r_0, c_0) &=& \quad (\ 6.3945, 0) \\
A_1 &= (r_1, c_1) &=& \quad (-0.9587, 0) \\
A_2 &= (r_2, c_2) &=& \quad (0.5841, 0.2565) \\
A_3 &= (r_3, c_3) &=& \quad (-0.2376, 0) \\
A_4 &= (r_4, c_4) &=& \quad (0.2296, 0)
\end{aligned}
$$

From the above fuzzy numbers, we can remark that the only variable that contributes to the ambiguity of the fuzzy linear regression is the variable F_r, for which the spread $c_2 \neq 0$, whereas all other independent variables have values for the coefficients $c_i = 0$.

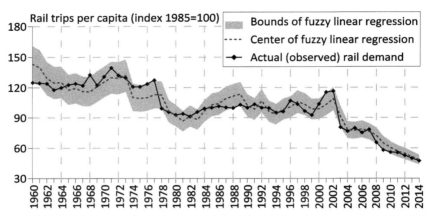

FIGURE 9.10 Comparison between actual and fitted, by the fuzzy linear regression model, rail passenger demand. *Source: Compiled by the authors.*

By substituting values of fuzzy numbers A_0, A_1, A_2, A_3, A_4 into Eq. (9.23), we can define the following fuzzy equation for the calculation of rail passenger demand:

$$\widehat{D}_r = 6.3945 - 0.9587 \cdot C_r + 0.5841 \cdot F_r - \\ - 0.2376 \cdot I_{co} + 0.2296 \cdot GDP \pm 0.2565 \cdot F_r \tag{9.24}$$

where $\widehat{D}_r$ is the estimated (fitted) by the fuzzy linear regression rail demand.

A first macroscopic assessment of the validity of the fuzzy model can be made by examining the signs of the regression coefficients. Indeed, the model has a negative sign for the relationship of rail demand to rail cost and private car ownership index and a positive sign for the relationship of rail demand to per capita GDP, frequency of rail services, and the intercept (+6.3945). These signs are compatible with findings from experience and experiments.

Fig. 9.10 illustrates a comparative presentation of the fitted values of rail demand by the fuzzy linear regression model with the actual values (recorded data). We can notice a satisfactory adjustment of the fuzzy model to actual data and its flexibility to follow accurately the turning points, that is, the points where changes of inclination of the demand curve are observed.

9.6.3 Comparison of the Fuzzy Model With the Classic Econometric Model

Fig. 9.11 illustrates a comparative analysis of the results of the fuzzy model given by Eq. (9.24) with the classic econometric model given by Eq. (9.22).

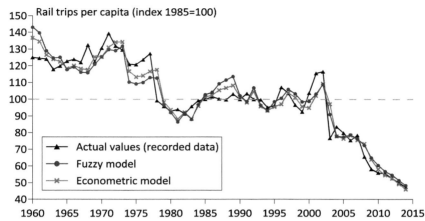

FIGURE 9.11 Comparison of results of the fuzzy model and the classic econometric model with actual values of rail passenger demand. *Source: Compiled by the authors.*

In the case of the fuzzy model, the center value was taken into account in the plot of Fig. 9.11. We can remark that both models can be considered as a satisfactory representation of rail passenger demand, as the values fitted by both models are very close to the data, and in addition the plots of both models accurately follow the turning points of the data of the problem.

9.6.4 Comparison of the Forecasting Ability of the Fuzzy Model and the Classic Econometric Model

The comparison of the forecasting ability of the fuzzy model and the classic econometric model will be based on the statistics presented in §5.11 and more particularly on values of the following indexes (illustrated in Table 9.5): root

TABLE 9.5: Root mean squared error (RMSE), mean absolute percentage error (MAPE), Theil's inequality coefficient (Theil's U), and bias (U^M), variance (U^S), and covariance (U^C) proportions for the fuzzy model and the classic econometric model.

Model	RMSE	MAPE	Theil's U	Theil's U decomposition ($U^M + U^S + U^C = 1$)		
				U^M	U^S	U^C
Econometric model	6.65	5.06	0.017	$7.85 \cdot 10^{-4}$	0.012	0.987
Fuzzy model	7.55	5.89	0.019	$1.28 \cdot 10^{-4}$	0.025	0.975

Source: Compiled by the authors.

mean squared error (RMSE), mean absolute percentage error (MAPE), Theil's inequality coefficient (Theil's U), and Theil's inequality coefficient decomposition in its proportions U^M, U^S, and U^C (see §5.11.5). From Table 9.5 it becomes clear that the classic econometric model has a slightly better explanatory behavior and ability than the fuzzy model. This is most likely due to the fact that the independent variables were properly selected, accurate data were provided for the various variables of the problem, and in any case the ambiguity related to the values of the various independent variables was very low.

9.7 APPLICATION OF FUZZY LINEAR REGRESSION ANALYSIS FOR AIR TRANSPORT DEMAND

In Chapter 7 (§7.4.6), we constructed an econometric model for the forecast of demand of international passengers for a representative case of a tourist airport. We analyzed that the critical driving force of demand of international passengers was the rate of exchange equivalence of the national currency at that time in relation to the currencies of origin countries of international passengers of the airport. An equivalence indicator was constructed, which takes into account both fluctuations in the currencies of the origin countries of passengers and the share of each country to international demand of the airport (Fig. 9.12). We set the value 100 for the year 1986.

The equation of the calibrated econometric model was:

$$\widehat{D}_{airport} = 1/2 \cdot \left[e^{0.004 \cdot EXR} \cdot 925,332 + EXR \cdot \left(0.175 \cdot EXR^2 - \right. \right. \\ \left. \left. - 43.212 \cdot EXR + 7,548 \right) + 906,696 \right] \tag{9.25}$$

where

$D_{airport}$ annual international passenger demand (dependent variable),
EXR   rate of exchange equivalence of the national currency to currencies of origin countries of international passengers.

The coefficient of determination of this econometric model was $R^2 = 0.87$.

The calibrated fuzzy linear regression model will have the form:

$$\widehat{D}_{airport} = A_0 + A_1 \cdot EXR \quad \text{or} \quad \widehat{D}_{airport, j} = (r_0 + r_1 \cdot EXR_j) \pm (c_0 + c_1 \cdot EXR_j) \tag{9.26}$$

where $A_i = (r_i, c_i)$ [$i = 0, 1$ and $j = 1, 2, ..., 12$ (12 is the number of annual data of years from 1986 to 1997)] are symmetric triangular fuzzy numbers. For $h = 0$ (since we have more than 10 observations for each variable) and by using Eqs. (9.13), (9.15), (9.17), and (9.18), we can define the numbers r and c,

FIGURE 9.12 Evolution of the exchange rate of the national currency to currencies of origin countries of international passengers at the airport of Rhodes. *Source: Modified from Ref. [18].*

which denote the center and the spread of a fuzzy number $A_i = (r_i, c_i)$ ($i = 0, 1$ and $j = 1, 2, ..., 12$). With the help of a computer software (in this case: Maple) we solve the linear programming problem of Eqs. (9.13), (9.15), (9.17), and (9.18), and we take:

$$A_0 = (r_0, c_0) = (636142.33, 0)$$
$$A_1 = (r_1, c_1) = (6957.44, 1351.01)$$

Thus, the fuzzy linear regression model takes the form:

$$\widehat{D}_{airport} = 636,142.33 + 6,957.44 \cdot EXR \pm 1,351.01 \cdot EXR \qquad (9.27)$$

where $\widehat{D}_{airport}$ is the estimated (fitted) airport demand by the fuzzy linear regression (Fig. 9.13).

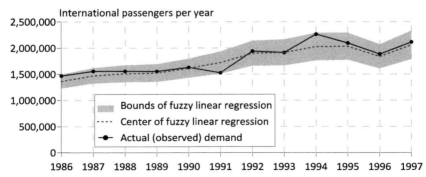

FIGURE 9.13 Fuzzy linear regression for the analysis of international passenger demand of the airport of Rhodes. *Source: Modified from Ref. [18].*

Fig. 9.14 illustrates a comparison of the performances of the fuzzy model and the classic econometric model with actual values (recorded data) of international passenger demand at the airport of Rhodes.

The comparison of the forecasting ability of the fuzzy model and the classic econometric model will be conducted on the basis of the values of the various statistical indexes as in §9.6.4 (Table 9.5). Table 9.6 makes clear that the fuzzy model provides a better value for the root mean squared error and the mean absolute percentage error, whereas both models have similar values for the Theil's inequality coefficient.

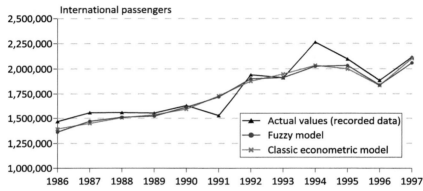

FIGURE 9.14 Comparison of results of the fuzzy model and the classic econometric model with actual values of international passenger demand at the airport of Rhodes. *Source: Compiled by the authors, based on data of Ref. [18].*

TABLE 9.6: Root mean squared error (RMSE), mean absolute percentage error (MAPE), Theil's inequality coefficient (Theil's U), and bias (U^M), variance (U^S), and covariance (U^C) proportions for the fuzzy model and the classic econometric model.

Model	RMSE	MAPE	Theil's U	Theil's U decomposition ($U^M + U^S + U^C = 1$)		
				U^M	U^S	U^C
Econometric model	105,522	4.61	0.0295	0.155	0.058	0.787
Fuzzy model	102,983	4.36	0.0292	0.177	0.064	0.759

Source: Compiled by the authors.

9.8 APPLICATION OF THE FUZZY METHOD FOR THE ESTIMATION OF TRANSPORT DEMAND AT URBAN LEVEL

9.8.1 Transport Demand at Urban Level, the 4-Step Model, and the Interfering Subjectivity

In Chapter 3 (§3.9.7) and Chapter 7 (§7.10), we analyzed the 4-step model (trip generation, trip distribution to origin—destination pairs, choice of mode of transport, route assignment), which is a combination of time series, gravity, and econometric models for the estimation of transport demand and of its characteristics at the urban level. The theoretical background of the model lies in theories of satisfaction of a transport need for a traveler with respect to a specific purpose, and more particularly in theories of maximization for a traveler of his or her individual utility, which can be represented in transport by the generalized cost and considers the travel times and costs of the various transport modes.

A fundamental weakness of the 4-step model relates to the transformation of the subjective assessment of a traveler for a particular transport mode or route into numerical values. For instance, should a traveler choose to use a metro system (with a travel time of 23 min and a cost of US$ 1.5) instead of his or her private car (with a travel time ranging from 29 to 44 min and a cost of US$ 4.9), he or she makes his or her choice at a more general and macroscopic level, without calculating his or her utility and each generalized cost accurately and in detail. In most of the cases, he or she makes an assessment in the form of linguistic variables of the type: "travel time of the metro is lower than travel time of a private car" or "the cost of the metro is much lower than the cost of a private car." Thus, the 4-step model is characterized by a great degree of subjectivity, as a result of the inherent uncertainty and ambiguity of assessments made by travelers. A classic approach consists in tackling this subjectivity through traffic counts and questionnaire surveys (steps 1 and 2 of trip generation and distribution), approximate calculations of the generalized cost, and the gravity formula (see §3.9.7 and §7.10.4.4) for the mean traveler.

In an attempt to make the 4-step model more objective, many variables of the problem are either omitted or introduced as dummy variables. In addition, approximate mean values are used for variables (such as travel time, cost) which have a great range of variations.

9.8.2 Transport Demand at Urban Level, Variables Involved, and the Fuzzy Method

Assessment of demand at the urban level is an ideal area for application of the fuzzy method. In most of the cases, symmetric triangular fuzzy numbers were used.

Thus, a fuzzy 4-step model can take into account a great number of trip generation variables: population, number of households, residential area, population density, student population, car ownership index, value of land, land use, distances to zones of production and attraction of trips, parking facilities, number of big residential buildings, and so on. Similarly, a fuzzy model can take into account a great number of trip attraction variables: number of working places; number of shops (categorized in relation to the number of visitors per day); number of students; number (and space) of administrative, industrial, financial, and business buildings; number (and capacity) of hospitals, cinemas, parks, exhibitions, etc.

9.8.3 How the Fuzzy Logic Transforms Linguistic Variables Into Fuzzy Numbers

When a driver selects a route A against a route B, he or she never conducts instantly accurate calculations of the comparative travel times and generalized costs of these alternative routes. This problem is approached in the 4-step model by the Logit model formula (see §7.10.5), according to which the choice of the driver is a function of the difference of travel times and of generalized costs of alternatives A and B. It is assumed that drivers behave in the same way all the time and that mean values represent accurately the behavior of the whole population.

The fuzzy method confronts the problem differently and its rules use linguistic variables and can be represented by the following approximate reasoning [508−510]:

Case 1   If travel time of path A is much shorter than travel time of path B, then preference of a driver for path A is much stronger.
Case 2   If travel time of path A is shorter than travel time of path B, then preference of a driver for path A is stronger.
Case 3   If travel time of path A is equal to travel time of path B, then preference of a driver for path A is medium.
Case 4   If travel time of path A is greater than travel time of path B, then preference of a driver for path A is weak.
Case 5   If travel time of path A is much greater than travel time of path B, then preference of a driver for path A is very weak.

Qualitative methods could approach the problem presented by the above statements in a totally empirical way with the use, e.g., of the Likert scale (see §4.4.6.4).

9.8.4 Successive Stages in the Application of the Fuzzy Method to the 4-Step Model

The fuzzy method, while departing from the same statements with qualitative methods, follows a different reasoning, which has the following stages:

1. Choose the appropriate type of fuzzy numbers. Symmetric triangular fuzzy numbers are most commonly used, but in some cases trapezoidal fuzzy numbers are also used.
2. Define membership functions of input and output variables, according to the results of questionnaire surveys or the assessment made by experts and specialists in the field. A number of trials are necessary for the finalization of values of the membership function, which can only be accomplished after a careful examination of the statistical dispersion of the survey data.
3. Define a rule of inference (such as the above statements of §9.8.3) between input and output variables.
4. Allocate appropriate numerical values to the linguistic variables which are represented by statements. Thus, the fuzzy numbers are converted into crisp numbers.
5. Choose an algorithm and software (such as MATLAB, etc.) for the transfer function between inputs and outputs.
6. Convert fuzzy output to crisp numbers by using a defuzzification method.

9.9 APPLICATION OF THE FUZZY METHOD TO TRANSPORT ECONOMICS PROBLEMS - MULTICRITERIA ANALYSIS

A typical problem in transport economics is the selection of the transport projects to be financed (and therefore realized) against other projects that are omitted. The various criteria of selection (cost—benefit analysis, net present value, internal rate of return) are based on a comparison of the various benefits, such as reduction of travel times (expressed in monetary values) and of operation costs of users of the specific project, with the costs (of construction and operation) of the infrastructure. However, other criteria, such as environmental effects, quality of service, reduction of accidents, accessibility, increase in economic output, and energy consumption, are not taken into account. Multicriteria analysis is a method that gives the ability to assess multiple and often conflicting criteria and objectives, which, however, may take very different values by different decision makers [2,511—516].

Multicriteria methods require a ranking and weighting of the attributes of each alternative to be evaluated. This weighting inevitably has a subjective character, presents an inherent vagueness and ambiguity, and makes use of linguistic variables. The fuzzy method is suitable to increase the accuracy and validity of the classic multicriteria methods.

Take a multiattribute decision-making process for a transport investment problem with a number of L_h ($h = 1, 2,..., m$) alternatives, a number C_k ($k = 1, 2,..., n$) of criteria—attributes, and a number x_{mn} of weights (or ratings) of alternative L_h with respect to criterion C_k. All of the above can be represented by the following matrix M:

$$M = \begin{array}{c|cccc} & C_1 & C_2 & \cdots & C_n \\ \hline L_1 & x_{11} & x_{12} & \cdots & x_{1n} \\ L_2 & x_{21} & x_{22} & \cdots & x_{2n} \\ \vdots & \vdots & \vdots & & \vdots \\ L_m & x_{m1} & x_{m2} & \cdots & x_{mn} \end{array} \qquad (9.28)$$

Application of the fuzzy method to our problem entails the use of fuzzy numbers (instead of usual real numbers) for the various weights (or ratings) x_{mn} of matrix M. The weights (or ratings) x_{mn} are based on the assessment of the various attributes, which may have the following linguistic form: very poor (VP), poor (P), medium poor (MP), fair (F), medium good (MG), good (G), very good (VG).

If we use nonsymmetric triangular fuzzy numbers, the above linguistic variables can be expressed by the upper, lower, and center value of fuzzy numbers, as in Fig. 9.15.

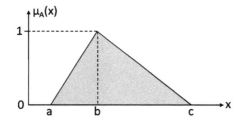

$$\mu_A(x) = \begin{cases} \dfrac{x-a}{b-a} & a < x \leq b \\[2mm] \dfrac{c-x}{c-b} & b < x < c \\[2mm] 0 & \text{otherwise} \end{cases}$$

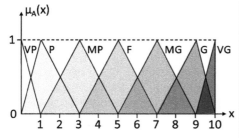

Lingustic variable	Fuzzy number A (a, b, c)
Very poor (VP)	(0, 0, 1)
Poor (P)	(0, 1, 3)
Medium poor (MP)	(1, 3, 5)
Fair (F)	(3, 5, 7)
Medium good (MG)	(5, 7, 9)
Good (G)	(7, 9, 10)
Very good (VG)	(9, 10, 10)

FIGURE 9.15 Fuzzy numbers for multicriteria assessment of transport infrastructure. *Source: Modified from Ref. [517].*

The fuzzy method was applied for assessment purposes among many alternative transport infrastructure projects, while taking into account the following criteria: travel times; accessibility and attraction; construction and operation costs; hydrological problems; impact on urban activities, economic activities, natural environment, the landscape, etc. [517].

After transforming the linguistic variables into fuzzy numbers, it becomes necessary to define some predetermined targets for the upper and lower values x_{mn} of matrix M, which were used as the crisp maximum and minimum values. Then, the fuzzy problem is transformed into a linear programming problem, in which the optimal solution consists in minimizing the difference of the final values x_{mn} from the crisp maximum and in maximizing that difference from the crisp minimum.

9.10 APPLICATIONS OF THE FUZZY METHOD FOR OTHER (THAN DEMAND) TRANSPORT PROBLEMS

9.10.1 A Great Variety of Applications

Fuzzy logic and fuzzy method are suitable for application to any kind of problem which presents some degree of uncertainty or ambiguity and can combine subjective and objective knowledge in a rational way. There is no sector of knowledge and science which has not been tempted to apply the fuzzy method. Thus, from economics, applied linguistics, engineering, sciences based on experimental data, and computational sciences to medicine and even theology and philosophy, many researchers have applied the fuzzy method [518,521−526], although some applications do not lead for the moment to directly usable findings. Transportation is a domain very susceptible to applications of the fuzzy method, since many choices for specific transport modes are based on imprecise knowledge of the existing data at a given moment and for this reason they are often expressed through linguistic variables. Any travel choice cannot be separated from subjective human perception and assessment. Thus, imprecision and vagueness are inherent to the behavior of and choices made by a traveler, whose information is often inaccurate, vague, and in some cases even nonmeasurable.

9.10.2 Route Choice Among Many Alternatives

Intelligent transport systems provide nowadays linguistic information to the driver of the type: "route A is in free flow" or "route D is crowded" or "route E is saturated." In relation to this information and by taking into account other variables such as cost, convenience, and existing weather conditions, the driver makes his or her decision. We analyzed in §9.8.3 how fuzzy method can transform the above linguistic variables into a measurable decision made by the driver [508,518].

9.10.3 Road Safety and Accident Analysis

Road safety is a crucial issue for any country or region and authorities are confronted with the problem of choosing accident-prone locations for which measures and improvement works should be undertaken. The factors related to the three components of road safety (the driver, the vehicle, the road and its environment) are assessed through linguistic information and affect the feeling of safety and the driving comfort.

In such an application of the fuzzy method for accident analysis, the following variables were taken into account: radius of curvature, longitudinal and transverse gradient, speed limits and usual running speeds, roughness and other characteristics of the pavement, weather conditions, lighting, land uses, vehicle type, accident time, accident location, accident type, severity of the accident, ratio of volume of traffic to capacity of the road [508,518,527,528].

9.10.4 Light Signaling and Optimization of Movements of Vehicles and Pedestrians

A central problem in traffic engineering is the calculation of the optimum cycle time of traffic lights, its split into the various phases, and the offset for the successive crossroads. Most algorithms are based on the optimization of the capacity of the various converging roads. However, other criteria should be taken into consideration, particularly:

- decrease of delays,
- avoidance of risks associated with rear-end collisions,
- minimization of air and noise pollution.

As the above criteria are usually expressed in the form of linguistic variables, they can be assessed with the use of the fuzzy method.

A common issue addressed by traffic engineers and researchers is to keep an equilibrium between movements of pedestrians and (both motorized and nonmotorized) vehicles in traffic lights. The usual way is to adapt times of the various phases in relation to movements of pedestrians, who when wishing to cross a street can push a button. Then the system must decide whether to terminate the green phase for vehicles and provide a green phase for pedestrians or not. The input variables of the problem are the following:

- cumulative waiting time (WT) for pedestrians,
- number of vehicles (NV) approaching the crossroad,
- time (S) between successive vehicles.

The fuzzy method can be used if we apply in the above problem a linguistic approach of the type:

> If WT is long, VT is very low and S is small, then the
> actual phase is terminated.

The fuzzy method employed in the above problem used triangular symmetric fuzzy numbers and provided better results than usual methods, as it succeeded simultaneously a minimization of both vehicles and pedestrians delays at the crossroads studied [529].

9.10.5 Logistics and Routing of Vehicles

A typical problem for any freight transport manager (especially of e-commerce companies), who receives every hour a great number of requests from clients to send specific volumes of goods to different destinations, is to match his or her available vehicles to transportation requests. However, each request is characterized by a large number of attributes: type of freight, weight and volume of freight, loading and unloading sites, distance, delivery times, eventual special conditions (vulnerable products, etc.). As the above attributes can be addressed with the application of linguistic forms, the problem is suitable for the application of the fuzzy method [509,518,530].

Routing of freight vehicles is scheduled as a function of travel times, travel costs, and the distance between origin and destination. Each one of these variables can be expressed through a number of characteristics in a linguistic form. Thus, travel times depend on the characteristics of the driver, traffic conditions, weather conditions, and type of driving. Some linguistic forms used, e.g., to assess travel times are: short, medium, long. These linguistic forms can be introduced as fuzzy numbers in fuzzy models for the optimization of the routing of freight vehicles [484].

9.10.6 Optimization of Capacity of Airports

Congestion situations are increasing in airports all over the world and cause delays, which are harmful for the air industry and its economics. The usual problem of a traffic controller and organization (such as the European Organisation for the Safety of Air Navigation, commonly known as Eurocontrol, in Europe and the Air Traffic Organization of the Federal Aviation Administration in the United States) in a congested airport is to decide which aircraft will not be served during a particular time period and to set a new departure time. The fuzzy method can prove helpful to deciding which aircraft will not be served so as to minimize the total delay of all aircraft. The number of aircraft, their size, and delay times are treated as fuzzy numbers through linguistic characteristics such as big, medium, and little. This method usually leads to higher priority for the landing of larger aircraft [508,518].

References

[1] M.A. Knapp, Social effects of transportation, The Annals of the American Academy of Political and Social Science 20 (1) (1902) 1−15.

[2] V. Profillidis, Transport Economics, fifth ed., Papasotiriou Publishing, Athens, 2016 in Greek.

[3] M. Parkin, M. Powell, K. Matthews, Economics, seventh ed., Pearson Education Ltd., Harlow, 2007.

[4] European Commission, EU Transport in Figures − Statistical Pocketbook 2016, 2016. https://ec.europa.eu/transport/facts-fundings/statistics/pocketbook-2016_en.

[5] OECD (Organisation for Economic Co-operation and Development), Data and Metadata for OECD Countries and Selected Non-member Economies. https://stats.oecd.org/.

[6] M. Janić, Advanced Transport Systems: Analysis, Modeling, and Evaluation of Performances, Springer-Verlag, London, 2014.

[7] V.A. Profillidis, Railway Management and Engineering, fourth ed., Ashgate, London, 2014.

[8] R. Van Nes, Design of Multimodal Transport Networks, Delft University Press, Delft, 2002.

[9] V. Profillidis, G. Botzoris, Air passenger transport and economic activity, Journal of Air Transport Management 49 (2015) 23−27.

[10] R. Cervero, K. Kockelman, Travel demand and the 3Ds: density, diversity and design, Transportation Research Part D: Transport and Environment 2 (3) (1997) 199−219.

[11] M. Horn, An extended model and procedural framework for planning multi-modal passenger journeys, Transportation Research Part B: Methodological 37 (7) (2003) 641−660.

[12] S. Souche, Measuring the structural determinants of urban travel demand, Transport Policy 17 (3) (2010) 127−134.

[13] C. Polat, The demand determinants for urban public transport services: a review of the literature, Journal of Applied Sciences 12 (12) (2012) 1211−1231.

[14] V. Profillidis, G. Botzoris, Econometric models for the forecast of passenger demand in Greece, Journal of Statistics and Management Systems 9 (1) (2006) 37−54.

[15] H.A. Adler, Economic Appraisal of Transport Projects: A Manual with Case Studies, Johns Hopkins University Press, Baltimore, MD, 1987.

[16] T. Litman, Generated traffic: implications for transport planning, Institute of Transportation Engineers Journal 71 (4) (2001) 38−47.

[17] D. Embley, B. Thalheim, The Handbook of Conceptual Modeling: Its Usage and Its Challenges, Springer-Verlag, Berlin, Heidelberg, 2011.

[18] V. Profillidis, Econometric and fuzzy models for the forecast of demand in the airport of Rhodes, Journal of Air Transport Management 6 (2) (2000) 95−100.

[19] S. Friedenthal, A. Moore, R. Steiner, A Practical Guide to SysML: The Systems Modeling Language, second ed., Morgan Kaufmann, Waltham, MA, 2012.

[20] P. Coscia, F. Castaldo, F.A. Palmieri, A. Alahi, S. Savarese, L. Ballan, Long-term path prediction in urban scenarios using circular distributions, Image and Vision Computing 69 (2018) 81–91.

[21] B. Thalheim, Towards a theory of conceptual modelling, in: C.A. Heuser, G. Pernul (Eds.), Advances in Conceptual Modeling – Challenging Perspectives, vol. 5833, Springer-Verlag, Berlin, Heidelberg, 2009, pp. 45–54.

[22] OECD (Organisation for Economic Co-operation and Development), Eurostat, UNECE (United Nations Economic Commission for Europe), Illustrated Glossary for Transport Statistics, fourth ed., OECD Publishing, Paris, 2010.

[23] Å. Andersson, Economic and social change – on the transforming of the logistical and economic systems, in: European Conference of Ministers of Transport (Ed.), Proceedings of the 13th International Symposium on Theory and Practice in Transport Economics, 9–11 May 1995, Luxembourg, OECD Publications, Paris, France, 1996, pp. 67–82.

[24] R. Katiyar, K. Ohta, Concept of daily travel time and its applicability to travel demand analysis, Journal of the Faculty of Engineering of the University of Tokyo 42 (2) (1993) 109–121.

[25] J.H. Ausubel, C. Marchetti, P.S. Meyer, Toward green mobility: the evolution of transport, European Review 6 (2) (1998) 137–156.

[26] J.H. Ausubel, C. Marchetti, The evolution of transport, The Industrial Physicist 7 (2) (2001) 20–24.

[27] A. Bleijenberg, The driving forces behind transport growth and their implications for policy, in: European Conference of Ministers of Transport (Ed.), Proceedings of the International Seminar: Managing the Fundamental Drivers of Transport Demand, 16 December 2002, Brussels, Belgium, OECD Publications, Paris, France, 2003, pp. 37–50.

[28] V. Profillidis, Air Transport – Airports, Papasotiriou Publishing, Athens, 2010 in Greek.

[29] G. Hupkes, The law of constant travel time and trip rates, Futures 14 (1) (1988) 38–46.

[30] V. Profillidis, G. Botzoris, A correlation of mobility and personal income, in: Hellenic Institute of Transportation Engineers (Ed.), Proceeding of the 6th International Congress on Transportation Research, 17–18 October 2013, Thessaloniki, Greece, 2013, pp. 649–659.

[31] H. Folmer, E. van Ierland, Valuation Methods and Policy Making in Environmental Economics, Elsevier Science Publishers, Amsterdam, 1989.

[32] E. Haezendonck, Transport Project Evaluation: Extending the Social Cost-Benefit Approach, Edward Elgar Publishing Ltd., Cheltenham, 2008.

[33] J. Roosen, Cost-benefit analysis, in: C. Klüppelberg, D. Straub, I. Welpe (Eds.), Risk – A Multidisciplinary Introduction, Springer International Publishing, Cham, 2014, pp. 309–331.

[34] H. Jones, F. Moura, T. Domingos, Transport infrastructure project evaluation using cost-benefit analysis, Procedia-Social and Behavioral Sciences 111 (2014) 400–409.

[35] A. Al-Kaisy, Y. Jung, H. Rakha, Developing passenger car equivalency factors for heavy vehicles during congestion, Journal of Transportation Engineering 131 (7) (2005) 514–523.

[36] L. Sherry, Capacity of a Single Runway, George Mason University – Center for Air Transportation Systems Research, Fairfax, VA, 2009.

[37] World Energy Council, Energy Efficiency Indicators. https://www.wec-indicators.enerdata.eu/.

[38] World Bank, Indicators. http://data.worldbank.org/indicator?tab=all.

[39] USDOT (United States Department of Transportation), Bureau of Transportation Statistics. https://www.bts.gov.

[40] Airlines for America, Data and Statistics. http://airlines.org/data/.

[41] C. McEvedy, R. Jones, Atlas of World Population History, Penguin, London, 1978.

[42] United Nations, The World at Six Billion, Department of Economic and Social Affairs — Population Division, Washington, DC, 1999.

[43] United Nations, World Population Prospects: The 2017 Revision, Department of Economic and Social Affairs — Population Division, New York, NY, 2017.

[44] United Nations, Patterns of Urban and Rural Population Growth, Department of Economic and Social Affairs — Population Division, New York, NY, 1980.

[45] Y.Y. Tseng, W.L. Yue, M.A. Taylor, The role of transportation in logistics chain, in: Proceedings of the Eastern Asia Society for Transportation Studies, vol. 5, 2005, pp. 1657—1672.

[46] R. Vickerman, Freight traffic, in: European Conference of Ministers of Transport (Ed.), Proceedings of the International Seminar: Managing the Fundamental Drivers of Transport Demand, 16 December 2002, Brussels, Belgium, OECD Publications, Paris, France, 2003, pp. 15—25.

[47] A. Ballis, J. Golias, Towards the improvement of a combined transport chain performance, European Journal of Operational Research 152 (2) (2004) 420—436.

[48] K. Selviaridis, M. Spring, V. Profillidis, G. Botzoris, Benefits, risks, selection criteria and success factors for third-party logistics services, Maritime Economics and Logistics 10 (4) (2008) 380—392.

[49] ICAO (International Civil Aviation Organization), Airport Planning Manual — Part 1: Master Planning, second ed., 1987. Montreal.

[50] W.A. Sahlman, How to write a great business plan, Harvard Business Review 75 (1) (1997) 98—108.

[51] TRB (Transportation Research Board), Guidebook for Developing General Aviation Airport Business Plans, Airport Cooperative Research Program — Report 77, Washington, DC, 2012.

[52] R. Benedicter, Science fiction "moonshots" — or step-by-step pragmatism? Two strategies on the future mobility today, in: European Transport Congress — Mobility 4.0, 16—17 June 2016, Vienna, Austria, 2016.

[53] P. Tapio, Towards a theory of decoupling: degrees of decoupling in the EU and the case of road traffic in Finland between 1970 and 2001, Transport Policy 12 (2) (2005) 137—151.

[54] A. Alises, J.M. Vassallo, A.F. Guzmán, Road freight transport decoupling: a comparative analysis between the United Kingdom and Spain, Transport Policy 32 (2014) 186—193.

[55] A. Alises, J.M. Vassallo, Comparison of road freight transport trends in Europe. Coupling and decoupling factors from an input—output structural decomposition analysis, Transportation Research Part A: Policy and Practice 82 (2015) 141—157.

[56] A.C. McKinnon, Decoupling of road freight transport and economic growth trends in the UK: an exploratory analysis, Transport Reviews 27 (1) (2007) 37—64.

[57] J. Vehmas, P. Malaska, J. Luukkanen, J. Kaivo-oja, O. Hietanen, M. Vinnari, J. Ilvonen, Europe in the Global Battle of Sustainability: Rebound Strikes Back? — Advanced Sustainability Analysis, Publications of the Turku School of Economics and Business Administration, Turku, Finland, 2003.

[58] M.R. Tight, P. Delle Site, O. Meyer-Rühle, Decoupling transport from economic growth: towards transport sustainability in Europe, European Journal of Transport and Infrastructure Research 4 (4) (2004) 381—404.

[59] G. Botzoris, A. Galanis, V. Profillidis, N. Eliou, Coupling and decoupling relationships between energy consumption and air pollution from the transport sector and the economic activity, International Journal of Energy Economics and Policy 5 (4) (2015) 949−954.

[60] V. Profillidis, G. Botzoris, A. Galanis, Decoupling of economic activity from transport-related energy consumption: an analysis for European Union member countries, International Journal of Innovation and Sustainable Development 12 (3) (2018) 271−286.

[61] D. Banister, D. Stead, Reducing transport intensity, European Journal of Transport and Infrastructure Research 2 (3−4) (2002) 161−178.

[62] B. Shamir, I. Salomon, Work-at-home and the quality of working life, Academy of Management Review 10 (3) (1985) 455−464.

[63] S.R. Sardeshmukh, D. Sharmaand, T. Golden, Impact of telework on exhaustion and job engagement: a job demands and resources model, New Technology, Work and Employment 27 (3) (2012) 193−207.

[64] S. Choo, P.L. Mokhtarian, I. Salomon, Does telecommuting reduce vehicle-miles travelled? An aggregate time series analysis for the US, Transportation 32 (1) (2005) 37−64.

[65] G. Botzoris, A. Galanis, V. Profillidis, Teleworking and sustainable transportation in the era of economic crisis, in: Publishing Institution of the University of Žilina (Ed.), Proceedings of Conference on Information and Management Sciences, 21−25 March 2016, Slovak Rep., 2016, pp. 25−29.

[66] E. Christou, P. Kassianidis, Consumer's perceptions and adoption of online buying for travel products, Journal of Travel and Tourism Marketing 12 (4) (2002) 93−107.

[67] UK Department for Transport, National Travel Survey Statistics. https://www.gov.uk/government/collections/national-travel-survey-statistics#publications.

[68] US Department of Commerce, Monthly and Annual Retail Trade. https://www.census.gov/retail/index.html.

[69] eMarketer, Worldwide Retail E-commerce Sales: eMarketer's Updated Estimates and Forecast Through 2019, New York, NY, 2015.

[70] Statista, Statistics and Market Data on Key Figures of E-commerce. https://www.statista.com/markets/413/topic/544/key-figures-of-e-commerce/.

[71] V. Profillidis, G. Botzoris, A. Galanis, Environmental effects and externalities from the transport sector and sustainable transportation planning − a review, International Journal of Energy Economics and Policy 4 (4) (2014) 647−661.

[72] A. Galanis, G. Botzoris, A. Siapos, N. Eliou, V. Profillidis, Economic crisis and promotion of sustainable transportation: a case survey in the city of Volos (Greece), Transportation Research Procedia 24 (2017) 241−249.

[73] D. Kim, J. Ko, Y. Park, Factors affecting electric vehicle sharing program participants' attitudes about car ownership and program participation, Transportation Research Part D: Transport and Environment 36 (2015) 96−106.

[74] B. Boyaci, K. Zografos, N. Geroliminis, An optimization framework for the development of efficient one-way car-sharing systems, European Journal of Operational Research 240 (3) (2015) 718−733.

[75] P. Delhomme, A. Gheorghiu, Comparing French carpoolers and non-carpoolers: which factors contribute the most to carpooling? Transportation Research Part D: Transport and Environment 42 (2016) 1−15.

[76] P. van der Waerden, A. Lem, W. Schaefer, Investigation of factors that stimulate car drivers to change from car to carpooling in city center oriented work trips, Transportation Research Procedia 10 (2015) 335−344.

[77]   T. Teubner, C.M. Flath, The economics of multi-hop ride sharing — creating new mobility networks through IS, Business and Information Systems Engineering 57 (5) (2015) 311–324.

[78]   S. Shaheen, A. Cohen, Growth in worldwide carsharing: an international comparison, Transportation Research Record: Journal of the Transportation Research Board 1992 (2007) 81–89.

[79]   S. Wagner, T. Brandt, D. Neumann, In free float: developing business analytics support for carsharing providers, Omega 59 (A) (2016) 4–14.

[80]   B. Boyaci, K.G. Zografos, N. Geroliminis, An integrated optimization-simulation framework for vehicle and personnel relocations of electric carsharing systems with reservations, Transportation Research Part B: Methodological 95 (2017) 214–237.

[81]   US Census Bureau, American Community Survey (ACS). https://www.census.gov/acs/www/data/data-tables-and-tools/.

[82]   S. Le Vine, A. Zolfaghari, J. Polac, Carsharing: Evolution, Challenges and Opportunities, Centre for Transport Studies, Imperial College London, 2014.

[83]   S. Shaheen, A. Cohen, Innovative Mobility Carsharing Outlook: Carsharing Market Overview, Analysis and Trends, Transportation Sustainability Research Center, University of California, Berkeley, Richmond, CA, 2015.

[84]   C. Schürmann, A. Talaat, Towards a European Peripherality Index: Final Report, Report for Directorate-General for Regional Policy of the European Commission, Institute of Spatial Planning, Dortmund, 2000.

[85]   B. van Wee, K. Geurs, Discussing equity and social exclusion in accessibility evaluations, European Journal of Transport and Infrastructure Research 11 (4) (2011) 350–367.

[86]   M.L. Manheim, Fundamentals of Transportation Systems Analysis, Volume 1: Basic Concepts, MIT Press, Cambridge, MA, 1979.

[87]   E. Cascetta, Transportation Systems Analysis — Models and Applications, second ed., Springer, New York, NY, 2009.

[88]   PIANC (Permanent International Association of Navigation Congresses), Life Cycle Management of Port Structures — Recommended Practice for Implementation, Report 103, Brussels, 2008.

[89]   J.P. Baumgartner, Prices and Costs in the Railway Sector, Laboratoire d'Intermodalité des Transports et de Planification, Lausanne, 2001.

[90]   British Petroleum (BP), Statistical Review of World Energy, 2017. http://www.bp.com/en/global/corporate/energy-economics/statistical-review-of-world-energy.html.

[91]   Enerdata, Global Energy Statistical Yearbook 2017, 2017. https://yearbook.enerdata.net/energy-consumption-data.html.

[92]   US Energy Information Administration (EIA), International Energy Outlook 2016, Washington, DC, 2016.

[93]   IEA (International Energy Agency) & UIC (International Union of Railways), Railway Handbook 2015 — Energy Consumption and CO_2 Emissions, Paris, 2015.

[94]   G. Kouroussis, D.P. Connolly, G. Alexandrou, K. Vogiatzis, The effect of railway local irregularities on ground vibration, Transportation Research Part D: Transport and Environment 39 (2015) 17–30.

[95]   K. Vogiatzis, P. Vanhonacker, Noise reduction in urban LRT networks by combining track based solutions, Science of the Total Environment 568 (2016) 1344–1354.

[96]   S. Vougias, T. Natsinas, Correlation of vehicular noise to various traffic and geometrical characteristics in Thessaloniki — Greece, Applied Acoustics 19 (6) (1986) 421–432.

[97]   C.N. Pyrgidis, Railway Transportation Systems: Design, Construction and Operation, CRC Press, Boca Raton, FL, 2016.

[98]   E. Moliner, V. Rosario, F. Vicente, A fair method for the calculation of the external costs of road traffic noise according to the Eurovignette directive, Transportation Research Part D: Transport and Environment 24 (2013) 52−61.

[99]   L.C. den Boer, A. Schroten, Traffic Noise Reduction in Europe, CE Delft, The Netherlands, 2007.

[100]   UIC (International Union of Railways), Environmental Noise Directive − Development of Action Plans for Railways, Paris, France, 2008.

[101]   H. van Essen, A. Schroten, M. Otten, D. Sutter, C. Schreyer, R. Zandonella, M. Maibach, C. Doll, External Costs of Transport in Europe, CE Delft, INFRAS and Frannhofer, Delft, The Netherlands, 2011.

[102]   L. Thompson, Changing railway structure and ownership: is anything working? Transport Reviews 23 (3) (2003) 311−355.

[103]   E. Quinet, A meta-analysis of Western European external costs estimates, Transportation Research Part D: Transport and Environment 9 (6) (2004) 465−476.

[104]   C. Macharis, E. Van Hoeck, E. Pekin, T. van Lier, A decision analysis framework for intermodal transport: comparing fuel price increases and the internalisation of external costs, Transportation Research Part A: Policy and Practice 44 (7) (2010) 550−561.

[105]   T. Levitt, The globalization of markets, Harvard Business Review 3 (1983) 92−102.

[106]   K. Ohmae, The Borderless World: Power and Strategy in the Global Marketplace, Harper Collins, London, 1992.

[107]   Financial Time Lexicon, Definition of Globalisation. http://lexicon.ft.com/Term?term= globalisation.

[108]   G.N. Mankiw, Principals of Macroeconomics, fourth ed., Thompson South-Western, Mason, OH, 2006.

[109]   T. Litman, Transit price elasticities and cross-elasticities, Journal of Public Transportation 7 (2) (2004) 37−58.

[110]   T. Litman, Understanding Transport Demands and Elasticities, Victoria Transport Policy Institute, Victoria, Canada, 2013.

[111]   T. Litman, Transit Price Elasticities and Cross-Elasticities, Victoria Transport Policy Institute, Victoria, Canada, 2016.

[112]   J. Preston, Public transport demand, in: C. Nash (Ed.), Handbook of Research Methods and Applications in Transport Economics and Policy, Edward Elgar Publications Ltd., Cheltenham, UK, 2015, pp. 192−211.

[113]   P. Black, T. Hartzenberg, B. Standish, Economics: Principles and Practice, Pearson Education, Cape Town, 1997.

[114]   T. Hartzenberg, S. Richards, B. Standish, V. Tang, A. Wentzel, Economics: Fresh Perspectives, Pearson Education and Prentice Hall, Cape Town, 2005.

[115]   N. Paulley, R. Balcombe, R. Mackett, H. Titheridge, J. Preston, M. Wardman, J. Shires, P. White, The demand for public transport: the effects of fares, quality of service, income and car ownership, Transport Policy 13 (4) (2006) 295−306.

[116]   J.M. Dargay, M. Hanly, The demand for local bus services in England, Journal of Transport Economics and Policy 36 (1) (2002) 73−91.

[117]   R. Fouquet, Trends in income and price elasticities of transport demand (1850−2010), Energy Policy 50 (2012) 62−71.

[118]   K. Orr, Data quality and systems theory, Communications of the ACM 41 (2) (1998) 66−71.

[119] G. Mintsis, S. Basbas, P. Papaioannou, C. Taxiltaris, I.N. Tziavos, Applications of GPS technology in the land transportation system, European Journal of Operational Research 152 (2) (2004) 399–409.

[120] D. Efthymiou, C. Antoniou, Use of social media for transport data collection, Procedia-Social and Behavioral Sciences 48 (2012) 775–785.

[121] T. Ruiz, L. Mars, R. Arroyo, A. Serna, Social networks, big data and transport planning, Transportation Research Procedia 18 (2016) 446–452.

[122] F. Hatziioannidu, A. Polydoropoulou, Passenger demand and patterns of tourists' mobility in the Aegean archipelago with combined use of big datasets from mobile phones and statistical data from ports and airports, Transportation Research Procedia 25 (2017) 2314–2334.

[123] A. Gandomi, M. Haider, Beyond the hype: big data concepts, methods, and analytics, International Journal of Information Management 35 (2) (2015) 137–144.

[124] Airbus, Mapping Demand 2016 − 2035, Toulouse-Blagnac, France, 2016.

[125] Boeing, Current Market Outlook 2016 − 2035, Seattle, WA, 2016.

[126] IATA (International Air Transport Association), Annual Review. http://www.iata.org/publications/Pages/annual-review.aspx.

[127] R. Doganis, Flying Off Course: Airline Economics and Marketing, fourth ed., Routledge, Oxfordshire, 2010.

[128] Z. Lei, A. Papatheodorou, Measuring the effect of low-cost carriers on regional airports' commercial revenue, Research in Transportation Economics 26 (1) (2010) 37–43.

[129] N.P. Dennis, End of the free lunch? The responses of traditional European airlines to the low-cost carrier threat, Journal of Air Transport Management 13 (5) (2007) 311–321.

[130] A. Graham, N.P. Dennis, Airport traffic and financial performance: a UK and Ireland case study, Journal of Transport Geography 15 (3) (2007) 161–171.

[131] A. Graham, Understanding the low cost carrier and airport relationship: a critical analysis of the salient issues, Tourism Management 36 (2013) 66–76.

[132] J.F. O'Connell, G. Williams, Passengers' perceptions of low-cost airlines and full-service carriers: a case study involving Ryanair, Aer Lingus, Air Asia and Malaysia Airlines, Journal of Air Transport Management 11 (4) (2005) 259–272.

[133] K. Button, S. Ison, The economics of low-cost airlines: introduction, Research in Transportation Economics 24 (1) (2008) 1–4.

[134] B. Lange, The Market: Long- and Short-Term Outlook, Airbus, Toulouse-Blagnac, France, 2016.

[135] C. Dionelis, J. Mourmouris, M. Giaoutzi, The European railways in the TEN context: from planning to implementation, Regional Science Inquiry Journal 4 (2) (2012) 125–137.

[136] UIC (International Union of Railways), Statistics. https://uic.org/statistics.

[137] V. Profillidis, G. Botzoris, High speed railways: present situation and future prospects, Journal of Transportation Technologies 3 (2A) (2013) 30–36.

[138] C. Nash, When to invest in high speed rail, Journal of Rail Transport Planning and Management 5 (1) (2015) 12–22.

[139] M. Leenen, A. Wolf, A. Peighambari, The Worldwide Market for Railway Industries, SCI Verkehr GmbH, Hamburg, Seattle, WA, 2014.

[140] OICA (Organisation Internationale des Constructeurs d'Automobiles), Facts and Figures. http://www.oica.net/.

[141] Wards, World Motor Vehicle Data − 2014 Edition, Southfield, MI, 2014.

[142] ACEA (Association des Constructeurs Européens d'Automobiles), Annual Statistics. http://www.acea.be/statistics.

[143] USDOT (United States Department of Transportation), Federal Highway Administration. https://www.fhwa.dot.gov/resources/pubstats/.

[144] UK Department for Transport, Statistical Data Sets. https://www.gov.uk/government/statistical-data-sets.

[145] J. Al-Matawah, K. Jadaan, Application of prediction techniques to road safety in developing countries, International Journal of Applied Science and Engineering 7 (2) (2009) 169–175.

[146] E. Papadimitriou, G. Yannis, Needs and priorities of road safety stakeholders for evidence-based policy making, Transport Policy 35 (2014) 286–294.

[147] E. Papadimitriou, S. Lassarre, G. Yannis, Pedestrian risk taking while road crossing: a comparison of observed and declared behaviour, Transportation Research Procedia 14 (2016) 4354–4363.

[148] WHO (World Health Organization), Global Status Report on Road Safety 2015, WHO Publications, Geneva, Switzerland, 2015.

[149] R. Lozano, et al., Global and regional mortality from 235 causes of death for 20 age groups in 1990 and 2010: a systematic analysis for the Global Burden of Disease Study 2010, The Lancet 380 (9859) (2012) 2095–2128.

[150] WHO (World Health Organization), World Health Statistics 2016: Monitoring Health for the Sustainable Development Goals, WHO Publications, Geneva, Switzerland, 2016.

[151] OECD (Organisation for Economic Co-operation and Development) & ITF (International Transport Forum), Road Safety Annual Report 2017, OECD Publishing, Paris, 2017.

[152] I. García, L.J. Miguel, Is the electric vehicle an attractive option for customers? Energies 5 (1) (2012) 71–91.

[153] R. Prud'homme, M. Koning, Electric vehicles: a tentative economic and environmental evaluation, Transport Policy 23 (2012) 60–69.

[154] T.R. Hawkins, B. Singh, G. Majeau-Bettez, A.H. Strømman, Comparative environmental life cycle assessment of conventional and electric vehicles, Journal of Industrial Ecology 17 (1) (2013) 53–64.

[155] L.K. Mitropoulos, P.D. Prevedouros, P. Kopelias, Total cost of ownership and externalities of conventional, hybrid and electric vehicle, Transportation Research Procedia 24 (2017) 267–274.

[156] J. Fontaínhas, J. Cunha, P. Ferreira, Is investing in an electric car worthwhile from a consumers' perspective? Energy 115 (2) (2017) 1459–1477.

[157] L. Matthews, J. Lynes, M. Riemer, T. Del Matto, N. Cloet, Do we have a car for you? Encouraging the uptake of electric vehicles at point of sale, Energy Policy 100 (2017) 79–88.

[158] D.L. Anderson, An Evaluation of Current and Future Costs for Lithium-Ion Batteries for Use in Electrified Vehicle Powertrains (M.Sc. thesis), Nicholas School of the Environment – Duke University, Durham, NC, 2009.

[159] OECD (Organisation for Economic Co-operation and Development) & IEA (International Energy Agency), Global EV Outlook – Beyond One Million Electric Cars, IEA Publications, Paris, 2016.

[160] Y. Tyrinopoulos, C. Antoniou, Factors affecting modal choice in urban mobility, European Transport Research Review 5 (1) (2013) 27–39.

[161] P. Bass, P. Donoso, M. Munizaga, A model to assess public transport demand stability, Transportation Research Part A: Policy and Practice 45 (8) (2011) 755–764.

[162]   D. Albalate, G. Bel, Factors Explaining Urban Transport Systems in Large European Cities: A Cross-Sectional Approach, Working Papers 2009/05, Research Institute of Applied Economics, University of Barcelona, 2009.

[163]   V. Profillidis, Theoretical and practical aspects concerning land access to sea ports, in: European Conference of Ministers of Transport (Ed.), Proceedings of the Round Table No 113: Land Access to Sea Ports, 10−11 December 1998, Paris, OECD Publications, Paris, France, 2001, pp. 147−156.

[164]   J.J. Corbett, J. Winebrake, The impacts of globalisation on international maritime transport activity, in: Organisation for Economic Co-operation and Development (Ed.), Proceedings of the Global Forum on Transport and Environment in a Globalising World, 10−12 November 2008, Guadalajara, Mexico, OECD Publications, Paris, France, 2008.

[165]   Y.H.V. Lun, K.-H. Lai, T.C.E. Cheng, Shipping and Logistics Management, Springer-Verlag, London, 2010.

[166]   A. Jugović, N. Komadina, A.P. Hadžić, Factors influencing the formation of freight rates on maritime shipping markets, Scientific Journal of Maritime Research 29 (2015) 23−29.

[167]   UNCTAD (United Nations Conference on Trade and Development), Review of Maritime Transport 2016, United Nations Publications, Geneva, Switzerland, 2016.

[168]   WSC (World Shipping Council), Global Trade. http://www.worldshipping.org/about-the-industry/global-trade.

[169]   G.S. Egiyan, 'Flag of convenience' or 'open registration' of ships, Marine Policy 14 (2) (1990) 106−111.

[170]   F.J.M. Llácer, Open registers: past, present and future, Marine Policy 27 (6) (2003) 513−523.

[171]   B.N. Metaxas, Flags of convenience, Marine Policy 5 (1) (1981) 52−66.

[172]   J.W. Creswell, Research Design: Qualitative, Quantitative and Mixed Methods Approaches, fourth ed., Sage Publications, Los Angeles, 2013.

[173]   B.S. Everitt, A. Skrondal, The Cambridge Dictionary of Statistics, fourth ed., Cambridge University Press, Cambridge, 2010.

[174]   OECD (Organisation for Economic Co-operation and Development), Glossary of Statistical Terms, OECD Publishing, Paris, 2007.

[175]   I. Martinez-Zarzoso, F.D. Nowak-Lehmann, Is distance a good proxy for transport costs? The case of competing transport modes, The Journal of International Trade and Economic Development 16 (3) (2007) 411−434.

[176]   L.A. Zadeh, The concept of a linguistic variable and its application to approximate reasoning − I, Information Sciences 8 (3) (1975) 199−249.

[177]   L.A. Zadeh, The concept of a linguistic variable and its application to approximate reasoning − II, Information Sciences 8 (4) (1975) 301−357.

[178]   A. Gelman, J. Hill, Data Analysis Using Regression and Multilevel/Hierarchical Models, Cambridge University Press, New York, NY, 2007.

[179]   N. Schaap, O. van de Riet, Behavioral insights model. Overarching framework for applying behavioral insights in transport policy analysis, Transportation Research Record: Journal of the Transportation Research Board 2322 (2012) 42−50.

[180]   P.C. Fishburn, Utility theory, Management Science 14 (5) (1968) 335−378.

[181]   L. Dell'Olio, A. Ibeas, J. de Oña, R. de Oña, Public Transportation Quality of Service − Factors, Models, and Applications, Elsevier, Cambridge, MA, 2017.

[182]   S. Francois, P. Astegiano, F. Viti, Analyzing the correlation between commuting satisfaction and travelling utility, Transportation Research Procedia 25 (2017) 2643−2652.

[183] C.V. Kumar, D. Basu, B. Maitra, Modeling generalized cost of travel for rural bus users: a case study, Journal of Public Transportation 7 (2) (2004) 59–72.

[184] Y. Crozet, Time and passenger transport, in: Proceedings of the Round Table 127 of European Conference of Ministers of Transport 'Time and Transport', 4–5 December 2003, Paris, OECD Publications, Paris, France, 2003, pp. 25–65.

[185] M. Andersson, K. Brundell-Freij, J. Eliasson, Validation of aggregate reference forecasts for passenger transport, Transportation Research Part A: Policy and Practice 96 (2017) 101–118.

[186] K.W. Axhausen, T. Gärling, Activity-based approaches to travel analysis: conceptual frameworks, models, and research problems, Transport Reviews 12 (4) (1992) 323–341.

[187] R. Kitamura, An evaluation of activity-based travel analysis, Transportation 15 (1) (1988) 9–34.

[188] M. Ghasri, T.H. Rashidi, S.T. Waller, Developing a disaggregate travel demand system of models using data mining techniques, Transportation Research Part A: Policy and Practice 105 (2017) 138–153.

[189] C. Glymour, D. Madigan, D. Pregibon, P. Smyth, Statistical themes and lessons for data mining, Data Mining and Knowledge Discovery 1 (1) (1997) 11–28.

[190] M.G. Karlaftis, E.I. Vlahogianni, Statistical methods versus neural networks in transportation research: differences, similarities and some insights, Transportation Research Part C: Emerging Technologies 19 (3) (2011) 387–399.

[191] A.P. Engelbrecht, Computational Intelligence: An Introduction, second ed., John Wiley & Sons, Chichester, 2007.

[192] A. Sadek, G. Spring, B. Smith, Toward more effective transportation applications of computational intelligence paradigms, Transportation Research Record: Journal of the Transportation Research Board 1836 (2003) 57–63.

[193] A.K. Kanafani, Transportation Demand Analysis, McGraw-Hill, New York, NY, 1983.

[194] M.G. Speranza, Trends in transportation and logistics, European Journal of Operational Research 264 (3) (2018) 830–836.

[195] OECD (Organisation for Economic Co-operation and Development) & ITF (International Transport Forum), Big Data and Transport: Understanding and Assessing Options, OECD Publishing, Paris, 2015.

[196] C.P. Chen, C.Y. Zhang, Data-intensive applications, challenges, techniques and technologies: a survey on big data, Information Sciences 275 (2014) 314–347.

[197] M. Chen, S. Mao, Y. Liu, Big data: a survey, Mobile Networks and Applications 19 (2) (2014) 171–209.

[198] W.A. Günther, M.H.R. Mehrizi, M. Huysman, F. Feldberg, Debating big data: a literature review on realizing value from big data, The Journal of Strategic Information Systems 26 (3) (2017) 191–209.

[199] D. Reinsel, J. Gantz, J. Rydning, Data Age 2025: The Evolution of Data to Life-Critical: Don't Focus on Big Data; Focus on the Data That's Big, International Data Corporation, Framingham, MA, 2017.

[200] A. Karkouch, H. Mousannif, H. Al Moatassime, T. Noel, Data quality in internet of things: a state-of-the-art survey, Journal of Network and Computer Applications 73 (2016) 57–81.

[201] K.W. Axhausen, Social factors in future travel: a qualitative assessment, IEE Proceedings - Intelligent Transport Systems 153 (2) (2006) 156–166.

[202] S. Kim, Forecasting short-term air passenger demand using big data from search engine queries, Automation in Construction 70 (2016) 98–108.

[203] M.A. Yazici, C. Kamga, A. Singhal, A big data driven model for taxi drivers' airport pick-up decisions in New York city, in: Proceedings of IEEE International Conference on Big Data, 6–9 December 2013, Silicon Valley, CA, USA, 2013, pp. 37–44.

[204] USDOT (United States Department of Transportation), Big Data's Implications for Transportation Operations — An Exploration, Cambridge (MA), 2014.

[205] R.L. Priem, Executive judgment, organizational congruence, and firm performance, Organization Science 5 (3) (1994) 421–437.

[206] N.C. Dalkey, O. Helmer, An experimental application of the Delphi method to the use of experts, Management Science 9 (3) (1963) 458–467.

[207] H. Linstone, M. Turoff, The Delphi Method: Techniques and Application, Addison-Wesley Publishing, Reading, MA, 1975 & 2002.

[208] C. Okoli, S.D. Pawlowski, The Delphi method as a research tool: an example, design considerations and applications, Information and Management 42 (1) (2004) 15–29.

[209] R. Tolley, L. Lumsdon, K. Bickerstaff, The future of walking in Europe: a Delphi project to identify expert opinion on future walking scenarios, Transport Policy 8 (4) (2001) 307–315.

[210] J. Dinwoodie, S. Tuck, P. Rigot-Müller, Maritime oil freight flows to 2050: Delphi perceptions of maritime specialists, Energy Policy 63 (2013) 553–561.

[211] B. Dimitrijević, V. Simić, V. Radonjić, A. Kostić-Ljubisavljević, The Delphi method as a research tool: an application in transportation and logistics systems evaluations, in: Proceeding of the 6th International Quality Conference, 8 June 2012, University of Kragujevac, Serbia, 2012, pp. 401–406.

[212] J. Landeta, J. Barruita, People consultation to construct the future: a Delphi application, International Journal of Forecasting 27 (1) (2011) 134–151.

[213] S.W. Schuckmann, T. Gnatzy, I.-L. Darkow, H.A. von der Grach, Analysis of factors influencing the development of transport infrastructure until the year 2030 — a Delphi based scenario study, Technological Forecasting and Social Change 79 (8) (2012) 1373–1387.

[214] S. Cafiso, A. Di Graziano, G. Pappalardo, Using the Delphi method to evaluate opinions of public transport managers on bus safety, Safety Science 57 (2013) 254–263.

[215] R. Weston, N. Davies, The future of transport and tourism: a Delphi approach, Tourism and Hospitality Planning and Development 4 (2) (2007) 121–133.

[216] M.G. Kendall, B.B. Smith, The problem of m rankings, The Annals of Mathematical Statistics 10 (3) (1939) 275–287.

[217] S. Siegel, N.J. Castellan, Nonparametric Statistics for the Behavioral Sciences, second ed., McGraw-Hill, New York, NY, 1988.

[218] R.C. Schmidt, Managing Delphi surveys using nonparametric statistical techniques, Decision Sciences 28 (3) (1997) 763–774.

[219] M. Marozzi, Testing for concordance between several criteria, Journal of Statistical Computation and Simulation 84 (9) (2014) 1843–1850.

[220] M. Mäkitalo, O.P. Hilmola, Analysing the future of railway freight competition: a Delphi study in Finland, Foresight 16 (6) (2010) 20–37.

[221] Y.C. Chang, C.J. Hsu, G. Williams, M.-L. Pan, Low cost carriers' destination selection using a Delphi method, Tourism Management 29 (5) (2008) 898–908.

[222] W.W. Cooper, A. Gallegos, M.H. Granof, A Delphi study of goals and evaluation criteria of state and privately owned Latin American airlines, Socio-Economic Planning Sciences 29 (4) (1995) 273–285.

[223] P. Gray, O. Helmer, The use of futures analysis for transportation research planning, Transportation Journal 16 (2) (1976) 5—12.

[224] A.T. Gumus, Evaluation of hazardous waste transportation firms by using a two step fuzzy-AHP and TOPSIS methodology, Expert Systems with Applications 36 (2) (2009) 4067—4074.

[225] J. He, W. Hung, Perception of policy-makers on policy-making criteria: the case of vehicle emissions control, Science of the Total Environment 417—418 (2012) 21—31.

[226] M. Linz, Scenarios for the aviation industry: a Delphi-based analysis for 2025, Journal of Air Transport Management 22 (2012) 28—35.

[227] T.C. Lirn, H.A. Thanopoutou, M.J. Beynon, A.K.C. Beresford, An application of AHP on transshipment port selection: a global perspective, Maritime Economics and Logistics 6 (1) (2004) 70—91.

[228] V. Marchau, R. van der Heijden, Policy aspects of driver support systems implementation: results of an international Delphi study, Transport Policy 5 (4) (1998) 249—258.

[229] M. McDonald, G. Marsden, M. Brackstone, Deployment of interurban ATT test scenarios (DIATS): implications for the European road network, Transport Reviews 21 (3) (2001) 303—335.

[230] K. Mulder, C. van de Weijer, V. Marchau, Prospects for external sources of vehicle propulsion: results of a Delphi study, Futures 28 (10) (1996) 919—945.

[231] M.I. Piecyk, A.C. McKinnon, Forecasting the carbon footprint of road freight transport in 2020, International Journal of Production Economics 128 (1) (2010) 31—42.

[232] A. Pirdavani, T. Brijs, G. Wets, A multiple criteria decision-making approach for prioritizing accident hotspots in the absence of crash data, Transport Reviews 30 (1) (2010) 97—113.

[233] A. Samuelsson, B. Tilanus, A framework efficiency model for goods transportation with an application to regional less-than-truckload distribution, Transport Logistics 1 (2) (1997) 139—151.

[234] Y. Shiftan, S. Kaplan, S. Hakkert, Scenario building as a tool for planning a sustainable transportation system, Transportation Research Part D: Transport and Environment 8 (5) (2003) 323—342.

[235] G.H. Tzeng, C.W. Lin, S. Opricovic, Multi-criteria analysis of alternative-fuel buses for public transportation, Energy Policy 33 (11) (2005) 1373—1383.

[236] S. Wibowo, H. Deng, A fuzzy rule-based approach for screening international distribution centres, Computers and Mathematics with Applications 64 (5) (2012) 1084—1092.

[237] Z. Liu, L. Zhang, L.V. Xue, J. Chen, Evaluation method about bus scheduling based on discrete Hopfield neural network, Journal of Transportation Systems Engineering and Information Technology 11 (2) (2011) 77—83.

[238] V. Profillidis, G. Botzoris, Analysis and modelling of road safety factors, in: Hellenic Institute of Transportation Engineers (Ed.), Proceeding of the 3rd Greek Conference on Road Safety, 10—11 October 2005, Volos, Greece, 2005.

[239] V. Profillidis, N. Eliou, G. Botzoris, Utilisation des techniques GPS pour évaluer la perception du danger routier par le conducteur, Transports 451 (2008) 304—309.

[240] S. Cafiso, A. Di Graziano, G. Pappalardo, Road safety issues for bus transport management, Procedia-Social and Behavioral Sciences 48 (2012) 2251—2261.

[241] A.D. Pearman, Scenario construction for transport planning, Transportation Planning and Technology 12 (1) (1988) 73—85.

[242] J. Van Doorn, Scenario writing: a method for long-term tourism forecasting, Tourism Management 7 (1) (1986) 33—49.

[243] A. Roukouni, F. Medda, M. Giannopoulou, A. Vavatsikos, A multi-attribute comparative evaluation of value capture financing mechanisms: a case study, in: J. Woltjer, E. Alexander, A. Hull, M. Ruth (Eds.), Evaluation in Integrated Land-Use Management: Towards an Area Oriented and Place-Based Evaluation for Infrastructure and Spatial Projects, Ashgate, Farnham, UK, 2015, pp. 75−95.

[244] ICCR (Interdisciplinary Centre for Comparative Research in the Social Sciences), Foresight for Transport; A Foresight Exercise to Help Forward Thinking in Transport and Sectoral Integration, Vienna, 2004.

[245] O. Tansey, Process tracing and elite interviewing: a case for non-probability sampling, Political Science and Politics 40 (4) (2007) 765−772.

[246] N.L. Reynolds, A.C. Simintiras, A. Diamantopoulos, Theoretical justification of sampling choices in international marketing research: key issues and guidelines for researchers, Journal of International Business Studies 34 (1) (2003) 80−89.

[247] R.L. Raschke, A.S. Krishen, P. Kachroo, P. Maheshwari, A combinatorial optimization based sample identification method for group comparisons, Journal of Business Research 66 (9) (2013) 1267−1271.

[248] R. de Oña, G. López, F.J.D. de los Rios, J. de Oña, Cluster analysis for diminishing heterogeneous opinions of service quality public transport passengers, Procedia-Social and Behavioral Sciences 162 (2014) 459−466.

[249] R. Johnson, D. Wichern, Multivariate Statistical Analysis, third ed., Prentice Hall, Englewood Cliffs, NJ, 1992.

[250] Y. Tyrinopoulos, G. Aifadopoulou, A complete methodology for the quality control of passenger services in the public transport business, European Transport 38 (2008) 1−16.

[251] Y. Tyrinopoulos, C. Antoniou, Public transit user satisfaction: variability and policy implications, Transport Policy 15 (4) (2008) 260−272.

[252] P. Lietz, Research into questionnaire design − a summary of the literature, International Journal of Market Research 52 (2) (2010) 249−272.

[253] N.C. Schaeffer, S. Presser, The science of asking questions, Annual Review of Sociology 29 (2003) 65−88.

[254] A. Fink, How to Ask Survey Questions, second ed., Sage Publications, Thousand Oaks, CA, 2003.

[255] R. Likert, A technique for the measurement of attitudes, Archives of Psychology 22 (140) (1932) 5−55.

[256] E. Grigoroudis, Y. Siskos, A survey of customer satisfaction barometers: some results from the transportation-communications sector, European Journal of Operational Research 152 (2) (2004) 334−353.

[257] J. Dawes, Do data characteristics change according to the number of scale points used? An experiment using 5-point, 7-point and 10-point scales, International Journal of Market Research 50 (1) (2008) 61−77.

[258] D.A. Hensher, Stated preference analysis of travel choices: the state of practice, Transportation 21 (2) (1994) 107−133.

[259] E.P. Kroes, R.J. Sheldon, Stated preference methods: an introduction, Journal of Transport Economics and Policy 22 (1) (1988) 11−25.

[260] L. Eboli, G. Mazzulla, A stated preference experiment for measuring service quality in public transport, Transportation Planning and Technology 31 (5) (2008) 509−523.

[261] P.N. Seneviratne, N. Martel, Variables influencing performance of air terminal buildings, Transportation Planning and Technology 16 (1) (1991) 3−28.

[262] P. Hackett, G. Foxall, Consumers' evaluations of an international airport: a facet theoretical approach, The International Review of Retail, Distribution and Consumer Research 7 (4) (1997) 339–349.

[263] A.R. Correia, S.C. Wirasinghe, A.G. de Barros, Overall level of service measures for airport passenger terminals, Transportation Research Part A: Policy and Practice 42 (2) (2008) 330–346.

[264] D. Wiredja, V. Popovic, A. Blackler, Questionnaire design for airport passenger experience survey, in: Proceedings of the 6th International Association of Societies of Design Research Congress, 2–5 November 2015, Brisbane, Australia, 2015, pp. 2236–2254.

[265] K. Proussaloglou, F. Koppelman, Air carrier demand, Transportation 22 (4) (1995) 371–388.

[266] F. Pakdil, Ö. Aydin, Expectations and perceptions in airline services: an analysis using weighted SERVQUAL scores, Journal of Air Transport Management 13 (4) (2007) 229–237.

[267] M. Anastasiadou, D. Dimitriou, A. Fredianakis, E. Lagoudakis, G. Traxanatzi, K.P. Tsagarakis, Determining the parking fee using the contingent valuation methodology, Journal of Urban Planning and Development 135 (3) (2009) 116–124.

[268] V. Profillidis, G. Botzoris, The market survey: an essential tool for the commerce and tariff policy of a public transport authority, in: Proceedings of the 2nd UITP International Marketing Conference, 12–14 November 2003, Union Internationale des Transports Publics, Paris, France, 2003.

[269] A.A. Ahern, N. Tapley, The use of stated preference techniques to model modal choices on interurban trips in Ireland, Transportation Research Part A: Policy and Practice 42 (1) (2008) 15–27.

[270] E. Nathanail, Measuring the quality of service for passengers on the Hellenic railways, Transportation Research Part A: Policy and Practice 42 (1) (2008) 48–66.

[271] L. Creemers, M. Cools, H. Tormans, P.J. Lateur, D. Janssens, G. Wets, Identifying the determinants of light rail mode choice for medium-and long-distance trips: results from a stated preference study, Transportation Research Record: Journal of the Transportation Research Board 2275 (2012) 30–38.

[272] L. Eboli, Y. Fu, G. Mazzulla, Multilevel comprehensive evaluation of the railway service quality, Procedia Engineering 137 (2016) 21–30.

[273] I. Politis, P. Papaioannou, S. Basbas, N. Dimitriadis, Evaluation of a bus passenger information system from the users' point of view in the city of Thessaloniki — Greece, Research in Transportation Economics 29 (1) (2010) 249–255.

[274] L. Dell'Olio, A. Ibeas, P. Cecin, The quality of service desired by public transport users, Transport Policy 18 (1) (2011) 217–227.

[275] R.G. Mugion, M. Toni, H. Raharjo, L. Di Pietro, S.P. Sebathu, Does the service quality of urban public transport enhance sustainable mobility? Journal of Cleaner Production 174 (2018) 1566–1587.

[276] R.C.P. Wong, W.Y. Szeto, L. Yang, Y.C. Li, S.C. Wong, Elderly users' level of satisfaction with public transport services in a high-density and transit-oriented city, Journal of Transport and Health 7 (2017) 209–217.

[277] G. Botzoris, A. Galanis, V. Profillidis, N. Eliou, Commuters perspective on urban public transport system service quality, WSEAS Transactions on Environment and Development 11 (2015) 182–192.

[278] M. Tsami, E. Nathanail, Guidance provision for increasing quality of service of public transport, Procedia Engineering 178 (2017) 551–557.

[279] D. Efthymiou, C. Antoniou, Understanding the effects of economic crisis on public transport users' satisfaction and demand, Transport Policy 53 (2017) 89−97.

[280] A. Pantouvakis, C. Chlomoudis, A. Dimas, Testing the SERVQUAL scale in the passenger port industry: a confirmatory study, Maritime Policy and Management 35 (5) (2008) 449−467.

[281] B. Wiegmans, P. Rietveld, P. Nijkamp, Container terminal handling quality, European Transport 25 (26) (2004) 61−80.

[282] I. Kolanovic, C.A. Dundović, A. Jugović, Customer based port services quality model, Traffic and Transportation 23 (6) (2011) 495−502.

[283] S.P. Washington, M.G. Karlaftis, F. Mannering, Statistical and Econometric Methods for Transportation Data Analysis, second ed., CRC Press, Boca Raton, FL, 2010.

[284] F. Galton, Regression towards mediocrity in hereditary stature, The Journal of the Anthropological Institute of Great Britain and Ireland 15 (1886) 246−263.

[285] R.A. Yaffee, M. McGee, An Introduction to Time Series Analysis and Forecasting: with Applications of SAS and SPSS, Academic Press, New York, NY, 2000.

[286] D.R. Cox, Interaction, International Statistical Review/Revue Internationale de Statistique 52 (1) (1984) 1−24.

[287] K. Pearson, Notes on regression and inheritance in the case of two parents, Proceedings of the Royal Society of London 58 (1895) 240−242.

[288] T.C. Krehbiel, Correlation coefficient rule of thumb, Decision Sciences Journal of Innovative Education 2 (1) (2004) 97−100.

[289] R.J. Brook, G.C. Arnold, Applied Regression Analysis and Experimental Design, CRC Press, New York, NY, 1985.

[290] J.M. Cortina, Interaction, nonlinearity, and multicollinearity: implications for multiple regression, Journal of Management 19 (4) (1993) 915−922.

[291] R.M. O'brien, A caution regarding rules of thumb for variance inflation factors, Quality and Quantity 41 (5) (2007) 673−690.

[292] C.M. Jarque, A.K. Bera, A test for normality of observations and regression residuals, International Statistical Review/Revue Internationale de Statistique 55 (2) (1987) 163−172.

[293] R.D. Cook, S. Weisberg, Residuals and Influence in Regression, Chapman & Hall, New York, NY, 1982.

[294] K.A. Bollen, R.W. Jackman, Regression diagnostics: an expository treatment of outliers and influential cases, Sociological Methods and Research 13 (4) (1985) 510−542.

[295] J. Durbin, G. Watson, Testing for serial correlation in least squares regression. I, Biometrika 37 (3/4) (1950) 409−428.

[296] J. Durbin, G. Watson, Testing for serial correlation in least squares regression. II, Biometrika 38 (1/2) (1951) 159−177.

[297] J. Durbin, G. Watson, Testing for serial correlation in least squares regression. III, Biometrika 58 (1) (1971) 1−19.

[298] G.S. Maddala, Introduction to Econometrics, second ed., McMillan Publishing, New York, NY, 1992.

[299] A.P. Field, Discovering Statistics Using SPSS, third ed., Sage, London, 2009.

[300] D.N. Gujarati, Basic Econometrics, fourth ed., McGraw-Hill/Irwin, New York, NY, 2003.

[301] L. Keele, N.J. Kelly, Dynamic models for dynamic theories: the ins and outs of lagged dependent variables, Political Analysis 14 (2) (2005) 186−205.

[302] J. Durbin, Testing for serial correlation in least-squares regression when some of the regressors are lagged dependent variables, Econometrica 38 (3) (1970) 410−421.

[303] T.S. Breusch, L.G. Godfrey, A review of recent work on testing for autocorrelation in dynamic economic models, in: D. Currie, R. Nobay, D. Peel (Eds.), Macroeconomic Analysis, Croom-Helm, London, 1981, pp. 63–105.

[304] G.M. Ljung, G.E. Box, On a measure of lack of fit in time series models, Biometrika 65 (2) (1978) 297–303.

[305] R.J. Hyndman, G. Athanasopoulos, Forecasting: Principles and Practice, OTexts, Melbourne, Australia, 2013.

[306] N.G. Mankiw, A quick refresher course in macroeconomics, Journal of Economic Literature 28 (4) (1990) 1645–1660.

[307] T.S. Breusch, A.R. Pagan, A simple test for heteroscedasticity and random coefficient variation, Econometrica 47 (5) (1979) 1287–1294.

[308] H. Glejser, A new test for heteroscedasticity, Journal of the American Statistical Association 64 (325) (1969) 316–323.

[309] D. Asteriou, S.G. Hall, Applied Econometrics, second ed., Palgrave Macmillan, New York, NY, 2011.

[310] A.C. Harvey, Estimating regression models with multiplicative heteroscedasticity, Econometrica 44 (3) (1976) 461–465.

[311] L.G. Godfrey, Testing for higher order serial correlation in regression equations when the regressors include lagged dependent variables, Econometrica 46 (6) (1978) 1303–1310.

[312] H. White, A heteroscedasticity-consistent covariance matrix estimator and a direct test for heteroscedasticity, Econometrica 48 (4) (1980) 817–838.

[313] R.F. Engle, Autoregressive conditional heteroscedasticity with estimates of the variance of United Kingdom inflation, Econometrica 50 (4) (1982) 987–1007.

[314] T. Bollerslev, R.Y. Chou, K.F. Kroner, ARCH modeling in finance: a review of the theory and empirical evidence, Journal of Econometrics 52 (1–2) (1992) 5–59.

[315] T.W. Gentry, B.M. Wiliamowski, L.R. Weatherford, A comparison of traditional forecasting techniques and neural networks, Intelligent Engineering Systems Through Artificial Neural Networks 5 (1995) 765–770.

[316] F. Bliemel, Theil's forecast accuracy coefficient: a clarification, Journal of Marketing Research 10 (4) (1973) 444–446.

[317] P.K. Watson, S.S. Teelucksingh, A Practical Introduction to Econometric Methods: Classical and Modern, University of the West Indies Press, Jamaica, 2002.

[318] V. Yorucu, The analysis of forecasting performance by using time series data for two Mediterranean islands, Review of Social, Economic and Business Studies 2 (2003) 175–196.

[319] R.S. Pindyck, D.L. Rubinfeld, Econometric Models and Economic Forecasts, fourth ed., McGraw-Hill/Irwin, New York, NY, 1998.

[320] A.D. Owen, G.D.A. Phillips, The characteristics of railway passenger demand. An econometric investigation, Journal of Transport Economics and Policy 21 (3) (1987) 231–253.

[321] A.S. Fowkes, C.A. Nash, A.E. Whiteing, Understanding trends in inter-city rail traffic in Great Britain, Transportation Planning and Technology 10 (1) (1985) 65–80.

[322] M. Wardman, Demand for rail travel and the effects of external factors, Transportation Research Part E: Logistics and Transportation Review 42 (3) (2006) 129–148.

[323] V. Stefanis, G. Botzoris, An aggregate econometric model for the forecast of rail passenger demand, Informatics and IT Today 2 (1) (2014) 12–19.

[324]   V. Profillidis, G. Botzoris, A comparative analysis of performances of econometric, fuzzy and time-series models for the forecast of transport demand, in: Proceedings of IEEE International Fuzzy Systems Conference, 23—26 July 2007, London, United Kingdom, 2007.

[325]   K.J. Button, Transport Economics, third ed., Edward Elgar Publishing Ltd., Cheltenham (UK), Northampton (MA), 2010.

[326]   Hellenic Statistical Authority, Statistics. http://www.statistics.gr/en/home/.

[327]   Stanford University, Econometric Benchmarks — Critical Values for the Durbin-Watson Test, 2018. https://web.stanford.edu/~clint/bench/dwcrit.htm.

[328]   P.J. Diggle, P. Heagerty, K. Liang, S.L. Zeger, Analysis of Longitudinal Data, second ed., Oxford University Press, Oxford, 2002.

[329]   G.M. Fitzmaurice, N.M. Laird, J.H. Ware, Applied Longitudinal Analysis, second ed., John Wiley & Sons, Hoboken, NJ, 2011.

[330]   V. Profillidis, G. Botzoris, S. Taxidis, A holistic approach of the correlation between GDP and air transport through panel data analysis, in: Hellenic Institute of Transportation Engineers (Ed.), Proceeding of the 7th International Congress on Transportation Research, 5—6 November 2015, Athens, Greece, 2015.

[331]   P.H. Franses, A method to select between Gompertz and logistic trend curves, Technological Forecasting and Social Change 46 (1) (1994) 45—49.

[332]   J. Dargay, D. Gately, M. Sommer, Vehicle ownership and income growth worldwide: 1960—2030, The Energy Journal 28 (4) (2007) 143—170.

[333]   Eurotunnel, Traffic Figures. https://www.getlinkgroup.com/uk/eurotunnel-group/operations/traffic-figures/.

[334]   D.L. Massart, L. Kaufman, P.J. Rousseeuw, A. Leroy, Least median of squares: a robust method for outlier and model error detection in regression and calibration, Analytica Chimica Acta 187 (1986) 171—179.

[335]   V. Profillidis, An ex-post assessment of a passenger demand forecast of an airport, Journal of Air Transport Management 25 (2012) 47—49.

[336]   J. Heizer, B. Render, Principles of Operations Management, sixth ed., Prentice Hall, Upper Saddle River, NJ, 2006.

[337]   G.E. Box, G.M. Jenkins, G.C. Reinsel, G.M. Ljung, Time Series Analysis: Forecasting and Control, fifth ed., John Wiley & Sons, Hoboken, NJ, 2015.

[338]   G.E. Halkos, I.S. Kevork, A comparison of alternative unit root tests, Journal of Applied Statistics 32 (1) (2005) 45—60.

[339]   G.E. Halkos, I.S. Kevork, Forecasting the stationary AR (1) with an almost unit root, Applied Economics Letters 13 (12) (2006) 789—793.

[340]   D.A. Dickey, W.A. Fuller, Distribution of the estimators for autoregressive time series with a unit root, Journal of the American Statistical Association 74 (366a) (1979) 427—431.

[341]   W.A. Fuller, Introduction to Statistical Time Series, second ed., John Wiley & Sons, New York, NY, 1996.

[342]   G.W. Schwert, Tests for unit roots: a Monte Carlo investigation, Journal of Business and Economic Statistics 7 (2) (1989) 147—159.

[343]   H. Akaike, A new look at the statistical model identification, IEEE Transactions on Automatic Control 19 (6) (1974) 716—723.

[344]   H. Bozdogan, Akaike's information criterion and recent developments in information complexity, Journal of Mathematical Psychology 44 (1) (2000) 62—91.

[345] G. Schwarz, Estimating the dimension of a model, The Annals of Statistics 6 (2) (1978) 461−464.

[346] E.J. Hannan, B.G. Quinn, The determination of the order of an autoregression, Journal of the Royal Statistical Society − Series B: Methodological 41 (2) (1979) 190−195.

[347] G.E. Box, G.M. Jenkins, Time Series Analysis: Forecasting and Control, second ed., Holden-Day, San Francisco, CA, 1976.

[348] J. Davidson, Econometric Theory, Blackwell Publishers, Oxford, 2000.

[349] C. Chatfield, The Analysis of Time Series, sixth ed., Chapman & Hall, New York, NY, 2003.

[350] J.G. MacKinnon, Numerical distribution functions for unit root and cointegration tests, Journal of Applied Econometrics 11 (6) (1996) 601−618.

[351] ICAO (International Civil Aviation Organization), Manual on Air Transport Forecasting, third ed., 2006. Montreal.

[352] Y. Yajima, Estimation of the degree of differencing of an ARIMA process, Annals of the Institute of Statistical Mathematics 37 (1) (1985) 389−408.

[353] J.A. Laval, C.S. Toth, Y. Zhou, A parsimonious model for the formation of oscillations in car-following models, Transportation Research Part B: Methodological 70 (2014) 228−238.

[354] C.W. Granger, Long memory relationships and the aggregation of dynamic models, Journal of Econometrics 14 (2) (1980) 227−238.

[355] C.W. Granger, Investigating causal relations by econometric models and cross-spectral methods, Econometrica 37 (3) (1969) 424−438.

[356] A. Graham, Managing Airports: An International Perspective, third ed., Elsevier, Oxford, 2008.

[357] N.P. Dennis, Long-term route traffic forecasts and flight schedule pattern for a medium-sized European airport, Journal of Air Transport Management 8 (5) (2002) 313−324.

[358] A. Graham, D. Metz, Limits to air travel growth: the case of infrequent flyers, Journal of Air Transport Management 62 (2017) 109−120.

[359] F. Kilipiris, Sustainable tourism development and local community involvement, Tourism and Hospitality Management 11 (2) (2005) 27−39.

[360] A. Chin, J. Tay, Developments in air transport: implications on investment decisions, profitability and survival of Asian airlines, Journal of Air Transport Management 7 (5) (2001) 319−330.

[361] M. Marazzo, R. Scherre, E. Fernandes, Air transport demand and economic growth in Brazil: a time series analysis, Transportation Research Part E: Logistics and Transportation Review 46 (2) (2010) 261−269.

[362] T. Koo, N. Halpern, A. Papatheodorou, A. Graham, P. Arvanitis, Air transport liberalisation and airport dependency: developing a composite index, Journal of Transport Geography 50 (2016) 83−93.

[363] A. Fragoudaki, Greek domestic air transport—industry and policy developments from post-World War II to post-liberalization, Journal of Air Transport Management 6 (4) (2000) 223−232.

[364] A. Kanafani, A.A. Ghobrial, Airline hubbing − some implications for airport economics, Transportation Research Part A: General 19 (1) (1985) 15−27.

[365] N.P. Dennis, Airline hub operations in Europe, Journal of Transport Geography 2 (4) (1994) 219−233.

[366] I. Pagoni, V. Psaraki-Kalouptsidi, The impact of carbon emission fees on passenger demand and air fares: a game theoretic approach, Journal of Air Transport Management 55 (2016) 41−51.

[367] UK Department for Transport, UK Aviation Forecasts 2013. https://www.gov.uk/government/uploads/system/uploads/attachment_data/file/223839/aviation-forecasts.pdf.

[368] R. Guo, Z.W. Zhong, Forecasting air passenger volume in Singapore: determining the explanatory variables for econometric models, MATTER: International Journal of Science and Technology 3 (1) (2017) 123−139.

[369] N.J. Ashford, S. Mumayiz, P.H. Wright, Airport Engineering: Planning, Design and Development of 21st Century Airports, John Wiley & Sons, Hoboken, NJ, 2011.

[370] R. Horonjeff, F.X. McKelvey, W.J. Sproule, S.B. Young, Planning and Design of Airports, fifth ed., McGraw-Hill, New York, NY, 2010.

[371] P.T. Wang, D.E. Pitfield, The derivation and analysis of the passenger peak hour: an empirical application to Brazil, Journal of Air Transport Management 5 (3) (1999) 135−141.

[372] M. Janić, The Sustainability of Air Transportation: A Quantitative Analysis and Assessment, Ashgate, London, 2007.

[373] Boeing, World Air Cargo Forecasts, Seattle, WA, 2016.

[374] V. Profillidis, Experiences from liberalisation of road and rail transport, Journal of Maritime Economics and Logistics 6 (2004) 270−273.

[375] M. Sanchez-Borras, C. Nash, P. Abrantes, A. Lopez-Pita, Rail access charges and the competitiveness of high-speed trains, Transport Policy 17 (2) (2010) 102−109.

[376] E. Bougna, Y. Crozet, Towards a liberalised European rail transport: analysing and modelling the impact of competition on productive efficiency, Research in Transportation Economics 59 (2016) 358−367.

[377] A. Fraszczyk, N. Amirault, M. Marinov, Rail marketing, jobs and public engagement, in: M. Marinov, A. Fraszczyk (Eds.), Sustainable Rail Transport, Springer, Cham, 2018, pp. 207−224.

[378] E.G. Tsionas, N.C. Baltas, D.P. Chionis, Rail infrastructure charging in Hellenic railways, Journal of Policy Modeling 33 (3) (2011) 370−380.

[379] C.H. Achen, Why lagged dependent variables can suppress the explanatory power of other independent variables, in: Annual Meeting of the Political Methodology Section of the American Political Science Association, 20−22 July 2000, Los Angeles, CA, USA, 2000.

[380] UK Department for Transport, Rail Demand Forecasting Estimation, 2016. https://www.gov.uk/government/publications/rail-demand-forecasting-estimation-study-phase-reports.

[381] M. Milenković, N. Bojović, Railway demand forecasting, in: U.B. Rai (Ed.), Handbook of Research on Emerging Innovations in Rail Transportation Engineering, IGI Global, Hershey, PA, USA, 2016, pp. 100−129.

[382] J.F. Odgers, L.A. van Schijndel, Forecasting annual train boardings in Melbourne using time series data, in: Australasian Transport Research Forum, 28−30 September 2011, Adelaide, Australia, 2011.

[383] P.S. Rao, Forecasting the demand for railway freight services, Journal of Transport Economics and Policy 12 (1) (1978) 7−26.

[384] K. Haase, G. Desaulniers, J. Desrosiers, Simultaneous vehicle and crew scheduling in urban mass transit systems, Transportation Science 35 (3) (2001) 286−303.

[385] R.E. Wener, G.W. Evans, A morning stroll: levels of physical activity in car and mass transit commuting, Environment and Behavior 39 (1) (2007) 62–74.

[386] T. Abdallah, Sustainable Mass Transit: Challenges and Opportunities in Urban Public Transportation, Elsevier, Cambridge, MA, 2017.

[387] D. McFadden, The measurement of urban travel demand, Journal of Public Economics 3 (4) (1974) 303–328.

[388] V. Profillidis, Light rail transit systems – present trends and future prospects, Journal of Light Rail Transit Association 56 (1995) 8–12.

[389] A. Schafer, D.G. Victor, The future mobility of the world population, Transportation Research Part A: Policy and Practice 34 (3) (2000) 171–205.

[390] G. Giuliano, J. Dargay, Car ownership, travel and land use: a comparison of the US and Great Britain, Transportation Research Part A: Policy and Practice 40 (2) (2006) 106–124.

[391] K.B. Medlock, R. Soligo, Car ownership and economic development with forecasts to the year 2015, Journal of Transport Economics and Policy 36 (2) (2002) 163–188.

[392] J. Holmgren, Meta-analysis of public transport demand, Transportation Research Part A: Policy and Practice 41 (10) (2007) 1021–1035.

[393] A. García-Ferrer, M. Bujosa, A. de Juan, P. Poncela, Demand forecast and elasticities estimation of public transport, Journal of Transport Economics and Policy 40 (1) (2006) 45–67.

[394] G. Bresson, J. Dargay, J.L. Madre, A. Pirotte, The main determinants of the demand for public transport: a comparative analysis of England and France using shrinkage estimators, Transportation Research Part A: Policy and Practice 37 (7) (2003) 605–627.

[395] D. Metz, Demographic determinants of daily travel demand, Transport Policy 21 (2012) 20–25.

[396] A. Roukouni, S. Basbas, A. Kokkalis, Impacts of a metro station to the land use and transport system: the Thessaloniki metro case, Procedia-Social and Behavioral Sciences 48 (2012) 1155–1163.

[397] K. Kepaptsoglou, A. Stathopoulos, M.G. Karlaftis, Ridership estimation of a new LRT system: direct demand model approach, Journal of Transport Geography 58 (2017) 146–156.

[398] J.M. Salanova, M. Estrada, G. Aifadopoulou, E. Mitsakis, A review of the modeling of taxi services, Procedia-Social and Behavioral Sciences 20 (2011) 150–161.

[399] K.I. Wong, S.C. Wong, Modeling urban taxi services in road networks: progress, problem and prospect, Journal of Advanced Transportation 35 (3) (2001) 237–258.

[400] E.J. Gonzales, C. Yang, E.F. Morgul, K. Özbay, Modeling Taxi Demand With GPS Data from Taxis and Transit, Mineta National Transit Research Consortium, San José, CA, 2014.

[401] J.M. Salanova, M. Estrada, Social optimal shifts and fares of taxi services, in: Proceedings of the 12th Conference on Transport Engineering, 7–9 June 2016, Valencia, Spain, 2016, pp. 1000–1007.

[402] Y.W. Lau, Modeling the Level of Taxi Service in Hong Kong (M.Sc. dissertation), The Hong Kong University of Science and Technology, Hong Kong, 1997.

[403] B. Schaller, A regression model of the number of taxicabs in US cities, Journal of Public Transportation 8 (5) (2005) 63–78.

[404] C. Caliendo, M. Guida, A. Parisi, A crash-prediction model for multilane roads, Accident Analysis and Prevention 39 (4) (2007) 657–670.

[405] R. Elvik, Assessing causality in multivariate accident models, Accident Analysis and Prevention 43 (1) (2011) 253–264.

[406]   L. Fridstrøm, S. Ingebrigtsen, An aggregate accident model based on pooled, regional time-series data, Accident Analysis and Prevention 23 (5) (1991) 363−378.

[407]   S. Cafiso, A. Di Graziano, G. Di Silvestro, G. La Cava, B. Persaud, Development of comprehensive accident models for two-lane rural highways using exposure, geometry, consistency and context variables, Accident Analysis and Prevention 42 (4) (2010) 1072−1079.

[408]   G. Yannis, A. Dragomanovits, A. Laiou, T. Richter, S. Ruhl, F. La Torre, L. Domenichini, D. Graham, N. Karathodorou, H. Li, Use of accident prediction models in road safety management − an international inquiry, Transportation Research Procedia 14 (2016) 4257−4266.

[409]   K. Button, Transport safety and traffic forecasting: an economist's perspective, IATSS Research 38 (1) (2014) 27−31.

[410]   R. Elvik, T. Vaa, A. Hoye, M. Sorensen, The Handbook of Road Safety Measures, second ed., Emerald Group Publishing, Bingley, 2009.

[411]   M.L. Manheim, Fundamentals of Transportation Systems Analysis − Basic Concepts, MIT Press, Cambridge, MA, 1979.

[412]   R.B. Mitchell, C. Rapkin, Urban Traffic − A Function of Land Use, Columbia University Press, New York, NY, 1954.

[413]   J.D. Ortúzar, L.G. Willumsen, Modelling Transport, second ed., John Wiley & Sons, Chichester, 1996.

[414]   M.G. McNally, The four-step model, in: D.A. Hensher, K.J. Button (Eds.), Handbook of Transport Modelling, second ed., Elsevier, Amsterdam, The Netherlands, 2008, pp. 35−53.

[415]   P.W. Bonsall, Principles of transport analysis and forecasting, in: C.A. O'Flaherty (Ed.), Transport Planning and Traffic Engineering, Elsevier, Amsterdam, The Netherlands, 1997, pp. 103−131.

[416]   E. Weiner, Urban Transportation Planning in the United States: An Historical Overview, fifth ed., US Department of Transportation, Washington, DC, 1987.

[417]   M.G. McNally, W.W. Recker, On the Formation of Household Travel/Activity Patterns: A Simulation Approach, University of California, Irvine, CA, 1986.

[418]   D. Teodorović, M. Janić, Transportation Engineering: Theory, Practice and Modeling, Butterworth-Heinemann, Oxford, 2016.

[419]   K.P. Furness, Time function iteration, Traffic Engineering and Control 7 (7) (1965) 458−460.

[420]   M.M.M. Abdel-Aal, Calibrating a trip distribution gravity model stratified by the trip purposes for the city of Alexandria, Alexandria Engineering Journal 53 (3) (2014) 677−689.

[421]   H.M. Celik, Sample size needed for calibrating trip distribution and behavior of the gravity model, Journal of Transport Geography 18 (1) (2010) 183−190.

[422]   L. de Grange, E. Fernández, J. de Cea, A consolidated model of trip distribution, Transportation Research Part E: Logistics and Transportation Review 46 (1) (2010) 61−75.

[423]   J.G. Rose, The calibration of trip distribution models − a new philosophy, Urban Studies 12 (8/9) (1975) 335−338.

[424]   B.P. Bhatta, O.I. Larsen, Are intrazonal trips ignorable? Transport Policy 18 (1) (2011) 13−22.

[425]   M.E. Ben-Akiva, S.R. Lerman, Discrete Choice Analysis: Theory and Application to Travel Demand, MIT Press, Cambridge, MA, 1985.

[426] F.S. Koppelman, C. Bhat, A Self Instructing Course in Mode Choice Modeling: Multinomial and Nested Logit Models, US Department of Transportation, Washington, DC, 2006.

[427] E.J. Gumbel, The return period of flood flows, The Annals of Mathematical Statistics 12 (2) (1941) 163−190.

[428] J.G. Wardrop, Some theoretical aspects of road traffic research, Proceedings of the Institution of Civil Engineers 1 (3) (1952) 325−362.

[429] Y. Sheffi, B. Eskandari, H.N. Koutsopoulos, Transportation mode choice based on total logistics costs, Journal of Business Logistics 9 (2) (1988) 137.

[430] A.Z. Zeng, C. Rossetti, Developing a framework for evaluating the logistics costs in global sourcing processes: an implementation and insights, International Journal of Physical Distribution and Logistics Management 33 (9) (2003) 785−803.

[431] J. Engblom, T. Solakivi, J. Töyli, L. Ojala, Multiple-method analysis of logistics costs, International Journal of Production Economics 137 (1) (2012) 29−35.

[432] D. Beagan, M. Fischer, A. Kuppam, Quick Response Freight Manual, US Department of Transportation − Federal Highway Administration, Washington, DC, 2007.

[433] R.B. Handfield, E.L. Nichols, Introduction to Supply Chain Management, Prentice Hall, Upper Saddle River, NJ, 1999.

[434] D.J. Bowersox, D.J. Closs, M.B. Cooper, Supply Chain Logistics Management, McGraw-Hill/Irwin, New York, NY, 2002.

[435] M. Hesse, J.P. Rodrigue, The transport geography of logistics and freight distribution, Journal of Transport Geography 12 (3) (2004) 171−184.

[436] J.Y. Chow, C.H. Yang, A.C. Regan, State-of-the art of freight forecast modeling: lessons learned and the road ahead, Transportation 37 (6) (2010) 1011−1030.

[437] A. Tamara, B. Taras, B. Viktor, B. Natalia, The choice of transport for freight and passenger traffic in the region, using econometric and fuzzy modeling, Procedia Computer Science 120 (2017) 830−834.

[438] S. Bougheas, P.O. Demetriades, E.L. Morgenroth, Infrastructure, transport costs and trade, Journal of International Economics 47 (1) (1999) 169−189.

[439] A. Nuzzolo, U. Crisalli, A. Comi, A demand model for international freight transport by road, European Transport Research Review 1 (1) (2009) 23−33.

[440] G.P. Kiesmüller, A.G. de Kok, J.C. Fransoo, Transportation mode selection with positive manufacturing lead time, Transportation Research Part E: Logistics and Transportation Review 41 (6) (2005) 511−530.

[441] W. Abdelwahab, M. Sargious, Modelling the demand for freight transport: a new approach, Journal of Transport Economics and Policy 26 (1) (1992) 49−70.

[442] G. De Jong, H. Gunn, W. Walker, National and international freight transport models: an overview and ideas for future development, Transport Reviews 24 (1) (2004) 103−124.

[443] M. Janic, Modelling the full costs of an intermodal and road freight transport network, Transportation Research Part D: Transport and Environment 12 (1) (2007) 33−44.

[444] T. Crainic, M. Gendreau, J. Potvin, Intelligent freight-transportation systems: assessment and the contribution of operations research, Transportation Research Part C: Emerging Technologies 17 (6) (2009) 541−557.

[445] M.G. Karlaftis, K. Kepaptsoglou, E. Sambracos, Containership routing with time deadlines and simultaneous deliveries and pick-ups, Transportation Research Part E: Logistics and Transportation Review 45 (1) (2009) 210−221.

[446] M. Doumpos, C. Zopounidis, Preference disaggregation and statistical learning for multi-criteria decision support: a review, European Journal of Operational Research 209 (3) (2011) 203–214.

[447] M. Minsky, Steps toward artificial intelligence, Proceedings of the IRE 49 (1) (1961) 8–30.

[448] S.H. Chen, A.J. Jakeman, J.P. Norton, Artificial intelligence techniques: an introduction to their use for modelling environmental systems, Mathematics and Computers in Simulation 78 (2–3) (2008) 379–400.

[449] I.A. Basheer, M. Hajmeer, Artificial neural networks: fundamentals, computing, design, and application, Journal of Microbiological Methods 43 (1) (2000) 3–31.

[450] J.J. Hopfield, Neural networks and physical systems with emergent collective computational abilities, Proceedings of the National Academy of Sciences of the United States of America 79 (8) (1982) 2554–2558.

[451] G.A. Carpenter, Neural network models for pattern recognition and associative memory, Neural Networks 2 (4) (1989) 243–257.

[452] W.S. McCulloh, W. Pitts, A logical calculus of the ideas immanent in nervous activity, The Bulletin of Mathematical Biophysics 5 (4) (1943) 115–133.

[453] B. Cheng, D.M. Titterington, Neural networks: a review from a statistical perspective, Statistical Science 9 (1) (1994) 2–30.

[454] K. Hornik, M. Stinchcombe, H. White, Multilayer feedforward networks are universal approximators, Neural Networks 2 (5) (1989) 359–366.

[455] M.N. Karim, S.L. Rivera, Comparison of feedforward and recurrent neural networks for bioprocess state estimation, Computers and Chemical Engineering 16 (s1) (1992) 369–377.

[456] H.G. Han, S. Zhang, J.F. Qiao, An adaptive growing and pruning algorithm for designing recurrent neural network, Neurocomputing 242 (2017) 51–62.

[457] M. Dougherty, A review of neural networks applied to transport, Transportation Research Part C: Emerging Technologies 3 (4) (1995) 247–260.

[458] M.Q. Raza, A. Khosravi, A review on artificial intelligence based load demand forecasting techniques for smart grid and buildings, Renewable and Sustainable Energy Reviews 50 (2015) 1352–1372.

[459] A. Sato, K. Yamada, Generalized learning vector quantization, Advances in Neural Information Processing Systems 8 (1995) 423–429.

[460] A. Barra, A. Bernacchia, E. Santucci, P. Contucci, On the equivalence of Hopfield networks and Boltzmann machines, Neural Networks 34 (2012) 1–9.

[461] A. Bielecki, M. Wójcik, Hybrid system of ART and RBF neural networks for online clustering, Applied Soft Computing 58 (2017) 1–10.

[462] D.E. Rumelhart, G.E. Hinton, R.J. Williams, Learning representations by back-propagating errors, Nature 323 (1986) 533–536.

[463] E. Yair, A. Gersho, The Boltzmann perceptron network: a soft classifier, Neural Networks 3 (2) (1990) 203–221.

[464] Z. Chen, S. Haykin, J.J. Eggermont, S. Becker, Correlative Learning: A Basis for Brain and Adaptive Systems, John Wiley & Sons, Hoboken, NJ, 2008.

[465] K.P.G. Alekseev, J.M. Seixas, A multivariate neural forecasting modeling for air transport – preprocessed by decomposition: a Brazilian application, Journal of Air Transport Management 15 (5) (2009) 212–216.

[466] C. Garrido, R. de Oña, J. de Oña, Neural networks for analyzing service quality in public transportation, Expert Systems with Applications 41 (15) (2014) 6830–6838.

[467] V. Profillidis, G. Botzoris, S. Taxidis, Multiparameter artificial neural network models for the forecast of air transport demand, in: Hellenic Institute of Transportation Engineers (Ed.), Proceeding of the 8th International Congress on Transportation Research, 27–29 September 2017, Thessaloniki, Greece, 2017.

[468] IATA (International Air Transport Association), International Air Transport Association – Vision 2050, Singapore, 2011.

[469] L. Xiao, X. Chen, X. Zhang, A joint optimization of momentum item and Levenberg-Marquardt algorithm to level up the BPNN's generalization ability, Mathematical Problems in Engineering (2014) 1–10.

[470] T.N. Lin, C.L. Giles, B.G. Horne, S.Y. Kung, A delay damage model selection algorithm for NARX neural networks, IEEE Transactions on Signal Processing 45 (11) (1997) 2719–2730.

[471] L.R. Weatherford, T.W. Gentry, B. Wilamowski, Neural network forecasting for airlines: a comparative analysis, Journal of Revenue and Pricing Management 1 (4) (2003) 319–331.

[472] T.H. Tsai, C.K. Lee, C.H. Wei, Neural network based temporal feature models for short-term railway passenger demand forecasting, Expert Systems with Applications 36 (2) (2009) 3728–3736.

[473] K. Adjenughwure, G. Botzoris, B. Papadopoulos, Neural, fuzzy and econometric techniques for the calibration of transport demand models, Journal of Mathematical Sciences and Engineering Applications 7 (5) (2013) 385–403.

[474] S. Sharif Azadeh, R. Labib, G. Savard, Railway demand forecasting in revenue management using neural networks, International Journal of Revenue Management 7 (1) (2013) 18–36.

[475] K. Kumar, M. Parida, V.K. Katiyar, Short-term traffic flow prediction for a non urban highway using artificial neural network, Procedia-Social and Behavioral Sciences 104 (2013) 755–764.

[476] E.I. Vlahogianni, Optimization of traffic forecasting: intelligent surrogate modeling, Transportation Research Part C: Emerging Technologies 55 (2015) 14–23.

[477] R.A. Jacobs, Increased rates of convergence through learning rate adaptation, Neural Networks 1 (4) (1988) 295–307.

[478] T. Tollenaere, SuperSAB: fast adaptive back propagation with good scaling properties, Neural Networks 3 (5) (1990) 561–573.

[479] B.L. Smith, M.J. Demetsky, Short-term traffic flow prediction: neural network approach, Transportation Research Record: Journal of the Transportation Research Board 1453 (1994) 98–104.

[480] J.Y. Potvin, D. Dubé, C. Robillard, A hybrid approach to vehicle routing using neural networks and genetic algorithms, Applied Intelligence 6 (3) (1996) 241–252.

[481] H.H. Aghdam, E.J. Heravi, D. Puig, A practical approach for detection and classification of traffic signs using convolutional neural networks, Robotics and Autonomous Systems 84 (2016) 97–112.

[482] Y. Zhu, C. Zhang, D. Zhou, X. Wang, X. Bai, W. Liu, Traffic sign detection and recognition using fully convolutional network guided proposals, Neurocomputing 214 (2016) 758–766.

[483] T. Becker, C. Illigen, B. McKelvey, M. Hülsmann, K. Windt, Using an agent-based neural-network computational model to improve product routing in a logistics facility, International Journal of Production Economics 174 (3) (2016) 156–167.

[484] K. Mattas, G. Botzoris, B. Papadopoulos, Application of fuzzy sets for the improvement of routing optimization heuristic algorithms, Transport and Telecommunication 17 (4) (2016) 350−361.

[485] M.S. Kaseko, S.G. Ritchie, A neural network-based methodology for pavement crack detection and classification, Transportation Research Part C: Emerging Technologies 1 (4) (1993) 275−291.

[486] F.M. Nejad, H. Zakeri, An optimum feature extraction method based on Wavelet − Radon transform and dynamic neural network for pavement distress classification, Expert Systems with Applications 38 (8) (2011) 9442−9460.

[487] K. Yurii, G. Liudmila, Application of artificial neural networks in vehicles' design self-diagnostic systems for safety reasons, Transportation Research Procedia 20 (2017) 283−287.

[488] T. Pamuła, Neural networks in transportation research − recent applications, Transport Problems 11 (2) (2016) 27−36.

[489] B. Kosko, Fuzzy systems as universal approximators, IEEE Transactions on Computers 43 (11) (1994) 1329−1333.

[490] J. de Andrés, A. Terceño, Applications of fuzzy regression in actuarial analysis, The Journal of Risk and Insurance 70 (4) (2003) 665−699.

[491] A. Falsafain, S.M. Taheri, M. Mashinchi, Fuzzy estimation of parameters in statistical models, World Academy of Science, Engineering and Technology 38 (2008) 318−324.

[492] L.A. Zadeh, Fuzzy sets, Information and Control 8 (3) (1965) 338−353.

[493] G. Klir, B. Yuan, Fuzzy Sets and Fuzzy Logic: Theory and Applications, Prentice Hall, Upper Saddle River, NJ, 1995.

[494] V. Profillidis, B. Papadopoulos, G. Botzoris, Similarities in fuzzy regression models and application on transportation, Fuzzy Economic Review 4 (1) (1999) 83−98.

[495] B.K. Papadopoulos, M.A. Sirpi, Similarities in fuzzy regression models, Journal of Optimization Theory and Applications 102 (2) (1999) 373−383.

[496] T. Terano, K. Asai, M. Sugeno, Fuzzy Systems Theory and its Applications, Academic Press Inc., San Diego, CA, 1992.

[497] V. Stefanis, V. Profillidis, B. Papadopoulos, G. Botzoris, Analysis and forecasting of intercity rail passenger demand by econometric and fuzzy regression models − similarities in fuzzy regression models, in: Proceedings of the 8th SIGEF Congress: New Logic for the New Economy, 20−21 September 2001, Naples, Italy, 2002.

[498] B. Kim, R.R. Bishu, Evaluation of fuzzy linear regression models by comparing membership functions, Fuzzy Sets and Systems 100 (1−3) (1998) 343−352.

[499] H. Tanaka, S. Uejima, K. Asai, Linear regression analysis with fuzzy model, IEEE Transactions on Systems, Man and Cybernetics 12 (6) (1982) 903−907.

[500] H. Tanaka, Fuzzy data analysis by possibilistic linear models, Fuzzy Sets and Systems 24 (3) (1987) 363−375.

[501] K.J. Kim, H. Moskowitz, M. Koksalan, Fuzzy versus statistical linear regression, European Journal of Operational Research 92 (2) (1996) 417−434.

[502] M. Hojati, C.R. Bector, K. Smimou, A simple method for computation of fuzzy linear regression, European Journal of Operational Research 166 (1) (2005) 172−184.

[503] E. Pasha, T. Razzaghnia, T. Allahviranloo, G. Yari, H.R. Mostafaei, Fuzzy linear regression models with fuzzy entropy, Applied Mathematical Sciences 1 (35) (2007) 1715−1724.

[504] H. Moskowitz, K. Kim, On assessing the H value in fuzzy linear regression, Fuzzy Sets and Systems 58 (3) (1993) 303−327.

[505] G. Botzoris, B. Papadopoulos, Fuzzy Sets Applications for the Design and Operation of Engineering Projects, Sofia Publishing, Thessaloniki, Greece, 2015 in Greek.

[506] H. Tanaka, J. Watada, Possibilistic linear systems and their application to the linear regression model, Fuzzy Sets and Systems 27 (3) (1988) 275−289.

[507] C. Tzimopoulos, K. Papadopoulos, B.K. Papadopoulos, Models of fuzzy linear regression: an application in engineering, in: T.M. Rassias, V. Gupta (Eds.), Mathematical Analysis, Approximation Theory and Their Applications, Springer International Publishing, Cham, 2016, pp. 693−713.

[508] D. Teodorović, Fuzzy sets theory applications in traffic and transportation, European Journal of Operational Research 74 (3) (1994) 379−390.

[509] D. Teodorović, G. Pavković, The fuzzy set theory approach to the vehicle routing problem when demand at nodes is uncertain, Fuzzy Sets and Systems 82 (3) (1996) 307−317.

[510] A. Sarkar, G. Sahoo, U.C. Sahoo, Application of fuzzy logic in transport planning, International Journal on Soft Computing 3 (2) (2012) 1−21.

[511] A.L. Bristow, J. Nellthorp, Transport project appraisal in the European Union, Transport Policy 7 (1) (2000) 51−60.

[512] K. De Brucker, C. Macharis, A. Verbeke, Multi-criteria analysis in transport project evaluation: an institutional approach, European Transport 47 (2011) 3−24.

[513] E. Kopytov, D. Abramov, Multiple-criteria analysis and choice of transportation alternatives in multimodal freight transport system, Transport and Telecommunication 13 (2) (2012) 148−158.

[514] C. Macharis, A. Bernardini, Reviewing the use of Multi-Criteria Decision Analysis for the evaluation of transport projects: time for a multi-actor approach, Transport Policy 37 (2015) 177−186.

[515] J.A. Annema, N. Mouter, J. Razaei, Cost-benefit analysis (CBA), or multi-criteria decision-making (MCDM) or both: politicians' perspective in transport policy appraisal, Transportation Research Procedia 10 (2015) 788−797.

[516] S. Rajak, P. Parthiban, R. Dhanalakshmi, Sustainable transportation systems performance evaluation using fuzzy logic, Ecological Indicators 71 (2016) 503−513.

[517] G. Leonardi, A fuzzy model for a railway-planning problem, Applied Mathematical Sciences 10 (27) (2016) 1333−1342.

[518] D. Teodorović, Fuzzy logic systems for transportation engineering: the state of the art, Transportation Research Part A: Policy and Practice 33 (5) (1999) 337−364.

[519] V. Profillidis, Differentiation of rail passenger demand in response to the increase of the quality of service - a case study, Rail International 12 (1995) 21−25.

[520] V. Profillidis, G. Botzoris, Internalization of external costs and impact on the demand of various transport modes, in: Hellenic Institute of Transportation Engineers, in: Proceeding of the 5th International Congress on Transportation Research 2010, Volos, Greece, 27−28 September 2010, pp. 148−161.

[521] B.R. Gaines, Foundations of fuzzy reasoning, International Journal of Man-Machine Studies 8 (6) (1976) 623−668.

[522] S. Spartalis, L. Iliadis, F. Maris, An innovative risk evaluation system estimating its own fuzzy entropy, Mathematical and Computer Modelling 46 (1−2) (2007) 260−267.

[523] H. Singh, M.M. Gupta, T. Meitzler, Z.G. Hou, K.K. Garg, A.M. Solo, L.A. Zadeh, Real-life applications of fuzzy logic, Advances in Fuzzy Systems 2013 (581879) (2013) 1−3.

[524] N. Kyriakoulis, A. Gasteratos, S.G. Mouroutsos, An adaptive fuzzy system for the control of the vergence angle on a robotic head, Journal of Intelligent & Fuzzy Systems 21 (6) (2010) 385–394.

[525] P.J. Van Dyk, A fuzzy interpretation of the Bible: going beyond modernism and post-modernism, Religion and Theology 9 (3) (2002) 163–182.

[526] N.H. Phuong, V. Kreinovich, Fuzzy logic and its applications in medicine, International Journal of Medical Informatics 62 (2–3) (2001) 165–173.

[527] N. Eliou, V. Profillidis, G. Botzoris, Drivers' risk perception analysis – advanced evaluation methodology based on fuzzy theory, in: Proceedings of the XIII Congress of International Association for Fuzzy-Set Management and Economy, 30 November – 2 December 2006, Hammamet, Tunisia, 2006.

[528] N. Eliou, V. Profillidis, G. Botzoris, Experimental monitoring of characteristics of risk perception by drivers and appropriate modelling with the use of the fuzzy method, in: Proceedings of the 10th International Conference on Application of Advanced Technologies in Transportation, 27–31 May 2008, Athens, Greece, 2008, pp. 3732–3746.

[529] J. Niittymaki, S. Kikuchi, Application of fuzzy logic to the control of a pedestrian crossing signal, Transportation Research Record: Journal of the Transportation Research Board 1651 (1998) 30–38.

[530] A. Baykasoğlu, K. Subulan, An analysis of fully fuzzy linear programming with fuzzy decision variables through logistics network design problem, Knowledge-Based Systems 90 (2015) 165–184.

Abbreviations

€	Euro
$	United States dollar
ACF	autocorrelation function
AI	artificial intelligence
AIC	Akaike information criterion
a.m.	ante meridiem (before noon)
ANN	artificial neural network
APEC	Asia–Pacific Economic Cooperation
AR	autoregressive
ARCH	autoregressive conditional heteroscedasticity
ARI	autoregressive integrated
ARIMA	autoregressive integrated moving average
ARMA	autoregressive moving average
ART	algebraic reconstruction technique
BIC	Bayesian information criterion
BLUE	best linear unbiased estimators
cov(X,Y)	covariance between two random variables X and Y
dB(A)	A-weighted decibels
df	degrees of freedom
E(X)	expected value of a random variable X
EU-15	European Union of 15 members (Austria, Belgium, Denmark, Finland, France, Germany, Greece, Ireland, Italy, Luxembourg, Netherlands, Portugal, Spain, Sweden, United Kingdom)
EU-28	European Union of 28 members (EU-15 plus Bulgaria, Czech Republic, Estonia, Croatia, Cyprus, Latvia, Lithuania, Hungary, Malta, Poland, Romania, Slovenia, Slovakia)
ex-USSR	former Union of Soviet Socialist Republics
FAA	Federal Aviation Administration
ft	feet (10 ft = 3.048 m)
GC	generalized cost
GDP	gross domestic product
GPS	global positioning system
GRP	gross regional product
GSM	global system for mobile
h	hour(s)
H_0	null hypothesis
H_1	alternative hypothesis
HQIC	Hannan–Quinn information criterion
IATA	International Air Transport Association
ICAO	International Civil Aviation Organization
IMA	integrated moving average
ITS	intelligence transport systems

LCA	low-cost airlines
LCVs	light commercial vehicles
LM	Lagrange multipliers
LMS	least median of squares
ln	natural logarithm
MA	moving average
MAD	mean absolute deviation
MAPE	mean absolute percentage error
ML	machine learning
MLN	multinomial Logit model
MSE	mean squared error
MTC	maximum throughput capacity
N	Newton
n.a.	nonavailable
OECD	Organization for Economic Co-operation and Development
OLS	ordinary least squares
p.a.	per annum
PACF	partial autocorrelation function
PCE	passenger car equivalents
p-km	passenger-kilometer(s)
p.m.	post meridiem (after noon)
PPP	purchasing power parity
r	Pearson correlation coefficient, when it refers to the sample
$\mathbf{R^2}$	coefficient of determination
$\mathbf{\bar{R}^2}$	adjusted coefficient of determination
RMSE	root mean squared error
$\mathbf{s^2}$	variance, when it refers to the sample
SARIMA	seasonal autoregressive integrated moving average
SE	standard error
SMS	short message service
SPSS	Statistical Package for the Social Sciences (computer software)
TEU	twenty-foot equivalent unit(s)
t-km	tonne-kilometer(s)
UAE	United Arab Emirates
UIC	Union Internationale des Chemins de Fer (International Union of Railways)
UITP	Union Internationale des Transports Publics (International Association of Public Transport)
UK	United Kingdom
UNCTAD	United Nations Conference on Trade and Development
USA	United States of America
V	velocity (speed)
VIF	variance inflation factor
ρ	Pearson correlation coefficient, when it refers to the population
σ^2	variance, when it refers to the population

Index

Note: 'Page numbers followed by "f" indicate figures, "t" indicate tables.'

A

Accessibility, 33
Accident analysis, 416
Accuracy, 48, 211–212
ACF. *See* Autocorrelation function (ACF)
Activation function structure, 356–359
    activation function—check of forecasting
        ability, 370
    analogies between artificial and biological
        neuron, 356–357, 357f
    ANN
        artificial neurons and, 357–358, 358f
        four functions of, 358
        transfer or activation function of, 359,
            359f
    conception of artificial neuron, 356
Adaline, 361
Adjusted coefficient of determination, 190,
    217–218
Administrative statistics, 48
Aggregate models, 100–101, 317
    aggregate forecast transformation, 296–298
AI. *See* Artificial intelligence (AI)
AIC. *See* Akaike information criterion (AIC)
AI—neural network methods
    analytical example of application of ANN
        for transport, 367–373
    application of ANN
        to assessing performance of transport
            systems, 382
        for forecast of maintenance needs of
            vehicles and transport infrastructure,
            381–382
        for forecast of rail transport demand,
            374–376
        for forecast of road traffic demand,
            377–379, 379f
        in problems of road safety, driver
            behavior, and self-driven vehicles,
            380–381
        for routing and scheduling of freight
            transport, 381

for short-term forecasts of air transport
    demand, 374
artificial neuron and activation function
    structure, 356–359
comparative analysis of ANN with other
    forecasting methods, 363–366
reasons for choosing AI methods for
    modeling transport demand, 353–355
structure and elements of biological
    neuron, 355–356, 355f
types of ANN, algorithms, and software,
    359–363
Air fare, 287–288
Air freight
    costs, 300
    demand, 59, 59f, 62
    yields, 300
Air freight transport demand, econometric
    models for, 298–301
    derived demand for high-value products, 298
    driving forces and plausible independent
        variables, 299–300
    forms, 301
Air passenger demand, 57–59, 58f, 62
Air traffic forecasts, 286
Air transport, 2
    activity, 62
    growth rates of, 54
Air transport demand. *See also* Public
    transport demand; Rail transport
    demand; Road transport demand
    aggregate forecast transformation at annual
        level, 296–298
    air trips per 1000 inhabitants, 293t
    ANN application for short-term forecasts
        of, 374
    application of fuzzy linear regression
        analysis for, 408–410, 410t
    availability of valid forecasts for evolution
        of independent variables, 289
    driving forces and plausible independent
        variables, 286–288

CPI Antony Rowe
Chippenham, UK
2019-01-07 15:51